World Economic and Financial Surveys

W9-DEN-048

WORLD ECONOMIC OUTLOOK
September 2002

Trade and Finance

International Monetary Fund

©2002 International Monetary Fund

Production: IMF Graphics Section
Cover and Design: Luisa Menjivar-Macdonald
Figures: Theodore F. Peters, Jr.
Typesetting: Choon Lee and Joseph A. Kumar

World economic outlook (International Monetary Fund)
    World economic outlook: a survey by the staff of the International
Monetary Fund.—1980– —Washington, D.C.: The Fund, 1980–

    v.; 28 cm.—(1981–84: Occasional paper/International Monetary
Fund ISSN 0251-6365)
    Annual.
    Has occasional updates, 1984–
    ISSN 0258-7440 = World economic and financial surveys
    ISSN 0256-6877 = World economic outlook (Washington)
    1. Economic history—1971–   —Periodicals.   I. International
Monetary Fund.   II. Series: Occasional paper (International
Monetary Fund)
    HC10.W7979   84-640155

                                            338.5'443'09048—dc19
                                                    AACR 2 MARC-S

Library of Congress   8507

    Published biannually.
ISBN 1-58906-179-9

Price: US$49.00
(US$46.00 to full-time faculty members and
students at universities and colleges)

Please send orders to:
International Monetary Fund, Publication Services
700 19th Street, N.W., Washington, D.C. 20431, U.S.A.
Tel.: (202) 623-7430   Telefax: (202) 623-7201
E-mail: publications@imf.org
Internet: http://www.imf.org

recycled paper

CONTENTS

Boxes

Tables

Figures

ASSUMPTIONS AND CONVENTIONS

A number of assumptions have been adopted for the projections presented in the *World Economic Outlook*. It has been assumed that real effective exchange rates will remain constant at their average levels during July 19–August 16, 2002, except for the currencies participating in the European exchange rate mechanism II (ERM II), which are assumed to remain constant in nominal terms relative to the euro; that established policies of national authorities will be maintained (for specific assumptions about fiscal and monetary policies in industrial countries, see Box A1); that the average price of oil will be $24.40 a barrel in 2002 and $24.20 a barrel in 2003, and remain unchanged in real terms over the medium term; that the six-month London interbank offered rate (LIBOR) on U.S. dollar deposits will average 2.1 percent in 2002 and 3.2 percent in 2003; that the three-month certificate of deposit rate in Japan will average 0.1 percent in 2002 and 2003; and that the three-month interbank deposit rate for the euro will average 3.4 percent in 2002 and 3.8 percent in 2003. These are, of course, working hypotheses rather than forecasts, and the uncertainties surrounding them add to the margin of error that would in any event be involved in the projections. The estimates and projections are based on statistical information available through early September 2002.

The following conventions have been used throughout the *World Economic Outlook:*

... to indicate that data are not available or not applicable;

— to indicate that the figure is zero or negligible;

– between years or months (for example, 2000–2001 or January–June) to indicate the years or months covered, including the beginning and ending years or months;

/ between years or months (for example, 2000/01) to indicate a fiscal or financial year.

"Billion" means a thousand million; "trillion" means a thousand million.

"Basis points" refer to hundredths of 1 percentage point (for example, 25 basis points are equivalent to ¼ of 1 percent point).

In figures and tables, shaded areas indicate IMF staff projections.

Minor discrepancies between sums of constituent figures and totals shown are due to rounding.

As used in this report, the term "country" does not in all cases refer to a territorial entity that is a state as understood by international law and practice. As used here, the term also covers some territorial entities that are not states but for which statistical data are maintained on a separate and independent basis.

FURTHER INFORMATION AND DATA

This report on the *World Economic Outlook* is available in full on the IMF's Internet site, *www.imf.org*. Accompanying it on the website is a larger compilation of data from the WEO database than in the report itself, consisting of files containing the series most frequently requested by readers. These files may be downloaded for use in a variety of software packages.

Inquiries about the content of the *World Economic Outlook* and the WEO database should be sent by mail, electronic mail, or telefax (telephone inquiries cannot be accepted) to:

World Economic Studies Division
Research Department
International Monetary Fund
700 19th Street, N.W.
Washington, D.C. 20431, U.S.A.
E-mail: weo@imf.org   Telefax: (202) 623-6343

PREFACE

The analysis and projections contained in the *World Economic Outlook* are integral elements of the IMF's surveillance of economic developments and policies in its member countries, developments in international financial markets, and the global economic system. The survey of prospects and policies is the product of a comprehensive interdepartmental review of world economic developments, which draws primarily on information the IMF staff gathers through its consultations with member countries. These consultations are carried out in particular by the IMF's area departments together with the Policy Development and Review Department, the International Capital Markets Department, the Monetary Affairs Department, and the Fiscal Affairs Department.

The analysis in this report was coordinated in the Research Department under the general direction of Kenneth Rogoff, Economic Counsellor and Director of Research. The project was directed by David Robinson, Deputy Director of the Research Department, together with Tamim Bayoumi, Division Chief, World Economic Studies Division.

Primary contributors to this report also include Luis Catão, Xavier Debrun, Hali Edison, Thomas Helbling, Maitland MacFarlan, James Morsink, Silvia Sgherri, Marco Terrones, Stephen Tokarick, and Cathy Wright. Augusto Clavijo, Emily Conover, Toh Kuan, and Bennett Sutton provided research assistance. Nicholas Dopuch, Mandy Hemmati, Casper Meyer, Yutong Li, Di Rao, and Anthony G. Turner managed the data base and the computer systems. Sylvia Brescia, Viktória Kiss, and Laura Leon were responsible for word processing. Other contributors include Anupam Basu, Andrew Berg, Peter Breuer, Jean-Pierre Chauffour, Ximena Cheetham, Manmohan Kumar, Guy Meredith, David Parsley, Andrew Rose, Antonio Spilimbergo, Krishna Srinivasan, and Shang-Jin Wei. Marina Primorac of the External Relations Department edited the manuscript and coordinated production of the publication.

The analysis has benefited from comments and suggestions by staff from other IMF departments, as well as by Executive Directors following their discussion of the report on September 3 and 4, 2002. However, both projections and policy considerations are those of the IMF staff and should not be attributed to Executive Directors or to their national authorities.

FOREWORD

This issue of the *World Economic Outlook* (WEO) contains two chapters on trade and its links with finance. Why so much emphasis on international trade in what is, after all, a quintessentially macroeconomic publication? A narrow explanation would be that forecasts of world trade have always been a central element of the WEO. Although these forecasts tend to attract somewhat less attention than our growth forecasts, they are absolutely fundamental to our picture of the global economy and its linkages—for example, global trade growth is a key variable we look at in assessing whether a global downturn should be judged a recession (see Box 1.1 in the April 2002 *World Economic Outlook*). But our real reasons for concentrating more on trade and its links with finance run much deeper. In our view, these linkages are inseparable, a fact that has recently come to the fore of thinking on international financial policy.[1] They are also timely issues, given renewed concern about the international debt problems facing some emerging markets that are relatively closed to trade,[2] the continuing multilateral negotiations on lowering tariff barriers under the Doha round (including the recent grant of "fast track" negotiating authority to President Bush), and heightened concerns that prolonged exchange rate misalignments may be exacerbating protectionist pressures in some major countries.

Much of the concern about exchange rate misalignments has focused on the U.S. current account deficit of about 4 percent of U.S. GDP. However, as one country's deficit is another country's surplus, it is best to look at this issue from a broader multilateral perspective. There is now a gap of some 2½ percent of *global* GDP between the current account surpluses of continental Europe and east Asia (dominated by the euro area and Japan, respectively) and the deficit countries, dominated by the United States. Indeed, relative to the size of trade flows, the present nexus of current account imbalances has risen to levels almost never seen in industrial countries in the postwar era. We do not view this as a problem specific to deficit countries, or to surplus countries; rather, it is a problem of the system as a whole. The first essay in Chapter II assesses the risks that these imbalances will unwind quickly, resulting in larger, and potentially disruptive, short-term exchange rate movements than if the imbalances unwind slowly. There is no easy prescription for mitigating these risks, though these concerns strengthen the case for policymakers in deficit countries to pursue medium-term fiscal consolidation, and for policymakers in surplus countries to press ahead rapidly with structural reforms to make their economies more flexible and to boost growth. Expanding global trade would also help, since the more open economies are to trade, the less exchange rate adjustment is required to achieve a given current account reversal.

Markets for basic agricultural commodities such as grain are often thought of as textbook examples of highly organized competitive markets in which prices respond rapidly to divergences between demand and supply. So it is something of a paradox that there are so many countries in which domestic agricultural markets are among the most heavily subsidized and protected. As the second essay in Chapter II notes, agricultural support by the industrial countries amounts to over 30 percent of agricultural output! Quantitatively, the largest burden of these subsidies falls on consumers and taxpayers in industrialized countries, but unfortunately the effects also fall heavily on the rest of the world, including many poor countries, most notably in sub-Saharan Africa. The essay documents these costs, which

---

[1] "Promoting Sustained Growth and International Financial Stability," address by Horst Köhler, IMF Managing Director, to the National Press Club, April 17, 2002.

[2] See also Chapter II of the April 2002 *World Economic Outlook*.

are particularly large for certain commodities such as cotton. It argues that industrial countries should be in the vanguard of multilateral efforts to get rid of farm subsidies given the large resources at their disposal and the small size of their farm sectors. In addition to the direct benefits, such an initiative would promote similar reforms in developing countries. This is of particular importance as the adverse effects of developing countries' own trade restrictions are significantly larger than the costs imposed by industrial country protection, not just on agriculture, but also on manufactures and services.[3]

The Asia crisis in 1997 and successive crises in Latin America have underlined the role of healthy corporate and bank balance sheets in maintaining financial stability. The third essay in Chapter II looks at trends in corporate health and financial vulnerabilities across 18 emerging markets, focusing particularly on differences between east Asian firms and their emerging European and Latin American counterparts. Two results from this study are particularly noteworthy. First, policies that promote openness to foreign investors have a positive effect in helping corporations reduce their leverage (debt to equity ratios) and to extend the maturity of their debts. This is not to deny the heightened risks of exchange rate mismatches, but, in terms of debt maturity and composition, openness helps rather than hurts. Second, leverage also seems to have much to do with the level of domestic financial development. In particular, corporations in countries at intermediate levels of financial development often have particularly high leverage ratios compared to countries with more primitive or more advanced financial systems, in part because their financial systems tend to be primarily based on bank lending and other debt instruments. The essay suggests that a higher level of economic development may help explain why east Asian firms still tend to have higher leverage ratios than their counterparts in emerging markets in Europe and Latin America, even after the Asian debt crisis of the 1990s. (Another likely factor is the increased ability of corporates to borrow in countries with more stable macroeconomic policy histories.) Past a certain point, however, as a country develops and its financial system matures, equity markets often become more important, leading to lower leverage ratios. If east Asian countries are indeed on the cusp where further level development begins to lead to lower leverage ratios, then this differential may abate in the coming decade.

Globalization is one of the major forces affecting the world. The relationship between its two main facets—trade integration and financial market integration—is the focus of Chapter III. Historically, international trade and finance have generally moved hand in hand. Empirically, the two are reinforcing each other, with greater financial integration tending to increase trade, and more trade requiring larger international financing. Indeed, the chapter finds that the benefits from opening up to the rest of the world are greatest in terms of reduced macroeconomic volatility and fewer financial crises when progress is made on opening to both trade and finance. Theoretically, there is also a fairly clear link. It is now well known that a fall in trade costs can significantly expand financial market integration measured by the level of risk sharing across countries. Indeed, one can potentially explain much of the differences in the level of capital market integration across countries by trade frictions broadly defined to include not only transport and tariffs, but also other factors such as differences in language and legal systems.[4]

While a steady fall in trade costs has certainly been the driving force for global integration throughout modern history, the roots of the change have differed somewhat over time. During the last great era of globalization, 1870–1914, integration was driven mainly by changes in technology. During the modern post–World War II era, however, policy has been at least as important. While financial and trade integration have generally moved in broad correspondence, there have been cases where policy-driven

[3]Jagdish Bhagwati, "The Poor's Best Hope," *The Economist,* June 22, 2002, pp. 24–26.
[4]See Maurice Obstfeld and Kenneth Rogoff, 2000, "The Six Major Puzzles in International Macroeconomics: Is There a Common Cause?" *NBER Macroeconomics Annual 2000* (Cambridge, Massachusetts: MIT Press).

liberalization in financial markets has leaped ahead first, and where the supporting changes needed to achieve trade integration never materialized. This can lead to problems, including financial crises, as was discussed in Chapter II of the April 2002 *World Economic Outlook*, and as we discuss again here.

Given the importance of opening up to finance and trade, Chapter III also contains a detailed investigation of why some regions seem to trade so much more than others. Much of the analysis is based on the so-called "gravity model" of trade, which controls for factors such as country size, distance from trading partners, and policy restrictiveness. Overall, the results suggest that while trade policy restrictiveness is quite important in explaining the lower trading levels of developing countries compared with their industrialized brethren, other factors, such as the level of economic development and inherited geography, turn out to be even more important. Low income per capita is central to explaining the relatively low level of "South-South" trade; as consumers in poor countries use a relatively narrow range of products, such countries will naturally trade less with each other, even relative to income. Many countries also suffer from the problem of geographic isolation and, in some cases, being landlocked. Indeed, geography alone accounts for roughly 40 percent of the difference in trade levels across countries. Trade and balance of payments restrictions, on the other hand, appear to account for between 10 and 20 percent of the shortfall in bilateral trade flows. We can conclude from this that, over the next century, we are likely to see increased globalization not only due to continued improvements in the global transportation and communications system, and active policy measures to reduce trade restrictions, but also simply due to further economic development. Globalization is not only a source of growth; it is a natural outcome of it.

Kenneth Rogoff
Economic Counsellor and Director, Research Department

Since late 2001, a global recovery has been under way, with trade and industrial production picking up across the globe. However, after a strong first quarter, concerns about the pace and sustainability of the recovery have risen significantly. Financial markets have weakened markedly, with equity markets falling sharply since end-March accompanied by a depreciation of the U.S. dollar; financing conditions for emerging markets have deteriorated, particularly in South America and Turkey; and incoming data in both the U.S. and the euro area have fallen short of expectations. The recovery is still expected to continue, but global growth in the second half of 2002 and in 2003 will be weaker than earlier expected (Figure 1.1 and Table 1.1), and the risks to the outlook are primarily on the downside. With inflationary pressures generally subdued, macroeconomic policies in advanced countries will now need to remain accommodative for longer than had earlier seemed necessary; if incoming data were to suggest that the recovery is faltering, additional monetary easing would need to be considered. Attention also needs to focus on policies to reduce dependence on the United States as the global engine of growth, and to support an orderly reduction in the global imbalances, which remain a serious risk to the world economy.

Since the turn of the year, a global recovery has been under way, led by the United States and underpinned by a pickup in global industrial production and trade (Figure 1.2). Even allowing for the recent substantial downward revision to GDP growth in 2001 in the United States, the global slowdown in 2000–01 has proved to be more moderate than most previous downturns. This owed much to an aggressive policy response, particularly following the events of September 11, in turn made possible by the improvement in economic fundamentals during the 1990s. Other contributing factors included the decline in oil prices in 2001; the resilience of the global financial infrastructure to a variety of substantial shocks; and a

Figure 1.1. Global Indicators[1]
(Annual percent change unless otherwise noted)

After a sharp slowdown in 2001, global output is projected to pick up in 2002–03, although remaining below trend.

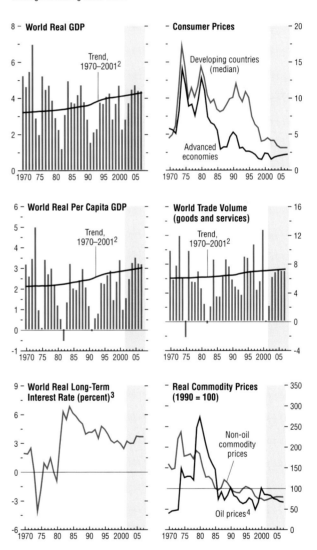

[1]Shaded areas indicate IMF staff projections. Aggregates are computed on the basis of purchasing-power-parity weights unless otherwise indicated.
[2]Average growth rates for individual countries, aggregated using purchasing-power-parity weights; the aggregates shift over time in favor of faster growing countries, giving the line an upward trend.
[3]GDP-weighted average of the 10-year (or nearest maturity) government bond yields less inflation rates for the United States, Japan, Germany, France, Italy, the United Kingdom, and Canada. Excluding Italy prior to 1972.
[4]Simple average of spot prices of U.K. Brent, Dubai, and West Texas Intermediate crude oil.

Table 1.1. Overview of the *World Economic Outlook* Projections
(Annual percent change unless otherwise noted)

	2000	2001	Current Projections 2002	Current Projections 2003	Difference from April 2002 Projections[1] 2002	Difference from April 2002 Projections[1] 2003
World output	**4.7**	**2.2**	**2.8**	**3.7**	**—**	**−0.3**
Advanced economies	3.8	0.8	1.7	2.5	—	−0.5
Major advanced economies	3.4	0.6	1.4	2.3	−0.1	−0.5
United States	3.8	0.3	2.2	2.6	−0.1	−0.8
Japan	2.4	−0.3	−0.5	1.1	0.5	0.3
Germany	2.9	0.6	0.5	2.0	−0.4	−0.7
France	4.2	1.8	1.2	2.3	−0.2	−0.7
Italy	2.9	1.8	0.7	2.3	−0.7	−0.6
United Kingdom	3.1	1.9	1.7	2.4	−0.3	−0.4
Canada	4.5	1.5	3.4	3.4	0.9	−0.2
Other advanced economies	5.3	1.6	2.6	3.3	0.1	−0.4
Memorandum						
European Union	3.5	1.6	1.1	2.3	−0.4	−0.6
Euro area	3.5	1.5	0.9	2.3	−0.5	−0.6
Newly industrialized Asian economies	8.5	0.8	4.7	4.9	1.1	−0.2
Developing countries	5.7	3.9	4.2	5.2	−0.1	−0.3
Africa	3.0	3.5	3.1	4.2	−0.3	—
Developing Asia	6.7	5.6	6.1	6.3	0.2	−0.1
China	8.0	7.3	7.5	7.2	0.5	−0.2
India	5.4	4.1	5.0	5.7	−0.5	−0.1
ASEAN-4[2]	5.1	2.6	3.6	4.2	0.3	0.1
Middle East and Turkey[3]	6.1	1.5	3.6	4.7	0.3	0.2
Western Hemisphere	4.0	0.6	−0.6	3.0	−1.3	−0.7
Brazil	4.4	1.5	1.5	3.0	−1.0	−0.5
Countries in transition	6.6	5.0	3.9	4.5	—	0.1
Central and eastern Europe	3.8	3.0	2.7	3.8	−0.3	−0.2
Commonwealth of Independent States and Mongolia	8.4	6.3	4.6	4.9	0.1	0.3
Russia	9.0	5.0	4.4	4.9	—	—
Excluding Russia	6.9	8.9	5.2	4.9	0.5	0.8
Memorandum						
World growth based on market exchange rates	3.9	1.1	1.7	2.8	−0.1	−0.4
World trade volume (goods and services)	**12.6**	**−0.1**	**2.1**	**6.1**	**−0.4**	**−0.5**
Imports						
Advanced economies	11.8	−1.3	1.7	6.2	−0.4	−0.4
Developing countries	15.9	1.6	3.8	7.1	−2.6	−0.6
Countries in transition	13.4	11.7	6.9	8.0	−1.1	0.3
Exports						
Advanced economies	12.0	−1.1	1.2	5.4	0.3	−0.9
Developing countries	15.0	2.6	3.2	6.5	−1.6	−0.5
Countries in transition	14.7	5.9	5.3	6.2	0.1	0.1
Commodity prices (U.S. dollars)						
Oil[4]	57.0	−14.0	0.5	−0.8	5.8	3.5
Nonfuel (average based on world commodity export weights)	1.8	−5.4	4.2	5.7	4.3	−1.5
Consumer prices						
Advanced economies	2.3	2.2	1.4	1.7	0.1	−0.1
Developing countries	6.1	5.7	5.6	6.0	−0.2	0.9
Countries in transition	20.2	15.9	11.3	8.8	0.5	0.1
Six-month London interbank offered rate (LIBOR, percent)						
On U.S. dollar deposits	6.6	3.7	2.1	3.2	−0.8	−1.3
On Japanese yen deposits	0.3	0.2	0.1	0.1	—	—
On euro deposits	4.6	4.1	3.4	3.8	−0.3	−0.8

Note: Real effective exchange rates are assumed to remain constant at the levels prevailing during July 19–August 16, 2002.
[1]Using updated purchasing-power-parity (PPP) weights, summarized in the Statistical Appendix, Table A.
[2]Includes Indonesia, Malaysia, the Philippines, and Thailand.
[3]Includes Malta.
[4]Simple average of spot prices of U.K. Brent, Dubai, and West Texas Intermediate crude oil. The average price of oil in U.S. dollars a barrel was $24.28 in 2001; the assumed price is $24.40 in 2002, and $24.20 in 2003.

degree of good luck, in that the impact of the terrorist attacks on confidence proved surprisingly short lived.

During the first quarter of 2002, activity was surprisingly strong, with GDP growth in a number of regions—particularly North America and emerging markets in Asia—exceeding expectations. Since that time the pace of recovery has slowed, except in emerging markets in Asia, and incoming data have generally been weaker than expected. Forward-looking indicators—while still stronger than at end-2001—have also fallen back markedly (Figure 1.2). Domestic demand growth so far has been relatively weak outside North America and the United Kingdom, the cyclically most advanced of the major industrial countries, making the upturn elsewhere heavily dependent on external demand. Moreover, there is as yet limited evidence of a pickup in global investment, which will be critical to maintain the momentum of the projected upturn in the second half of the year.

Notwithstanding the upturn, global financial markets have weakened significantly.[1] Industrial country equity markets have fallen sharply—and with surprising synchronicity—since end-March (Figure 1.3). This has reflected a combination of factors, including downward revisions of earlier—and always optimistic—profit forecasts; concerns about the sustainability of the recovery; and widespread concerns about accounting and auditing practices, particularly in the United States. While a portion of those losses have been recouped since late July, markets remain volatile. In the face of increased risk and uncertainty, demand for government bonds and high-quality corporate paper has risen, which—together with expectations that monetary tightening will be postponed—has driven long-run interest rates down significantly. Spreads for riskier borrowers have risen, and risk appetite has also declined, although not to the point of outright risk aversion. In currency markets, the U.S. dollar has

[1]See the September 2002 *Global Financial Stability Report* for a detailed discussion of financial market developments and risks.

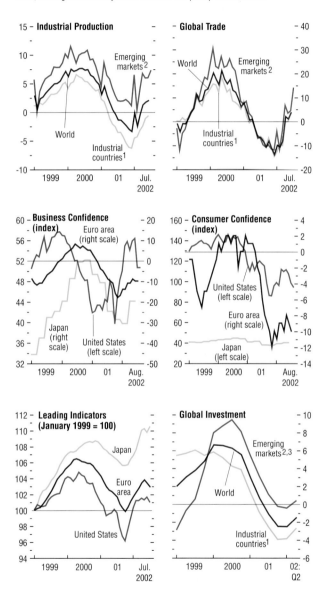

Figure 1.2. Current and Forward-Looking Indicators
(Percent change from a year earlier unless otherwise indicated)

Current and forward-looking indicators have generally strengthened since late 2001, although there is as yet little evidence of a pickup in investment.

Sources: Haver Analytics. Business confidence for the United States, the National Association of Purchasing Managers; for the euro area, the European Commission; and for Japan, Bank of Japan. Consumer confidence for the United States, the Conference Board; for the euro area, the European Commission; and for Japan, the Economic Planning Agency. Leading indicators produced by OECD, *Main Economic Indicators*.
[1]Australia, Canada, Denmark, euro area, Japan, New Zealand, Norway, Sweden, Switzerland, the United Kingdom, and the United States.
[2]Argentina, Brazil, Chile, China, Colombia, Czech Republic, Hong Kong SAR, Hungary, India, Indonesia, Israel, Korea, Malaysia, Mexico, Peru, the Philippines, Poland, Russia, Singapore, South Africa, Taiwan Province of China, Thailand, Turkey, and Venezuela.
[3]2002:Q1–Q2 data for China, India, and Russia are interpolated.

Figure 1.3. Developments in Mature Financial Markets

Equity markets have fallen sharply since end-March, accompanied by a depreciation of the U.S. dollar, and some increase in risk aversion.

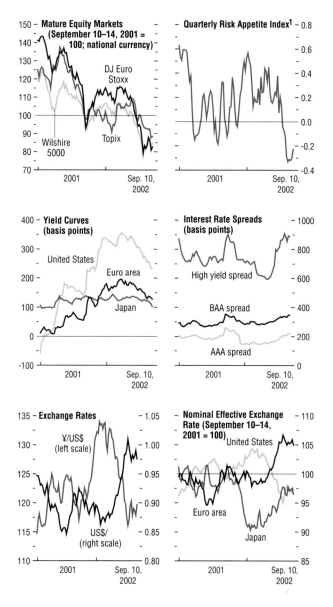

Sources: Bloomberg Financial Markets, LP; State Street Bank; and IMF staff estimates.
[1]IMF/State Street risk appetite indicators.

depreciated markedly against the euro and yen, although more moderately in trade-weighted terms. In part, this appears to have reflected a diminution in the attractiveness of U.S. assets, a slowdown in euro area institutions' diversification away from euro-denominated assets,[2] and growing concerns about the large U.S. current account deficit.

While the timing of market adjustments is always difficult to predict, these developments should not be particularly surprising. Recent issues of the *World Economic Outlook* and the *Global Financial Stability Report* have explicitly warned about the risk of a further decline in equity markets, and the overvaluation of the U.S. dollar has also been a long-standing concern in these pages. From a medium-term perspective, recent developments in equity and currency markets may help reduce global imbalances, but—as discussed in detail in Box 1.1—they make the short-term outlook more difficult. The fall in equity markets, if sustained, will significantly affect U.S. consumption and investment, although the impact will be partly offset by lower long-run interest rates as well as the weaker dollar. In the euro area and Japan, the effect of equity market declines is smaller, but not negligible; however, long-term interest rates have fallen less than in the United States and stronger currencies will weaken exports, so far the mainstay of recovery. This is of particular concern in Japan, where the upturn is likely to be weakest, and which has least room for offsetting policy maneuver.

There has also been substantial turbulence in many emerging markets, partly reflecting higher risk aversion and global uncertainties but also, more fundamentally, country-specific factors. From mid-April, sentiment toward Latin America and Brazil in particular has deteriorated, prompted by rising political uncertainties and concerns about debt dynamics. As spreads rose, these concerns became increasingly self-reinforcing, culminating in mid-June with a full-scale

---

[2]See "What is Driving the Weakness of the Euro and Strength of the Dollar," in Chapter II of the May 2001 *World Economic Outlook*.

Box 1.1. How Will Recent Falls in Equity Markets Affect Activity?

Industrial country equity markets have fallen precipitately between late March and early September of this year, with prices down by one-fifth or so in all major industrial countries. Indeed, over these five months the fall in prices is of a comparable magnitude to that between the bursting of the technology bubble in early 2000 and late March this year, with the exception of Japan (first table). While any fall in equity values of this size and speed is notable, this one is of particular interest for several reasons. First, it has been accompanied by additional significant shifts in asset prices, including a depreciation of the dollar against other major currencies as well as a generalized decline in long-term interest rates as fears of inflation and expectations of monetary tightening recede. Second, the recent fall has been widespread, while over the previous two years it was focused on the technology sector. Third, the timing is unusual as activity is recovering from the downturn in 2001, and partly reflects concerns over accounting scandals.

This box examines the likely impact of these equity price falls on activity, and how they may be mitigated or exacerbated by changes in other asset market prices. A fall in equity markets affects the real economy through three main channels: it increases borrowing costs for households and corporations as collateral is eroded; it raises the cost of equity capital for firms, lowering investment; and it reduces household wealth and hence consumption.[1] The size and nature of these effects differ considerably across countries, depending on the size of the equity market, the proportion of equities held by households, and the extent to which corporations rely on equity markets for funding. In general, it is found to be largest in countries with market-based financial systems, including North America and the United Kingdom, characterized by high equity market capitalization,

Note: The main authors of this box are Tamim Bayoumi and David J. Robinson.

[1]See "Asset Prices and the Business Cycle," in the May 2000 *World Economic Outlook,* for a detailed description of the channels through which asset price movements affect activity.

Changes in Equity Prices
(Percent)

	United States	Euro Area	Japan	United Kingdom
End-March 2002 to early September[1]				
Total	−21	−27	−16	−22
Technology	−34	−40	−25	−32
Nontechnology	−17	−24	−13	−20
End-March 2000 to end-March 2002[2]				
Total	−28	−28	−39	−18
Technology	−63	−64	−63	−69
Nontechnology	4	−7	−26	−24

Source: Datastream.
[1]Average March 25–29, 2002 to September 2–6, 2002.
[2]Average March 27–31, 2000 to March 25–29, 2002.

broader ownership of equities by households, and significant financing of firms through equity issues. In contrast, the impact in bank-based economies—such as continental Europe and Japan—is generally found to be smaller, although not negligible (and because banks in these countries have large equity holdings, there can be substantial effects on their balance sheets, particularly in Japan given the precarious state of the banking system and negative impact of falling equity prices on bank capital). In both cases, the impact of equity markets on activity appears to have been increasing over time, as financial systems get deeper and more flexible, a trend that is likely to continue in the future.

It should be emphasized at the outset that any calculation of the impact on activity is highly speculative as asset prices can move rapidly (particularly in volatile trading conditions of the type experienced lately) and estimated impacts on activity are imprecise, and in any case can vary with circumstances. With these caveats in mind, the second table reports rough estimates of the impact on consumer spending assuming that the equity price falls as of the first full week in September are sustained. The calculations are based on IMF staff estimates of the marginal propensities to consume, after two years, out of equity wealth of 4¼ cents per dollar in the United States and the United Kingdom and 1 cent in the euro

Box 1.1 *(concluded)*

Impact on Activity of Asset Price Changes, Late March to Early September 2002[1]
(Percent of GDP unless otherwise stated)

	United States	Euro Area	Japan	United Kingdom
Equity markets				
Stock market capitalization	−23	−20	−12	−23
Marginal propensity to consume out of wealth				
(cents per dollar)	4¼	1	1	4¼
Impact on spending	**−1**	**−¼**	**¼**	**−1**
Monetary conditions				
Effective exchange rate (percent)	−9	5	7	−1
Real 10-year bond yield[2] (percentage points)	−1¼	−¾	¼	−¾
Impact on spending[3]	**1**	**−¼**	**−¼**	**½**

Source: IMF staff calculations.
[1]Average March 25–29 versus September 2–6, 2002.
[2]Government bond yield, except in the case of the United States where AAA corporate bonds were used, adjusted for the change in projected inflation between the April 2002 *World Economic Outlook* and this one.
[3]Coefficients on the bond yield are −0.55 for the United States, −0.35 for the United Kingdom, and −0.27 for the euro area and Japan; on the real effective exchange rate −0.05 for Japan and the United States, −0.07 for the euro area, and −0.18 for the United Kingdom. The coefficients are derived from the Goldman-Sachs financial conditions index for the United States and United Kingdom (although in the United States, Goldman Sachs uses A bonds rather than AAA bonds), and IMF staff estimates of a similar index for the euro area and for Japan (where the coefficient on bond yields was made equal to that in the euro area).

area and Japan. (See "Is Wealth Increasingly Driving Consumption?" Chapter II in the April 2002 *World Economic Outlook*.)[2] Such numbers are broadly consistent with other academic work and with macroeconomic models such as MULTIMOD or Oxford Analytics.

Taken in isolation, the estimated fall in consumer spending from equity prices is about 1 percentage point of GDP in the United States and the United Kingdom and a ¼ percentage point in the euro area and Japan over the next two years, reflecting different propensities to consume out of wealth. That said, other sources of private wealth can provide an offset. In particular, buoyant housing markets can provide some support to demand (especially as the stock of housing wealth is estimated to be larger than that of equities, and an increase in housing wealth has a larger impact on consumption than a similar increase in equity wealth). Over recent years, real house prices have risen significantly in the United Kingdom and some smaller European countries, and to a lesser extent the United States and France, but have declined in Japan and Germany (see the figure).

[2]Estimates of the impact on investment are less precise, but could raise the impact by one-half or more.

The second table also reports the likely first-year impact of associated changes in monetary conditions over the past five months, comprising changes in effective exchange rates and lower long-term interest rates (short-term policy interest rates have remained unchanged in the major economies except Canada). Lower long-term rates and exchange rate depreciation boost activity in the United States and, to a lesser extent, the United Kingdom, while in Japan, and the euro area to a lesser extent, the erosion in activity due to the appreciation in the exchange rate is estimated to be somewhat larger than the benefit from lower real long-term interest rates.[3]

The net result of all of these asset price changes is likely to be a broad-based slowdown in activity in industrial countries. Aggregating the impact is complicated by the fact that wealth effects are generally thought to have a longer-lasting effect than interest and exchange rates,

[3]It should, however, be noted that futures markets also imply a greater change in the expected monetary stance in the euro area than elsewhere, which is not reflected in changes in bond yields. In addition, the appreciation in the euro may help support activity in the short term by reducing inflation and boosting real incomes.

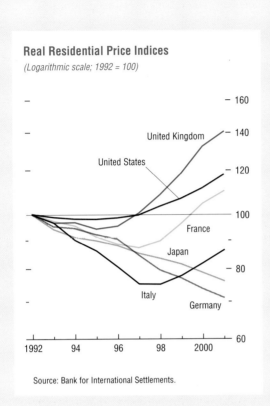

Real Residential Price Indices
(Logarithmic scale; 1992 = 100)

Source: Bank for International Settlements.

peaking after about two years rather than one, and because aggregation compounds the uncertainties inherent in each individual calculation. That said, it appears reasonable to assume that the effects of lower wealth will outweigh looser monetary conditions in the United States (taking into account the potential impact on investment), although—as in France—this may be partly offset by continuing strength in the housing market. In the United Kingdom, buoyant household consumption suggests that the effect of housing prices may have more than offset the adverse effects of equity market declines. In other major economies, the appreciation in the effective exchange rate will be a more important factor,

exacerbating the decline in the value of equities and, in the case of Japan and Germany, housing.

Developments in equity markets in industrial countries also feed through to emerging market countries. Given the increasing correlation between equity markets across the world, declines in industrial country equity markets have been mirrored in most emerging markets (although country-specific factors continue to play an important and in some cases offsetting role). With financial systems in most developing countries still largely bank-based, and equity markets often small, the direct impact on activity in general will be moderate (although most countries will be affected by weaker activity in industrial countries).

In practice, the indirect impact through financial markets is often more important. On the positive side, as discussed above, lower equity prices have been accompanied by lower interest rates in industrial countries, which benefits emerging market countries. However, the general shift out of risky assets has raised spreads for emerging markets. Since late March, the rise in the emerging market bond index plus spread has been on the order of 2 percentage points (with a similar increase in spreads in U.S. junk bonds, generally regarded as being in the same asset class), significantly larger than the fall in bond rates, implying some tightening of financing conditions for the average borrower.

In sum, recent movements in asset prices appear to be providing a downward impetus to global activity, although the main sources vary across regions, with equity declines dominating in North America and the United Kingdom, exchange rate appreciation mattering more in the euro area and Japan, and increasing bond spreads being the main conduit to emerging markets.

sell-off of emerging market debt and a decline in emerging market financing (Figure 1.4). Since early August, financing conditions have improved, led by Brazil where spreads have tightened significantly since the announcement of a new IMF

package, accompanied by a commitment by the major presidential candidates to pursue sound economic policies. However, spreads still remain at high levels, and unsecured access remains difficult to subinvestment-grade borrowers in Latin

Figure 1.4. Emerging Market Financial Conditions

Emerging market spreads have risen markedly, particularly in Argentina and Brazil, accompanied by signs of increased contagion.

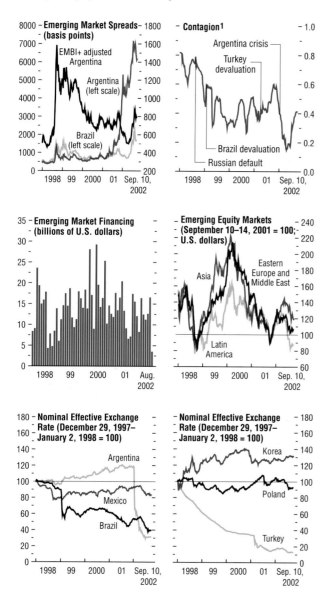

Sources: Bloomberg Financial Markets, LP; and IMF staff estimates.
[1]Average of 60-day rolling cross-correlation of emerging debt markets.

America. Equity markets in most emerging markets have fallen back over recent months, although developments in foreign exchange markets have been mixed. In some Latin American countries and Turkey, currencies have fallen sharply against the dollar, and by even more in trade-weighted terms. Elsewhere, currencies have generally risen against the dollar, but weakened against the euro and yen. With some exceptions, this has generally resulted in a modest depreciation in trade-weighted exchange rates.

While the global recovery is expected to continue, it will be weaker than earlier expected. Global growth is projected at 2.8 percent in 2002, rising to 3.7 percent in 2003, underpinned by the turn in the inventory cycle and continued accommodative policies, with interest rate increases in the United States and the euro area now expected to be deferred to 2003. While global growth in 2002 is the same as that projected in the April 2002 *World Economic Outlook*, this reflects the stronger-than-expected outturn in the first quarter of 2002, as well as upward revisions for Asia, partly offset by much lower growth in Latin America. From the second quarter onward, the pace of recovery has generally been marked down to reflect the impact of recent financial market developments (Figure 1.5); correspondingly, GDP growth in 2003 is somewhat lower than earlier projected. Looking across individual countries and regions, we find the following:

- Among the industrial countries, the recovery in the United States is now expected to be considerably weaker than earlier thought with GDP growth in 2002—and more so 2003—marked down significantly (Table 1.2). In the euro area, projections have also been reduced; in the short run GDP growth will be boosted by a turn in the inventory cycle, but final domestic demand growth is likely to pick up more slowly than previously expected. In Japan, where the economy appears to have bottomed out, GDP growth has been revised upward in both 2002 and 2003. However, with final domestic demand still weak, there are downside risks to the outlook given the appreciation of the yen and the more subdued recovery elsewhere.

- The outlook for the major emerging market countries has become increasingly diverse. In Latin America, the outlook has seriously deteriorated, and output is expected to decline in 2002. Growth is picking up in Mexico and is expected to in Chile; both countries are relatively open and have strong credit ratings. However, Argentina is experiencing an almost unprecedented collapse in economic activity (outside transition and conflict countries), Uruguay is facing serious difficulties, and the outlook for Brazil, Venezuela, and a number of smaller countries has deteriorated markedly. In emerging markets in Asia, in contrast, the recovery has so far proved stronger than expected, driven by the rebound in global trade and a nascent recovery in information technology (see Appendix 1.1), and in some countries—notably China, India, and Korea—domestic demand. While there are signs that final domestic demand growth is becoming more broadly based, the recovery remains dependent on external demand, and the prospect of a weaker global recovery has added to downside risks. In the Middle East, while the outlook for oil prices is somewhat stronger, the forecast has remained broadly unchanged; however, the difficult security situation has affected growth in Israel and its neighbors. GDP growth in Turkey has somewhat exceeded expectations, although political turmoil and a sharp deterioration in financial indicators, combined with its large financing needs, have increased risks looking forward. The outlook for the countries in transition remains solid, underpinned by strong growth in Russia and Ukraine, and in central and eastern Europe, by buoyant foreign direct investment.

- Among the poorest countries, GDP growth in Africa has held up surprisingly well, supported by improved macroeconomic policies, fewer conflicts, and debt relief under the HIPC (heavily indebted poor countries) Initiative. Serious problems exist in certain parts of the continent, however—most importantly, a

Figure 1.5. Global Outlook
(Percent change from four quarters earlier)

While GDP growth is expected to continue to pick up during 2002 and 2003, the recovery will be slower than earlier anticipated.

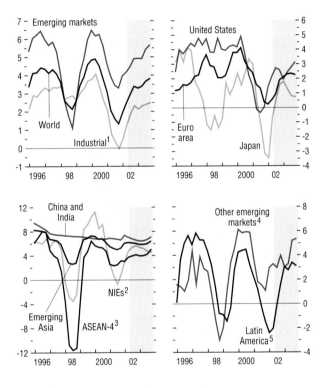

Sources: Haver Analytics; and IMF staff estimates.
[1]Australia, Canada, Denmark, euro area, Japan, New Zealand, Norway, Sweden, Switzerland, the United Kingdom, and the United States.
[2]Hong Kong SAR, Korea, Singapore, and Taiwan Province of China.
[3]Indonesia, Malaysia, the Philippines, and Thailand.
[4]Czech Republic, Hungary, Israel, Poland, Russia, South Africa, and Turkey.
[5]Argentina, Brazil, Chile, Colombia, Mexico, Peru, and Venezuela.

Table 1.2. Advanced Economies: Real GDP, Consumer Prices, and Unemployment
(Annual percent change and percent of labor force)

	Real GDP				Consumer Prices				Unemployment			
	2000	2001	2002	2003	2000	2001	2002	2003	2000	2001	2002	2003
Advanced economies	**3.8**	**0.8**	**1.7**	**2.5**	**2.3**	**2.2**	**1.4**	**1.7**	**5.9**	**5.9**	**6.4**	**6.5**
Major advanced economies	3.4	0.6	1.4	2.3	2.3	2.1	1.2	1.6	5.7	6.0	6.6	6.7
United States	3.8	0.3	2.2	2.6	3.4	2.8	1.5	2.3	4.0	4.8	5.9	6.3
Japan	2.4	−0.3	−0.5	1.1	−0.8	−0.7	−1.0	−0.6	4.7	5.0	5.5	5.6
Germany	2.9	0.6	0.5	2.0	2.1	2.4	1.4	1.1	7.8	7.8	8.3	8.3
France	4.2	1.8	1.2	2.3	1.8	1.8	1.8	1.4	9.5	8.6	9.0	8.9
Italy	2.9	1.8	0.7	2.3	2.6	2.7	2.4	1.8	10.6	9.5	9.3	8.9
United Kingdom[1]	3.1	1.9	1.7	2.4	2.1	2.1	1.9	2.1	5.5	5.1	5.2	5.3
Canada	4.5	1.5	3.4	3.4	2.7	2.5	1.8	2.1	6.8	7.2	7.6	6.7
Other advanced economies	5.3	1.6	2.6	3.3	2.4	2.9	2.3	2.2	6.2	5.7	5.8	5.7
Spain	4.2	2.7	2.0	2.7	3.5	3.2	2.8	2.4	13.9	10.5	10.7	9.9
Netherlands	3.4	1.2	0.4	2.0	2.3	5.1	3.8	2.4	2.6	2.0	2.9	3.2
Belgium	4.0	1.0	0.6	2.2	2.7	2.4	1.6	1.2	6.9	6.6	6.9	7.1
Sweden	3.6	1.2	1.6	2.5	1.0	2.6	2.3	2.2	4.7	4.0	4.2	4.2
Austria	3.0	1.0	0.9	2.3	2.0	2.3	1.8	1.6	3.7	3.6	4.3	3.8
Denmark	3.0	1.0	1.5	2.2	2.9	2.2	2.2	2.1	5.2	5.0	5.1	5.1
Finland	5.6	0.7	1.1	3.0	3.0	2.7	2.2	1.9	9.8	9.1	9.4	9.3
Greece	4.1	4.1	3.7	3.2	2.9	3.7	3.8	3.3	11.2	10.4	10.2	10.3
Portugal	3.2	1.7	0.4	1.5	2.8	4.4	3.7	2.7	4.0	4.1	4.7	5.1
Ireland	11.5	5.9	3.8	5.3	5.3	4.0	4.4	3.0	4.3	3.9	4.5	4.7
Luxembourg	7.5	3.5	2.7	5.1	3.2	2.7	2.0	1.8	2.6	2.6	2.9	2.8
Switzerland	3.0	0.9	—	1.9	1.6	1.0	0.7	1.0	2.0	1.9	2.7	2.7
Norway	2.4	1.4	1.7	1.9	3.1	3.0	1.5	2.5	3.4	3.6	3.6	3.6
Israel	7.4	−0.9	−1.5	1.8	1.1	1.1	6.2	3.0	8.8	9.3	10.7	10.9
Iceland	5.5	3.1	−0.5	1.7	5.0	6.7	5.2	2.2	1.3	1.7	2.3	2.6
Cyprus	5.1	4.0	2.5	4.0	4.1	2.0	2.5	2.2	3.4	3.6	3.8	4.0
Korea	9.3	3.0	6.3	5.9	2.3	4.1	2.7	3.3	4.1	3.7	3.0	3.0
Australia	3.1	2.6	4.0	3.8	4.5	4.4	2.8	2.5	6.3	6.7	6.3	6.0
Taiwan Province of China	5.9	−1.9	3.3	4.0	1.3	—	0.4	1.6	3.0	4.6	5.0	4.9
Hong Kong SAR	10.4	0.2	1.5	3.4	−3.7	−1.6	−3.0	−0.5	4.9	5.0	7.5	7.1
Singapore	10.3	−2.0	3.6	4.2	1.1	1.0	—	1.0	3.1	3.3	3.0	2.3
New Zealand[2]	3.8	2.5	3.0	2.9	2.7	2.7	2.6	1.9	6.0	5.3	5.4	5.6
Memorandum												
European Union	3.5	1.6	1.1	2.3	2.3	2.6	2.1	1.8	8.2	7.4	7.7	7.6
Euro area	3.5	1.5	0.9	2.3	2.4	2.6	2.1	1.6	8.8	8.0	8.4	8.2

[1]Consumer prices are based on the retail price index excluding mortgage interest.
[2]Consumer prices excluding interest rate components.

deepening famine in southern Africa. Growth in 2003 is projected to pick up to 4.2 percent, aided by stronger commodity prices. However, it should be noted that—in part due to unanticipated natural disasters and conflicts—WEO forecasts have consistently overestimated African growth in the past.[3]

Inflationary pressures across the globe remain relatively subdued and—despite some concerns in the euro area—wage increases have generally been moderate. Partly reflecting the pickup in

global activity, commodity prices have turned upward. Since early August, spot oil prices have risen markedly owing to concerns about a further deterioration in the security situation in the Middle East (at the time the *World Economic Outlook* went to press, oil price futures for 2003 were about 5 percent higher than assumed in the WEO baseline). Nonetheless, inflation is expected to remain moderate in 2003, a testament to the increased effectiveness and credibility of anti-inflationary policies in both industrial and emerging markets in recent years. However, deflation remains a serious issue in Japan, and will be exacerbated by the recent appreciation of

[3]See Box 3.1 in the December 2001 Interim *World Economic Outlook.*

the yen; it is also a concern in China and Hong Kong SAR, although in these cases the recent depreciation of the U.S. dollar will be helpful. In contrast, inflationary risks have sharply increased in a number of countries in Latin America, especially Argentina, where, despite some recent progress, a sustainable monetary framework is not yet in place.

Developments since the first quarter have intensified concerns about the durability and sustainability of the recovery. While it is possible that the outlook could be better than projected, for example if productivity growth in the United States were to surprise on the upside, the risks to the forecast—judged in April to be relatively balanced—are primarily to the downside.

- *The recovery continues to depend heavily on the outlook for the United States,* especially with the pickup in western Europe not yet self sustaining and domestic demand growth in Japan likely to remain constrained by banking and corporate sector difficulties for some time. There is a significant risk of a more subdued recovery, especially if the impact of recent equity market declines in both the United States and Europe proves greater than presently expected; if housing markets, which have been providing significant support to demand in the United Kingdom and some smaller European countries, and to a lesser extent the United States (Box 1.1), were to weaken; if final domestic demand in Germany, which has a strong influence on the rest of the euro area, remains weak; or if the tentative recovery in Japan is derailed by adverse shocks—such as an appreciation of the yen—as on previous occasions in the 1990s. Such an outcome would clearly also have an important impact on emerging market economies.
- *Oil prices could spike sharply if the security situation in the Middle East were to deteriorate further.* Depending on its extent and duration, this increase could have a significant negative effect on global growth both directly and indirectly through its effects on confidence (see Appendix 1.1). It would also increase the like-

lihood of other risks to the outlook occurring, and exacerbate their impact.

- *Equity markets remain very volatile, and could fall further.* While a considerable portion of the irrational exuberance that characterized stock valuations in the late 1990s may now have been eliminated, recent accounting and auditing scandals have seriously weakened confidence. The U.S. authorities have moved quickly to strengthen corporate governance and auditing, and other initiatives are also under consideration. It is encouraging that the deadline for certification of financial statements by major U.S. corporations in mid-August passed without significant disruption. Nonetheless, there remains a risk that markets could overshoot on the downside—particularly if new accounting scandals were to emerge or if productivity growth and profitability disappointed—with the impact aggravated by relatively high levels of corporate and household debt in some countries. The fall in equity markets could also pose risks for some financial institutions, particularly in Europe and Japan.
- *Risks in emerging markets, in particular South America and Turkey, have increased.* As described above, the tightening in emerging market financing conditions has resulted in a serious deterioration in the outlook for a number of countries in South America, and has begun to affect a number of those elsewhere. To date, most countries outside South America retain access to global capital markets, and—with some exceptions—flexible exchange rate regimes have facilitated a relatively smooth adjustment to the movements in major currencies. The prospect of more widespread contagion is also reduced by the relatively low level of capital flows, as well as less extensive leverage in global financial markets (Table 1.3). Nonetheless, were problems in South America to intensify—especially if accompanied by weaker growth in industrial countries—the potential for a more widespread impact on the emerging market asset class, including through cross-border bank lending, would increase significantly.

Table 1.3. Emerging Market Economies: Net Capital Flows[1]

(Billions of U.S. dollars)

	1994	1995	1996	1997	1998	1999	2000	2001	2002	2003
Total[2]										
Private capital flows, net[3]	151.7	211.5	228.8	102.2	62.1	84.8	29.4	24.9	62.4	64.9
Private direct investment, net	80.6	98.2	114.4	141.7	153.6	164.0	158.0	172.1	151.3	160.9
Private portfolio investment, net	113.0	42.7	90.2	46.7	−0.1	34.3	−4.3	−42.6	−3.0	−4.0
Other private capital flows, net	−41.9	70.5	24.1	−86.2	−91.5	−113.4	−124.3	−104.6	−85.9	−91.9
Official flows, net	3.5	26.5	−2.3	68.3	69.9	12.2	0.2	15.4	20.6	18.2
Change in reserves[4]	−68.9	−118.2	−108.1	−68.8	−48.2	−87.9	−113.2	−119.9	−146.6	−129.7
Memorandum										
Current account[5]	−71.6	−91.1	−96.5	−69.1	−52.3	34.1	128.4	94.7	61.3	41.7
Africa										
Private capital flows, net[3]	14.3	12.7	11.9	9.4	11.6	15.1	6.1	6.9	8.8	8.9
Private direct investment, net	3.0	1.9	3.6	7.8	6.4	9.3	7.7	22.3	11.8	10.1
Private portfolio investment, net	3.6	2.5	2.8	7.0	3.7	8.2	−2.2	−9.0	−1.0	−1.3
Other private capital flows, net	7.8	8.3	5.5	−5.4	1.5	−2.5	0.6	−6.4	−2.0	0.1
Official flows, net	3.2	4.1	−3.6	2.0	3.3	0.7	1.7	1.3	1.0	0.4
Change in reserves[4]	−5.3	−2.5	−7.9	−11.1	2.5	−3.5	−13.3	−12.7	−4.7	−8.4
Developing Asia[6]										
Private capital flows, net[3]	70.3	96.9	122.1	7.1	−45.9	6.8	−12.9	16.7	31.6	7.9
Private direct investment, net	44.7	52.6	53.4	56.8	59.7	61.2	54.2	47.1	58.7	59.0
Private portfolio investment, net	20.8	22.7	32.8	7.3	−17.9	14.4	4.3	−13.5	0.7	−9.7
Other private capital flows, net	4.7	21.6	35.9	−56.9	−87.7	−68.8	−71.4	−16.8	−27.8	−41.3
Official flows, net	3.2	4.5	−12.4	16.9	26.1	4.4	5.1	−5.7	−1.4	3.3
Change in reserves[4]	−57.8	−43.3	−46.9	−15.4	−67.4	−78.9	−48.7	−84.7	−97.4	−67.8
Memorandum										
Hong Kong SAR										
Private capital flows, net[3]	−4.1	−3.5	−7.1	11.7	−8.5	1.0	4.2	−5.1	−10.4	−10.9
Middle East and Turkey[7]										
Private capital flows, net[3]	15.7	9.9	7.2	15.0	9.1	0.2	−22.4	−48.4	−19.6	−9.4
Private direct investment, net	4.8	6.5	4.8	5.5	6.4	5.5	7.9	10.8	8.8	11.5
Private portfolio investment, net	7.6	2.0	1.8	−0.9	−13.2	−3.2	−13.7	−22.0	−9.8	−6.6
Other private capital flows, net	3.3	1.4	0.6	10.4	15.8	−2.1	−16.7	−37.1	−18.6	−14.4
Official flows, net	3.5	4.5	6.6	9.3	3.0	2.1	0.4	6.6	8.8	4.7
Change in reserves[4]	−4.7	−11.6	−22.2	−19.4	9.7	−6.3	−27.0	−6.7	−10.8	−10.4
Western Hemisphere										
Private capital flows, net[3]	47.1	43.5	64.9	69.3	72.7	49.7	48.6	22.8	10.3	26.5
Private direct investment, net	22.8	24.2	40.3	56.1	60.1	64.1	64.7	66.9	40.4	45.6
Private portfolio investment, net	65.0	0.8	39.5	25.9	22.3	11.9	4.7	−2.2	1.0	7.6
Other private capital flows, net	−40.7	18.5	−14.9	−12.7	−9.8	−26.3	−20.8	−41.9	−31.1	−26.7
Official flows, net	4.7	19.2	4.7	14.9	16.0	1.5	−3.5	21.1	15.8	14.6
Change in reserves[4]	4.0	−23.3	−28.9	−13.5	8.4	7.9	−2.5	1.2	−3.3	−16.5
Countries in transition										
Private capital flows, net[3]	4.3	48.4	22.6	1.3	14.6	13.0	10.0	26.8	31.2	31.1
Private direct investment, net	5.3	13.1	12.3	15.5	20.9	23.9	23.4	25.1	31.5	34.7
Private portfolio investment, net	16.1	14.6	13.3	7.5	5.0	2.9	2.6	4.2	6.1	6.0
Other private capital flows, net	−17.1	20.7	−3.0	−21.6	−11.3	−13.8	−16.0	−2.5	−6.4	−9.6
Official flows, net	−11.2	−5.8	2.3	25.3	21.4	3.6	−3.6	−7.9	−3.6	−4.8
Change in reserves[4]	−5.1	−37.5	−2.2	−9.5	−1.4	−7.1	−21.7	−17.1	−30.5	−26.7
Memorandum										
Fuel exporters										
Private capital flows, net[3]	18.6	23.4	−4.8	−9.6	−5.4	−28.5	−53.3	−43.6	−31.4	−24.8
Nonfuel exporters										
Private capital flows, net[3]	133.2	188.0	233.6	111.8	67.4	113.4	82.7	68.6	93.8	89.8

[1]Net capital flows comprise net direct investment, net portfolio investment, and other long- and short-term net investment flows, including official and private borrowing. Emerging markets include developing countries, countries in transition, Korea, Singapore, Taiwan Province of China, and Israel.
[2]Excludes Hong Kong SAR.
[3]Because of data limitations, "other private capital flows, net" may include some official flows.
[4]A minus sign indicates an increase.
[5]The sum of the current account balance, net private capital flows, net official flows, and the change in reserves equals, with the opposite sign, the sum of the capital and financial account and errors and omissions. For regional current account balances, see Table 27 of the Statistical Appendix.
[6]Includes Korea, Singapore, and Taiwan Province of China in this table.
[7]Includes Israel and Malta.

- *While the fall in the dollar has so far been orderly, the U.S. current account deficit remains very high, and—as discussed in Chapter II—a more abrupt and disruptive adjustment cannot be ruled out.* Given the synchronicity of the global slowdown, the U.S. current account deficit has improved very little since 2000, and in the short run appears likely to widen (Table 1.4). The question is not whether the U.S. deficit will be sustained at present levels forever—it will not—but more when and how the eventual adjustment takes place. While history is modestly reassuring, the overvaluation of the dollar has not yet been corrected and an abrupt and disruptive adjustment remains a significant risk. A particular concern is that medium-term growth in countries with surpluses—including Japan, emerging markets in Asia, and to a lesser extent Europe—is constrained to differing degrees by structural problems. This makes it more difficult to achieve an orderly rebalancing of domestic demand from deficit to surplus countries, increasing the prospect that the adjustment in the U.S. current account will be accompanied by weaker global growth. Moreover, if in some countries current account surpluses do not decline, the adjustment that will fall on other countries—and therefore the potential appreciation in their exchange rates—will be correspondingly greater.

With macroeconomic policies in most industrial countries still accommodative, a shift to a more neutral stance will eventually be needed. At the same time, however, the short-term outlook has deteriorated, and the risks appear to be primarily on the downside; inflation remains relatively subdued; and anti-inflationary credibility is high. The situation varies somewhat across countries, reflecting their relative cyclical positions, as well as the relative risks associated with greater equity market and exchange rate uncertainty (Box 1.2). However, in most cases the balance of risks appears to favor maintaining relatively accommodative policies for longer than earlier seemed necessary, and in Japan further easing is warranted. If incoming data were to suggest that

Table 1.4. Selected Economies: Current Account Positions
(Percent of GDP)

	2000	2001	2002	2003
Advanced economies	**−0.9**	**−0.8**	**−0.8**	**−0.9**
Major advanced economies	−1.5	−1.4	−1.5	−1.5
United States	−4.2	−3.9	−4.6	−4.7
Japan	2.5	2.1	3.0	2.9
Germany	−1.1	0.1	1.9	2.1
France	1.5	1.8	1.9	1.4
Italy	−0.5	0.1	0.2	0.2
United Kingdom	−2.0	−2.1	−2.1	−2.3
Canada	2.6	2.8	1.7	1.9
Other advanced economies	1.9	2.4	2.3	2.1
Spain	−3.4	−2.6	−1.7	−1.8
Netherlands	3.8	2.8	3.2	3.0
Belgium-Luxembourg	4.5	5.2	4.7	4.5
Sweden	3.3	3.2	3.2	3.2
Austria	−2.5	−2.2	−2.3	−2.3
Denmark	1.6	2.6	2.8	3.4
Finland	7.4	6.5	7.3	7.6
Greece	−6.8	−6.2	−5.1	−5.4
Portugal	−10.4	−9.2	−8.0	−7.5
Ireland	−0.6	−1.0	−0.7	−0.9
Switzerland	12.9	10.0	10.5	11.0
Norway	15.0	15.4	11.4	9.5
Israel	−1.7	−1.7	−1.9	−1.8
Iceland	−10.1	−4.4	−2.0	0.1
Cyprus	−5.2	−4.4	−5.5	−3.6
Korea	2.7	2.0	1.5	0.9
Australia	−4.0	−2.6	−3.6	−3.9
Taiwan Province of China	2.9	6.7	5.8	5.9
Hong Kong SAR	5.4	7.3	9.2	9.7
Singapore	16.7	20.4	21.7	22.3
New Zealand	−5.5	−2.9	−3.5	−4.1
Memorandum				
European Union	−0.4	—	0.6	0.5
Euro area[1]	−0.3	0.4	1.1	1.0

[1]Calculated as the sum of the balances of individual euro area countries.

the recovery is faltering, additional monetary easing would also need to be considered elsewhere. Against this background, the main policy priorities appear to be the following.

- *Macroeconomic policies in industrial countries should continue to be supportive of activity.* In the United States, the Federal Reserve has held interest rates steady, and a continued accommodative stance remains appropriate; if the outlook weakens further, additional interest rate cuts should be considered. With the budget deficit (excluding social security) projected to remain in deficit in coming years, medium-term fiscal consolidation is a priority

Box 1.2. Market Expectations of Exchange Rate Movements

After continuing to strengthen in the face of last year's global downturn, the U.S. dollar has fallen sharply against other major currencies since mid-April. Yet it remains well above longer-term historical values, while the U.S. current account deficit has swelled to a record level. These developments raise the question of whether a much larger, and possibly disorderly, adjustment in major exchange rates presents a risk to the global outlook.

In assessing this issue, it is interesting to consider how market participants view the outlook for exchange rates, both in terms of direction and volatility. Futures and options prices can be used to shed light on market perceptions, specifically by constructing implied "probability density functions" (PDFs) for future exchange rate values. Under the assumption that market participants are risk neutral, PDFs indicate the perceived likelihood of the exchange rate reaching different levels at a future date.[1]

Such implied PDFs for the yen-dollar rate are shown in the figure (top panel). They reflect expectations for the 3-month-ahead level of the exchange rate at three different dates: January 2, 2002, June 27, 2002, and August 16, 2002. The mean of the yen-dollar PDF shifted down over this period, in line with the appreciation in the yen against the dollar. Indeed, covered interest arbitrage ensures that the mean of the PDF (i.e., the forward rate in markets) equals the spot rate plus an adjustment for the interest differential on short-term assets in the two currencies. As interest rates have been stable in recent months, so has the gap between spot and forward exchange rates. The forward yen-dollar rate implies further yen appreciation, as the short-term interest rate on yen assets is below that on U.S. dollar assets; conversely, the for-

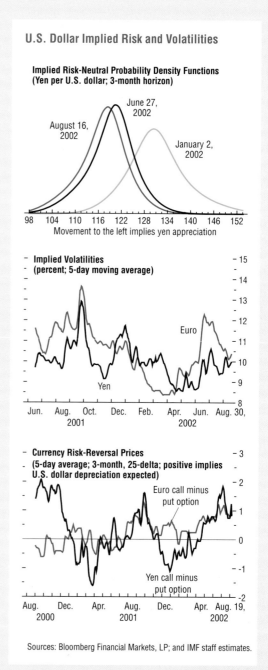

U.S. Dollar Implied Risk and Volatilities

Implied Risk-Neutral Probability Density Functions
(Yen per U.S. dollar; 3-month horizon)

Sources: Bloomberg Financial Markets, LP; and IMF staff estimates.

Note: The main authors of this box are Peter Breuer and Guy Meredith.

[1]The risk-neutrality assumption implies that changes in options prices reflect changes in expected volatility ("riskiness"), as opposed to investor attitudes toward risk. See Breuer (2002) for an approach to accounting for risk aversion in constructing PDFs.

ward euro-dollar rate implies euro depreciation given the higher yield on euro assets.

Because of the mechanical link between spot rates, forward rates, and the interest differential, "higher moments" of the PDF often reveal more interesting information about market expectations. For instance, the expected *volatility* of the future exchange rate is reflected in the variance of the implied PDF. The path of expected volatility for the yen-dollar and euro-dollar rates since mid-2001 is shown in the figure (middle panel). Expected volatility rose following the onset of dollar weakness in April. The rise in euro-dollar volatility was particularly sharp during June, but most of this increase was retraced over the summer. Yen-dollar volatility has been more stable, showing only a modest increase from the trough in the spring. On balance, these data do not suggest that markets perceive an abnormally high risk of abrupt currency movements relative to recent history.

Another interesting feature of implied PDFs is their "skew." Skew reflects asymmetries in the shape of the two sides of the PDF, which arise when markets perceive the risk of equal-sized currency movements in opposite directions as differing. In practice, skew is measured by the cost of insuring against a dollar depreciation relative to a dollar appreciation of the same degree—the risk-reversal price.[2] Recent data on risk-reversal prices are shown in the figure (bottom panel). The relative cost of insuring against dollar depreciation versus both the euro and yen has risen significantly since the begining of the year. This suggests that markets place greater weight on the possibility of a sharp dollar depreciation relative to the forward rate than was the case earlier, even as the

spread between the forward and spot rate has remained roughly constant.

It must be emphasized that the assumption of risk neutrality is needed to interpret PDFs as measures of market expectations. Furthermore, the value of market expectations as predictors of future exchange rates depends on whether markets efficiently use all available information. Many studies have indicated that the forward rate is a biased predictor of the future spot rate, indicating that at least one, and possibly both, of these assumptions do not hold.[3] There has been less conclusive analysis of the relationship between higher moments of implied PDFs and future exchange rates, so it is more difficult to gauge their usefulness as predictors of exchange rate movements or volatility.

Independent of the forecasting power of market expectations, however, implied PDFs provide information that is potentially useful in assessing the interaction between market developments and policy actions. For instance, an environment of high uncertainty about future exchange rates could raise concerns about excessive market reactions to policy initiatives, while a significant skew in expectations implies the risk of large one-way movements in rates. Either situation might create a rationale for taking a cautious approach to policy actions to avoid destabilizing currency markets. Recent market information does not suggest that perceptions of volatility or asymmetric outcomes have become abnormal from a historical perspective, suggesting that policies would not be constrained by concerns about exceptional market sensitivity.

---

[2]A risk reversal is the price of an out-of-the-money foreign currency call option relative to the price of an equally out-of-the-money short foreign currency put option.

[3]See Meredith and Ma (2002).

(Table 1.5), especially in view of impending demographic pressures. In the euro area, concerns about inflationary pressures have been mitigated by the appreciation of the euro as well as the weaker-than-expected recovery. Correspondingly, the scope for easing has increased, and should be used if activity

remains weak and inflationary pressures ease as expected. In Japan, aggressive monetary easing remains essential to address deflationary pressures. If structural reforms—which could adversely affect activity in the short run—are significantly accelerated, further steps to contain the withdrawal of stimulus

Table 1.5. Major Advanced Economies: General Government Fiscal Balances and Debt[1]
(Percent of GDP)

	1986–95	1996	1997	1998	1999	2000	2001	2002	2003	2007
Major advanced economies										
Actual balance	−3.9	−3.6	−2.1	−1.6	−1.1	−0.1	−1.7	−3.0	−2.8	−0.9
Output gap[2]	−0.5	−1.1	−0.5	−0.5	−0.1	0.7	−1.1	−2.2	−2.4	—
Structural balance	−3.6	−3.0	−1.7	−1.3	−1.0	−0.8	−1.3	−2.2	−1.9	−0.9
United States										
Actual balance	−4.5	−2.4	−1.3	−0.1	0.6	1.5	−0.2	−2.6	−2.8	−1.0
Output gap[2]	−1.3	−1.6	−0.5	0.3	1.1	1.6	−1.2	−2.0	−2.6	—
Structural balance	−4.0	−1.9	−1.1	−0.2	0.3	0.9	0.1	−1.9	−1.9	−1.0
Net debt	53.2	59.2	57.0	53.4	48.9	43.9	43.0	44.1	45.0	41.7
Gross debt	67.3	72.8	70.3	66.6	63.4	57.7	56.4	57.0	57.4	51.5
Japan										
Actual balance	−0.4	−4.9	−3.7	−5.5	−7.0	−7.3	−7.1	−7.2	−6.1	−1.0
Excluding social security	−3.2	−7.0	−5.8	−7.1	−8.5	−8.4	−7.4	−7.1	−5.9	−1.5
Output gap[2]	0.7	0.9	1.0	−1.7	−2.2	−1.1	−2.4	−3.8	−3.8	0.2
Structural balance	−0.6	−5.2	−4.1	−4.9	−6.1	−6.8	−6.1	−5.7	−4.6	−1.0
Excluding social security	−3.4	−7.2	−6.0	−6.8	−8.0	−8.1	−6.8	−6.2	−5.0	−1.5
Net debt	13.8	21.6	27.9	38.1	45.2	57.5	65.5	74.0	80.2	80.3
Gross debt	71.8	91.7	97.4	108.6	120.9	135.6	145.1	155.1	161.2	152.3
Euro area										
Actual balance	−4.6	−4.2	−2.6	−2.3	−1.3	0.1	−1.6	−1.9	−1.5	−0.5
Output gap[2]	−0.2	−1.8	−1.6	−1.0	−0.6	0.5	−0.4	−1.7	−1.8	—
Structural balance[4]	. . .	−3.1	−1.5	−1.5	−0.8	−1.1	−1.4	−1.1	−0.6	−0.4
Net debt	46.1	58.4	62.9	61.4	60.8	58.7	57.9	58.1	57.3	53.3
Gross debt	60.9	76.1	75.4	73.7	72.6	70.2	69.2	69.4	68.2	60.2
Germany[3]										
Actual balance	−2.2	−3.4	−2.7	−2.2	−1.5	1.1	−2.8	−2.9	−2.2	−0.6
Output gap[2]	0.2	−0.5	−1.0	−0.9	−0.7	0.3	−1.0	−2.3	−2.3	—
Structural balance[4]	−1.8	−2.8	−1.7	−1.4	−1.0	−1.5	−2.2	−1.6	−0.9	−0.6
Net debt	27.6	51.1	52.3	52.2	52.5	51.5	50.8	52.5	53.1	49.2
Gross debt	45.1	59.8	61.0	60.9	61.2	60.2	59.5	61.2	61.8	57.9
France										
Actual balance	−3.5	−4.1	−3.0	−2.7	−1.6	−1.3	−1.4	−2.5	−2.1	−1.4
Output gap[2]	−0.5	−3.3	−3.1	−1.8	−1.1	0.6	—	−1.1	−1.2	—
Structural balance[4]	−3.0	−1.9	−1.0	−1.5	−0.9	−1.6	−1.6	−1.9	−1.4	−1.3
Net debt	30.3	48.1	49.6	49.8	48.8	47.6	48.2	47.6	47.3	53.3
Gross debt	39.0	57.0	59.3	59.5	58.5	57.3	56.9	57.2	57.0	53.3
Italy										
Actual balance	−10.4	−7.1	−2.7	−2.8	−1.8	−0.5	−2.2	−2.0	−1.5	−0.8
Output gap[2]	−0.1	−1.7	−1.6	−1.7	−2.0	−1.0	−1.0	−2.3	−2.0	—
Structural balance[4]	−10.4	−6.2	−1.9	−2.0	−0.9	−1.3	−1.8	−1.7	−1.2	−0.8
Net debt	97.8	116.1	113.8	110.1	108.4	104.6	103.9	104.0	100.9	89.7
Gross debt	103.7	122.7	120.2	116.4	114.5	110.6	109.8	109.8	106.6	94.8
United Kingdom										
Actual balance	−3.4	−4.2	−1.6	0.2	1.4	4.0	0.2	−0.8	−1.1	−1.4
Output gap[2]	−0.2	−1.3	−0.4	0.5	0.2	1.1	0.4	−0.9	−1.1	—
Structural balance[4]	−3.3	−3.4	−1.0	0.3	1.2	1.3	−0.1	−0.6	−0.5	−1.4
Net debt	24.2	46.2	44.6	41.9	39.0	34.0	30.8	29.5	29.0	28.5
Gross debt	42.6	51.8	49.6	46.6	43.8	40.4	37.9	36.3	35.7	35.1
Canada										
Actual balance	−6.6	−2.8	0.2	0.1	1.7	3.1	1.8	1.1	1.2	1.2
Output gap[2]	0.3	−1.4	−0.9	−0.8	0.5	1.2	−0.8	−0.6	−0.1	—
Structural balance	−6.6	−2.0	0.8	0.5	1.6	2.5	2.2	1.6	1.2	1.1
Net debt	70.1	88.1	85.6	81.8	75.6	65.4	61.2	57.4	53.1	39.7
Gross debt	101.9	120.7	118.8	115.3	112.6	102.1	100.9	95.4	89.0	69.5

Note: The methodology and specific assumptions for each country are discussed in Box A1.

[1]Debt data refer to end of year; for the United Kingdom they refer to end of March.

[2]Percent of potential GDP.

[3]Data before 1990 refer to west Germany. For net debt, the first column refers to 1988–94. Beginning in 1995, the debt and debt-service obligations of the Treuhandanstalt (and of various other agencies) were taken over by general government. This debt is equivalent to 8 percent of GDP, and the associated debt service to ½ to 1 percent of GDP.

[4]Excludes one-off receipts from the sale of mobile telephone licenses (the equivalent of 2.5 percent of GDP in 2000 for Germany, 0.1 percent of GDP in 2001 and 2002 for France, 1.2 percent of GDP in 2000 for Italy, and 2.4 percent of GDP in 2000 for the United Kingdom). Also excludes one-off receipts from sizable asset transactions.

that is in prospect from the latter part of FY2002 may be desirable.

- In *emerging markets*, the deterioration in the outlook has partly reflected lower risk appetite and contagion, but country-specific factors—including political uncertainties and concerns about debt dynamics—have played a more important role. Particularly in Latin America and Turkey, a restoration of financial market confidence will require that these issues be comprehensively addressed. Elsewhere, policy priorities vary widely, as described in detail below. However, given the more difficult global economic outlook, macroeconomic policies in countries with room for policy maneuver—as in industrial countries—will likely have to remain accommodative longer than earlier expected.

- *Medium-term policies should continue to foster sustained and broad-based economic growth and an orderly reduction in global imbalances.* Since the mid-1990s, much attention has been given to the pickup in productivity growth in the United States, particularly in relation to other major industrial countries. This pickup appears due in part to the greater flexibility of the U.S. economy (Box 1.3). In the euro area, flexibility can be boosted by reform of labor and product markets—measures that would also help raise employment rates, which remain well below U.S. levels. In Japan, reform of banking and corporate sectors takes center stage; despite different circumstances, that is also a priority for emerging markets in Asia. Higher potential growth in the rest of the world is desirable in its own right, but would also help reduce dependence on the United States as the global engine of growth, and promote an orderly correction of the global imbalances. Beyond that, as discussed in the *Global Financial Stability Report,* there is a clear need to strengthen corporate governance and transparency in the United States and elsewhere. While corporate malpractice has been a common feature of past technological revolutions, the weaknesses

in accounting and auditing practices likely exacerbated the information technology (IT) bubble and contributed to the global imbalances. The recent reform package in the United States provides a welcome improvement in the framework for regulating corporate governance and accounting; the challenge going forward will be to ensure its effective implementation and enforcement.

- *Continued efforts are required to strengthen resilience to future economic shocks.* In industrial countries, aging populations pose a serious threat to future fiscal and economic stability, particularly in Japan, many countries in Europe, and to a lesser degree the United States. While the solutions are multidimensional—raising potential growth would help substantially—accelerated reforms of pension and health systems, supported by medium-term fiscal consolidation, are now urgent. Fiscal issues are also a key concern in Latin America, where high levels of public debt constitute a continuing and major source of vulnerability and constrain the scope for countercyclical policies, and increasingly in Asia, where public debt has risen sharply recently. With Asia facing a period of substantial structural change, particularly as it adapts to the challenges and opportunities posed by China's rapid development, completion of remaining corporate and financial sector reforms is also a priority.

Since the mid-1990s, most countries in Africa have made substantial progress in achieving macroeconomic stability, but GDP growth remains well below what is needed to achieve sustained poverty reduction. In part, this reflects low investment and savings, but it also reflects the low efficiency with which existing resources are used.[4] Low efficiency, in turn, stems from a host of problems, including the impact of conflicts and disease, weak institutions and infrastructure, poor governance, and low life expectancy, the last much exacerbated by the HIV/AIDS pandemic. The New Partnership for Africa's Development, put forward by African leaders in late 2001, sets

---

[4]Hall and Jones (1999).

Box 1.3. Reversal of Fortune: Productivity Growth in Europe and the United States

The surge in labor productivity growth in the United States since the mid-1990s has attracted significant attention—not just for its beneficial effects on output performance, earnings, and inflation, but also because it has not been matched elsewhere, particularly in Europe. This box assesses the level and growth rate of productivity in the United States and four major European countries in recent years and shows the following: (1) the persistent differences in GDP per capita between the United States and Europe are due much more to differences in labor utilization than those in labor productivity (as measured by output per hour); (2) productivity growth in Europe exceeded that in the United States up to the mid-1990s, but since then European performance has slackened while the United States has picked up and taken a lead; and (3) there is a consensus that high tech sectors have played an important role in the acceleration of productivity growth in the United States; these benefits are yet to be fully realized in Europe.

Following rapid catch-up in the three decades after World War II, GDP per capita in Europe since the late 1970s has generally settled at about 65–70 percent of the U.S. level (see the table). This persistent gap does not appear to be due to differences in productivity (output per hour); rather it reflects marked differences in the operations of labor markets and in labor utilization. Three elements stand out: labor force

Note: The main authors of this box are Manmohan S. Kumar and Maitland MacFarlan.

participation rates, especially of females and of individuals aged 55 and above, are substantially lower in continental Europe; unemployment rates are much higher in Europe; and average annual hours worked per employee are about 20 to 30 percent lower than in the United States. These three elements more than account for the gap in GDP per capita between the United States and the major continental economies; output per hour in France, Germany, and Italy is similar to, or exceeds, the U.S. level. The United Kingdom has similar high rates of participation and employment to the United States but, as on the continent, hours worked are lower; overall, output per hour appears to be lower than in the United States.

The past decade reveals some striking differences in the factors driving growth in output per capita across the two regions. For much of the 1990s, U.S. GDP growth per capita exceeded that in Europe. In the first half of the decade, however, growth in output per hour in the United States lagged substantially behind that in Europe. This continued the trends that had been evident since as far back as the 1960s, with the average annual growth in U.S. productivity per hour less than half that in Europe (as well as in Japan). (See the figure.) Indeed, it was this persistent shortfall in U.S. productivity growth that led to pessimistic assessments of U.S. productivity and growth prospects in the 1980s and even as late as the mid-1990s (see, for instance, Gordon, 1996). Over this period, however, the United States was able to maintain its lead in terms of GDP per capita through higher utilization of labor, as

Growth and Productivity in the United States and Europe

	2001				1990–95	1995–2001	1990–95	1995–2001
	GDP per capita	GDP per hour	Average hours worked	Labor force participation	Growth in GDP per capita		Growth in GDP per hour	
United States	100.0	100.0	100.0	100.0	1.2	2.4	1.0	2.4
Germany[1]	71.8	106.2	69.7	93.2	0.8	1.5	2.3	1.8
France	72.3	115.0	73.8	88.5	0.9	2.0	1.7	1.7
Italy	69.0	117.0	77.2	79.0	1.5	1.8	2.5	1.1
United Kingdom	66.3	85.1	80.6	97.5	1.2	2.4	2.5	1.8

Sources: IMF staff estimates and Organization for Economic Cooperation and Development (2002).
[1]Growth data for Germany—average from 1992–95 only.

Labor Productivity
(Percent; 5-year moving average; output per hour)

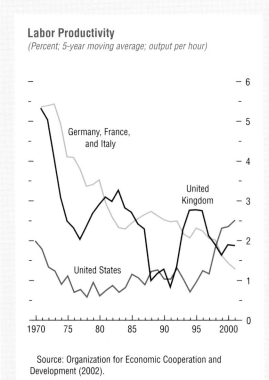

Germany, France, and Italy

United Kingdom

United States

1970   75   80   85   90   95   2000

Source: Organization for Economic Cooperation and Development (2002).

noted above. Moreover, during the first half of the 1990s, the relative weakness in hourly productivity growth in the United States was more than offset by stronger employment growth and total hours worked, leading to a widening differential with Europe in terms of GDP per capita.

In the second half of the decade, there was a marked and surprising acceleration in U.S. productivity growth. In sharp contrast, productivity growth slowed substantially in Germany, Italy, and the United Kingdom and showed no change in France—in all cases falling well behind that in the United States. Rising productivity growth in the U.S. was accompanied by an acceleration in employment growth: even though European employment growth also picked up strongly over this period, it still lagged behind that in the United States. As a result of higher growth in both productivity and employment, growth in GDP per capita in the U.S. exceeded that in Europe even more than in the first half of the 1990s.

What accounts for these divergences in relative productivity performance in the second half of the decade? In the United States, the bulk of the acceleration in productivity growth reflects the production and use of information technology.[1] The take-up of new technologies has been slower in Europe, which meant that—at least until very recently—Europe did not benefit to the same degree from the productivity boost that came for the technology revolution.[2] But in addition, there were a number of other developments—particularly in labor markets—that may have contributed to the pickup in employment growth in Europe, but that also probably contributed to the slowing in productivity growth.

In particular, the relatively rapid employment growth in the euro area in the second half of the 1990s resulted in part from strong wage moderation as well as from steps taken to liberalize labor markets. These entailed reductions in tax wedges (especially in France and Italy), and provision for more flexible employment contracts, which opened up employment opportunities, especially for temporary and part-time workers.[3] Over this period, the long-standing trends of falling participation and rising rates of unemployment were reversed. It is striking that for much of this period part-time employment, especially of females, accounted for the bulk of the employment gains. For some countries such as France, this employment growth may have been concentrated primarily among lower skill workers; in general, though, much of the gains occurred among higher skilled nonmanual workers. (See, for example, European Commission, 2000.) But even there, growth was concentrated in sectors typically associated with low productivity—

[1]See Nordhaus (2001), Baily (2002), Gust and Marquez (2002), Oliner and Sichel (2002), and the October 2001 *World Economic Outlook.*

[2]A large number of factors, including cross-country regulatory differences, may affect the reallocation of labor and capital and the rate of adoption of information technologies. See, for example, Gust and Marquez (2002).

[3]The steps also included employment subsidies for private employers and public employment schemes.

Box 1.3 *(concluded)*

notably the service sectors, including health and social services. In addition, the increase in youth employment, likely to reflect relatively lower-skilled workers, may also have contributed to the weaker productivity growth. (See Kumar and MacFarlan, forthcoming.)

The downturn in labor productivity growth in Europe may have been just a temporary side effect of the labor market adjustments noted above: there is some indication that productivity growth picked up in 2000, before the current cyclical downturn. More broadly, however, the weakness of labor productivity growth may also reflect slower growth in capital-labor ratios in Europe, which had been unusually high. This slowdown in the growth of labor productivity in itself need not be a cause for concern, as it would normally be associated with some concomitant increase in capital productivity, which may leave total factor productivity broadly unchanged. Recent data suggest, however, that total factor productivity growth in Europe may also have declined somewhat, while in the United States it may have increased.

There is a great deal of uncertainty about the future evolution of productivity growth, not least reflecting the recent turmoil in the high tech sector and its longer-term implications. However, the fact that, in the United States, high rates of productivity growth have been maintained even during the recent period of weak activity—when productivity would normally have been expected to decline as employment reductions lagged behind the fall in output—augurs well for the sustainability of the robust performance of recent years. For Europe, there is some evidence that the information technology diffusion is following similar patterns to that experienced in the United States, but at a somewhat slower pace.[4] This, together with a cyclical pickup, should support a rebound in productivity growth, but, to take full advantage of the benefits of new technologies, it is essential to broaden structural reforms in labor, product, and financial markets. Such reforms would also help accelerate participation and employment growth more broadly in these economies, setting up a virtuous cycle of higher productivity, higher domestic demand growth, and higher GDP per capita.

[4]See, for instance, Ark, Inklaar, and McGuckin (2002).

out a bold and consistent strategy to address these issues. But while the first responsibility lies with Africa's governments and people, external support is also essential. The G-8 Africa Action Plan announced at the Kananaskis Summit in June—along with the commitment to double aid flows at the Monterrey Summit three months earlier—is therefore particularly welcome. Higher aid flows will, over time, result in a large increase in public expenditures in recipient countries. Correspondingly, receiving countries will need to press ahead with efforts to improve their absorptive capacity, including strengthening public expenditure management systems and addressing governance issues. This would be facilitated if, on the donors' side, new aid commitments were as concrete and predictable as possible.

As the IMF's Managing Director has repeatedly stressed, while increased aid flows are essential, trade—the theme of this issue of the *World Economic Outlook*—is even more important.[5] Industrial country barriers impose significant costs on the developing world, by some estimates not that much smaller than annual aid flows (Chapter II). Moreover, as discussed in Chapter III, openness to trade is an essential underpinning of financial liberalization. As has been seen in Latin America, if countries have open financial markets but are relatively closed to trade, this can substantially increase the risk of crisis.

[5]"Building a Better Future in Africa," address by Horst Köhler, Ghana, May 2002 (available via the Internet: www.imf.org/external/np/speeches/2002/050302.htm).

The biggest gains come from countries liberalizing their own markets, and the biggest barriers to developing country trade are in fact in developing countries themselves. Even so, industrial countries—which have relatively much smaller agricultural and industrial sectors, and are much more able to manage the transitional costs of restructuring—have a special responsibility to lead the way. Given this, the intensification of protectionist pressures earlier this year, including as a result of the passage of the U.S. Farm Bill, is particularly regrettable, although recent proposals to reduce agricultural protection announced by the United States and the European Commission are encouraging. Every effort needs to be made to ensure that protectionist pressures are contained and that substantive progress is made with the Doha Round.

North America: How Well Will the Recovery be Sustained?

In the United States, growth picked up strongly in late 2001 and early 2002, although since then it has slowed markedly. Recent data revisions reveal that GDP growth in much of 2000 and the first half of 2001 was considerably weaker than earlier thought, although the 2001 recession was still somewhat shorter and milder than the historical norm. This owed much to the aggressive and timely policy response of U.S. policymakers to the downturn, in turn aided by the significant improvement in the fiscal position during the 1990s as well as the credibility of monetary policy management. But it also reflected strong productivity growth in the second half of 2001 and early 2002; these productivity gains supported higher real wages and prevented a further decline in profits, which by early 2001 had fallen close to historic lows (Figure 1.6).

During the first quarter of 2002, the recovery was driven by an upturn in the inventory cycle and by robust household spending, particularly on automobiles and housing. The latter reflected the combined impact of past policy easing, solid wage growth, and buoyant real estate values, which have helped offset the negative

Figure 1.6. United States: Productivity, Profitability, and Investment

With corporate profits still relatively low, companies have cut back employment sharply, resulting in strong productivity growth. Despite high real wage growth, unit labor costs have fallen and profits have also begun to pick up.

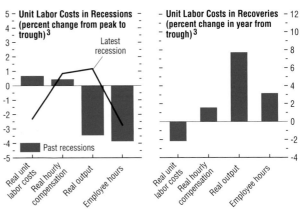

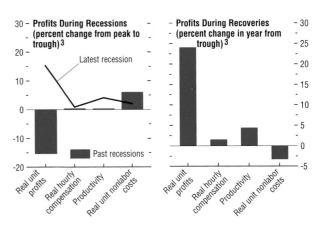

Sources: DRI-WEFA, Inc.; and IMF staff estimates.
[1]Shading indicates business cycle from peak to trough.
[2]Profits before tax, adjusted for inventory valuation and capital consumption.
[3]All data for nonfinancial corporate sector. Latest recession assumed to begin in the first quarter of 2001 and end in the fourth quarter of 2001.

effect of lower equity prices.[6] In the second quarter, however, GDP growth slowed significantly, reflecting partly a sharp jump in import growth but also a weakening in consumption. At the same time, financial market conditions have deteriorated markedly. The S&P 500 has fallen sharply since end-March, reflecting mounting concerns about corporate accounting and auditing practices, a revision of earlier optimistic profit forecasts, and concerns about the sustainability of the recovery. Associated with this, and also reflecting growing concerns about the financing of the current account deficit, the U.S. dollar depreciated significantly against the euro and the yen, although more moderately in trade-weighted terms. Business and consumer confidence have also weakened markedly, although they remain above their late 2001 lows.

Looking forward, the outlook depends crucially on the strength of final demand in the second half of the year and beyond. Clearly, the recent sharp decline in equity markets will have a significant impact on demand looking forward, particularly in 2003, although this will be partly offset by the recent fall in long-run interest rates and the depreciation of the dollar (Box 1.1). While consumption has picked up in recent months, this has largely reflected higher auto sales—underpinned by generous incentives—which are unlikely to be sustained. Correspondingly, much continues to depend on a pickup in private investment. While the recovery is expected to continue, its pace is likely to be significantly more moderate than earlier thought, with growth remaining below potential until well into 2003. Consumption growth is expected to remain subdued, mainly reflecting the effects of lower equity prices, and investment is projected to recover more slowly than earlier thought. The current account deficit, which widened sharply in the second quarter, is expected to rise to 4.6 percent of GDP in 2002.

Considerable uncertainties remain, however, particularly with respect to developments in financial markets. First, as discussed above, equity

markets could fall further, and the impact of such a decline on demand could be exacerbated by the relatively high level of household and corporate debt. Second, the projected recovery in investment could be delayed. There have been some signs of a pickup in investment—including an upturn in equipment and software spending in the second quarter—and lower interest rates and earlier investment incentives should help. However, excess capacity in some sectors and the general tightening of financial market and credit conditions pose downside risks. Finally, the possibility of an abrupt and disruptive adjustment in the U.S. dollar remains a concern, for both the United States and the rest of the world (Chapter II). The extent of these risks will depend importantly on whether the recent rise in productivity growth, which remains broadly intact despite recent data revisions, can be sustained. If productivity growth remains solid, this will provide support to profits (as was the case in previous recoveries—Figure 1.6) and consumption (through higher real wages), and will reduce the risk of an abrupt adjustment in the dollar. If not, there would be a considerably greater possibility of a slower and weaker pickup in demand, and a correspondingly weaker recovery.

Given the less favorable outlook, and relatively subdued inflation, the Federal Reserve has kept its target for the federal funds rate unchanged, but noted in August that the risks were weighted mainly toward conditions that might generate economic weakness. In view of the heightened uncertainties surrounding the outlook, the Federal Reserve has room to wait to withdraw stimulus until the recovery is more clearly established, and if incoming data were to weaken further, additional interest rate cuts would need to be considered. On the fiscal side, the combination of tax cuts, additional expenditures after the September 11 attacks, and the automatic stabilizers have played an important role in supporting demand. But this has taken a substantial toll on the fiscal position, with the FY2002 budget now expected to show a deficit of 1¾ percent of GDP,

---

[6]See "Is Wealth Increasingly Driving Consumption?" in Chapter II of the April 2002 *World Economic Outlook*.

rather than the 3 percent of GDP surplus antici-pated a year ago. Of more concern, the medium-term outlook has also weakened consid-erably. Given the forthcoming fiscal pressures from the aging population—albeit less than in many other industrial countries—and the desir-ability of strengthening domestic savings, it will be important to reestablish a framework that sets the clear goal of balancing the budget (exclud-ing Social Security) over the business cycle. With the budget already anticipating tight—and prob-ably unrealistic—restraint on nondefense discre-tionary expenditures, reaching this goal will likely require some increase in revenues over the medium term. This should be accompanied by steps to safeguard the longer-term health of the Medicare and Social Security systems. Continued efforts are also required to improve corporate governance, building on the reforms under way—including by ensuring that the new over-sight board develops needed reforms to account-ing rules and that these and other reform measures are effectively enforced.

In Canada, the economy has rebounded faster than in any other G-7 country, underpinned by the near completion of the inventory correction, robust consumer spending, and the recent rebound in investment. The strength of the Canadian economy, especially in relation to the United States, reflects a number of factors, including a more moderate capital overhang, less dependence on the IT sector, the relatively depreciated value of the Canadian dollar, and the impact of the U.S. housing boom on the resource sector. Economic indicators continue to point to strong growth in the period ahead although, as in the United States, demand growth will be affected by the recent decline in equity markets. While fiscal policy has provided moderate support to activity, the federal budget remains in significant surplus. General govern-ment debt has fallen significantly in recent years, but is still close to 60 percent of GDP; corre-

spondingly, the authorities remain appropriately committed to a balanced budget and further debt reduction over the medium term. Given the strength of the recovery, the Bank of Canada raised interest rates by 75 basis points through July, but paused in September, partly reflecting the weakening recovery in the United States. Looking forward, the pace of monetary tighten-ing will need to continue to balance the cur-rently strong domestic demand conditions in Canada against uncertain prospects for external demand, particularly from the United States, and the impact of financial market developments.

Japan: Are Growth Prospects Picking Up at Last?

Activity appears to have bottomed out in Japan after the third, and most severe, recession in the last decade. A modest rebound is projected for the remainder of this year and in 2003, although it remains subject to downside risks. The funda-mental issue in Japan, however, continues to be how to achieve more rapid underlying rates of output growth, and break the decade-long pat-tern of anemic performance interspersed with recession. This cannot be achieved by macroeco-nomic policies alone, but requires decisive action to deal with long-standing structural impedi-ments. Such action is most important in the banking sector, where a vicious circle needs to be broken in which large unrecognized nonper-forming loans make banks unwilling to lend, hurting financial intermediation and activity, and thereby creating new nonperforming loans to replace those being written off.

Activity appears to have stabilized in early 2002. The revised national income accounts indicate that activity accelerated modestly over the first half of this year, underpinned by net exports, while private domestic demand remained rela-tively weak.[7] More recent indicators suggest that business investment is likely to begin to recover

---

[7]A major overhaul of the methodology of the Japanese national accounts was introduced in August. Revisions of the data back to early 2001 using the new methodology indicate a smoother path for activity that is also more consistent with higher frequency data.

Figure 1.7. Japan: Costs of Muddling Through
(Logarithmic scale and index 1989 = 100 unless otherwise indicated)

Since the bursting of the asset price bubble in the early 1990s, the Japanese government has failed to put into place bold structural initiatives, at considerable long-term cost.

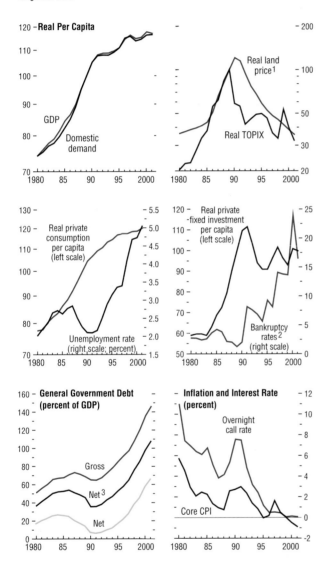

Sources: CEIC Data Company Limited; Nikkei Telecom; Nomura Security; and IMF staff estimates.
[1]Average of all areas for urban land prices in six big cities.
[2]Business failures: amount of liability in trillions of yen.
[3]Excluding social security.

by late 2002, although retail sales remain sluggish. High levels of slack remain, and deflation of about 1 percent a year persists, magnifying real debt burdens. Wealth destruction continues, with equity prices down since the start of the year and land prices continuing to fall, putting additional pressure on bank balance sheets.

Real GDP is projected to fall by ½ percent in 2002 (on an annual basis) before staging modest positive growth of about 1 percent in 2003. This anticipates a gradual recovery in private domestic demand, with private consumption growing somewhat in the second half of 2002 and business investment recovering late in the year. The contribution from net exports, however, is expected to weaken as rising domestic demand boosts imports and the appreciation of the yen erodes competitiveness. Higher private spending is partly offset by fiscal consolidation, with government investment declining in the latter part of 2002 as spending associated with past fiscal stimulus packages wanes, while the 2003 structural fiscal deficit is projected to fall by about 1 percent of GDP, although some of this decline may be offset by tax cuts that are likely to be announced soon.

While the economy could recover more rapidly, particularly if global activity picks up more quickly than currently expected, downside risks predominate. The recent appreciation of the yen highlights the susceptibility of the recovery to external influences, including further appreciation or weaker global recovery. A further fall in equity prices could also affect activity by eroding confidence and dealing a further blow to the difficult financial position of the banks, already weakened by slow growth and falling asset prices.

Over the last decade, the authorities have adopted a gradualist approach to reform, rather than taking decisive action to solve long-standing structural weaknesses exposed by the bursting of the asset price bubble in the early 1990s. This approach has come at a considerable cost to the Japanese economy in terms of activity, wealth destruction, and unemployment (Figure 1.7). Countercyclical macroeconomic policies have been unable to ignite self-sustaining growth or avoid deflation becoming entrenched, despite stimulus measures that helped to increase net debt excluding social security to over 100 percent of GDP, and gross debt to 140 percent of GDP, and reduced short-term interest rates to zero.

In a break with the past, in 2001 the government of newly elected prime minister Koizumi presented a broad strategy to address Japan's fundamental economic problems. This strategy encompassed banking reform, fiscal consolidation, and corporate restructuring and deregulation, and the government is expected to announce another economic package that will provide further details of its reform proposals in coming weeks. Existing initiatives include recently completed special inspections of the accuracy of classification of major bank loans to particularly weak large corporations; accelerating major banks' disposal of the worst nonperforming loans; encouraging a reduction of banks' equity holdings; setting procedures for formal and informal rehabilitation of distressed companies; a ¥30 trillion (6 percent of GDP) limit on central government bond issuance in this fiscal year; and establishing broad goals for medium-term fiscal consolidation. While these are welcome steps, additional initiatives appear necessary to address the structural impediments confronting the Japanese economy and hence to significantly improve medium-term growth prospects, so as to achieve the following:

- *Improve banks' financial health and profitability* through full recognition of the quality of all bank loans; recapitalize viable banks, possibly using public funds, but subject to strong conditionality; promote the exit of nonviable banks; and scale down the role of government financial institutions. Forcefully tackling the underlying problems faced by the banks is a prerequisite for the planned removal of the blanket guarantee on demand deposits next April.

- *Accelerate corporate restructuring* by giving banks stronger time-bound incentives to agree realistic restructuring plans with viable firms and to carry out the rapid and complete disposal of the assets of nonviable ones.

- *Increase the credibility of the medium-term fiscal consolidation strategy* by setting a medium-term

debt target and broad objectives for major budget categories, to help maintain investor confidence in an environment of high and rapidly rising debt.

Turning to the short-term macroeconomic stance, bolder monetary stimulus should be used to support the emerging recovery; given the difficult underlying fiscal position, however, consolidation should be initiated unless bold structural policies are undertaken. Specifically,

- *A more aggressive monetary stimulus is needed to support economic activity*, comprising a public commitment to end deflation in no more than 12–18 months, backed by further quantitative easing. The recent appreciation of the yen bolsters the case for further easing, as it will negatively affect activity and prices if sustained. Although there is a possibility that aggressive quantitative easing could result in excessive yen weakness, the regional impact should likely be manageable given the movement toward flexible exchange rates and healthier reserve and external debt positions. Regional effects would be further mitigated if quantitative easing were combined with the initiatives needed to revive Japan's medium-term growth; and

- *In the absence of appropriate restructuring initiatives, the focus of fiscal policy should move toward the initiation of gradual consolidation to stabilize the debt ratio in the medium term.* Given the unsustainable fiscal situation—net debt excluding social security is projected to rise to over 120 percent of GDP by the end of fiscal year 2002/03—it is critical that the authorities clarify their medium-term consolidation strategy. That said, if appropriate structural policies are followed, which could engender a negative short-run impact on activity, steps should be taken to attain a neutral fiscal stance in the short term.

Western Europe: A Tepid Recovery So Far

Recovery in the euro area appears to be lagging behind that of other regions, especially North America and emerging markets in Asia.

Figure 1.8. United States, Euro Area, and United Kingdom: Contribution to Change in GDP Growth[1]

Recent GDP growth in the United States and the United Kingdom has been driven largely by private consumption, government spending, and in the United States, the inventory correction, while the much weaker growth in the euro area stems mainly from net exports.

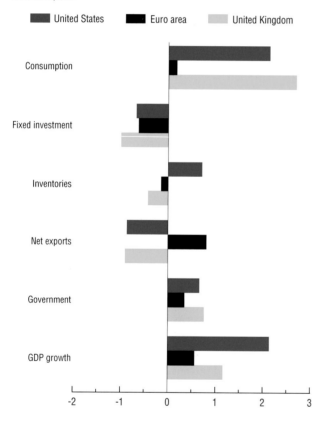

Source: Haver Analytics.
[1]GDP growth rate in the year to 2002:Q2.

Reflecting this, the modest pickup in growth since late 2001 has been led by the external sector, with exports gradually rising but imports falling further (Figure 1.8). But, as reflected in the weakness of imports, domestic demand remains sluggish across much of the region in early 2002, with private consumption still subdued and area-wide investment spending yet to recover from its fall in 2001. Recent indicators of activity and confidence—including retail sales, second quarter GDP, and the key IFO index of business sentiment in Germany—have generally disappointed, suggesting that the regional recovery will be more muted than earlier expected. Nevertheless, several factors should support some strengthening of growth later in 2002 and in 2003. The inventory cycle, which has yet to turn substantially in Europe, should provide a boost to activity later this year. Support should also come from a recovery in consumption, underpinned by recent increases in earnings growth, falling inflation, and the surprisingly robust labor market performance over recent years. And investment spending should strengthen as corporate earnings (which have held up better than in the United States) and capacity utilization pick up. Overall, GDP growth in the euro area is now expected to be 0.9 percent in 2002 and 2.3 percent in 2003, both about ½ percent lower than the projections in the April *World Economic Outlook*.

Questions remain about the resilience and dynamism of the expected recovery, however. The robustness of export-led growth could come under pressure if external demand disappoints or the euro continues to strengthen. Furthermore, while equity market capitalization is much lower in Europe than in the United States and equities are not as widely held by households, euro area stock markets have fallen even more sharply than those in the United States since 2000. This may have a dampening effect on confidence and demand, and add to balance sheet pressures on insurance companies and other financial institutions. Prospects for industrial production and domestic demand in Germany appear particularly uncertain, and further weaknesses there would have important implications for Europe as a whole. The severe floods during the summer of 2002 are estimated to have had a negligible net impact on area-wide activity. In Germany and Austria, any initial adverse effects on output will probably be more than offset later in 2002 and in 2003 by increased spending arising from flood relief and reconstruction efforts.

Substantial variations in economic performance persist across the region, reflecting differences in the impact of recent global shocks—for example, from higher oil prices and weaker international trade—together with differences in fiscal pressures and underlying structural conditions. Among the larger economies, domestic demand has been particularly weak in Germany and Italy, while France has been somewhat more resilient, helped by labor market reforms that have boosted employment over recent years. This variation in economic performance may also partly reflect differential movements in house prices, which have been rising in France but steadily declining in Germany. In addition, ongoing restructuring of the banking system in Germany may have contributed to slower credit growth. Elsewhere, recent growth has been relatively slow in Austria, Belgium, the Netherlands, and Portugal, while stronger economic performance is evident in Greece, Ireland, and Spain.

Inflation has been close to or above the 2 percent ceiling of the European Central Bank (ECB) during much of the economic slowdown, and core inflation (excluding energy, food, alcohol, and tobacco) has remained at about 2½ percent since the beginning of 2002. Concerns have been heightened by a gradual upward trend in wage growth, which, while partly a catch-up from weak growth in earlier years, has been accompanied by falling productivity and hence a sharp rise in unit labor costs. Inflation is expected to diminish in the period ahead, however, as the impact of temporary factors fades (including past increases in oil and fresh food prices, and the euro changeover), as productivity stages a cyclical rebound, and if the recent strengthening in the euro is sustained. The sizable output gap in the euro area should also help contain core

inflation. Earlier in the year, with core inflation edging up and growth expected to recover from around midyear on, the ECB appropriately put interest rates on hold. In recent months, however, the euro's appreciation has led to an implicit tightening of monetary conditions, there are signs of core inflation starting to come down, and, as discussed above, the recovery has appeared increasingly hesitant. Hence, with risks to the outlook now more weighted to the downside and little room for maneuver on fiscal policy (see below), if monetary easing is not warranted now, a bias in that direction is.

On the fiscal front, the euro area's structural deficit is projected to begin narrowing again this year, although policy requirements differ significantly among member states—largely reflecting the failure of the largest countries to match the consolidation efforts of most smaller countries during the period of relatively strong growth in the late 1990s. Germany is expected to be close to the 3 percent limit of the Stability and Growth Pact in 2002 (a limit that Portugal may again exceed this year), implying that significant efforts will be needed in the coming years to bring the deficit down to close to balance. Following revised budget estimates and recent tax decisions in France, the fiscal position now appears much more difficult. And Italy will also need to make substantially firmer efforts to meet the commitment of fiscal balance, to be achieved in 2005 (rather than 2003, as envisaged earlier). More generally, most euro area economies face the need for further strengthening of fiscal positions over the medium term, especially to provide scope for reductions in high tax burdens and to meet public pension and health care obligations, which are projected to rise significantly over the next 10 to 20 years. Credible steps by the three largest countries toward achieving underlying fiscal balance would permit an easier monetary policy.

These fiscal challenges, and the broader need to improve the euro area's growth potential, highlight the need for further structural reforms throughout the region. Some important steps have been taken over recent years—for example, with countries providing greater scope for the use of part-time, temporary, and contractual employees, and some also lowering tax wedges on lower-paid workers and allowing greater flexibility in work arrangements. Such measures, supported by overall wage moderation, contributed to the pickup in employment growth and reduction in unemployment in the second half of the 1990s, including the absorption into employment of many females and younger workers (see Box 1.3). But these efforts need to be intensified and broadened to promote growth in employment and potential output, which would help in meeting the challenges ahead from population aging. While area-wide unemployment has come down substantially, it remains high compared with other advanced economies; and labor force participation rates—especially of people aged over 55—are very low relative to the United States and other countries. Support also needs to come from further product market and financial sector reforms—both areas now all the more important given the scope for increased area-wide integration and efficiency gains since the introduction of the euro.

Turning to other European economies, growth in the United Kingdom slowed sharply in the final quarter of 2001, but rebounded in the second quarter of this year. Private consumption has remained relatively robust, especially in comparison with the large euro area economies, and has been supported by firm labor markets, increased household borrowing, and rapidly rising house prices—up about 20 percent in the year to August. The manufacturing sector has shown signs of improvement following a severe contraction in output and fixed investment since 2000. Looking ahead, growth is expected to pick up in the second half of 2002 and reach about 2½ percent in 2003. This recovery should be helped by the recent weakening of sterling (especially against the euro) and stronger demand for exports. With inflation below target (2 percent in July), weak equity prices, and risks to the global recovery, the Monetary Policy Committee's unchanged interest rate stance is appropriate. Some firming in monetary policy may be needed

when the projected recovery is clearly established, particularly if house prices continue to rise rapidly. This monetary stance will need to be supported by ongoing fiscal prudence as recovery proceeds, with fiscal policy—which includes a major expansion of public spending over the coming years—continuing to be anchored to a sound medium-term framework.

Elsewhere, growth in Denmark, Norway, and Sweden appears to be picking up steadily, and is expected to reach about 1½ percent in 2002 and 2–2½ percent in 2003. These improvements should be supported by further strengthening in private consumption, which, helped by generally firm labor market conditions and earnings growth, has been relatively robust during the slowdown; and by a pickup in exports—including, in Sweden, a rebound in the high tech sector. Manufacturing activity and investment still appear weak, however, and are expected to lag the overall recovery. With inflation pressures still of some concern and growth picking up, monetary policy was tightened in Sweden in early 2002. Further monetary policy adjustments should wait until the recovery is firmly embedded, especially in view of the recent currency appreciation. With inflation remaining very low, the authorities in Switzerland have lowered policy interest rates to help ease safe-haven-related appreciation pressures on the Swiss franc. The Swiss economy is expected to stagnate in 2002, but growth is projected to rebound to about 2 percent in 2003.

Latin America: Heightened Economic and Financial Uncertainties

In contrast with signs of strengthening in most other regions, economic and financial conditions in Latin America deteriorated in the first half of 2002 and remain fragile. Regional output contracted by 2½ percent in the first quarter (compared with the final quarter of 2001), and is expected to fall in 2002 as a whole (Table 1.6). Financial indicators for the region have come under particular pressure: bond spreads widened significantly in the first half of 2002—including sharp increases in Brazil, Ecuador, and

Table 1.6. Selected Western Hemisphere Countries: Real GDP, Consumer Prices, and Current Account Balance
(Annual percent change unless otherwise noted)

	Real GDP				Consumer Prices[1]				Current Account Balance[2]			
	2000	2001	2002	2003	2000	2001	2002	2003	2000	2001	2002	2003
Western Hemisphere	**4.0**	**0.6**	**−0.6**	**3.0**	**8.1**	**6.4**	**8.6**	**9.3**	**−2.4**	**−2.8**	**−1.9**	**−1.6**
Mercosur[3]	**2.9**	**0.1**	**−2.6**	**2.4**	**5.0**	**4.9**	**11.4**	**13.5**	**−3.8**	**−3.5**	**−1.3**	**−0.1**
Argentina	−0.8	−4.4	−16.0	1.0	−0.9	−1.1	29.0	48.0	−3.1	−1.6	10.8	15.4
Brazil	4.4	1.5	1.5	3.0	7.0	6.8	6.5	4.3	−4.2	−4.6	−3.8	−3.6
Chile	4.4	2.8	2.2	4.2	3.8	3.6	2.1	2.8	−1.4	−1.9	−1.6	−2.0
Uruguay	−1.4	−3.1	−11.1	−4.5	4.8	4.4	24.2	49.9	−2.6	−2.5	1.6	1.5
Andean region	**2.9**	**2.0**	**−0.4**	**2.4**	**16.1**	**10.6**	**10.2**	**10.4**	**4.8**	**0.2**	**0.2**	**0.4**
Colombia	2.7	1.4	1.2	2.0	9.2	8.0	5.7	5.0	0.5	−2.2	−2.4	−2.4
Ecuador	2.3	5.6	3.5	3.5	96.2	37.7	12.7	8.9	5.3	−3.4	−8.6	−6.6
Peru	3.1	0.2	3.5	3.0	3.8	2.0	0.4	2.0	−2.9	−2.0	−2.0	−2.3
Venezuela	3.2	2.8	−6.2	2.2	16.2	12.5	22.7	25.2	10.8	3.2	5.7	6.4
Central America and Caribbean	**6.0**	**0.2**	**1.7**	**3.9**	**8.7**	**6.5**	**4.8**	**4.0**	**−3.5**	**−3.2**	**−3.1**	**−3.4**
Dominican Republic	7.2	2.8	3.5	5.3	7.7	8.9	4.8	4.5	−5.2	−3.9	−3.9	−3.8
Guatemala	3.6	1.8	2.3	3.5	5.1	8.7	5.0	3.9	−5.5	−4.6	−4.5	−4.1
Mexico	6.6	−0.3	1.5	4.0	9.5	6.4	4.8	3.7	−3.1	−2.9	−2.8	−3.2

[1]In accordance with standard practice in the *World Economic Outlook*, movements in consumer prices are indicated as annual averages rather than as December/December changes during the year, as is the practice in some countries.
[2]Percent of GDP.
[3]Includes Argentina, Brazil, Paraguay, and Uruguay, together with Bolivia and Chile (associate members of Mercosur).

Venezuela, together with further deterioration in Argentina and Uruguay; most currencies weakened, with the Brazilian *real* falling to an all-time low and the Venezuelan bolivar also depreciating significantly; and debt markets remained largely closed to all but investment-grade issuers—that is, Chile and Mexico (Figure 1.9). The latter two countries continue to resist the region's difficulties reasonably well, helped by sound policy management, relatively low public debt (Chile), and strong links to the United States (Mexico).

Much of the output decline in Latin America during the first few months of 2002 was accounted for by the crisis in Argentina and its spillover effects on some neighboring countries, especially Uruguay and Paraguay. More broadly, though, while direct contagion from Argentina still appears limited, this crisis has provided investors with a "wake-up call" to underlying vulnerabilities that persist in the region. In particular, the recent upsurge in difficulties being experienced by many regional economies stems from interactions between domestic political uncertainties and economic weaknesses, including high debt levels, large external financing requirements, and—in some cases—fragile banking systems. Furthermore, the deterioration in

financial market sentiment toward Brazil—with by far the largest external financing requirement in the region—may have exacerbated the problems being faced by other Latin American economies. Looking ahead, the improvement in global growth should provide some support for regional activity over the coming year. But short-term risks still appear to be predominantly on the downside, and any turnaround in confidence and prospects will be heavily contingent on the abatement of current political, economic, and financial market uncertainties.

Argentina is experiencing an economic contraction of unprecedented magnitude in its economic history, with the cumulative fall in output in the four years to the end of 2002 expected to be over 20 percent—about twice that experienced in the Great Depression of the 1930s. GDP fell 6 percent in the first quarter (over the previous quarter), with consumption and especially investment contracting sharply, and unemployment has increased to about 25 percent. While the trade and current account balances have improved, this reflects the collapse of imports; exports have also fallen, largely because of a cutoff in trade finance. Inflation picked up significantly during the first part of 2002 and,

Figure 1.9. Selected Western Hemisphere Countries: Exchange Rates and EMBI Yield Spreads

There has been a marked weakening in exchange rates and rise in bond spreads for most Latin American countries over recent months.

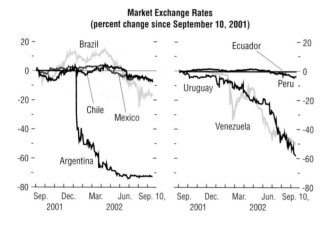

Market Exchange Rates
(percent change since September 10, 2001)

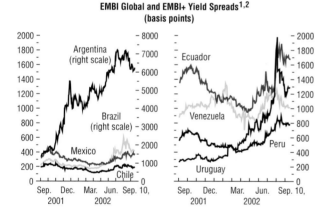

EMBI Global and EMBI+ Yield Spreads[1,2]
(basis points)

Sources: Bloomberg Financial Markets, LP; and J.P. Morgan Chase.
[1]EMBI Global: Chile and Uruguay.
[2]EMBI+: Argentina, Brazil, Ecuador, Mexico, Peru, and Venezuela.

while monthly inflation rates have recently moderated, this in part reflects temporary factors, including the continuing freeze on public service prices. Rapid progress is needed in four key areas: finalizing a fiscal framework that, to the extent possible, balances medium-term debt sustainability requirements and current cyclical considerations; developing a comprehensive strategy to address the very difficult financial condition of the banking sector, and applying this transparently and uniformly; establishing a sustainable monetary anchor for the authorities' economic program; and reinforcing the independence of the central bank.

Some countries neighboring Argentina—notably Uruguay, but also Paraguay and Bolivia—have also been affected by the Argentine crisis through trade, tourism, and financial channels (to varying degrees among the countries concerned). Banks in Uruguay have suffered a particularly severe run on dollar deposits, with heavy withdrawals by Argentine deposit holders then spreading to domestic depositors, and this led to a temporary suspension of banking operations in late July. Paraguay and Bolivia have experienced similar, if lesser, pressures, although deposit withdrawals in Bolivia were driven mostly by uncertainty surrounding the general elections. Seeking to limit the drain on reserves, the Uruguayan authorities allowed the peso to float as of June 20, and further support has come from an augmentation of Uruguay's stand-by credit arrangement with the IMF. Indicating an improvement in sentiment, there was a significant slowing in the outflow of deposits during August, especially on the part of domestic deposit holders. Nevertheless, a continuing vulnerability in Uruguay and some other regional economies—already highlighted by the problems in Argentina—is the high level of dollarization of the banking system (Figure 1.10). As a result, the authorities have only limited scope to use monetary policy to respond to current pressures, and banks are facing significant balance sheet problems as exchange rates weaken. In such circumstances, policy attention needs to focus on strengthening the banking system, in part through a more rigorous supervisory framework, as well as on tackling underlying sources of risk—especially by improving fiscal performance.

Having resisted direct contagion from the crisis in Argentina reasonably well, Brazil faced a sharp deterioration in financial market sentiment in the second quarter, notwithstanding the sound macroeconomic policies pursued since the 1998 crisis (Box 1.4). The decline in market confidence—reflected in a sharp fall in the Brazilian *real* and widening of bond spreads—appeared to be driven largely by uncertainties about the prospective policy stance following the October presidential elections. This situation has raised particular concerns, given the high level of Brazil's public debt, the scale of its gross financing requirements, and its important role in emerging debt markets. Responding to these concerns, the IMF has agreed with the Brazilian authorities on a new $30 billion stand-by arrangement, to be disbursed mainly in 2003. The floor on net international reserves has been lowered by $10 billion. The new program envisages the maintenance of a primary surplus target of no less than 3¾ percent of GDP during 2003, to be revisited each quarter, and the inclusion of no less than that target in Brazil's budgetary guidelines law for 2004 and 2005. Accompanying this agreement have been commitments by the major presidential candidates to follow prudent macroeconomic policies, and expressions of intent from foreign banks to sustain their general level of business in Brazil, including trade lines. Greater stability appears to have returned to financial markets in recent weeks, including a significant fall in bond spreads, although they remain very high. These developments have helped to improve confidence and reduce uncertainty, and should thereby support the continuation of the authorities' policy strategy directed toward strengthening macroeconomic stability and growth. But important vulnerabilities remain—including with respect to the debt amortization and rollover schedule in the months ahead. Over the medium term, the policy goal should be to reduce the country's debt burden through the maintenance of high

Figure 1.10. Selected Western Hemisphere Countries: Public Debt and Foreign Exchange Deposits

The significant dollarization of public debt and private bank deposits in most Latin American countries acts as a constraint on the use of easier monetary and exchange rate policies to ease the region's economic difficulties.

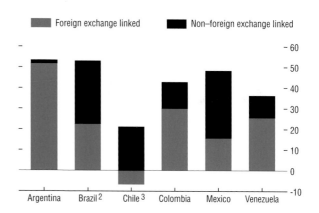

Foreign and Domestic Government Debt, end-2001[1] (percent of GDP)

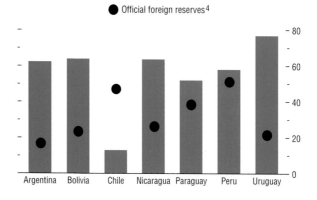

Foreign Exchange Deposits, 2001 (percent of broad money)

Sources: National authorities; IMF, *International Financial Statistics;* and IMF staff estimates.

[1]Unless noted otherwise, data refer to gross stocks of government debt, including that of public enterprises, but excluding central bank liabilities.

[2]Includes also central bank liabilities (monetary base) net of liquid foreign exchange assets.

[3]Consolidated debt of the Chilean government, central bank, and state-owned enterprises, net of official reserves and deposits in the financial system. Figures do not include recognition bonds related to pension system conversion.

[4]Percent of broad money; estimated using central bank's Gross International Reserves.

Box 1.4. Brazil: The Quest to Restore Market Confidence

Following more than two decades of macro-economic instability in Brazil, the *real* plan in 1994—centered on the introduction of a new currency, the *real*, and the adoption of a crawling peg policy vis-à-vis the dollar—proved a turning point for macroeconomic policies. In the four years that followed, inflation was brought down to 5 percent and GDP growth averaged 4 percent; at the same time, considerable progress was made in structural reform, notably in the areas of large scale privatization, demonopolization and deregulation of key sectors, external liberalization, and financial reform. However, the *real* plan was less successful in addressing structural fiscal problems. After an initial tightening, the consolidated public sector—encompassing the central government, the social security system, the central bank, the states and municipalities, and the public enterprises (all levels of government)—posted an average primary deficit of 0.4 percent of GDP between 1996 and 1998, while net domestic public debt rose from 21 percent of GDP in 1994 to 30 percent of GDP in 1997. Partly for this reason, and also because of a sharp appreciation of the exchange rate as stabilization took hold, the current account deficit widened to 4 percent of GDP by 1997.

These underlying vulnerabilities were exposed by the Asian crisis in 1997 and even more so by the Russia and LTCM crisis of 1998, as capital flows to Latin America dropped precipitously. In response to growing pressures on the *real*, the authorities chose to defend the crawling peg regime by raising interest rates, substituting substantial dollar-linked and overnight interest rate–linked debt for fixed-rate debt, and tightening fiscal policy, supported, from December 1998, by an $18 billion stand-by arrangement with the IMF. The issuance of indexed debt allowed the authorities to avoid "locking in" high interest rates on long-term fixed-rate domestic debt, but at a cost of increased vulnerability to subsequent shocks to interest rates and the exchange rate. While financial pressures initially abated, they quickly reemerged, partly

reflecting concerns that the projected fiscal stabilization could not be achieved, and, following an initial widening of the exchange rate band, the *real* was floated on January 15, 1999. This, together with subsequent increases in interest rates, stemmed capital outflows, and the currency stabilized quickly, albeit at a much more depreciated level. After an initial spike in prices, inflation fell back to 6 percent by the end of 2000, aided by the successful introduction and implementation of an inflation-targeting framework. Real GDP growth resumed at 4.4 percent in 2000, after near-stagnation in 1998 and 1999.

In the aftermath of the floating of the *real*, Brazil tightened fiscal policy, posting a primary surplus of 3.2 percent of GDP in 1999 and 3.5 percent in 2000, implying a fiscal adjustment of nearly 4 percentage points of GDP. Brazil also implemented fiscal institutional reforms that substantially strengthened the management of its public finances. The centerpiece of the institutional strengthening effort was the enactment in May 2000 of a Fiscal Responsibility Law, which set out, for all levels of government, fiscal rules aimed at ensuring medium-term fiscal sustainability. In addition, the Budget Guidelines Law sets medium-term fiscal targets as indicative guidelines for the annual budget law. Subnational finances have also been strengthened through the conclusion by 1999, and subsequent continued enforcement, of debt restructuring arrangements between the National Treasury and the states and over 180 municipalities.

Nonetheless, despite the large increase in the primary surplus, the public debt continued to grow rapidly, for several reasons. First, the high interest rates used to defend the currency in 1998 resulted in a sharp increase in interest payments. In addition, the devaluation of 1999 sharply increased the *real* value of dollar-linked public debt that had been issued as part of the defense of the crawling peg policy. Finally, about 11 percentage points of the increase in the debt ratio was due to the recognition of the so-called "skeletons," or implicit public sector liabilities, which were gradually made explicit. Overall, net public debt (domestic and external) rose from 35 per-

Note: The main author of this box is Andrew Berg. The box covers developments up to September 13, 2002.

Brazilian Net Public Debt and its Composition
(Percent of GDP)

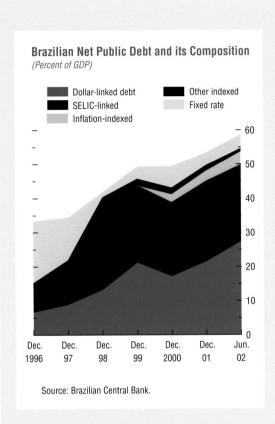

Source: Brazilian Central Bank.

cent of GDP in 1997 to 50 percent by the end of 2000.[1] Moreover, public debt remained highly indexed, with 45 percent linked to the SELIC overnight interest rate and a further 35 percent linked to the U.S. dollar by end-2000 (see the figure).

In 2001, Brazil experienced a series of domestic and external shocks, including a domestic energy crisis, spillovers from developments in Argentina, and slower growth in the global economy. Output growth slowed, the *real* weakened substantially in real terms, and spreads on Brazilian sovereign bonds widened along with those of emerging market indices in general. In response, the authorities tightened fiscal policy, supported by a $15 billion stand-by arrangement with the IMF. The authorities indicated that they did not intend to draw under the program

[1]Net debt is defined as total debt less the value of various government assets, such as government bank deposits.

unless conditions in local and external markets deteriorated. In the weeks immediately following the events of September 11, the *real* depreciated and spreads increased further, in part owing to investors' concern about the ability of Brazil to confront large external and domestic financing requirements during a period of global instability, and the authorities purchased $5 billion under the recently negotiated stand-by arrangement with the IMF. By early 2002 the *real* and bond prices had rebounded to roughly mid-2001 levels, and there was some evidence of a recovery in real GDP growth as the energy crisis waned. Most of the recently purchased IMF resources were repaid ahead of schedule in April 2002. However, given the weakening of the *real* over the course of the year, net public debt continued to rise, reaching 53 percent of GDP by the end of 2001.

The respite proved relatively short-lived, and from the second quarter of 2002 the macroeconomic situation has deteriorated sharply. Although macroeconomic policies have remained on track—with primary surplus targets exceeded despite lower than expected GDP growth—sovereign spreads doubled from 750 basis points to 1500 basis points between end-March and end-June and the *real* weakened by 18 percent to 2.8 reais per dollar. The reasons for this deterioration are varied. Perhaps most fundamentally, market participants began to focus their attention on the political uncertainties associated with the October presidential election and what this implied for the existing policy framework. In this context, the surprisingly large losses suffered by major international banks in Argentina were leading them to reassess and in some cases reduce sharply their exposure to Brazil. At the same time, the external environment worsened as global risk appetite fell, industrial stock markets dropped sharply, and doubts about the direction of the global economy resurfaced.

In response, on June 13 the authorities announced a further tightening of fiscal policy—raising the primary surplus target from 3½ to 3¾ percent of GDP—as well as their intent to purchase as much as $10 billion from the previ-

Box 1.4 *(concluded)*

ously approved IMF package following the completion of the Third Review under the program on June 18. Upon completion of the review, the net international reserves floor was lowered from $20 billion to $15 billion, allowing the authorities more leeway to sell their foreign exchange reserves in the market and buy back their external debt. Notwithstanding these measures, the situation deteriorated further in July and early August. First, markets grew increasingly nervous about the outcome of the election and what that might imply for the sustainability of Brazil's public finances, especially following polls in early July. Meanwhile, the weaker *real* continued to increase the value of dollar-indexed debt as a share of GDP, with net public debt rising to 58 percent of GDP at the end of June. Reflecting—and at the same time magnifying—these concerns, international credit lines continued to be cut and private borrowers found it increasingly difficult to roll over international credits. By August 6, spreads had risen to above 20 percentage points while the *real* had weakened to 3.11 reais per dollar (down 24 percent from end-May).

On August 7, the Brazilian authorities reached an agreement with the IMF on a new stand-by arrangement that commits US$30 billion of additional financing by the IMF, 80 percent of which is to be disbursed during 2003. To ensure fiscal sustainability over the medium term, the new program envisages the maintenance of a primary surplus target of no less than 3¾ percent of GDP during 2003, and the inclusion of no less than that level of primary surplus target in the budgetary guidelines.[2] At the same time, the arrangement gives the authorities more room to intervene in the foreign exchange market, with the net international reserve floor stipulated under the previous stand-by arrangement with Brazil reduced by US$10 billion to US $5 billion immediately upon Executive Board approval of the program, which came on September 6.

_____

[2]The 2003 budget law for the central government and federally owned enterprises has been submitted to congress in August 2002, in line with the projection of the program.

The new program is designed to provide a bridge to the new administration, which will take office on January 1, 2003, and to support a policy strategy that will underpin macroeconomic stability. Under plausible macroeconomic assumptions, predicated on continuing improvement in market sentiment over time, the minimum consolidated primary surplus of 3¾ percent of GDP is consistent with a gradual reduction of the net debt ratio over the medium term. The program envisages quarterly reviews of the primary surplus target in light of macroeconomic developments. While initial market reaction to the package was positive, the *real* and sovereign spreads gave up their gains in the following days, partly reflecting a mixed reaction from the main opposition candidates to the announced program and new poll results. Corporations continued to experience difficulties rolling over trade credit lines from foreign banks. To help mitigate this issue, the national development bank (BNDES) has set up a program to provide credit lines to exporters, and the central bank has begun auctioning foreign exchange to domestic banks involved in export financing, for them to on-lend to Brazilian exporters. Meanwhile, foreign banks have, after meetings with the authorities in recent weeks, expressed their intent to sustain their general level of business in Brazil, including trade lines. These developments, in addition to commitments by the major presidential candidates to follow prudent macroeconomic policies, among other factors, have led to greater stability in financial markets in recent weeks. Bond spreads have fallen sharply from their July/August peaks to levels not seen since mid-July; at the time the *World Economic Outlook* went to press the exchange rate had not made up as much ground. Markets remain focused both on short-run concerns about the need to roll over maturing government debt and the availability of external finance and longer-run questions regarding the public debt burden. To assuage these concerns, it is critical to provide confidence that an appropriate policy framework will remain in place after the elections; in this respect, the assurances already given by the major presidential candidates that they will maintain an adequate primary surplus and honor contracts are key ingredients.

primary surpluses, accompanied by structural reforms directed at reducing fiscal rigidities, which should help reduce the real interest rate, and strengthening and broadening sources of economic growth, including through greater openness to foreign trade.

Many other countries in Latin America—including Ecuador, Peru, and Venezuela—have also experienced a sharp rise in risk perceptions since the first quarter. As in Brazil, this deterioration appears to reflect the interactions among increased regional (and to some extent global) uncertainties, domestic political tensions, and underlying economic vulnerabilities that stem in most cases from the level and composition (by currency and maturity) of public debt. However, policy weaknesses, including substantial fiscal slippages and lack of progress with structural reforms, have also played an important role. In Ecuador, for example, the economic benefits arising from dollarization in early 2000 and from strong oil prices risk being undermined by delays in controlling public spending, due in part to large public sector wage increases, and in reforming public enterprises and the social security system. These developments have put upward pressure on the real exchange rate and widened the current account deficit. In Venezuela, a contraction in economic activity is expected this year as a result of cuts in oil output and the impact of prevailing uncertainties on the non-oil sector. Notwithstanding relatively high oil export prices, the fiscal deficit is expected to remain large at 3.7 percent of GDP in 2002, putting severe strains on sources of domestic and international finance. Further efforts to strengthen revenue and restrain spending are urgently required. Also needed is a program to address financial sector weaknesses, especially as deposit withdrawals and the decline in economic activity have increased the fragility of the banking system. Risk perceptions regarding Peru have also risen as a result of increased pressures on the government to relax macroeconomic policies in the run-up to regional elections in November.

In all of these countries, fiscal adjustment—involving expenditure restraint and improvements in revenues—is the core policy requirement for reducing economic vulnerabilities. This needs to be supported by firm monetary policies and wide-ranging structural reforms, including measures to address banking sector weaknesses and to liberalize external trade. Such mutually reinforcing policies are needed to restore investor confidence, lower interest rates, attract external financing, and reinvigorate growth.

Elsewhere in the region, Mexico and Chile have not escaped the region's difficulties entirely. The Mexican peso has weakened since the start of the year (although this may not be entirely unwelcome, given its earlier appreciation); Chile has been hit by a reduction of its exports to Argentina and some Chilean firms have also suffered losses in that country; and both countries' bond spreads have risen somewhat (although they remain low compared with other regional economies). Overall, though, these countries appear in relatively good shape to withstand current pressures and to resume stronger growth rates later in 2002 and in 2003, supported by the gradual firming of activity in the United States (of particular importance to Mexico) and in other advanced economies. Underpinning these countries' comparative resilience have been their strong records of policy performance, reflected in their investment-grade ratings and, in Chile, the low level of public debt. Given the substantial risks still present in the outlook, maintaining a firm and credible policy stance remains essential to limit the impact of the difficulties elsewhere in Latin America. Mexico's substantial external financing needs still leave it exposed to changes in investor sentiment, and recent tax reforms have not succeeded in raising non-oil revenues as intended. Key measures to reduce the associated risks include implementation of the authorities' medium-term program of fiscal and structural reform directed at reducing external vulnerabilities, strengthening productivity growth, and improving international competitiveness. In addition, with inflation having picked up recently, a firm monetary stance will need to be maintained to keep the inflation target within reach. The widening of the Argentina crisis could weaken

Table 1.7. Selected Asian Countries: Real GDP, Consumer Prices, and Current Account Balance
(Annual percent change unless otherwise noted)

	Real GDP				Consumer Prices[1]				Current Account Balance[2]			
	2000	2001	2002	2003	2000	2001	2002	2003	2000	2001	2002	2003
Emerging Asia[3]	**7.0**	**5.0**	**5.9**	**6.1**	**1.8**	**2.5**	**2.0**	**3.1**	**2.8**	**3.0**	**2.6**	**2.1**
Newly industrialized												
Asian economies	**8.5**	**0.8**	**4.7**	**4.9**	**1.1**	**1.9**	**1.1**	**2.2**	**4.4**	**6.0**	**5.7**	**5.5**
Hong Kong SAR	10.4	0.2	1.5	3.4	−3.7	−1.6	−3.0	−0.5	5.4	7.3	9.2	9.7
Korea	9.3	3.0	6.3	5.9	2.3	4.1	2.7	3.3	2.7	2.0	1.5	0.9
Singapore	10.3	−2.0	3.6	4.2	1.1	1.0	—	1.0	16.7	20.4	21.7	22.3
Taiwan Province of China	5.9	−1.9	3.3	4.0	1.3	—	0.4	1.6	2.9	6.7	5.8	5.9
ASEAN-4	**5.1**	**2.6**	**3.6**	**4.2**	**3.0**	**6.6**	**6.2**	**5.5**	**7.8**	**5.9**	**3.8**	**2.1**
Indonesia	4.8	3.3	3.5	4.5	3.8	11.5	11.9	8.7	5.3	4.7	2.7	2.0
Malaysia	8.3	0.5	3.5	5.3	1.6	1.4	1.8	2.5	9.4	8.2	6.9	6.4
Philippines	4.4	3.2	4.0	3.8	4.3	6.1	4.0	5.0	11.3	6.3	3.3	−3.3
Thailand	4.6	1.8	3.5	3.5	1.6	1.7	0.7	1.9	7.6	5.4	3.5	2.4
South Asia[4]	**5.3**	**4.0**	**4.8**	**5.5**	**4.0**	**3.8**	**4.5**	**5.1**	**−1.2**	**−0.1**	**0.1**	**−0.1**
Bangladesh	5.6	4.7	4.0	4.0	2.3	1.9	4.8	6.2	−1.3	−0.8	—	−0.3
India	5.4	4.1	5.0	5.7	4.0	3.8	4.5	5.1	−0.9	—	0.1	—
Pakistan	4.3	3.6	4.6	5.0	4.4	3.1	3.4	4.0	−1.9	0.3	1.3	0.1
Formerly centrally												
planned economies[5]	**7.9**	**7.2**	**7.4**	**7.2**	**0.4**	**0.7**	**−0.3**	**1.6**	**1.9**	**1.5**	**1.4**	**0.8**
China	8.0	7.3	7.5	7.2	0.4	0.7	−0.4	1.5	1.9	1.5	1.5	1.0
Vietnam	5.5	5.0	5.3	6.5	−1.7	0.1	4.1	3.8	2.1	2.2	−2.5	−4.0

[1]In accordance with standard practice in the *World Economic Outlook*, movements in consumer prices are indicated as annual averages rather than as December/December changes during the year, as is the practice in some countries.
[2]Percent of GDP.
[3]Includes developing Asia, newly industrialized Asian economies, and Mongolia.
[4]Includes Bangladesh, India, Maldives, Nepal, Pakistan, and Sri Lanka.
[5]Includes Cambodia, China, Lao People's Dem. Rep., Mongolia, and Vietnam.

the pickup in growth expected in Chile next year. Given its generally stronger debt position and financial sector, however, Chile should continue to outperform other countries in the region.

Emerging Markets in Asia: Consolidating the Recovery

In emerging markets in Asia, activity has picked up markedly since the beginning of the year, with industrial production and exports rebounding in response to the global upturn and the improvement in the IT sector. With second quarter data continuing to exceed expectations, and signs of a broadening pickup in domestic demand—aided by supporting macroeconomic policies—regional GDP growth is projected to increase to 6 percent in 2002 and to remain at that level in 2003 (Table 1.7). However, the outlook remains highly dependent on external developments, including the possibility of a slower-than-expected recovery in the United

States and Europe, and a loss of momentum in the IT sector. Asia is also relatively vulnerable to higher oil prices, were the security situation in the Middle East to deteriorate (see Appendix 1.1).

The impact of the recent turmoil in financial markets has so far been moderate. While equity markets have fallen back, the decline has been less than in other emerging markets. Most countries retain access to international capital markets, and contagion from Latin America has been limited. While spreads in the Philippines have risen somewhat, this appears primarily due to concerns about the fiscal position, and they remain significantly below their levels in late 2001. Except in China, Hong Kong SAR, and Malaysia, regional currencies have risen against the U.S. dollar since late March, as the latter fell back against the euro and yen. But trade-weighted exchange rates have generally depreciated moderately (except in Indonesia and Korea), suggesting that fears that movements in the U.S. dollar could adversely affect competitiveness or lead to deflationary pressures are as yet misplaced.

Assuming the recovery continues to unfold as expected, the focus of policies will need to shift increasingly to addressing medium-term challenges. These include the following.

- *Creating the conditions for a sustainable strengthening of domestic demand,* which remains below precrisis levels in some countries (in part reflecting structural problems). Stronger domestic demand is needed both to underpin balanced growth and to help resolve global imbalances (see the first essay in Chapter II).
- *Strengthening resilience to shocks.* Higher public sector debt—in many cases the legacy of the 1997/98 crisis—has increased macroeconomic vulnerabilities in a number of countries (Figure 1.11). Dependence on semiconductors—whose prices are highly volatile and linked to the industrial country cycle (Figure 1.12)—has also risen in many cases, even allowing for the relatively high import content of electronics production. Correspondingly, these countries will need to manage greater variability in output and the external current account, putting an increasing premium on maintaining adequate room for policy maneuver.
- *Ensuring that economies are flexible and dynamic* enough to manage—and indeed take advantage of—the substantial changes in intraregional comparative advantage in prospect, including as a result of China's rapid growth and entry into the World Trade Organization (WTO). In the longer run, successful completion of China's own bank and corporate reforms will be of critical importance for both China and the region.

While the policy priorities needed to meet these challenges vary across countries, there are a number of common themes. These include pressing ahead with the outstanding structural reform agenda, especially in banks and corporates; designing and implementing medium-term plans to ensure fiscal sustainability; and ensuring that exchange rate regimes are managed appropriately flexibly, without reversion to the de facto soft pegs seen in earlier years.

Figure 1.11. Asia: Deteriorating Fiscal Positions
(Percent of GDP)

Fiscal positions in most countries have deteriorated significantly since the mid-1990s, accompanied by a sharp rise in public sector debt, mostly domestic currency–denominated.

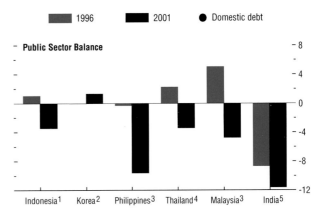

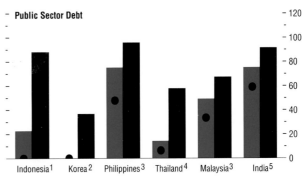

Sources: National authorities; and IMF staff estimates.
[1] End-March 1997 (prior to 2000, fiscal years covered April–March).
[2] Consolidated central government balance. Owing to lack of data, public sector debt for 2001 refers to calendar year 2000.
[3] Calendar years.
[4] Fiscal years 1995/96 and 2000/01.
[5] Fiscal years 1996/97 and 2001/02.

Figure 1.12. Has Asia Become a Commodity Producer?

Over the past decade, production of semiconductors has increased sharply in many Asian countries. Since semiconductors—like primary commodities—have highly volatile prices and react strongly to the industrial country cycle, this has increased vulnerability to external shocks.

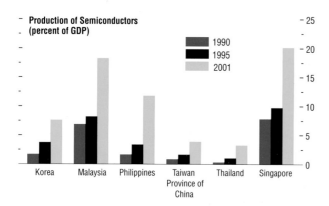

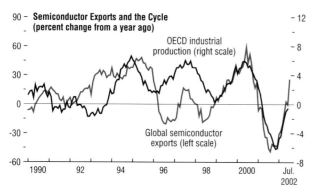

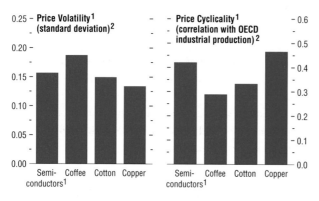

Sources: Reed Electronic Research (2001); OECD Direct; Semiconductor Industry Association; and IMF staff estimates.
[1]For semiconductors, refers to volatility and cyclicality of export value in U.S. dollars, given the lack of price data.
[2]All series detrended using bandpass filter.

Among the newly industrialized economies (NIEs) and ASEAN-4 countries (Indonesia, Malaysia, the Philippines, and Thailand), the expansion is so far best established in Korea, driven by buoyant domestic demand (in part underpinned by strong consumer lending) and also, more recently, by exports. With house prices rising rapidly, and inflation expected to rise in 2002 and 2003, interest rates were raised in May. The appreciation of the won will help moderate inflationary pressures, which, together with heightened external uncertainties, suggests that further interest rate increases may not be needed in the short run. Elsewhere, while final domestic demand appears to be picking up, the recovery is still dependent on exports and a turnaround in the inventory cycle; with inflation subdued and downside risks to global demand, monetary policies should remain accommodative for the time being. Given rising debt burdens, fiscal policies will need to shift increasingly from providing countercyclical support to consolidation, including in Indonesia, the Philippines, and also Hong Kong SAR, where a sizable structural deficit has emerged. Progress in structural reform varies, being more advanced in Korea (although there remains a need to strengthen insolvency procedures) and Malaysia. A more substantial agenda remains in other regional economies, including corporate debt restructuring and asset recovery (Indonesia); resolving the debt overhang and reviving bank intermediation (Thailand); and resolving banking sector fragility and accelerating implementation of power reforms (the Philippines).

In China, GDP growth has continued to exceed expectations, buoyed by strong public investment and export growth. Import growth has also picked up significantly, providing support to the recovery elsewhere in the region. Aided by continued strong inflows of foreign direct investment, the balance of payments has strengthened markedly, with reserves rising by $31 billion in the first half of the year. With moderate deflation reemerging at end-2001, monetary policy was eased in February and has since remained on hold. On the fiscal side, there is scope to achieve a moderate budgetary consolidation, especially given the difficult fiscal outlook, including high off-balance-sheet fiscal liabilities. Over the medium term, both growth and fiscal sustainability depend importantly on structural reforms, especially making further progress toward developing a sound and commercially oriented banking system, and completing the restructuring of state enterprises. Such reforms are all the more important following China's entry into the WTO. With the economy facing a period of major structural change, a gradual move toward more flexible exchange rate management would facilitate adjustment—especially given the strength of the balance of payments and the weakening of the U.S. dollar—supported by further development of foreign exchange market infrastructure.

In India, a cyclical recovery is now under way, although agriculture has been negatively affected by a poor monsoon and the regional security situation and higher oil prices are sources of risk. Inflation remains moderate and the external position is comfortable. However, trend growth has declined since the mid-1990s as the benefits of earlier structural reform have faded. With the fiscal deficit among the highest in the world, fiscal consolidation has become urgent, and pending fiscal responsibility legislation offers an opportunity to set out a clear and explicit medium-term fiscal consolidation path. Recent efforts to strengthen state finances are welcome, but the FY2002/03 budget envisages only modest deficit reduction, and even this may be difficult to achieve given relatively optimistic revenue projections. On the structural side, significant progress has been made in privatization, more market-based pricing of petroleum products, and interest rate liberalization. However, a large unfinished agenda remains, including further opening up to trade and foreign investment (Box 1.5), removing restrictions on agricultural and industrial activity; and strengthening the financial system.

Elsewhere on the subcontinent, Pakistan has continued to make progress toward macroeconomic stability, reflected in rising GDP growth

and a strengthened external position, although the deterioration in the regional security situation is again a risk. The proposed FY2002/03 budget will help arrest adverse debt dynamics and shift expenditure toward human development. Higher military expenditures as a result of regional tensions have complicated the outlook, however, and enforcing higher tax collection will require strong political resolve. Fiscal reform—linked to financial and public enterprise restructuring—is also critical in Bangladesh, where expansionary macroeconomic policies and loss of structural reform momentum have increased the risks to the outlook. In both countries, continued efforts to strengthen governance are also a priority.

In Australia and New Zealand, GDP growth in 2001 was among the highest in industrial countries, underpinned by supportive macroeconomic policies, highly competitive exchange rates, higher housing wealth, and rising long-term migration (New Zealand). With demand remaining robust in the first quarter of 2002, the RBA and RBNZ began to withdraw earlier monetary easing, although both central banks have held interest rates steady in recent months as the global outlook has weakened. Fiscal positions in both countries remain sound, although each faces rising pressures from aging populations. In Australia, additional measures may be required to finance major structural reforms that are needed over the medium term, while ensuring the objective of balancing the budget on average over the business cycle. In New Zealand, where productivity growth has disappointed in recent years, the authorities' focus on innovation and skill development is appropriate, and should be accompanied by additional efforts to reduce disincentives to work, save, and invest.

European Union Candidates: Surprisingly Resilient, but Some Policy Pressures

Growth among the EU candidates in central and eastern Europe and the Baltic region has, in general, been relatively well sustained during the global slowdown. For most of these countries,

Box 1.5. Where Is India in Terms of Trade Liberalization?

There is an acute awareness in India that more needs to be done to reap the full benefits of globalization so as to realize India's great economic potential. As Governor Jalan of the Reserve Bank of India has said: "... *Despite all the talk, we are nowhere even close to being globalized in terms of any commonly used indicator of globalization. In fact, we are still one of the least globalized among major countries—however we look at it* ... "[1] This box focuses primarily on India's integration with the world through trade rather than through capital account opening, reflecting the relative priorities in India's own reform process.

For most of India's postindependence period, trade policies were largely geared toward self-reliance through import substitution. Quantitative import restrictions and other nontariff barriers were pervasive and import tariffs were extremely high, resulting in a strong antiexport bias. In a major departure from this approach, India began a process of trade liberalization in the early 1990s as part of the wide-ranging reforms implemented in response to a major balance of payments crisis. In addition to trade liberalization, the reform program included gradual liberalization of the capital account and foreign investment regime. These policies resulted in strong trade and growth performance.

Since 1997, however, the pace of tariff reform has slowed. While the statutory peak rate was gradually reduced, higher duties continued to apply to a number of items, the rates on certain tariff lines were increased, and additional surcharges were introduced. As a result, the average tariff rate remained broadly unchanged at over 30 percent during 1997 to 2001. The remaining quantitative import restrictions were removed in two steps during 2000 and 2001 but, in some cases, new nontariff barriers were imposed. Export and import growth rates slowed and the share of trade in GDP remained flat. However, a sharp expansion of services exports—especially software, communications, and management services—mitigated the slowdown in goods

exports, reflecting the fact that the service industry has been relatively free of regulatory barriers.

Notwithstanding the reforms of the 1990s, India remains in the group of countries with the most restrictive trade regimes. India's average tariff remains one of the highest in the world, and the tariff shows substantial escalation in some sectors. A range of nontariff barriers continues to be in use, including some import bans, import restrictions through state trading monopolies, and stringent standards or certification requirements. India has also become one of the major users of antidumping measures, with some 250 actions initiated during 1995–2001. Overall, measured by the IMF's trade restrictiveness index, India stands at 8 (on a scale of 1 to 10) compared with 5 for China and 4–5 for other countries in east Asia.

Furthermore, effective protection in India and the antiexport bias may have been increased by the way trade has been liberalized, with tariffs on inputs and intermediate goods lowered at a faster pace than tariffs on outputs. Trade development has also been restrained by various domestic impediments to investment and growth. These include a relatively restrictive foreign investment regime; the policy of reserving the production of a large number of goods exclusively for small-scale industries; the poor quality of public infrastructure, such as transportation and power; the slow pace of industrial restructuring, reflecting weak bankruptcy laws and regulations that severely limit labor market flexibility; and transaction costs associated with administrative hurdles.

Reflecting these restraints, India is still lagging behind the rest of Asia in terms of opening up to international trade. Between 1980 and 2000, India's trade openness increased by about 50 percent while that of China surged by 150 percent. A similar pattern emerges in terms of shares of world trade.[2] While India's share of world merchandise exports increased from 0.5 percent to less than 0.7 percent over the last 20 years, China's share more than tripled to almost 4 percent (see the figure). Foreign direct investment inflows to India also remain very

Note: The main author of this box is Jean-Pierre Chauffour. For a more comprehensive discussion of this issue, see Subramanian, Tamirisa, and Bhavnani, forthcoming.

[1]Address at the Thirty Sixth Convocation of the Indian Statistical Institute by Reserve Bank of India Governor Bimal Jalan, Kolkata, January 15, 2002.

[2]China's rising export share in world markets is overstated, however, because a significant portion of China's exports reflects processing trade.

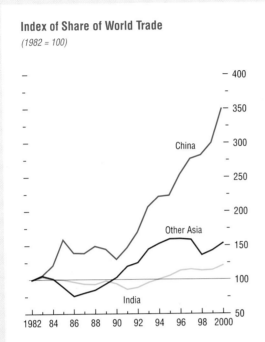

Index of Share of World Trade
(1982 = 100)

China

Other Asia

India

Sources: IMF, *International Financial Statistics;* and IMF staff estimates.

low in comparison to some other emerging countries. It should be noted, however, that thanks to India's competitive edge in the information technology sector, India's trade performance looks more favorable when trade in services is included.

The fact that India lags in global integration is confirmed by trade gravity models, which explain bilateral trade in terms of countries' characteristics such as economic mass, distance apart, geographical contiguity, common language, and free trade agreements. According to one set of estimates, India's merchandise trade between 1995 and 1999 was, on average, about 36 percent below its "expected" level.[3] This represents an improvement since the early 1990s, however, when undertrading

[3]This estimate is based on the model discussed in Chapter III of this *World Economic Outlook.* Other gravity model estimates of undertrading are even larger: Subramanian, Tamirisa, and Bhavnani (forthcoming) find that India's merchandise trade during 1995 to 1998 was about 70 to 80 percent less than expected given its income and geography.

is estimated to have been about 50 percent. When policy variables are included, gravity model estimates suggest that India's relatively restrictive policies account for about 25 percent of the shortfall in its trade openness compared with other developing countries over 1995–99, with the remainder attributable to India's relatively low per capita income, geographic factors, and restrictions imposed by other countries.

The authorities announced their intentions to advance liberalization with the export and import (EXIM) policy for 2002–07. This aims to identify potential markets and new areas of comparative advantage to raise India's share of world exports to 1 percent by 2007. Key elements include establishing new private sector–run special economic zones, making labor markets more flexible, significantly reducing the number of goods reserved for the small-scale sector, reducing red tape, and upgrading export infrastructure. At a microeconomic level, strategic sectors were identified for special focus, with the three "E"s—electronics, electrical, and engineering goods—figuring prominently in the list of items with the greatest export potential.

To achieve the authorities' objective for trade integration, however, more efforts are needed to eliminate the antiexport bias. Priorities should include significantly reducing and simplifying the tariff structure—for example, to bring the average tariff rate down to or below the "Asian level" of 12 percent—and removing the remaining nontariff and administrative barriers on imports and exports. Additional support would come from liberalizing the foreign investment regime and allowing the exchange rate to respond more flexibly to structural changes in the economy. As an indication of the potential impact of such reforms, estimates from the gravity model noted above suggest that if India unilaterally liberalized its trade and balance of payments regime, its average bilateral trade flow would increase by about 44 percent. More broadly, the array of domestic reforms needed to unshackle Indian industry and improve its global competitiveness would receive further support from reductions in industrial countries' trade barriers, which, as in other developing and emerging markets, impede India from fully exploiting its areas of comparative advantage.

Table 1.8. European Union Candidates: Real GDP, Consumer Prices, and Current Account Balance
(Annual percent change unless otherwise noted)

	Real GDP				Consumer Prices[1]				Current Account Balance[2]			
	2000	2001	2002	2003	2000	2001	2002	2003	2000	2001	2002	2003
EU candidates	**4.9**	**—**	**3.0**	**4.1**	**24.7**	**21.2**	**16.8**	**11.9**	**−5.1**	**−2.6**	**−3.4**	**−3.5**
Turkey	7.4	−7.4	3.9	5.0	54.9	54.4	47.1	28.6	−4.9	2.3	−0.8	−1.0
Accession candidates	3.8	3.0	2.7	3.7	13.1	9.8	6.2	5.7	−5.3	−4.3	−4.5	−4.4
Baltics	**5.5**	**6.2**	**4.6**	**5.2**	**2.2**	**2.7**	**2.3**	**2.8**	**−6.2**	**−6.7**	**−6.9**	**−6.6**
Estonia	7.1	5.0	4.5	5.0	4.0	5.8	3.7	3.0	−5.8	−6.1	−6.9	−7.4
Latvia	6.8	7.6	5.0	6.0	2.6	2.5	3.0	3.0	−6.9	−10.0	−8.5	−7.5
Lithuania	3.8	5.9	4.4	4.8	1.0	1.3	1.1	2.5	−6.0	−4.8	−5.9	−5.7
Central Europe	**3.9**	**2.2**	**2.1**	**3.3**	**8.9**	**6.2**	**3.2**	**3.5**	**−5.2**	**−3.9**	**−4.1**	**−4.2**
Czech Republic	3.3	3.3	2.7	3.2	3.9	4.7	2.7	3.0	−5.3	−4.6	−5.2	−4.6
Hungary	5.2	3.8	3.5	4.0	9.8	9.2	5.5	5.2	−2.8	−2.2	−3.8	−3.7
Poland	4.0	1.0	1.0	3.0	10.1	5.5	2.1	2.3	−6.3	−4.0	−3.6	−4.2
Slovak Republic	2.2	3.3	4.0	3.7	12.0	7.3	4.2	7.1	−3.6	−8.6	−8.5	−7.2
Slovenia	4.6	3.0	2.5	3.2	8.9	8.4	7.7	5.5	−3.4	−0.4	−0.8	−0.6
Southern and South Eastern Europe	**2.9**	**4.8**	**4.0**	**4.9**	**32.9**	**25.0**	**18.1**	**14.1**	**−5.1**	**−5.7**	**−5.3**	**−4.9**
Bulgaria	5.4	4.0	4.0	5.0	10.4	7.5	6.4	4.3	−5.6	−6.1	−5.6	−5.5
Cyprus	5.1	4.0	2.5	4.0	4.1	2.0	2.5	2.2	−5.2	−4.4	−5.5	−3.6
Malta	5.2	−1.0	2.0	4.9	2.4	2.9	2.0	2.0	−14.9	−5.0	−5.7	−4.4
Romania	1.8	5.3	4.3	4.9	45.7	34.5	24.2	19.1	−3.9	−5.9	−5.1	−4.9

[1]In accordance with standard practice in the *World Economic Outlook*, movements in consumer prices are indicated as annual averages rather than as December/December changes during the year as is the practice in some countries.
[2]Percent of GDP.

growth rates of at least 2½ to 4½ percent are expected in 2002, roughly the same on average as in 2001 (if Turkey is excluded) and with further strengthening projected for 2003 as the global economy improves (Table 1.8). Conditions and prospects differ among individual countries, however: the Polish economy is still relatively weak, although recently released indicators of economic activity have been more encouraging than in previous months; the Czech Republic was severely hit by the recent floods, as were other countries in the region to a lesser degree; and Turkey remains vulnerable to changes in financial market sentiment (see below). Moreover, the region as a whole has not escaped the impact of global financial market developments, with equity prices having fallen significantly—by 50 percent or more in most cases—since 2000. Over the same period, several countries—including the Czech Republic, Hungary, and Poland—have also experienced substantial effective exchange rate appreciations, although this has been partly reversed in Poland over recent months as a result of lower interest rates and an increase in policy uncertainties. While the central European and

Baltic countries' access to international finance continues to be strong, and bond spreads are low compared with other emerging markets, most of these economies remain vulnerable to a change in market sentiment as a result of their persistently high current account deficits.

Regional activity has been supported by strong inflows of foreign direct investment (FDI), providing the major source of external financing and helping sustain domestic demand. Such inflows no doubt reflect the benefits of generally stable and credible macroeconomic policies, together with market-friendly business climates. More specifically, much FDI has been attracted by these countries' relatively low-cost production bases and their increasing access to the EU market—especially given expectations of EU accession beginning within the next few years. Indeed, over the past decade countries in central Europe and the Baltics have been substantially more successful than other transition economies in building up FDI—a tendency that appears closely related, probably as both cause and effect, to their relative progress with enterprise reforms (Figure 1.13). In addition, domestic demand has been boosted in most countries by robust wage growth, falling inflation, and—in some cases—sizable fiscal stimulus packages. Export growth—although slowing somewhat since 2000—has also been surprisingly well sustained despite the EU slowdown and widespread exchange rate appreciations, with most countries continuing to gain market share (Figure 1.14).

While the policies needed to sustain and strengthen growth differ around the region, depending on current cyclical conditions and areas of prospective pressure, fiscal restraint—with supportive structural reforms—remains a priority in most countries. Over the short term, this would contribute to a better balance between macroeconomic policies; and, over the medium to long term, it would help accommodate ongoing spending pressures associated with EU and NATO accession, as well as rising public pension obligations. In Poland, the public expenditure restraint shown in the 2002 budget represents an important step toward reining in the growing fiscal imbalance. Fiscal consolidation—including through structural measures to better target social transfers and improve the overall quality of spending—needs to continue in the period ahead to limit the buildup of public debt. Such restraint should also provide scope for further easing of monetary policy to support recovery. In this regard, the significant monetary easing over the past year, including the further reduction in the main policy interest rate on August 28, has been appropriate given the weak state of the economy, the strength of the zloty, and the undershooting of the inflation target.

The cyclical position in Hungary has remained stronger than in Poland, with growth of about 3½ percent expected in 2002 and 4 percent in 2003. In this context, fiscal stimulus as large as that in the works in 2002—following substantial stimulus in 2001—does not appear necessary. Such stimulus, which reflects considerable public sector wage increases, could put at risk the inflation target, leading to further increases in interest rates (which the central bank has already begun to raise), and complicate the task of keeping the external current

Figure 1.13. Foreign Direct Investment and Enterprise Restructuring in Transition Economies

FDI among transition economies is positively related to progress with enterprise restructuring.

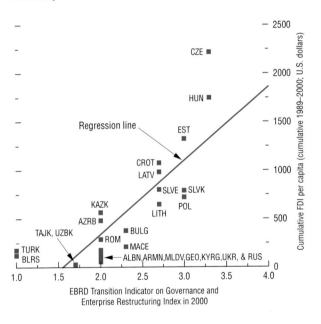

Sources: European Bank for Reconstruction and Development (2000); and IMF staff estimates.

Figure 1.14. Selected European Union Accession Countries: Exports and Market Share Growth
(Percent)

Although export growth has slowed since 2000, most EU accession countries have continued to experience firm export performance along with gains in market share during the current global slowdown.

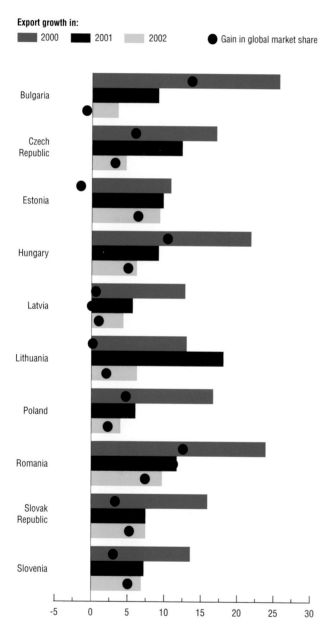

account deficit within prudent limits. These pressures would be eased through determined efforts to hold down expenditures and move toward significant medium-term consolidation.

The same policy priority applies to the new government in the Czech Republic, where the fiscal deficit appears set to increase substantially in 2002. Part of this increase is likely to arise from reconstruction spending following the recent floods—where the government estimates overall damage to be 2½–4 percent of GDP. However, since the bulk of this spending is likely to take place after this year, the increase in the deficit is largely attributable to higher spending unrelated to the floods. Such an expansion appears unwarranted, given the economy's recent resilience and the expected acceleration in growth in 2003, and medium-term fiscal pressures arising from costs associated with EU accession, bank restructuring, and growing future imbalances in the pension system. On the monetary side, the sizable appreciation of the exchange rate has contributed to an undershooting of the inflation target and allowed the central bank to lower interest rates, which have recently been below those in the euro area. With growth picking up in the Slovak Republic, concerns also center on recent fiscal slippages and on the high current account deficit. Responding to these developments, the central bank increased interest rates at the end of April; nevertheless, the currency depreciated significantly. Further interest rate increases could be needed if external pressures do not abate and no fiscal adjustment occurs.

Turning to southeastern Europe, macroeconomic developments in Bulgaria and Romania are largely on track. With further support coming from the projected recovery in western Europe, these countries are expected to continue growing by 4–5 percent this year and next. External deficits remain rather high, however, and so both countries will need to maintain a firm fiscal stance coupled with ongoing efforts to restructure their economies and boost external competitiveness. In Bulgaria, priorities include lowering public subsidies, moving forward with the privatization program, increasing labor market flexibility, and improving the business environment. High inflation remains a key concern in Romania, and needs to be tackled both through sound macroeconomic policies and by wage restraint—including in the government sector and state-owned enterprises. After posting strong output growth in 2000 and 2001, the Cypriot economy is experiencing a slowdown, driven by a decline in tourism arrivals. Nevertheless, underlying economic fundamentals remain solid.

While slowing somewhat from 2001, solid growth is expected to continue in the Baltic countries over 2002 and 2003, driven by robust domestic demand and accompanied by generally low inflation. Ongoing fiscal restraint and economic adjustment is particularly important in these countries, given their hard exchange rate pegs and persistently high current account deficits. While financed largely from FDI inflows, these external deficits nevertheless represent a potential source of vulnerability. In this regard, Estonia's strong policy record would be further enhanced if the public revenues from stronger-than-expected growth were saved rather than spent, especially in view of possible increases in budgetary tension in future years. With Latvia's current account deficit remaining very high, the government that takes office following the October parliamentary elections will need to formulate a 2003 budget that targets further reduction of the fiscal deficit. And favorable economic and policy developments in Lithuania would receive further support from structural reforms directed at reforming the tax system, strengthening the financial sector, and improving the country's external competitiveness.

Economic and financial conditions in Turkey improved significantly in the first few months of 2002, with industrial production and tourism receipts picking up, inflation declining—helped by a relatively stable exchange rate—and the fiscal position remaining on track. In May to July, however, financial sentiment deteriorated significantly, reflected in weakening of the exchange rate and stock prices and widening bond spreads. This deterioration stemmed mainly from political uncertainties regarding the viabil-

ity of the government coalition, but also from the more generalized weakening in international financial markets. Given the persistently high level of interest rates and the need to roll over large volumes of short-term domestic debt, much of which is foreign exchange–linked or floating rate, a key requirement is to provide clear reassurances to markets about Turkey's political, economic, and financial stability, including through continued strong implementation of the program strategy. In late July, parliament set a date for general elections, and passed several laws needed to meet the Copenhagen criteria for EU accession. Political stability following these elections will be particularly important in improving market conditions and bringing interest rates down to sustainable levels. Macroeconomic policies should continue to be directed toward a public sector primary surplus target of 6½ percent of GDP and a sustainable reduction in inflation, including through ongoing preparations for the eventual introduction of a formal inflation targeting framework. Significant progress has been made on bank reform, which has been skillfully handled, with the bank audit and recapitalization exercise now completed. Structural reform priorities in the period ahead include further improvements in bank supervision; determined efforts to move ahead with privatization; further measures to strengthen the business climate; and improvements in public financial management.

Commonwealth of Independent States (CIS): Persistent Dichotomy Between Advanced and Less Advanced Reformers

The impact of the global slowdown on CIS countries has been relatively mild. This region's resilience has been aided by strong domestic demand in Russia—the region's largest economy, with substantial (although possibly declining) linkages to the rest of the CIS (Figure 1.15)—and in Ukraine. During 2002, however, notwithstanding strengthening external demand, GDP growth across the region is expected to moderate, reflecting two main factors (Table 1.9). First,

Figure 1.15. Developments in Exports, FDI, and Demand for Money in the Commonwealth of Independent States (CIS)

Russia absorbs a large share of exports from other CIS countries, although this share appears to be declining.

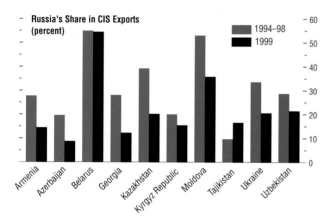

Foreign investment appears strongly biased toward natural resource extraction, especially oil.

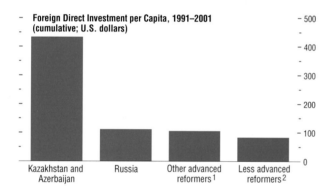

Progress with disinflation has contributed to an increase in the demand for money in Russia.

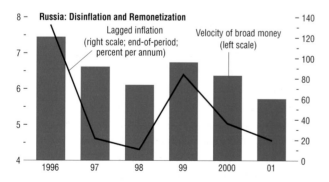

Sources: IMF, *Direction of Trade Statistics;* and IMF staff estimates.
[1]Armenia, Georgia, Kyrgyz Republic, Moldova, and Ukraine.
[2]Belarus, Tajikistan, and Uzbekistan.

growth in Russia and, to a lesser extent, Kazakhstan has slowed as a result of lower oil revenues, reflecting the lagged impact of weaker prices observed in late 2001 and early 2002. In Russia, the resulting fall in earnings of the energy sector may lead to cuts in investment spilling over to other sectors and countries (notably Ukraine, which has a substantial metal working industry), although the recent firming in oil prices should help to mute these effects. Second, agricultural growth—which was very high in 2001 owing to recovery from drought in 2000 and, in Ukraine, structural reforms—is projected to return to more normal levels. In general, however, with the exception of some less advanced reformers, GDP growth is expected to remain relatively well sustained. To date, contagion from the deteriorating situation in Latin America has been limited, largely reflecting the lack of trade linkages with this region together with the very limited global financial integration of most CIS countries.

Looking forward to 2003, GDP growth is expected to remain solid, supported by continued—if weaker—global recovery and the firming of oil prices. Within this, however, there is a persistent dichotomy across the region. In Russia and other more advanced reformers, domestic demand is expected to remain supportive of economic activity, mainly owing to strong private consumption and earlier progress made with reforms. By contrast, growth in the less advanced reformers is generally expected to lag behind, reflecting macroeconomic instability, lack of corporate restructuring (Belarus), and the unfavorable investment climate. Growth may remain relatively strong in Tajikistan, however, owing to strong growth in agriculture and satisfactory performance in the industrial sector. Beyond the pace of the global recovery, the key uncertainty in the outlook relates to developments in commodity prices, given the importance of the oil sector in Russia, and excessive dependence on a few commodities elsewhere (especially Uzbekistan and Tajikistan). The war in Afghanistan has had mixed effects: some countries are benefiting from reconstruction or leasing and airport fees (Kyrgyz Republic), but in others higher per-

Table 1.9. Commonwealth of Independent States: Real GDP, Consumer Prices, and Current Account Balance

(Annual percent change unless otherwise noted)

	Real GDP				Consumer Prices[1]				Current Account Balance[2]			
	2000	2001	2002	2003	2000	2001	2002	2003	2000	2001	2002	2003
Commonwealth of Independent States	**8.4**	**6.3**	**4.6**	**4.9**	**25.0**	**19.9**	**14.6**	**10.7**	**13.2**	**7.5**	**4.9**	**4.3**
Russia	9.0	5.0	4.4	4.9	20.8	20.7	15.8	11.0	17.5	10.3	7.0	6.3
Excluding Russia	7.0	8.9	5.2	4.9	34.9	18.0	11.9	10.1	1.6	−1.2	−1.7	−2.3
More advanced reformers	**6.8**	**9.6**	**5.8**	**5.6**	**19.7**	**9.4**	**5.1**	**7.3**	**2.1**	**−1.0**	**−1.8**	**−3.0**
Armenia	6.0	9.6	7.5	6.0	−0.8	3.2	2.8	2.8	−14.1	−7.2	−8.6	−8.2
Azerbaijan	11.1	9.0	7.9	7.3	1.8	1.5	2.4	3.3	−2.4	−1.3	−17.7	−30.4
Georgia	1.9	4.5	3.5	4.0	4.0	4.7	5.9	5.0	−5.4	−6.7	−6.2	−8.0
Kazakhstan	9.8	13.2	8.0	7.0	13.3	8.3	5.8	6.2	3.2	−6.9	−3.6	−2.5
Kyrgyz Republic	5.4	5.3	4.4	3.8	18.7	7.0	4.1	4.5	−7.5	−3.3	−3.8	−5.4
Moldova	2.1	6.1	4.8	5.0	31.3	9.8	6.6	8.4	−8.4	−7.4	−7.3	−7.7
Ukraine	5.9	9.1	4.8	5.0	28.2	12.0	5.1	9.1	4.7	3.7	2.6	1.7
Less advanced reformers[3]	**5.1**	**4.6**	**3.4**	**3.6**	**89.4**	**45.1**	**32.6**	**17.8**	**−0.6**	**−1.8**	**−1.4**	**−0.2**
Belarus	5.8	4.1	3.5	3.8	168.9	61.3	43.1	22.5	−2.5	−2.2	−1.4	0.5
Tajikistan	8.3	10.2	7.0	6.0	32.9	38.6	10.7	7.6	−6.5	−7.0	−4.2	−4.6
Uzbekistan	3.8	4.5	2.7	3.0	25.0	27.2	23.2	13.5	1.6	−1.0	−1.1	−0.7
Memorandum												
Net energy exporters[4]	9.3	6.1	4.7	5.0	19.6	19.2	14.7	10.5	16.1	8.9	5.8	5.2
Net energy importers[5]	5.2	7.0	4.2	4.4	45.2	22.1	14.2	11.6	1.0	0.6	0.2	—
Highly indebted countries[6]	4.1	6.5	5.0	4.7	13.0	9.3	5.7	5.3	−8.3	−6.4	−6.3	−7.1

[1]In accordance with standard practice in the *World Economic Outlook*, movements in consumer prices are indicated as annual averages rather than as December/December changes during the year as is the practice in some countries.
[2]Percent of GDP.
[3]Updated data for Turkmenistan not available.
[4]Includes Azerbaijan, Kazakhstan, Russia, and Turkmenistan.
[5]Includes Armenia, Belarus, Georgia, Kyrgyz Republic, Moldova, Tajikistan, Ukraine, and Uzbekistan.
[6]Armenia, Georgia, Kyrgyz Republic, Moldova, and Tajikistan.

ceived risks may have reduced foreign lending and investment (Tajikistan).

On the external side, the regional current account surplus is projected to decline in both 2002 and 2003. This is mainly because of a lower surplus in Russia, driven by strong domestic demand and a real appreciation of the ruble; and in Azerbaijan, where oil sector investment is projected to rise sharply. Elsewhere, changes are more moderate, although the current account surplus in Ukraine is also expected to decline as a result of the slower growth in Russia, solid domestic demand and real exchange rate appreciation. Large deficits are expected to persist in many countries, particularly among the region's poorest economies, where the level of external debt remains a serious threat to fiscal and external sustainability (Georgia, Kyrgyz Republic, Moldova, and Tajikistan). While continued domestic adjustment and structural reforms will be required in these cases, the international

community should provide more help through specific technical and financial assistance, including grants and, in some cases, debt relief. In that respect, the international financial institutions have recently proposed a specific initiative (the CIS-7 initiative). This aims to strengthen policy design and implementation, foster regional cooperation, heighten donors' awareness of the region's difficulties, and improve coordination among donors in the seven low-income CIS countries (the four listed above plus Armenia, Azerbaijan, and Uzbekistan).

While inflation has continued to decline across the region, aided by progress in fiscal consolidation, it remains an area of concern in Russia and a number of the less advanced reformers. In Russia, the main source of monetary expansion has come from the strength of the external position—mainly the current account surplus—which, given the desire to avoid an overly rapid appreciation of the ruble, has put upward pressure on liquidity in the absence of full sterilization. With the current account surplus projected to decline in 2002, monetary growth should moderate somewhat, but the central bank will need to stand ready to absorb liquidity as necessary to contain inflationary pressures. To facilitate this, it will be important to limit the extent of any fiscal relaxation in the 2003 budget. Among the less advanced reformers, inflation is primarily generated by continued state interventions in the economy (such as subsidies to public enterprises)—often off-budget—thereby boosting credit and money supply growth. In many countries in the region, the inflationary impact of rapidly increasing monetary aggregates has been moderated by higher money demand (remonetization), accompanied by a reduction in barter transactions. While this trend is both welcome and likely to continue for a while, the corresponding rapid increase in credit expansion—which raises questions about credit quality and risk—will need to be carefully monitored.

The main medium-term challenge for CIS countries remains to accelerate the reform process, particularly in the areas of institution building and governance. Key measures should include effective enforcement of legislation establishing basic market institutions; the liberalization of factor and goods markets; enterprise restructuring; and strengthening the financial sector. Over the past three years, Russia has made significant progress in critical areas of reform such as the tax system—which was made simpler and more transparent; fiscal management—including relations with decentralized entities; pension reform; labor law; agricultural land law; and administrative barriers to business. In other CIS countries, progress has generally been slower and implementation uneven, reflecting the opposition of powerful vested interests. While the solution to these problems lies largely in the countries themselves, it is to be hoped that accelerated reforms in Russia will—given its central role in the region—spur more rapid progress elsewhere (as the prospect of

integration to the European Union has for EU candidates).

Beyond this, countries in the region face a number of specific challenges. In particular, many countries remain heavily dependent on primary commodities, increasing vulnerability to external shocks and complicating macroeconomic management, particularly on the fiscal side. More specifically, significant uncertainty over revenues has led some countries to establish stabilization funds (for example, in Kazakhstan) in an attempt to insulate public expenditure from swings in revenues, or to formulate contingent expenditure plans (Kazakhstan and Russia) so as to preserve fiscal discipline in case of a shortfall in revenues. However, the efficient operation of stabilization funds may pose problems, notably in terms of transparency, while cutting expenditure plans if the economy experiences an adverse shock to the terms of trade may be difficult. Economic diversification therefore remains a priority, and would be facilitated by acceleration of reforms to improve the business climate and help correct the current bias of foreign direct investment towards exhaustible-resource extraction (Figure 1.15). Greater integration in the world economy, notably through WTO accession, would also contribute to reducing reliance on Russia as the main engine of growth.

Africa: Establishing the Conditions to Grow out of Poverty

GDP growth in Africa is projected to decline by 0.4 percentage points to 3.1 percent in 2002, equivalent to per capita income growth of about 0.5 percent (Table 1.10). While Africa will benefit from the expected strengthening of global activity, this may be offset by a combination of internal and external factors, including developments in commodity prices—still the driving force of economic performance in most countries of the region. In oil-exporting economies, growth prospects have been weakened by lower oil revenues, reflecting the lagged effect of earlier price declines and, in some cases, produc-

Table 1.10. Selected African Countries: Real GDP, Consumer Prices, and Current Account Balance
(Annual percent change unless otherwise noted)

	Real GDP				Consumer Prices[1]				Current Account Balance[2]			
	2000	2001	2002	2003	2000	2001	2002	2003	2000	2001	2002	2003
Africa	**3.0**	**3.5**	**3.1**	**4.2**	**14.3**	**13.1**	**9.6**	**9.5**	**1.2**	**0.3**	**−1.7**	**−1.6**
Maghreb	**2.4**	**4.4**	**3.2**	**4.0**	**1.3**	**2.6**	**3.3**	**2.7**	**7.3**	**7.0**	**3.5**	**3.7**
Algeria	2.5	2.8	2.1	2.9	0.3	4.2	4.0	3.0	16.9	12.4	8.1	8.9
Morocco	1.0	6.5	4.4	4.1	1.9	0.6	2.1	2.1	−1.4	4.9	1.3	0.5
Tunisia	4.7	5.0	3.8	6.4	3.0	1.9	3.4	3.0	−4.2	−4.2	−4.6	−3.8
Sub-Sahara[3]	**3.1**	**3.8**	**3.3**	**4.8**	**24.9**	**21.6**	**13.3**	**14.2**	**−1.0**	**−3.0**	**−5.6**	**−5.4**
Cameroon	4.2	5.3	4.4	4.7	0.8	2.8	4.0	3.0	−1.7	−2.2	−3.8	−4.3
Côte d'Ivoire	−2.3	0.1	3.0	4.5	2.5	4.4	3.0	3.0	−2.8	−2.3	1.0	−0.8
Ghana	3.7	4.2	4.5	5.0	25.2	32.9	14.6	10.8	−8.4	−4.0	−6.2	−5.9
Kenya	−0.1	1.2	1.4	2.8	10.0	5.8	2.0	4.7	−2.7	−3.0	−4.6	−5.9
Nigeria	4.3	2.8	−2.3	3.7	6.9	18.9	15.9	13.2	11.9	6.0	−5.4	−1.5
Tanzania	5.1	5.6	5.8	6.0	6.2	5.2	4.4	3.9	−1.6	−1.6	−4.9	−4.6
Uganda	5.0	5.6	5.7	6.5	6.3	4.6	−1.8	1.0	−12.1	−11.3	−12.4	−13.1
South Africa	**3.4**	**2.2**	**2.5**	**3.0**	**5.4**	**5.7**	**7.9**	**6.0**	**−0.4**	**−0.1**	**0.8**	**0.6**
Memorandum												
Oil importers	2.9	3.6	3.3	4.4	13.8	11.7	8.0	8.8	−3.0	−2.2	−3.2	−3.4
Oil exporters	3.3	3.4	2.2	3.4	16.3	18.0	15.4	12.0	13.0	7.1	2.3	3.2

[1]In accordance with standard practice in the *World Economic Outlook*, movements in consumer prices are indicated as annual averages rather than as December/December changes during the year, as is the practice in some countries.
[2]Percent of GDP.
[3]Excludes South Africa.

tion cuts due to lower OPEC production quotas (Nigeria). Recent increases in oil prices will help to offset these effects, but will clearly weaken prospects among oil importers, which include many of the poorest countries. The protracted weakness in cotton and coffee prices will also continue to bear down on the performance of many countries in 2002. Country-specific factors have also played a role, including the spreading impact of drought and the resulting sharp decline in agricultural output in a number of countries in southern Africa, putting millions on the brink of starvation; continued conflicts and political instability, including in Liberia, Sudan, and Zimbabwe; and, in Morocco, a return to lower growth rates following the sharp, post-drought recovery in 2001. GDP growth is projected to pick up to 4.2 percent in 2003, aided by rising non-oil commodity prices (especially coffee, cotton, metals), and stronger external demand as the global recovery gains momentum. As noted above, however, the WEO projections for African growth have in the past been consistently optimistic, and much will depend on further improvements in

political stability as well as the absence of natural disasters.

On the external side, the regional current account deficit is expected to increase to 1.7 percent of GDP in 2002. This is mainly due to a decline in the surpluses of energy producers (particularly Nigeria and Algeria), offset in part by the emergence of a current account surplus in South Africa as a result of higher prices for gold and other metals and stronger external demand. In sub-Saharan Africa, with the notable exception of Côte d'Ivoire (where exports are being boosted by a sharp increase in cocoa prices), current account deficits remain relatively large, due to weak non-oil commodity prices and high oil prices by historical standards, and still high external debt-servicing costs. Over time, the latter should be reduced through the Heavily Indebted Poor Countries (HIPC) Initiative: through July 2002, some 22 (out of 26 eligible) African countries had begun to receive nominal debt service relief totaling $32.2 billion, which, on average, will halve the net present value of their debt. Recent commitments to increase international aid flows and raise the proportion provided as grants will also contribute to relaxing financing constraints.

Since the mid-1990s, African countries have made substantial progress toward macroeconomic stability, with CPI inflation expected to fall to single-digit levels in 2002 for the first time ever, and remain there in 2003. To a considerable extent, this has reflected increasing fiscal discipline across the region: excluding Nigeria, central government deficits in sub-Saharan Africa have been more than halved since the mid-1990s. Where fiscal discipline has improved, fiscal policy has been able to accommodate a larger availability of financing and to increase spending on behalf of the poor. Progress has been particularly notable in long-lasting high-inflation cases such as the Democratic Republic of Congo, because of the monetary and fiscal tightening that accompanied the decision to float the currency and lift exchange controls, and Ghana, as a result of fiscal discipline and greater central bank independence. However, inflationary pressures remain a serious concern in a number of countries, in particular Angola, Nigeria, Zambia, and Zimbabwe, generally reflecting excessive fiscal expansion, accompanied by rapid money supply growth.

Africa continues to face an enormous range of political and economic problems. Civil unrest, political instability and armed conflicts still threaten macroeconomic stability and longer-term growth prospects in a significant number of countries; natural disasters regularly damage subsistence crops; and the HIV/AIDS pandemic—as well as other infectious diseases—has seriously affected prospects across the continent, particularly in southern Africa (including a significant reduction in life expectancy, notably in Botswana and Zimbabwe). These are accompanied by a variety of other problems, including low levels of investment and savings and limited direct investment inflows (Box 1.6); poor infrastructure, including public utilities

and the health and education sectors; pervasive market distortions (especially in agriculture); underdeveloped legal and regulatory frameworks; and weak governance. These problems are often self-reinforcing: for instance, low life expectancy reduces the returns from education, and political instability and governance problems can magnify the impact of natural disasters (as appears to be the case, for example, in the famine in southern Africa).

Given the gains made in establishing macroeconomic stability in a growing number of African economies, the pressing need now is to address these underlying problems, and improve the overall environment for investment and growth. As stressed in the New Partnership for Africa's Development (NEPAD) put forward by African leaders in late 2001, the solutions are multidimensional in nature. However, one key element is to make further progress in strengthening the economic infrastructure—including basic market institutions such as the protection of property rights and, more generally, the rule of law, democratic accountability, the fight against corruption, and bureaucratic quality. A growing number of studies have found that these factors play a central role in explaining growth differences across countries.[8] Economic performance and human development are positively related to the quality of institutions (Figure 1.16, top two panels). The relationship between human development and institutional quality remains positive and significant even after taking into account the effect of GDP per capita on human development (as illustrated by the bottom panel of Figure 1.16).

Against this background, the emphasis placed in the NEPAD on developing economic infrastructure and institutions is particularly welcome. While much remains to be done, a number of countries have made important progress in key areas such as governance (for example, Botswana and Tanzania); economic liberalization (for example, Mozambique, Senegal,

---

[8]See Hall and Jones (1999).

and Uganda); and fiscal management, including tax collection, public expenditure management, civil service reform, and priority given to poverty reduction (for example, Burkina Faso, Mozambique, and Mali). For its part, the international community is beginning to support these efforts through additional financial and technical assistance, including increased aid commitments announced in Monterrey and the G-8 Africa Action Plan announced last June. However, these efforts need to be accompanied by faster and more aggressive trade liberalization, which—as discussed in Chapter II—would particularly benefit sub-Saharan Africa.

Looking more specifically at the region's largest economies, economic activity in South Africa has held up well in the face of the global downturn, and higher gold prices and external demand should stimulate stronger growth later this year and in 2003. The short-term outlook for inflation, however, is being affected by the sharp depreciation of the rand in 2001 and the target of 3–6 percent inflation in 2002 is likely to be missed. Inflationary pressures should, nevertheless, ease considerably toward the end of the year in response to the recovery in the value of the rand and four consecutive 100 basis point hikes in the repurchase rate by the central bank. Monetary and fiscal policies should remain firmly committed to maintaining macroeconomic stability, and inflation is expected to fall back into its targeted range in 2003. Modest current account surpluses are expected for 2002 and 2003.

As Nigeria cuts back oil production in line with its OPEC quota, GDP is projected to contract by 2.3 percent in 2002. Political uncertainties have lowered prospects for improving macroeconomic stability and promoting reforms in the near future, and Nigerian debt prices have recently fallen sharply as a result of heightened uncertainties regarding the status of debt payments. Excessive government expenditure and monetary expansion continue to feed inflation, and—along with the drop in exports—are leading to an unsustainable increase in the current account deficit and a sizable decline in

Figure 1.16. Impact of Institutional Quality in Africa

Institutional quality is positively related to human development, even after taking into account its positive contribution to GDP per capita.

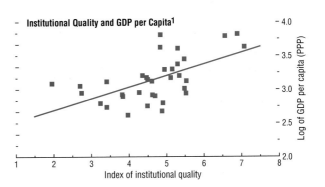

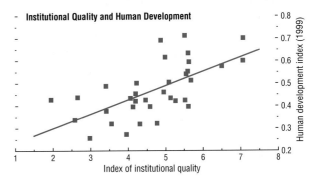

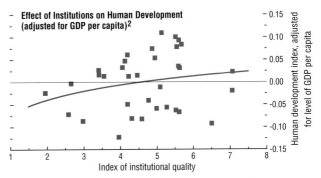

Sources: World Bank, *African Indicators;* Political Risk Services Group, *International Country Risk Guide (ICRG);* and UNDP, *Human Development Report.*
[1]The institutional quality index combines equally weighted ratings of government stability, democratic accountability, bureaucratic quality, law and order, and corruption. The sample consists of 34 African countries.
[2]The adjusted, or "unexplained" part of the human development index (HDI) is the residual from a log-linear regression of HDI on GDP per capita.

Box 1.6. Foreign Direct Investment in Africa

The stock of foreign direct investment (FDI) in Africa increased almost fivefold, to just under $150 billion, between 1980 and 2000. Despite this increase, however, Africa's share of global FDI has declined substantially, even compared with other developing country regions (see the table). Most FDI has been directed toward the primary sector, with the nine oil-exporting countries accounting for about 75 percent of FDI inflows during the 1990s. Privatization of state-owned enterprises has also provided an important source of foreign investment for a number of countries, including South Africa—by far the largest economy in the region.

A number of smaller countries, however, have been able to attract sizable FDI flows—representing a substantial share of their GDP and gross capital formation—outside the energy sector. Reflecting this, the 34 least developed countries approximately doubled their share in FDI inflows to Africa over the 1990s. This box considers briefly the experiences and prospects of seven small, non-oil-producing countries—Botswana, Lesotho, Namibia, Mauritius, Mozambique, Swaziland, and Uganda—all of which received relatively large flows of FDI in the 1990s (and, in some cases, the 1980s). It discusses in particular the four influences that may have been largely responsible for channeling FDI flows to Africa: the availability of natural resources; recent economic and structural reforms; host country policies that actively target export-oriented foreign investment; and specific locational advantages.

Natural Resources

It is in mining of high-value minerals and petroleum that Africa is particularly prominent as a host to FDI and where great potential for future FDI exists. While many countries are abundant in some type of natural resources, only some—including Botswana and Namibia—have been successful in obtaining *diversified* FDI.

Note: The main authors of this box are Anupam Basu and Krishna Srinivasan. For a fuller discussion of this topic, see Basu and Srinivasan (2002).

In both these countries, macroeconomic stability within the framework of a stable democratic political system has allowed access to relatively large FDI inflows. Also important in attracting FDI are their good governance and low levels of corruption, investment in human and physical capital, and the protection of property and contractual rights.

Economic Reforms

A few countries, including Mozambique and Uganda, were shunned by investors in the past but have recently attracted significant investor interest in response to their implementation of far-reaching economic and structural reforms. After witnessing economic decline in the context of political instability, civil strife, and ill-conceived policies over a long period since independence, in both Mozambique and Uganda the progression toward political stability and the pursuit of market-oriented economic reform has allowed private sector activity to become increasingly important in fueling economic expansion. A reduced role for the state, including through a rapid acceleration in the privatization of state-owned assets, the prioritizing of government spending to improve the quality and availability of physical and human capital, and the removal of impediments to foreign investment have yielded results in terms of larger access to global capital flows. Significant foreign participation in each country's privatization program has been backed by deliberate government efforts to reassure investors about the safety of their investment—including by signing international agreements governing investment protection and by eliminating discrimination between domestic and foreign investors. Attention has also been given to investment that would boost exports; for example, the Industrial Free Zones that came into effect in Mozambique in 1998 require a minimum export content of 85 percent. In this context, preferential access to the European Union and other markets under the Cotonou Agreement and the Generalized System of Preferences has provided further incentives for investment location.

Foreign Direct Investment Inward Stock by Host Region, 1980–2000, Share of Global Stock

	1980	1985	1990	1995	1999	2000
Developed countries[1]	58.2	60.1	73.5	69.3	63.5	65.8
Developing countries[2]	41.8	39.9	26.3	29.4	34.5	32.2
Africa	5.3	3.8	2.6	2.6	2.7	2.3
Latin America and the Caribbean	8.1	8.9	6.2	6.9	10.0	9.6
Developing Europe	—	—	0.1	0.1	0.2	0.2
Asia	28.1	27.0	17.4	19.8	21.5	20.0
The Pacific	0.2	0.1	0.1	0.1	0.1	0.1
Central and Eastern Europe	—	—	0.2	1.2	2.0	2.0

Source: World Investment Report (WIR).
[1]For expositional purposes, excludes South Africa; WIR includes South Africa in the list of developed countries.
[2]For expositional purposes, includes South Africa; WIR includes South Africa in the list of developed countries.

Policies targeting export-oriented foreign investment

Mauritius has been particularly successful in targeting and attracting export-oriented FDI. An investment-friendly climate has been underpinned by political stability, macroeconomic discipline, and the availability of bilingual and cheap labor, with further support provided by public investment in education and infrastructure. An important role has also been played by the creation of export-processing zones: these now account for over two-thirds of merchandise exports—especially textiles and clothing, almost all of which are destined for the European Union or the United States.

Locational advantages

The imposition of global sanctions on South Africa had positive effects on some other countries in the region, including Lesotho and Swaziland, which served as the conduit of trade between South Africa and a number of third countries. Multinational firms that wished to evade the sanctions located their subsidiaries in Lesotho or in neighboring Swaziland to produce goods that were primarily exported to South Africa. In addition to very specific locational advantages, these two countries enjoyed (partly through their relationship with South Africa) political stability, the adoption of reasonably sound macroeconomic policies, and the presence of a cheap, productive, and skilled labor force; to a smaller extent, the provision of tax incentives also influenced investment location decisions. More recently, however, the pace of new FDI has declined, although rein-

vestment of earnings by foreign subsidiaries in these countries has continued.

Conclusions

While Africa is undoubtedly rich in natural resources, a critical mass of mutually reinforcing measures clearly needs to be in place before the region can secure a larger share in global FDI flows. Progress toward conflict resolution is essential, because political stability is an important determinant of investment location. Political stability, however, is a necessary but not sufficient condition to ensure access to large FDI flows; a favorable economic environment is also crucial. Even countries well positioned to attract FDI as a result of their natural resources or locational advantages have sought to strengthen investment prospects by implementing sound macroeconomic policies and far-reaching structural reforms. Moreover, among countries without these natural endowments, a number have been successful in attracting FDI by establishing a policy environment conducive to investment. For example, privatization of state assets has generally been a key element in economic liberalization and a catalyst for increased foreign investment. Export processing zones and tax incentives could help to attract FDI inflows, but the potential benefits arising from these approaches need to be weighed against risks of eroding the tax base and encouraging rent-seeking activities and corruption. Hence, broad-based liberalization and adjustment remains the preferred approach to strengthening the investment climate and securing greater access to global FDI flows.

international reserves. In response to the deterioration in the macroeconomic situation and to protect international reserves, the Central Bank of Nigeria introduced a more market-based foreign exchange regime in July, centered on an auction mechanism for selling the government's oil receipts. As a result, the differential between the official and parallel market exchange rates has narrowed considerably. While a positive step, the priorities for policymakers should be to restore macroeconomic stability, implying a significant fiscal adjustment, and to unify the exchange rate and strengthen banking sector supervision.

The outlook for Algeria remains affected by civil unrest, political violence, and very high unemployment, especially among youth. Real growth, expected to remain weak at about 2.1 percent this year, is supported by domestic demand, including investment, but is negatively influenced by the reduction in Algeria's OPEC quota, which came into effect on January 1, 2002. Moderately expansionary fiscal policy, combined with lower hydrocarbon revenue under current price and output assumptions, is expected to lead to smaller current account surpluses. Inflation, which increased sharply in 2001, is expected to slow down somewhat this year. With investment concentrated in oil and gas production capacities, oil market developments remain a key source of vulnerability, underlining the need to press ahead with efforts to diversify the economy.

Middle East: Growing Divergences This Year; Better Prospects for 2003

Conditions and prospects in the Middle East are being shaped by a combination of global and local influences—notably the general economic slowdown and oil market developments; the difficult regional security situation; and country-specific policy pressures. The impact and relative importance of these various forces vary widely among the countries concerned, however. Among the region's oil exporters, growth in Saudi Arabia and Kuwait has weakened quite

sharply over the past two years, partly as a result of lower oil GDP (arising from production quotas and the lagged impact of oil price declines) and of the global slowdown more generally (Table 1.11). In contrast, reflecting recent progress with diversification, Iran has been better able to offset weaker activity in its oil sector through growth in non-oil activities, and robust growth of 5 to 6 percent looks set to continue. Elsewhere, security concerns, which are affecting the entire region, are the main reason for the substantial weakening in growth in Israel and the West Bank and Gaza. And, in Egypt, the further slowing in business activity and output in 2002 is a result of the sharp decline in tourism after September 11 and difficulties in the domestic policy framework, complicated to some extent by the political and security situation in the region. The severe economic and financial vulnerabilities faced by Lebanon are primarily a result of policies that have led to persistent budget deficits and high levels of public debt. In Jordan, on the other hand, robust export performance and growth over recent years have been underpinned by the authorities' firm commitment to macroeconomic stability and structural reforms.

Looking ahead, GDP growth across the region is expected to pick up later in 2002 and in 2003—particularly if global output strengthens as projected, if oil prices remain relatively firm, and if there is an easing in security tensions. While recent increases in oil prices would normally be expected to have a positive impact on prospects for energy exporters, the associated possibility of military conflict clearly represents a downside risk for the region. Sustaining stronger growth rates will also be contingent on progress in addressing growing policy challenges. In Saudi Arabia, for example, lower oil prices earlier in the year led to a significant deterioration in the fiscal situation. Domestic debt is high, and the economy remains vulnerable to potential oil market fluctuations. As a result, expenditure restraint and increases in non-oil revenues should continue to be pursued, possibly even more vigorously. Rapid progress with the author-

Table 1.11. Selected Middle Eastern Countries: Real GDP, Consumer Prices, and Current Account Balance
(Annual percent change unless otherwise noted)

	Real GDP				Consumer Prices[1]				Current Account Balance[2]			
	2000	2001	2002	2003	2000	2001	2002	2003	2000	2001	2002	2003
Middle East[3]	**5.7**	**4.2**	**3.5**	**4.6**	**9.8**	**8.0**	**9.4**	**9.2**	**11.8**	**7.6**	**4.4**	**3.2**
Oil exporters[4]	**6.2**	**4.6**	**3.9**	**4.9**	**12.6**	**10.0**	**11.7**	**11.2**	**16.0**	**10.5**	**6.2**	**4.7**
Saudi Arabia	4.9	1.2	0.7	3.3	−0.6	−0.8	—	1.1	7.6	7.8	2.1	0.2
Iran, Islamic Rep. of	5.7	4.8	5.8	5.5	12.6	11.4	15.0	15.0	13.4	4.8	3.2	2.5
Kuwait	3.8	−1.0	−1.0	1.7	1.7	2.5	2.5	2.5	38.8	31.9	29.0	27.8
Mashreq[5]	**4.2**	**3.2**	**2.4**	**3.6**	**1.8**	**1.9**	**2.7**	**3.3**	**−2.2**	**−2.2**	**−2.3**	**−2.6**
Egypt	5.1	3.3	2.0	3.7	2.8	2.4	2.5	3.4	−1.2	—	−0.2	0.1
Jordan	4.0	4.2	5.1	6.0	0.7	1.8	3.2	2.1	0.7	−0.1	−0.4	−1.7
Memorandum												
Israel	7.4	−0.9	−1.5	1.8	1.1	1.1	6.2	3.0	−1.7	−1.7	−1.9	−1.8

[1]In accordance with standard practice in the *World Economic Outlook*, movements in consumer prices are indicated as annual averages rather than as December/December changes during the year, as is the practice in some countries.
[2]Percent of GDP.
[3]Includes Bahrain, Egypt, Islamic Rep. of Iran, Iraq, Jordan, Kuwait, Lebanon, Libya, Oman, Qatar, Saudi Arabia, Syrian Arab Republic, United Arab Emirates, and Republic of Yemen.
[4]Includes Bahrain, Islamic Rep. of Iran, Iraq, Kuwait, Libya, Oman, Qatar, Saudi Arabia, and United Arab Emirates.
[5]Includes Egypt, Jordan, Lebanon, and Syrian Arab Republic.

ities' reform program is also important—particularly through the restructuring and privatization of state-owned enterprises, expedited integration of the segmented labor market, and capital market development.

In Iran, macroeconomic policies should build on the successful unification of exchange rates and introduction of a managed float in March 2002, particularly by reducing fiscal and monetary pressures that have developed recently and by improving policy coordination. The recent surge in public spending growth—which has been driven in large part by the exchange rate unification (which led to implicit subsidies that previously arose through the exchange rate system being recognized explicitly in the public accounts) but also by increases in other outlays—should be reined in. Such restraint would help to reduce persistent double-digit inflation. Also important are ongoing structural reforms, including further trade and price liberalization, subsidy reforms, measures to strengthen the operations and supervision of the financial sector, and public enterprise restructuring and privatization.

In Egypt, economic prospects have strengthened following a recovery in tourism. The upturn would be more solid, however, with a bet-

ter functioning exchange rate regime. Further flexibility in the official exchange rate would permit a reunification of the official and parallel currency markets, restoring much-needed liquidity to the former. Egypt's consolidated fiscal position has deteriorated from approximate balance in the late 1990s to a deficit of about 2½ percent of GDP, largely on account of the automatic stabilizers as growth slowed, but the limits to this flexibility have now been reached. The 2002/03 budget appropriately targets a reduced deficit, such a consolidation made all the more urgent by the large increases in public debt over recent years. With the move to greater exchange rate flexibility, monetary policies will need to take on a more central and transparent role as nominal anchor. In Jordan, the authorities' sound policy record would be reinforced by further fiscal consolidation, supported by implementation of their bold strategy on pension reforms and other structural measures. Lebanon faces extremely difficult debt dynamics, notwithstanding the reduction in the fiscal deficit from 25 percent of GDP in 2000 to a projected 17 percent of GDP in 2002. With gross public debt (including debt owed to the central bank and some other public institutions) over 170 percent of GDP, the immediate priority should be to tackle fiscal pressures

Figure 1.17. Middle East: Trade Restrictions

The Mashreq countries have relatively high trade restrictions and low levels of trade.

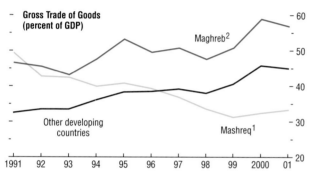

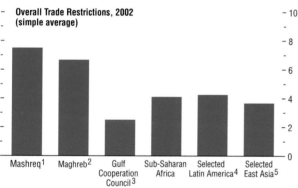

Sources: IMF, *Trade Policy Information Database (TPID);* and IMF staff estimates.
[1]Egypt, Jordan, Lebanon, and Syrian Arab Republic.
[2]Algeria, Morocco, and Tunisia.
[3]Bahrain, Kuwait, Oman, Qatar, Saudi Arabia, and the United Arab Emirates.
[4]Argentina, Brazil, Chile, and Mexico.
[5]Malaysia, Singapore, and Thailand.

by curtailing public spending and boosting revenues. Trade liberalization, together with privatization and other structural reforms, also needs to be part of the reform strategy to improve growth prospects.

In this regard, the economies of Egypt and several others in the region remain heavily protected by tariff and nontariff barriers, even after substantial tariff reductions in some cases (including Egypt) in the 1990s. Illustrating this, it is notable that the level of trade restrictiveness for most countries both in the Mashreq (including Egypt, Lebanon, and the Syrian Arab Republic) and in the Maghreb (especially Morocco and Tunisia) is much higher than in other developing countries (Figure 1.17). Moreover, gross trade in the Mashreq is particularly low, reflecting the impact of trade restrictions, real exchange rate appreciations during the 1990s, and political uncertainties.[9] This suggests there is substantial scope for increased regional and international trade integration to help support stronger growth (see Chapter III).

The increased political and economic uncertainties arising from security concerns have, as noted, led to significant downward revisions in growth projections for Israel in 2002 and 2003. These concerns have added to the pressures that were already apparent in 2001 as a result of the global slowdown and problems in the IT sector. With confidence declining, the sheqel has weakened substantially since the end of 2001—putting upward pressure on inflation, which is expected to rise to about 6 percent this year. In response to these currency and inflation pressures, the Bank of Israel has increased interest rates in several steps so far in 2002. A pickup in exports—supported by the lower sheqel and stronger global growth— should contribute to economic recovery in 2003, however, especially if regional tensions abate. The West Bank and Gaza has also been severely affected by the security situation, with

[9]See Blavy (2001).

real GDP expected to fall by about 20 percent in 2002. An easing of these tensions, together with international support to restore infrastructure and basic economic institutions, will be needed to lay the groundwork for a return to growth.

Appendix 1.1. Commodity Markets[10]

After bottoming out in late 2001, commodity prices recovered in the first months of this year, as prospects for global recovery improved. Prices generally stabilized in the second quarter, however, in the absence of further major surprises to the global growth outlook (Figure 1.18). In addition to global demand prospects, crude oil prices have been significantly influenced by political events in the Middle East and Venezuela, against the background of a relatively tight balance between world demand and supply. Non-oil commodity prices have broadly stabilized in the aggregate since April, although the picture for individual commodities varies.

Crude Oil

A combination of improved world growth prospects, cuts in OPEC production targets, and especially political uncertainty in the Middle East caused OPEC's reference oil prices to rise back within the $22–$28 target range early in the year (Figure 1.19). Nevertheless, prices have remained below the peaks reached in 2000. Prices increased sharply in the second half of August as regional security tensions increased, easing back somewhat in mid-September as these tensions appeared to partly abate. Recent price fluctuations have been driven mostly by developments in the Middle East and Venezuela, owing to their implications for supply disruptions. While Iraq's temporary suspension of exports has been lifted, unresolved issues remain with the United Nations regarding the pricing of oil exports and the details surrounding resumption of arms inspections. Global inventories of both crude oil and products have

Figure 1.18. Oil and Non-oil Price Indices
(1990 = 100)

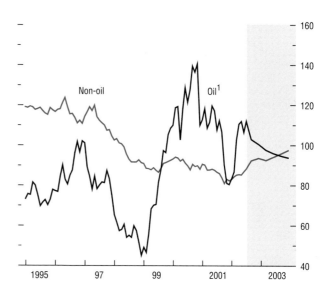

Source: IMF staff estimates.
[1]Simple average of spot prices of U.K. Brent, Dubai, and West Texas Intermediate crude oil.

[10]The main author of this appendix is Guy Meredith.

Figure 1.19. OPEC Target and Actual Production of Oil[1]
(Millions of barrels a day unless otherwise indicated)

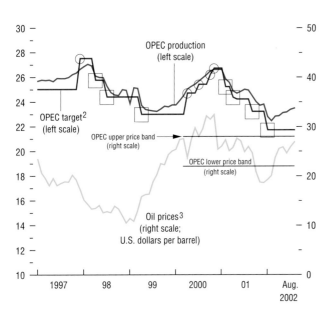

Source: Bloomberg Financial Markets, LP.
[1]Excluding Iraq.
[2]Circles denote increases in OPEC target production and squares denote decreases in OPEC target production.
[3]Simple average of spot prices of U.K. Brent, Dubai, and West Texas Intermediate crude oil.

fallen back to about the same level as last year, given recent drawdowns due to temporary cuts in supply from Iraq.

At its meeting in late June, OPEC announced it will leave oil production quotas unchanged for the third quarter. Nevertheless, actual production has edged up relative to target in recent months, as has occurred following past production cuts. Meanwhile, production restraint agreed to earlier by non-OPEC producers has weakened. Both Russia and Norway, the two largest non-OPEC producers, have announced plans to raise production in the third quarter. In early July, Russia sent its first oil shipment to the United States, following talks between Presidents Bush and Putin that could lead the United States to broaden its supply base and Russia to increase energy exports.

OPEC is to review output quotas at its meeting in Osaka on September 19 (just after the *World Economic Outlook* goes to press). Crude oil futures currently imply a substantial decline in spot prices in coming quarters, back toward the WEO baseline assumption, consistent with an expected easing in the tight supply situation and, most recently, indications of a possible reduction in political tensions following Iraq's decision to allow arms inspections to resume. Meanwhile, the volatility of future oil prices implied by options markets has declined since late last year, suggesting that perceived uncertainty about future market conditions has fallen (Figure 1.20). As discussed earlier in this chapter, however, the possibility of further sharp increases in oil prices arising from a deterioration in the Middle East security situation remains an important downside risk to the global outlook. In this regard, some indicators of the impact of changes in oil prices on regional output and trade balances are provided in Table 1.12.

Nonfuel Commodities

Conditions in markets for agricultural commodities have been more balanced than during 2001, when weak demand and expanding supply put severe downward pressure on many prices.

Table 1.12. The Impact of a $5 a Barrel, Permanent Increase in Oil Prices After a Year
(Percent of GDP)

	Real GDP	Trade Balance
World GDP	**−0.3**	—
Industrial Countries	**−0.3**	**−0.2**
United States	−0.4	−0.1
Euro area	−0.4	−0.1
Japan	−0.2	−0.2
Other	−0.2	0.2
Developing countries	**−0.2**	**0.2**
Of which:		
Latin America	−0.1	—
Asia	−0.4	−0.5
Emerging Europe and Africa	0.1	0.2

Source: IMF staff estimates based on IMF (2000).

Although demand has generally not picked up as much as had been expected, there has been some drawdown of inventories, partly due to the effects of adverse weather on production. The scope for significant price increases in the near term, however, is limited by continued high inventory levels and excess capacity. Passage of the U.S. Farm Bill, which both increases price support and expands support to new crops, is another factor dampening the prospect for higher agricultural prices. Proposals to reform agricultural subsidies in the European Union have been introduced, but passage remains uncertain, and the near-term effect on support levels would be modest. As discussed in the next section, the projected El Niño in 2002–03 could also affect commodity markets, although the expected intensity is modest relative to the last event in 1997–98.

Grain prices edged up during the first half of 2002, largely due to adverse weather conditions in the United States, Canada, and Australia and consequent declines in global stocks. In the near term, however, further price increases are limited by increased competition from other producers such as Argentina and Brazil, while the European Union may reinstate export subsidies. *Vegetable oils and meals* prices have shown a more pronounced recovery than other agricultural commodities, largely reflecting a reversal of extremely depressed levels in 2000–01. Palm and

Figure 1.20. NYMEX Oil: Implied Volatilities from Options Prices
(Standard deviation expressed in percent)

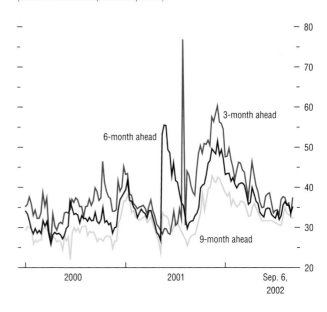

Source: Bloomberg Financial Markets, LP.

coconut oil prices have increased owing to small crops in major producer countries and reduced inventories; palm oil prices have also been affected by large purchases in India and Pakistan to guard against possible supply disruptions stemming from political conflict.

Beef prices have eased in recent months, as drought conditions in parts of the United States and Australia have led to increased slaughter rates, and owing to strong competition from pork and poultry. World *sugar* prices are expected to decline in 2002 owing to large crops in Brazil and China. *Coffee* prices continue to slide, in spite of Brazil's announced intention to retain some production to contain the fall in prices in the face of large anticipated production increases. Coffee growers worldwide are expected to increase their production for the coming crop year by 10 percent. *Cocoa bean* prices have reached a four-year high, in the face of declining supply; production in Côte d'Ivoire, the world's largest producer, dropped by about 14 percent during the 2001 crop year.

Within industrial inputs, *timber* prices remained strong in the first half of 2002, largely owing to a trade dispute between the United States and Canada and also reflecting strong U.S. housing starts. Prices eased back in July and August as inventories were drawn down. *Cotton* production estimates for the current year have increased, as favorable crop conditions have raised yields above historical averages. Reduced planting areas in South America in reaction to low world prices, however, will offset some of the effect of increased yields on production. World stocks of raw cotton will fall in the period ahead if global economic recovery leads to increased demand for cotton yarn and textiles, and weather conditions return to average.

Metal prices generally followed global cyclical developments through the first half of the year, picking up in the first quarter as growth prospects improved, and then stabilizing in the second quarter. Stocks of key metals, such as copper and aluminum, generally remain at comfortable levels, and the supply situation is relatively stable. Looking ahead, the main factor driving metal prices is likely to be evolving prospects for global industrial production.

Semiconductor Markets

Signs of a robust recovery in semiconductor markets earlier in 2002 have faded in recent months. Continuing difficulties among large telecommunications companies, notably WorldCom and Qwest, have dampened demand prospects in this sector. At the same time, retail sales of electronics products, including computers and cellular phones, have remained sluggish. Shipments of semiconductors have picked up only modestly from last year's depressed levels. Memory chip prices have fallen back after a short-lived rebound early in the year, and both Intel and AMD have introduced major price cuts for microprocessors (Figure 1.21). The outlook for memory chip prices is clouded by the announcement by U.S. authorities of an antitrust investigation among producers, but the introduction of double-data-rate (DDR) technology could spur new demand.

Exceptions to the generally subdued picture involve increased defense spending in the IT sector, expanding demand in parts of Asia (particularly Taiwan Province of China and China), and stronger demand for flat-screen monitors. But the outlook for the market as a whole remains clouded by the weak financial position of many companies and overcapacity in the telecommunications sector, both of which will limit IT investment in the period ahead. There are, as yet, few signs of a major replacement cycle in personal computers, as users do not appear to have a compelling need for new hardware or operating systems. Uncertainties about the prospects for the proposed industry standard on "digital rights management" (DRM) schemes for personal computers may also be a factor limiting upgrade demand.

El Niño and Commodity Prices

Climatic conditions have an important effect on commodity markets, most directly by altering production conditions. Less visibly, weather patterns also influence other aspects of the world economy, for instance by stimulating building construction, including in areas where the weather is atypically good, or disrupting transportation links as a result of floods and storms.

One of the most widely watched global weather indicators is the El Niño Southern Oscillation (ENSO) phenomenon. ENSO refers to a reversal of the typical water temperature and air pressure systems in the South Pacific, having far-reaching effects on global weather. ENSO events have been systematically tracked since the late 1800s, and tend to recur at a frequency of roughly four to five years. The intensity of the phenomenon varies, with particularly large events having occurred in 1981–82 and 1997–98. Based on available indicators, another ENSO event is expected in the fall of 2002, although it is not projected to be as strong as in 1997–98 (Figure 1.22).

The effects of ENSO on the world economy have been of particular interest since the widespread impact of the major 1981–82 event. In part because of this experience, there is a perception that ENSO is likely to have damaging effects on commodity production and world output more generally. Conceptually, however, the effects of ENSO are less clear-cut. Certain types of commodity production can actually be stimulated by the associated change in weather patterns, as can some activities unrelated to commodities, such as building construction, both as result of rebuilding and (in some countries) more favorable weather for the construction industry.[11] There is also a tendency for fewer tropical storms in the Atlantic to be observed during ENSO events, causing less disruption to activity on the U.S. east coast.[12]

[11]Rebuilding may, however, be more difficult in poorer countries with less resources.

[12]The U.S. National Oceanographic and Atmospheric Agency (NOAA) discusses the effect of ENSO on the U.S. economy in "The Economic Implications of an El Niño," available via the Internet: www.noaanews.noaa.gov/magazine/stories/mag24.htm.

Figure 1.21. Comparison of the Semiconductor Indices, CPU, and DRAM Indices

(April 2000 = 100)

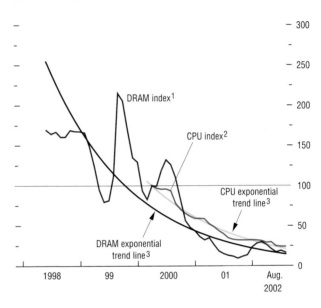

Sources: Bloomberg Financial Markets, LP; Thomson Financial's DataStream; and IMF staff calculations.

[1]DRAM index is the DataStream quoted price for a SDRAM Module 100Mhz 128Megabytes (16X8Megabyte), indexed to April 2000 and spliced with a more complete index in January of 2001, which comprises varying types of DDR and SDRAM.

[2]CPU index is constructed from Intel Celeron Processors weighted by their "clock speed" and length of time on market.

[3]Trend lines are calculated by using a least squares best fit approach to the Log 10 of the indices and using the results as exponents to the factor of 10.

In a recent study of the effect of ENSO on commodity prices, Brunner (2000) found that nonfuel commodity prices tend to rise in response to ENSO events. But the impact on world GDP seems, if anything, to be (slightly) positive, while there is a negligible impact on consumer price inflation. This section extends Brunner's analysis to include more recent data and consider alternative definitions of economic activity. It appears that his conclusions are robust: whether measured by GDP or industrial production, world output tends to rise in response to ENSO events, notwithstanding the positive impact on commodity prices. Overall consumer prices are largely unaffected by ENSO activity. One implication is that although an ENSO recurrence in 2002–03 could have serious effects on individual countries, notably on the Pacific coast of Latin America, it would not, in itself, present a downside risk to global recovery or an upside risk to inflation.

To analyze the impact of ENSO, vector autoregressions (VARs) were performed using a four-variable system consisting of deviations in a measure of ENSO (either surface water temperature or air pressure) from "normal" levels; growth in real commodity prices (the IMF's index of nonfuel commodity prices deflated by G-7 consumer prices); growth in real activity (either G-7 GDP or world industrial production); and inflation in a broad price index (G-7 consumer prices). Quarterly data from 1961 to 2001 were used. Preliminary testing indicated that four lags on each variable captured the main interactions in the system, so this common lag structure was imposed in the equations.

The statistical significance of the lagged impact of ENSO on the other variables is reflected in likelihood ratio statistics. Of the two measures of ENSO, preliminary results indicated that ocean surface temperature had a stronger effect on the system as a whole than did atmospheric pressure. The marginal significance of this measure of ENSO on both the overall system and the individual equations is as follows. The results are similar regardless of whether real

Figure 1.22. Recent and Projected ENSO Effects

(SST anomalies from seasonal averages in degrees Kelvin)

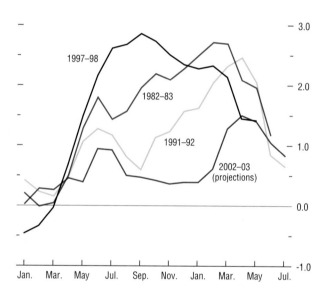

Source: National Oceanic Atmospheric Administrations (NOAA).

activity is measured by GDP or industrial production. ENSO plays a significant role in influencing the economic variables as a group, but with the effect falling almost entirely on nonfuel commodity prices as opposed to real activity or CPI inflation.

The time path of the impact of an ENSO shock on the endogenous variables is indicated by impulse response functions. These are illustrated in Figure 1.23 for 16 quarters following a temporary shock to the ENSO variable (here measured as atmospheric pressure, with industrial production as the activity variable). It is apparent that the ENSO effect itself dies out relatively quickly—about three quarters following an innovation. The initial impact is to raise non-oil commodity price inflation for several quarters, with the effect eventually reversing sign, as expected in the case of a temporary shock. Industrial production also rises in response to an ENSO shock, although the effect is minor. A similar pattern is evident when GDP is used as the activity variable. Finally, G-7 consumer prices are almost unaffected by ENSO, falling slightly on impact and rising slightly over time.

The overall picture provided by the significance tests and impulse responses, then, is that ENSO does have a significant positive impact on commodity prices. At the same time, the effect on global activity is, if anything, positive (though insignificant in statistical terms). However, this is subject to two important caveats (beyond the usual concerns about drawing inferences from relatively short historical samples). First, as already noted, the impact on some individual countries could be much greater; Ecuador and Peru, for instance, have experienced significant negative shocks from recent ENSO events.

Second, the analysis does not take account of the broader impact of climatic changes on economic wealth, as opposed to the current flow of production (GDP). Because measured output does not include capital losses from storm damage, forest fires, and other natural phenomena related to ENSO, it should not be concluded

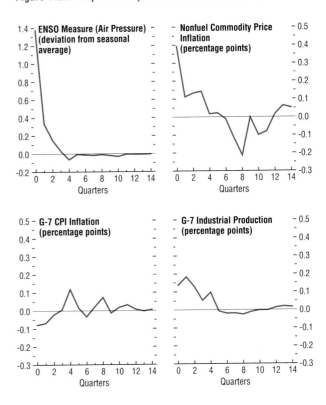

Figure 1.23. Impulse Response Functions for an ENSO Shock

Sources: National Oceanic Atmospheric Administrations (NOAA); and IMF staff calculations.

that ENSO is a "good thing" from the point of view of global welfare.

References

Ark, Bart van, Robert Inklaar, and Robert H. McGuckin, 2002, "Changing Gear; Productivity, ICT, and Service Industries: Europe and the United States," paper presented at Brookings Seminar on Productivity Measurement in the Service Industry, Washington, D.C, May 22.

Baily, Martin Neil, 2002, "The U.S. Outlook: Capital Spending and Productivity Growth," paper presented at the Institute for International Economics Conference, "Global Economic Prospects," Washington D.C., April. Available via the Internet: www.iie.com/papers/baily0402.pdf.

Basu, Anupam, and Krishna Srinivasan, 2002, "Foreign Direct Investment in Africa—Some Case Studies," IMF Working Paper 02/61 (Washington: International Monetary Fund).

Blavy, Rodolphe, 2001, "Trade in the Mashreq: An Empirical Examination," IMF Working Paper 01/163 (Washington: International Monetary Fund).

Breuer, Peter, 2002, "How Does the Volatility Risk Premium Affect the Informational Content of Currency Options?" forthcoming IMF Working Paper (Washington: International Monetary Fund).

Brunner, Allan D., 2000, "El Niño and World Primary Commodity Prices: Warm Water or Hot Air?" IMF Working Paper 00/203 (Washington: International Monetary Fund).

Campa, José Manuel, and Linda S. Goldberg, 2002, "Exchange Rate Pass-Through into Import Prices: A Macro or Micro Phenomenon?" NBER Working Paper No. 8934 (Cambridge, Massachusetts: National Bureau of Economic Research).

European Commission, 2000, *Employment in Europe 2000* (Brussels: European Commission).

Gordon, Robert J., 1996, "Problems in the Measurement and Performance of Service-Sector Productivity in the United States," NBER Working Paper No. 5519 (Cambridge, Massachusetts: National Bureau of Economic Research).

Gust, Christopher, and Jaime Marquez, 2002, "International Comparisons of Productivity Growth: The Role of Information Technology and Regulatory Practices," International Finance Discussion Paper No. 727 (Washington: Federal Reserve Board).

Hall, Robert E., and Charles I. Jones, 1999, "Why Do Some Countries Produce So Much More Output per Worker Than Others?" *Quarterly Journal of Economics*, Vol. 114 (February), pp. 83–116.

International Monetary Fund, 2000, "The Impact of Higher Oil Prices on the Global Economy." Available on the Internet: www.imf.org/external/pubs/ft/oil/2000/index.htm.

Kumar, Manmohan, and Maitland MacFarlan, forthcoming, "Reversal of Fortunes—Temporary or Permanent? A Comparison of U.S. and European Productivity Growth," IMF Working Paper (Washington: International Monetary Fund).

Meredith, Guy, and Yue Ma, 2002, "The Forward Premium Puzzle Revisited," IMF Working Paper 02/28 (Washington: International Monetary Fund).

Nordhaus, William D., 2001, "Productivity Growth and the New Economy," NBER Working Paper No. 8096 (Cambridge, Massachusetts: National Bureau of Economic Research).

Organization for Economic Cooperation and Development, 2002, *Economic Outlook* (Paris: OECD).

Oliner, Stephen D., and Daniel E. Sichel, 2002, "Information Technology and Productivity: Where Are We Now and Where Are We Going?" Finance and Economics Discussion Paper No. 2002–29 (Washington: Federal Reserve Board). Available via the Internet: www.federalreserve.gov/Pubs/FEDS/2002/200229/200229pap.pdf.

Subramanian, Arvind, Natalia Tamirisa, and Rikhil Bhavnani, forthcoming, "Are Developing Countries Integrated in the Global Economy?" IMF Working Paper (Washington: International Monetary Fund).

This chapter contains three essays on current policy issues associated with trade and finance: two on vulnerabilities to the world economic outlook (global external imbalances and corporate financial structures in emerging markets) and one on industrial country barriers to agricultural trade. The topics covered are of particular interest in light of recent events, including fluctuations in major exchange rates, renewed concern about emerging markets, and continuing multilateral negotiations on lowering trade barriers under the Doha round, including the granting of "fast track" negotiating authority to the U.S. president.

The first essay examines the concerns raised by large external imbalances between the main industrialized countries. Rather than focusing on the situation in the United States, as has generally been done in the existing literature, it considers these developments from a multilateral point of view (including the role of emerging markets in east Asia since the 1997 crisis). This perspective provides a series of additional insights, including the importance of looking at *relative* saving and investment rates across countries rather than *absolute* values; the impact of currency movements on global wealth holdings; and the constraints on the rotation of demand from the deficit countries to surplus countries caused by structural impediments in continental Europe and east Asia. Using a range of approaches, the essay concludes that the current imbalances are not viable over the medium term. It then analyzes the potential for the adjustment to occur in a rapid and potentially disruptive manner, and policies that could help mitigate this risk.

The second essay reviews the global consequences of extremely high levels of agricultural sector protection in industrialized countries.

Industrial countries provide protection to their farming sectors amounting to some 30 percent of gross farm income, which results in large distortions in global agricultural markets. Using a variety of approaches, the essay documents the benefits that could be achieved from reducing agricultural support. It finds that the largest gains go to the countries that liberalize. Thus, while developing countries would substantially benefit from the removal of industrial country agricultural protection—and industrial countries should take the lead in moving forward with this, not least because they would also gain in the longer run—developing countries would benefit even more from removing their own restrictions. The essay also notes, however, that some countries lose from liberalization of specific commodities.

The final essay examines differences in corporate structures and financial vulnerabilities across emerging market countries. It evaluates how institutions, macroeconomic developments, and firm- and sector-specific factors have affected the evolution of corporate leverage, liquidity, and profitability indicators across these countries since the early 1990s. In particular, the essay assesses the relative importance of these factors in explaining regional and country differences in vulnerabilities, and the resulting policy implications. One important finding is that corporate vulnerability tends to peak at moderate levels of financial development, underscoring the need for particular efforts to strengthen financial system monitoring and supervision at that stage.

How Worrisome Are External Imbalances?[1]

External imbalances across the main industrial country regions widened steadily during the

---

[1]The main authors of this essay are Tamim Bayoumi and Marco Terrones; Augusto Clavijo provided research assistance.

1990s. Current account surpluses in many countries and regions, including Japan, the euro area, and (in the late 1990s) emerging markets in east Asia, were counterbalanced by deficits elsewhere, most notably in the United States. Indeed, in the United States and Japan, the ratio of the current account balance to trade flows—perhaps the best measure of the degree of underlying imbalance—have risen to levels almost never seen in industrial countries in the postwar period. As a result, Japan is exporting 1½ percent of world saving and the United States is absorbing 6 percent.

In an extension of the existing literature, this essay analyzes the growing imbalances from a multilateral perspective, rather than focusing on the situation in the United States.[2] This change in focus generates a number of new analytic insights, including the importance of looking at *relative* saving and investment rates across countries rather than *absolute* values, the impact of currency movements on global wealth holdings, the constraints on the rotation of demand from the deficit countries to surplus countries caused by structural impediments in continental Europe and east Asia, and the consequences of external imbalances across the main deficit and surplus countries for the rest of the world.

One of the major concerns associated with the global imbalances is the possibility of an abrupt and disruptive adjustment of major exchange rates. At the outset, it should be emphasized that exchange rates are highly volatile and unpredictable, and economists have had little success in forecasting exchange rate movements over the short term (Meese and Rogoff, 1983). Over the medium term, however, real exchange rates do tend to revert back toward fundamental values (Taylor, 2001, and Engel, 2002). While it is difficult to know when adjustment will take place, it is essential to anticipate the potential risks and costs that may be associated with

adjustment, and whether these can be mitigated by policy actions. In this essay, we focus on the following key analytic issues.

- How concerned should policymakers be about external current account deficits, especially if they result from private sector decisions?
- What are the causes of the imbalances that have developed over the past decade?
- Are the present imbalances viable in the medium term and, if not, what can we say about how they will adjust?
- Can macroeconomic policies, both in the deficit and surplus countries, reduce the risk of a disruptive exchange rate and current account adjustment and, if so, how?

Why Are Imbalances an Issue?

Why should net flows of goods and assets between countries be a concern? Some have suggested that current account deficits are becoming an outmoded concept in an increasingly integrated world, where current and capital flows are driven primarily by private, rather than public, decisions (the so-called Lawson doctrine, first put forward by U.K. Chancellor Lawson in the late 1980s). While there is clearly an element of truth in such arguments, there are a number of reasons to believe that current accounts still matter.

- *First, relatively small external adjustments across countries imply significant changes in the tradable goods sector and in real exchange rates.* For all the recent emphasis on globalization, levels of integration between countries remain moderate, especially for the major currency areas.[3] With euro area, Japanese, and U.S. exports making up only 10–20 percentage points of their respective GDPs, an adjustment of a few percentage points of GDP in current accounts requires large changes in the tradable goods sectors, and consequently significant movements in real exchange rates.

[2]Existing work includes Mann (1999, 2002), Cooper (2001), Hervey and Merkel (2000), McKinnon (2001), Obstfeld and Rogoff (2000), and Ventura (2001).

[3]Obstfeld and Rogoff (2001). For example, after controlling for other relevant factors, the typical Canadian province trades some twenty times as much with other Canadian provinces than with U.S. states just across the border (McCallum, 1995; see also Anderson and van Wincoop, 2001).

- *Second, rapid movements in exchange rates can lead to disruptive changes in the macroeconomy.* In the 1970s and 1980s this was seen primarily in prices, with depreciation putting upward pressure on prices and wages, and often requiring a tightening of monetary policy. Since that time, pass-through of exchange rates to prices has fallen significantly in most countries as monetary policy has become more credible (Taylor, 2000; Choudhri and Hakura, 2001; and Gagnon and Ihrig, 2001). As a result, the impact of exchange rate changes is felt increasingly through changes in corporate profits, investment, and asset prices.
- *Third, while the increase in the imbalances in recent years has reflected private sector decisions, this does not exclude excesses.* To err is human, and this is as true of private sector investors as anyone else. Indeed, the financial excesses of recent years associated with the information technology (IT) revolution have much in common with those of earlier technological revolutions, when investors overestimated the profits associated with accelerations in productivity growth, leading to costly misallocations of resources (White, 1990, and Chapter III of the October 2001 *World Economic Outlook*).[4]
- *Finally, instability in the lead country can have an adverse impact on the international financial system.* The international financial system has generally been at its most stable when the external position of the lead country is strong, such as Britain during the classical gold standard, and less stable when external position of the lead country is under more strain

(Skidelsky, 2001, documents how financial positions affected the negotiating positions of the United States and the United Kingdom at the Bretton Woods conference). Recently, dollar strength has contributed to protectionist pressures in the United States and the imposition of tariffs on steel, increasing trade tensions at a time when multilateral negotiations on reducing trade barriers are getting under way.[5]

Evolution of Global Imbalances

External imbalances across major trading regions rose steadily during the 1990s, driven by movements in trade balances. There is now a gap of some 2½ percent of global GDP between the current account surpluses of continental Europe and east Asia (dominated by the euro area and Japan, respectively) and the deficit countries, dominated by the United States (Figure 2.1).[6] While such groupings inevitably obscure some country detail (for example, Canada is included in the deficit country group although its long-standing current account deficit turned into a surplus in 1999 as the Canadian dollar depreciated against its United States counterpart), they are a useful vehicle for discussing broad global trends. It is noticeable that a similar pattern of imbalances involving the same country groupings occurred in the first half of the 1980s, before dwindling in the second half of the decade as the dollar (in particular) reversed its earlier appreciation. Movements in the external positions of the deficit countries

---

[4]From a historical perspective, it is also noticeable that the imbalances are between regions with relatively similar economic structures and levels of development, and hence, one would expect, similar investment opportunities. By contrast, the large and highly persistent imbalances seen in the late nineteenth century (with which the current situation is sometimes compared) reflected the export of capital from the European industrial core to areas of new European settlement, where the introduction of modern techniques created higher rates of return. Also, in the earlier period, current account surpluses (deficits) were more sustainable as countries tended to run trade balances of the opposite sign.

[5]The link between deficits and protectionist pressures is extensively documented in the trade literature, as deficits are perceived to reflect unfair trading practices by other countries (Takacs, 1981, and Dornbusch and Frankel, 1987). See also McKinnon (2001).

[6]The continental European countries comprise the euro area plus Denmark, Norway, Sweden, and Switzerland; east Asia comprises Japan and emerging markets in east Asia, made up of Hong Kong SAR, Indonesia, Korea, Malaysia, the Philippines, Singapore, Thailand, and Taiwan Province of China, but not China itself as its capital markets remain relatively closed; and the deficit countries consist of Australia, Canada, New Zealand, the United Kingdom, and the United States.

Figure 2.1. Selected External Sector Variables

As in the early 1980s, rising current account imbalances in the 1990s reflect movements in trade balances and real exchange rates.

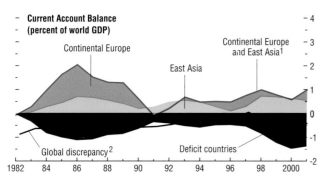

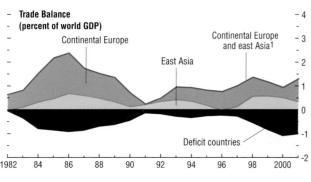

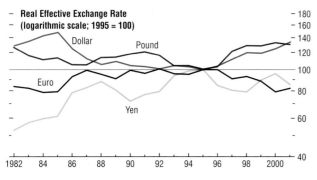

Sources: IMF, *International Financial Statistics;* and IMF staff calculations.
[1]Continental Europe and east Asia is represented by the solid blue line.
[2]Reflects errors, omissions and asymmetries in balance of payments statistics on current account, as well as the exclusion of data for international organizations and a limited number of countries.

have been largely offset by movements in the surpluses of continental Europe over the 1980s and 1990s and, since the 1997 financial crisis, emerging markets in east Asia, while Japan's surplus has been rather more constant. That said, a significant part of the deterioration in the external position of the deficit countries since 1997 has no counterpart in external statistics elsewhere, but is reflected in an expansion in the global current account discrepancy (Box 2.1 discusses this and other statistical issues).

Despite these fluctuations across regions, the current account deficit to GDP ratio for these three major areas as a group has changed little over time, with both saving and investment ratios to GDP remaining relatively stable (upper panel, Figure 2.2). As a result, variations in external positions within this group have not had a major impact on borrowing by the rest of the world, in part because many developing countries' ability to borrow money on global capital markets is already constrained. The major exception is Latin America, where countries are open to capital flows but have underlying financing needs that are generally close to their access limits, making them susceptible to changes in external financing conditions, in particular U.S. interest rates (Edwards, 1996, and Calvo, Leiderman, and Reinhart, 1993).

Real demand has consistently grown faster than real GDP as productivity accelerated in the deficit countries in the 1990s (most notably in the United States), while the opposite pattern is generally seen elsewhere (Table 2.1). The expansion in demand in the deficit countries partly reflected excessively buoyant expectations of future profits in the IT sector (Ventura, 2001; although Hervey and Merkel, 2000, take a different view). This affected the deficit countries most because IT was a generally a larger part of their economies and demand was more responsive to movements in wealth. Buoyant profit expectations in the deficit countries drew large capital inflows, supporting the 40 percent appreciation of the dollar and 20 percent depreciation of the euro between 1995 and early this year that facilitated the changes in real net exports associ-

Table 2.1. Growth of Output, Domestic and External Demand, 1982–2001
(Percent a year)

	1982–86	1987–91	1992–96	1997–2001
Deficit countries				
Domestic demand	3.8	2.0	3.1	4.1
Real GDP	3.2	2.4	3.0	3.5
External demand	0.6	−0.4	—	0.6
Continental Europe				
Domestic demand	1.7	3.4	0.9	2.6
Real GDP	1.8	3.3	1.3	2.6
External demand	−0.1	0.2	−0.4	—
East Asia[1]				
Domestic demand	3.6	6.7	3.5	0.4
Real GDP	3.8	6.1	3.9	1.4
External demand	−0.2	0.5	−0.4	−1.0

[1]Excluding Indonesia and Malaysia.

ated with divergences between the growth of output and demand.[7] In contrast, cyclical effects have generally been small, reflecting the synchronicity of the global business cycle, although they played some role in the early 1990s when recessions were atypically asynchronous across the main industrial country regions.

Were the higher current account deficits of the deficit countries in the 1990s financing private investment, private consumption, or the fiscal position?[8] The evolution of current accounts across regions depends upon the *relative* rather than *absolute* movements in saving and investment rates—for example, if saving rates in all regions rise by the same amount, this provides more resources for investment everywhere, but has no direct impact on current account positions. As can be seen from the lower panel of Figure 2.2, initially the higher current account deficit was driven by an increase in private investment relative to the other regions (mainly reflecting spending on IT goods associated with buoyant expectations about the new technology). Since 1999, however, the current account

Figure 2.2. Private Sector Saving and Investment, and Public Sector Balance
(Percent of GDP)

Investment and saving positions have been relatively stable for the regions as a whole, despite significant relative movements between the deficit countries and the rest.

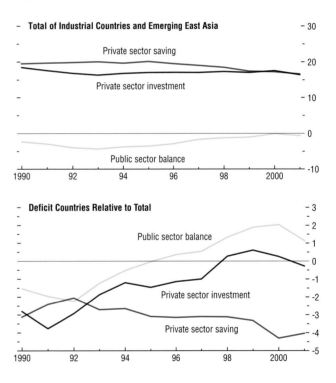

Sources: OECD, *Annual National Accounts;* IMF, *International Financial Statistics;* and IMF staff calculations.

[7]A similar pattern with regard to domestic demand and the exchange rate occurred in the early 1980s, driven by fiscal expansion in the deficit countries that raised interest rates and drew in foreign capital.

[8]See also Mann (1999, 2002) on the evolution of U.S. saving and investment rates.

Box 2.1. The Global Current Account Discrepancy and Other Statistical Problems

In principle, since one country's export is another country's import, current account balances across the world should sum to zero. In practice, however, this is not the case. Indeed, since 1997, the world as a whole has apparently been running an increasing current account deficit—the so-called global current account discrepancy—which by 2001 is estimated to have amounted to 2 percent of global imports (see the figure).[1] Clearly, this significantly complicates the analysis of global imbalances. For instance, it raises the question how much of the U.S. current account deficit is simply the result of measurement errors. In addition, even if the U.S. current account deficit is correctly measured, the discrepancy means that a significant portion of the recent increase has no counterpart in the rest of the world.

While a discrepancy is difficult to analyze by its very nature, recent work by Marquez and Workman (2001) suggests that the global current account discrepancy may in part reflect the following economic factors:

- *transportation lags*, if exports are recorded in one year, while the corresponding imports are not recorded until the next;
- *underreporting of investment income*, partly related to tax evasion and the growth of offshore centers;
- *asymmetric valuation*, where the export and import of the same good are valued at different prices; and
- *data quality issues*, especially for transportation services and workers' remittances.

To test these hypotheses, Marquez and Workman developed and estimated a small model of the discrepancy, which fit developments through 1998 reasonably well. Marquez recently provided updated projections from this model for the *World Economic Outlook*, and found that the model continues to track the overall behavior of the discrepancy up to 2002 reasonably well.

Note: The main author of this box is Tamim Bayoumi.
[1]The September 2002 *Global Financial Stability Report* has a full description of recent developments in the current account discrepancy.

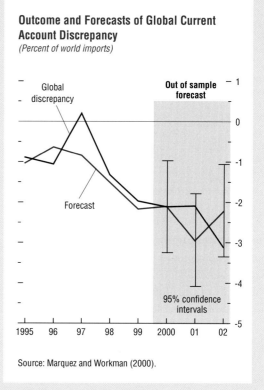

Outcome and Forecasts of Global Current Account Discrepancy
(Percent of world imports)

Source: Marquez and Workman (2000).

During the late 1990s, the rise in the discrepancy appears mainly to have been attributable to data quality issues. More recently, this effect has leveled off, and the rise in the absolute value of the discrepancy in 2001 largely reflects underreporting of investment income.

To the extent that the model tracks the discrepancy reasonably well, it implies that the rise in the absolute value of the discrepancy over the late 1990s reflects a continuation of existing trends, rather than a new phenomenon. This somewhat reduces the level of concern about the measurement of the U.S. current account deficit and its counterpart in the rest of the world. That said, these results have to be treated with caution, not least because the model performs rather less well when trying to explain individual components of the discrepancy. In addition, estimation over more recent data provides some evidence of parameter instability, hardly surprising in the modeling of a discrepancy whose size and composition presumably changes over time.

The global current account discrepancy is far from the only statistical problem facing balance of payments analysts. Measurement of international investment positions, which have grown rapidly in recent years, is also a serious problem.[2] The quality of the official data on investment positions put together using surveys and capital flows is improving, but remain imperfect.[3] Many

[2]In addition, data on net investment positions across a much wider range of countries using only accumulated capital flows and a consistent methodology are available in the academic literature (Lane and Milesi-Ferretti, 2001).

[3]The quality of the international investment data is likely to improve further in the near future. Some steps have already been taken, in part due to a Coordinated Portfolio Investment Survey (CPIS) introduced by the IMF. Twenty-nine countries participated in the first CPIS, compiling data on the stock of cross-border assets of equity and long-term debt securities at year-end 1997. A second CPIS involving 65 economies is currently being conducted to obtain end-2001 data, and from then on surveys will be annual, improving the frequency of benchmarks and hence the accuracy of the data.

industrial countries have only recently begun to compile data and methodologies differ—in particular, the foreign direct investment position is variously measured at book value, historic cost, or market prices. The data are also subject to large revisions, particularly when benchmark surveys are conducted.

In the United States, a country whose data has been among the more carefully compiled, the net liability position was recently revised down several percentage points of GDP as a result of the end-2000 benchmark survey, with a knock-on effect on net income flows that reduced the current account deficit by about ¼ percent of GDP (see Warnock and Cleaver, 2002, for a fuller discussion of the underlying issues). While this is significant, it does not fundamentally change the qualitative assessment of current trends. Despite all these statistical problems, it remains clear from a number of angles that there are large external imbalances between the deficit countries on the one hand and surplus countries on the other, and that these are resulting in diverging net asset positions.

deficit has mainly reflected lower relative private saving rates (accompanied by a partly cyclical fall in public savings and private investment rates), most likely reflecting the greater demand response to the increase in wealth in the 1990s in the deficit countries, which tend to have direct finance–based financial systems (Bertaut, 2002, and Chapter II of the May 2001 *World Economic Outlook*).[9]

In short, the expansion in the imbalances in the deficit countries in the 1990s reflected faster growth combined with financial excesses involving buoyant expectations about future economic

prospects associated with the IT revolution. These developments supported real demand and induced autonomous capital inflows that allowed the real exchange rate to appreciate. A number of factors suggest that financial excesses played a significant role in the large increase in the growth of real demand relative to output in the deficit countries. First, although traditional trade models imply that faster growth creates a deficit, this result is not generally seen in the data. Rather, the responsiveness of real exports to foreign activity increases (Krugman, 1989). Indeed, the authors' analysis of the impact of

[9]While slow-moving demographic trends across industry country groups could be responsible for the gradual movements in relative private saving through much of the 1990s, this has not been a significant driver of imbalances over most of the period. In addition, the most important demographic shifts are occurring between industrial and developing countries, rather than within industrial country groups. See Chapter III of the May 2001 *World Economic Outlook*.

medium-term trends in output growth on the current account and real exchange rate across 19 industrial countries finds that a medium-term acceleration in growth has a limited impact on the current account and real exchange rate. Second, the same staff study found some link between the size of the IT sector in the late 1990s and real exchange rates and current account deficits across the same 19 countries. Finally, as discussed further below, simulations using MULTIMOD, the IMF's macroeconomic model, find that, in addition to an acceleration in productivity growth in deficit countries, a shift in investor preferences toward the assets of deficit countries is needed to mimic the experience of the late 1990s.

The dynamism of demand in the deficit countries in the 1990s has provided important support for global activity, most notably in emerging markets in east Asia since 1997, but—as discussed below—current gaps between the growth in real domestic demand and real output cannot be sustained indefinitely. The underlying issue is whether the eventual rotation in real demand growth away from these countries to continental Europe and east Asia will occur in a smooth manner or not. In the late 1980s, the deceleration in real domestic demand in the deficit countries was cushioned by buoyant demand in the euro area and Japan (largely reflecting German unification and an asset price bubble, respectively). While this was stabilizing at the time, it proved unsustainable, and led to recessions in the euro area and Japan in 1992–93 as well as problems that linger to this day, including in the Japanese banking system and German construction industry. Given existing structural impediments in the euro area and east Asia, it appears unlikely that these regions are currently in a position to significantly offset a

rapid deceleration in demand elsewhere (such a pattern certainly did not occur over the 2001 global slowdown). Indeed, an appreciation in their currencies could even reduce the growth of output and demand, particularly in Japan with its limited room for policy maneuver. The implication is that, in current circumstances, a rapid reduction in external imbalances would most likely lead to a slowing of global output, underlining the urgency of pursuing structural reforms in continental Europe and east Asia, most notably in Japan.

Large external surpluses and deficits have also led to increasing divergences in net foreign asset positions across countries, with Japan building up net assets and the United States, net liabilities (Figure 2.3).[10] Indeed, the foreign asset position in both countries is approaching or beyond their own historical records. In the late 1990s, the U.S. deficit was financed increasingly by equity flows from the euro area (comprising both foreign direct investment and portfolio equity flows).[11] This was associated with buoyant expectations about future profits, particularly in the United States, and a general shift in investor preferences toward common stocks. Given the dominance of U.S. equity markets in global capitalization (a dominance not seen in bond markets), rising global equity prices led to significant autonomous inflows into the United States, an appreciation of the dollar, and a depreciation of the euro.[12] By contrast, the shift in investor preferences away from common stocks in 2001 and 2002 has been associated with falls in global equity prices and, more recently, an appreciation of the euro and depreciation of the dollar.

Finally, currency movements associated with reducing imbalances would shift wealth from surplus to deficit regions, with consequences for demand.[13] The large increase in gross foreign

[10]Other factors, including rising equity prices on the 1990s, help explain why on occasion movements in net foreign asset ratios do not correspond to those of current account ratios.

[11]The September 2002 *Global Financial Stability Report* discusses financing issues in greater depth. See also Cooper (2001) and Chapter II of the October 2001 *World Economic Outlook.*

[12]Portfolio diversification in the euro area prompted by the creation of the single currency probably also played a role.

[13]See also Mann (2002), who notes that because U.S. liabilities are denominated in dollars the U.S. economy is better protected against dollar depreciations than other countries.

assets and liabilities across countries in recent years has made national wealth holdings increasingly dependent on exchange rates (Figure 2.4). While the analysis is complicated by data limitations, a broad sense of the magnitudes involved can be obtained from data on the impact of exchange rate changes in U.S. foreign assets and liabilities (similar data are not available for other major countries). The 25 percent appreciation in the nominal effective value of the dollar between end-1995 and end-2001 led to a cumulative reduction of 12 percent in the value of assets held by U.S. citizens abroad. Based on end-2001 holdings, a reversal of the appreciation of the dollar since end-1995 could lead to an increase in the U.S. net asset position of some 7 percent of U.S. GDP. The potential loss to holders of U.S. assets would be closer to 10 percent of U.S. GDP because of the buildup of net liabilities, of which about 1½ percent of GDP would fall on central banks' reserve holdings, with the remainder distributed widely (including to financial firms and others that have provided hedging services). Additional wealth reallocations would also come from movements in the currencies of other deficit countries against the surplus countries.

Are the Imbalances Viable and How Might They Adjust?

Current account forecasts in this *World Economic Outlook,* which are based on the assumption that real exchange rates remain unchanged, imply that net foreign asset positions as a ratio to GDP will continue to diverge. In particular, in the absence of revaluations of asset prices, the current forecast implies that Japanese net assets as a ratio to GDP would rise by about one-third (to about 40 percent of GDP) between now and 2007, and U.S. net liabilities would double (again to about 40 percent of GDP). In both cases, this would be unprecedented by the countries' own historical standards. Indeed, even the existing net asset positions of these two countries are difficult to explain on the basis of underlying fundamentals.

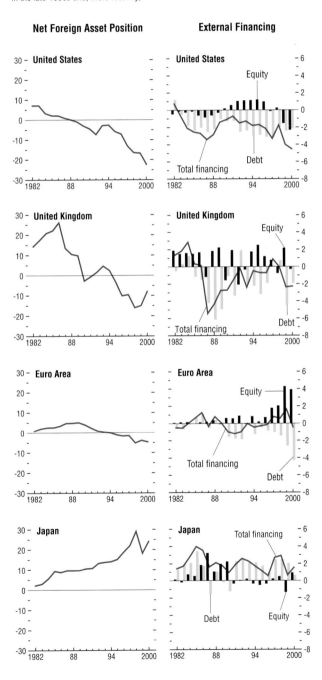

Figure 2.3. Net Foreign Positions and External Financing Flows
(Percent of GDP)

Imbalances have caused divergences in net asset positions, notably between growing net liabilities in the United States and the United Kingdom, and assets of Japan. There was also a notable increase in net equity outflows from the euro area in the late 1990s and, more recently, in inflows to the United States.

Figure 2.4. Assets and Liabilities Positions
(Percent of world GDP)

Gross assets and liabilities have grown rapidly in both deficit and surplus countries and regions, but remain relatively low in Japan.

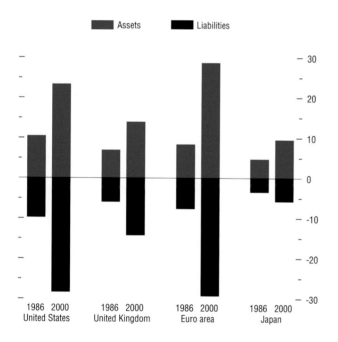

Sources: IMF, *Balance of Payments Statistics.*

For example, a recent paper relating international asset positions across a wide range of countries to government debt, relative GDP per capita, and demographic trends finds that these fundamentals predict net foreign asset ratios of only a few percent of GDP for Japan and the United States (Lane and Milesi-Ferretti, 2001). This implies that net foreign asset ratios are unlikely to maintain their current trajectories over the medium term.

Large external adjustments would be needed to stabilize net foreign asset positions as a ratio to GDP. (A slow divergence of net foreign asset positions may be justified by fundamentals; in particular, more rapid aging in Japan compared with the United States probably implies some accumulation of net foreign assets by Japan and decumulation by the United States.) External stability calculations focus on the balance of trade in goods and nonfactor services (which excludes payments on capital and unrequited transfers), rather than the current account, just as fiscal sustainability calculations focus on the primary balance (which excludes interest payments), rather than the overall balance (Lane and Milesi-Ferretti, 2001).[14] Even taking account of the fact that the United States has consistently experienced higher rates of return on its assets than most other countries, stabilizing the net foreign asset position would require adjustments in the trade balance of over 3½ percent of GDP in Japan, the United States, and the United Kingdom (Table 2.2, based on calculations in Lane and Milesi-Ferretti, 2001). Past experience indicates that significant reductions in external deficits generally occur through a combination of a slowdown in output growth, which lowers demand relative to output through its effect on consumption and investment, and a depreciation of the real exchange rate, which switches spending from foreign to domestic goods. The

[14]Indeed, in the simple case where all countries have the same rate of return on their assets, stabilizing net foreign assets (liabilities) as a ratio to GDP implies running a trade deficit (surplus), as the real economy needs to release (generate) foreign exchange.

time over which external adjustment occurs is also important. An extended period allows more time for countries to adjust their production structure, thereby reducing the size of the needed exchange rate adjustment (Obstfeld and Rogoff, 2000).

To assess the likely speed and nature of the adjustment, it is useful to begin by examining the historical experience. The existing literature has looked at the experience of current account reversals in developing and industrial countries (see Milesi-Ferretti and Razin, 1998, on developing countries; and Freund, 2000, on industrial countries).[15] The authors have extended this analysis by focusing on the experience of countries experiencing large deficits (in addition to those with current account reversals) and conducting a regression analysis to examine which factors help determine the response to these events. Turning to the experience of countries that have run a current account deficit of over 4 percentage points of GDP for three years in a row, the first result is that such events are rare.[16] Only 12 episodes were identified using data on 21 industrial countries since 1973, all involving relatively small and open economies (it is unclear whether adjustment in these types of countries would be more or less difficult than in larger and more closed economies).[17] The main conclusions of this analysis, illustrated in Figure 2.5, are the following (see Box 2.2 for more details):

- *Large deficits are generally not sustained for long.* After three years of large deficits, the average country experienced an improvement in the current account of 2 percentage points of GDP over the next three years. This was associated with a significant depreciation of the real exchange rate and a fall in output growth, both beginning a year or more before the current account adjustment (due to J-curve

Table 2.2. Average Trade Balance on Goods and Nonfactor Services
(Percent of GDP)

	Actual 2000–02	Needed to Stabilize International Investment Position as Ratio of GDP (1990–98)	Implied Adjustment
Major deficit countries			
United States	−4.4	−0.4	4.0
United Kingdom	−3.2	1.2	4.4
Major surplus areas			
Euro area	1.6	1.4[1]	−0.2
Japan	2.2	−1.4	−3.6

Source: IMF staff calculations based on work in Lane and Milesi-Ferretti (2001).
[1]Weighted average of Belgium, France, Germany, Italy, the Netherlands, and Spain.

effects, as volumes of exports and imports respond sluggishly to exchange rate depreciation). Within the sample, about one-fourth of the countries were able to maintain an appreciated exchange rate and large current account deficit, while one-fourth experienced a more rapid and potentially disruptive adjustment with a sharp current account reversal, rapid depreciation in the currency, and a significant fall in output growth.

- *The size of the adjustment depends upon initial conditions, structural factors, and policies.* Regressions examining the determinants of the adjustment indicate that the current account adjustment (real exchange rate depreciation) increases the larger the initial deficit (real appreciation), the more closed the economy, and the more expansionary the subsequent fiscal policy. As an expansionary fiscal policy lowers government net saving, this implies that such a policy results in larger and potentially disruptive increases in private sector net saving. By contrast, the impact on real GDP growth appears to be largely independent of these factors.

---

[15]The experience of countries running surpluses has not been studied in any depth, as surpluses are less likely to lead to a disruptive adjustment. See also Edwards (2001).

[16]This is the approximate size of the actual and projected U.S. deficit ratio between 2000 and 2002 (although double that of the United Kingdom).

[17]On the one hand, small open economies tend to be more constrained in terms of access to financing and borrowing in their own currency. On the other hand, external adjustment is easier as they have larger traded goods sectors.

Figure 2.5. Adjustment of External Imbalances in Industrial Countries, 1973–2001

Countries experiencing large deficits tend to experience reversal in their external position, including depreciation in their exchange rate and reduction in growth.

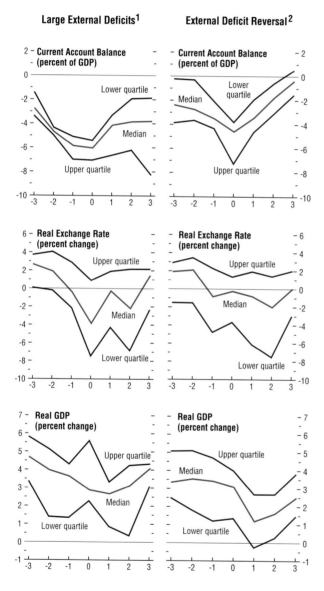

[1]A current account deficit of over 4 percent of GDP for three years.
[2]See Freund (2000) for the definition.

Given the limited number of countries experiencing large current account deficits, the study followed up on earlier work by examining the experience of deficit countries undergoing a significant current account adjustment. This approach has the advantage of identifying almost three times as many events, including several involving major industrial countries, but of course presupposes that a current account adjustment will occur. The results from this exercise were broadly similar, except (almost by definition) the response of the current account is larger and less varied, and the fall in activity is also more marked. These results correspond closely to those in Freund (2000), who did a similar analysis using a shorter sample period.

The historical analysis suggests the likelihood of a reduction in external imbalances over the next few years, involving slowing output growth in the deficit countries and a depreciation of their currencies a year or so before these reductions are seen. Given the size of the deficit countries in the global economy, this in turn implies—all else being equal—appreciations of the currencies of the surplus countries. History also suggests that a rapid and potentially more disruptive adjustment is a significant possibility.

An alternative way to examine possible adjustment paths is to create scenarios using MULTIMOD. First, a scenario was developed that mimicked many of the developments across the industrial country regions since 1996. The acceleration in deficit country output growth was created by introducing a gradual increase in assumed underlying productivity growth in the deficit countries (particularly the United States). To mirror the size of the increase in external deficits in the deficit countries, as well as the rise in exchange rates and equity prices, it was further assumed that these increases in productivity growth also led to a reduction in the relative risk premium on deficit countries' assets (again, most notably in the United States). Finally, to mimic the increase in equity prices elsewhere and the benefits of structural reforms and the IT revolution, a gradual increase in productivity growth in the surplus

Table 2.3. Scenario of Higher Expected Productivity and Alternative Scenario Where Expectations Are Overoptimistic
(Deviations from pre-1996 baseline)

	1996–99	2000	2001	2002	2003	2004	2005
United States							
Real GDP growth							
Higher productivity	1.0	0.9	1.4	0.8	0.8	1.0	1.3
Overoptimistic productivity	. . .	. . .	. . .	. . .	−3.1	0.5	0.8
Change	. . .	. . .	. . .	. . .	−3.9	−0.5	−0.5
Current account to GDP							
Higher productivity	−0.5	−1.3	−1.6	−1.9	−2.3	−2.7	−3.0
Overoptimistic productivity	. . .	. . .	. . .	. . .	−2.2	−2.1	−2.2
Change	. . .	. . .	. . .	. . .	−0.1	−0.6	−0.8
Real exchange rate							
Higher productivity	9.0	17.3	19.2	16.1	9.9	3.1	−3.4
Overoptimistic productivity	. . .	. . .	. . .	. . .	4.8	−3.3	−9.1
Change	. . .	. . .	. . .	. . .	−5.1	−6.4	−5.7
Euro area							
Real GDP growth							
Higher productivity	−0.3	−0.1	−0.2	0.2	0.5	0.5	0.6
Overoptimistic productivity	. . .	. . .	. . .	. . .	0.3	0.8	0.3
Change	. . .	. . .	. . .	. . .	−0.2	0.3	−0.3
Current account to GDP							
Higher productivity	0.4	1.5	2.0	2.5	2.6	2.8	2.6
Overoptimistic productivity	. . .	. . .	. . .	. . .	2.1	2.0	1.9
Change	. . .	. . .	. . .	. . .	−0.5	−0.8	−0.7
Real exchange rate							
Higher productivity	4.0	−10.3	−11.5	−11.2	−9.4	−6.9	−4.0
Overoptimistic productivity	. . .	. . .	. . .	. . .	−7.0	−3.3	−0.3
Change	. . .	. . .	. . .	. . .	2.4	6.6	3.7
Japan							
Real GDP growth							
Higher productivity	−0.2	−0.4	−0.1	0.3	0.2	0.3	0.3
Overoptimistic productivity	. . .	. . .	. . .	. . .	−1.1	0.4	—
Change	. . .	. . .	. . .	. . .	−1.3	0.1	−0.3
Current account to GDP							
Higher productivity	0.6	1.5	2.2	3.0	3.1	3.3	3.3
Overoptimistic productivity	. . .	. . .	. . .	. . .	2.8	2.1	1.9
Change	. . .	. . .	. . .	. . .	−0.3	−1.2	−2.2
Real exchange rate							
Higher productivity	−5.2	−6.1	−7.5	−6.5	−2.9	0.8	4.4
Overoptimistic productivity	. . .	. . .	. . .	. . .	0.5	5.3	9.2
Change	. . .	. . .	. . .	. . .	3.4	4.5	4.8
Other industrial countries							
Real GDP growth							
Higher productivity	−0.2	−0.2	—	−0.1	0.3	0.5	0.6
Overoptimistic productivity	. . .	. . .	. . .	. . .	−0.2	0.7	0.3
Change	. . .	. . .	. . .	. . .	−0.5	0.2	−0.3
Current account to GDP							
Higher productivity	0.7	1.6	2.0	2.4	2.7	3.2	3.7
Overoptimistic productivity	. . .	. . .	. . .	. . .	2.2	2.1	2.2
Change	. . .	. . .	. . .	. . .	−0.5	−1.1	−1.4
Real exchange rate							
Higher productivity	−0.6	−0.3	0.1	1.2	1.9	2.7	3.5
Overoptimistic productivity	. . .	. . .	. . .	. . .	1.9	2.6	3.1
Change	. . .	. . .	. . .	. . .	—	−0.1	−0.4

Source: IMF MULTIMOD simulations.

countries from 2004 was introduced. This base-line "high productivity" scenario is reported in Table 2.3. The key issue is how such a scenario might play out. If the expected acceleration in productivity elsewhere occurs, as assumed in the baseline scenario, the imbalances erode in a benign fashion. There is a smooth rotation of demand and a gradual depreciation of the dol-

Box 2.2. How Have External Deficits Adjusted in the Past?

This box provides details of the authors' analysis of the historical experience with external deficits since 1973. It extends earlier work examining current account reversals (Milesi-Ferretti and Razin, 1998, and Freund, 2000) by also investigating the experience of countries with large deficits and by using regression techniques to examine the importance of various factors in determining the response to a large deficit or current account reversal.

More specifically, the authors examined the experience of 21 industrial countries over 1973–2001.[1] The first event studied was of countries whose current account deficits had exceeded 4 percent of GDP for three consecutive years.[2] These events are rare—only 12 cases were found—and all involved relatively small and open economies, underlining the unusual nature of the current experience in the United States.[3] In addition, following Freund (2000), the experience of industrial countries undergoing large and persistent current account adjustments or reversals was studied.[4] This yielded 33 episodes, and hence the possibility for a richer econometric specification, including events experienced by major economies such as France (1982), the United Kingdom (1974 and 1990), and the United States (1987).

For each country group, the staff's econometric analysis examined the determinants of the change in the current account balance as a ratio to GDP, annualized real exchange rate appreciation, and annualized rate of output growth between the four years culminating in the event and the three subsequent years. The explanatory variables were of three types.

- *Initial conditions.* The relationship between the subsequent adjustment and the size of the initial deficit, rate of real exchange rate appreciation, and level of output growth was examined. All variables were averaged over the four years culminating in the event, and hence were predetermined.
- *Structural factors.* The role of underlying structural factors, in particular a country's openness to trade, can also matter. A less open economy would appear to require a larger exchange rate adjustment to effect the same external adjustment as a more open one. These factors were also measured using the average over the four years culminating in the event, and were hence also predetermined.
- *Macroeconomic policies.* Changes in the fiscal balance and real short-term interest rates between the initial buildup to the event and the subsequent period were included to examine the role of policy in exacerbating or mitigating adjustment. This was done by taking the change in both variables between the average in the four years running up to the event and the three subsequent years. Potential biases due to the joint impact of activity on the current account and the policy response were examined by including the change in the output growth rate in the regressions. As the impact on coefficients was found to be small, the simpler regressions excluding the change in output growth are reported.

The econometric results support the view that initial conditions, structural factors, and fiscal policy response all play an important role in the adjustment of large external imbalances, while the impact of real short-term interest rates is almost always small and insignificant (see the table). The results are qualitatively similar for large current account deficits and reversals, although the coefficients tend to be smaller in the latter case. Given the small sample of countries with large deficits, the latter coefficients are likely to be more reliable (Goldberger, 1991).[5]

Note: The main author of this box is Marco Terrones.
[1]The sample comprises Australia, Austria, Belgium, Canada, Denmark, Finland, France, Germany, Greece, Ireland, Italy, Japan, the Netherlands, New Zealand, Norway, Portugal, Spain, Sweden, Switzerland, the United Kingdom, and the United States.
[2]This criterion was selected to resemble the experience of the United States over recent years.
[3]Given the small sample, the staff also examined the 19 cases of countries with current account deficits of over 3 percentage points of GDP for three years in a row, which included the United Kingdom in 1990.
[4]See Freund (2000) for the definition.

[5]Indeed, the analysis of countries running deficits of 3 percent for three years in a row produced similar coefficients to those found when analyzing current account reversals.

Regression Results on the Adjustment of External Imbalances

Explanatory Variables	Change in the current account[1] (Percent of GDP)		Change in annualized real rate of appreciation[1] (Percent)		Adjustment of output growth[1] (Percent)	
	Large deficits	Reversals[2]	Large deficits	Reversals	Large deficits	Reversals
Initial conditions[3]						
Initial current account balance	−2.30*	−0.49*	. . .	. . .	. . .	. . .
Initial rate of real appreciation	. . .	. . .	−1.93*	−1.14*	. . .	. . .
Initial output growth	. . .	. . .	. . .	. . .	−0.36	−0.80*
Structural factors						
Openness[4]	−0.14*	—	−0.08*	0.02	−0.03	0.01
Policy responses						
Improvement in fiscal balance[1]	−0.37*	−0.15**	0.43*	0.51*	−0.08	−0.01
Higher real interest rates[1]	0.05	−0.01	0.01	0.01	0.02	0.01
Constant	−0.05*	—	−0.06*	−0.02	0.02	0.01
Memorandum						
R^2	0.89	0.37	0.98	0.54	0.22	0.54
Number of observations	12	32	12	32	12	32

Note: One and two asterisks represent statistical significance at 5 and 10 percent, respectively.
[1]Difference between the three-year annual average following the event with the previous four years.
[2]This regression equation also included the initial terms of trade growth, which was statistically significant.
[3]Annual averages of the four-year period running up to the event.
[4]Measured as the ratio of the sum of exports and imports of goods and services to GDP.

The following results stand out from the analysis.

- *Current account.* The current account improvement increases as the size of the initial current account deficit increases. In the reversals case, the coefficient of −½ implies that over the next three years countries with larger initial deficits still have a somewhat weaker external position than those with smaller initial deficits, although the gap narrows. Countries that are more open to international trade also tend to experience a more modest current account improvement. Turning to policies, countries that tighten their fiscal policy (that is, reduce their fiscal deficit as a ratio to GDP by a greater amount) generally experience a smaller current account adjustment. Apparently, the relative improvement in public net saving is on average more than offset by the opposite response in the private sector saving-investment balance.

- *Real exchange rate appreciation.* Countries with larger real appreciations in the run-up to an event have a larger real depreciation subse-

quently. Indeed, by the end of the full period, the earlier appreciation is basically offset. As expected, the rate of depreciation of the real exchange rate decreases the more open the economy. On the policy front, a tighter fiscal policy reduces the real exchange rate depreciation, while there is no significant effect from a tighter monetary policy.

- *Output growth.* The adjustment in output growth seems to depend only on the initial rate of economic growth, and to fall by more the faster the expansion in output before the event. The outcome appears largely independent of the other explanatory variables, including openness and the fiscal stance.

These results suggest that the adjustment process largely depends on the initial imbalance, the degree of openness of the economy, and the policy response. In particular, fiscal policy appears to be a potentially useful instrument for reducing the risk of a rapid and potentially disruptive adjustment in the current account and private sector net saving balance.

lar over several years, creating an immediate response in trade volumes (although the nominal current account balance continues to expand, reflecting J-curve effects).

In contrast, if it is assumed that recent views of underlying productivity growth have been too high, a more disruptive adjustment is possible. In particular, if the increase in underlying productivity growth is halved in all countries, this leads to a marked deceleration in the growth of global output in 2003, notably in the deficit countries but also elsewhere, particularly in Japan given the limited room for easing policy (this is the "overoptimistic productivity" scenario in Table 2.3). The exchange rates of the deficit countries also depreciate faster in the short term, and this, together with relatively larger fall in activity, results in a rapid improvement in their external position. Similarly disruptive outcomes can be generated by lowering expected income growth, even if it is assumed to be unrelated to forecast productivity. In particular, significant falls in output growth and reductions in external imbalances can be created by reducing expectations of future growth of wages and profits that are assumed to have been overoptimistic and mutually inconsistent. This illustrates how unexpected financial shocks (such as a reevaluation of accounting standards or future profit trends) can feed through into the real economy.

Policy Implications

The results of this analysis can be briefly summarized as follows. First, current account imbalances matter because of the limited integration of goods markets across countries. Second, the growth in imbalances reflects both the dynamism of the deficit countries in the late 1990s and financial excesses linked with the IT revolution. Third, using a range of theoretical and empirical approaches, existing imbalances appear unlikely to be viable over the medium term. If the adjustment occurs gradually it would likely be relatively benign, but a rapid adjustment could result in a diminution in global

growth if lower demand in the deficit countries is not offset by higher demand elsewhere, significant dislocation in tradable good sectors around the world, protectionist pressures, and changes in wealth.

How should policymakers respond in such circumstances? Given the unpredictability of exchange rate movements over the short term, macroeconomic policies should not be directed to a specific current account balance. However, given the possibility of a disruptive outcome due to a range of unexpected events, it would be prudent for policymakers to orient their medium-term objectives with a view to minimizing the risk of a less benign outcome, particularly if this achieves other desirable medium-term objectives. In the deficit countries, this analysis reinforces the argument for credible plans for medium-term fiscal consolidation—already needed in both deficit and surplus countries for a number of other reasons, including to prepare for aging populations—as a tighter fiscal policy appears to diminish the likelihood of a rapid adjustment of large current account deficits. At the same time, consideration could be given to other structural issues, including reforms of accounting rules and enforcement procedures aimed at maintaining investor confidence, where recent reforms in the United States (which houses the world's largest and most dominant equity markets) provide a good start, as well as other policies to encourage private saving in a nondistortionary manner (see also McKinnon, 2001).

In the surplus countries, the main policy imperative is to press ahead rapidly with needed structural reforms to make economies more flexible, boost potential growth, and support demand. In continental Europe, the main priorities are reducing labor markets' rigidities and increasing competition in product markets; and in east Asia, pushing ahead with banking and corporate reform and, in some cases, more flexible exchange rate arrangements. By creating a more dynamic environment, such reforms would increase the likelihood of a smooth rotation of demand from the deficit countries to the surplus countries, thereby minimizing the chances of a significant deceleration of global growth or unsustainable booms such as occurred in Japan and Germany in the late 1980s.

How Do Industrial Country Agricultural Policies Affect Developing Countries?[18]

Industrial economies provide extremely high levels of support to their farmers. The OECD has calculated that total transfers from consumers and taxpayers to farmers averaged about 30 percent of gross farm income in 2001, cost over $300 billion (1.3 percent of GDP), and amounted to six times overseas development aid.[19] Support to agriculture is much higher than that given to almost any other significant sector of industrial economies, and—as discussed below—is generally provided in a manner that is highly inefficient at achieving its underlying social aims. The high levels of support largely reflect the influence of special interests, which gain significantly, while the larger losses to consumers are more diffuse and less visible.

While agricultural support benefits some farmers in industrial countries, it can actually hurt others by increasing the prices they pay for inputs and depressing world prices for those who receive relatively little support. Furthermore, it imposes substantial costs on consumers and taxpayers in industrial countries, and on commodity producers in the rest of the world, many of whom are poor. Indeed, the vast majority of the world's poor are farmers in developing countries, whose product prices are depressed by industrial country farm-support programs. The nature and extent of these costs depend importantly on the type of support: trade measures— tariffs and export subsidies—are generally the most inefficient and depress international prices the most, while production subsidies and direct income support are somewhat less damaging.

The immediate costs come through three main channels.

- First, to the extent that agricultural support policies in industrial countries raise prices to consumers—for example, through tariffs and export subsidies—consumers' real income and purchases of agricultural products are reduced.

- Second, agricultural support encourages greater domestic production, moving resources away from more productive activities. Together with lower domestic consumption, this means that exports are greater (or, if the country is an importer, imports are less).

- Third, the greater net exports of farm products generated by agricultural support tend to increase supply on world markets, driving down international food prices. This hurts other commodity producers, including those in developing countries (although, as discussed below, net buyers of food in developing countries could gain).

Beyond these immediate costs, however, agricultural support has a number of other damaging effects. First, protection imposes substantial long-run costs by inducing countries to specialize in areas that are not to their long-run advantage, and by reducing trade and its associated benefits for growth. While these costs are difficult to calculate precisely, they may in practice be several times greater than those described above. Second, most industrial country support aims to stabilize prices facing domestic farmers and often also consumers, and thereby insulate them from global shocks. However, these efforts may not be successful, as they tend to reduce the effectiveness of each country's attempts at stabilization and may lead to increased instability in countries that do not intervene (Tyers and Anderson, 1992). This instability can cause serious fiscal and balance of payments difficulties for commodity producers.

---

[18]The main author of this essay is Stephen Tokarick; Bennett Sutton provided research assistance, and Yongzheng Yang ran the GTAP simulations.

[19]Based on the producer support estimate (PSE), which measures gross transfers from consumer and taxpayers to agricultural producers as a percentage of gross farm receipts.

Figure 2.6. Composition of Producer Support Estimates (PSE)
(Percent of farm receipts)

The average PSE has declined modestly in recent years. The composition of support has shifted slightly away from tariffs and subsidies.

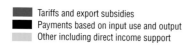

- Tariffs and export subsidies
- Payments based on input use and output
- Other including direct income support

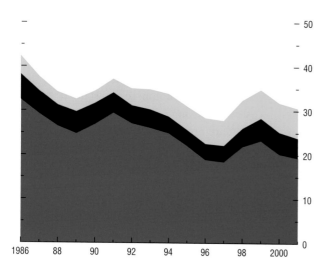

Source: Organization for Economic Cooperation and Development (2002).

Types of Agricultural Support Policies in Industrial Countries

Support to industrial country farmers averaged 31 percent of farm income in 2001, about two-thirds of which comes in the form of price-based support (Figure 2.6).[20] Support levels varied widely across countries, ranging from 69 percent in Switzerland to a low of 1 percent in New Zealand (Figure 2.7).[21] In general—and unsurprisingly—support was smallest in countries that have efficient, export-oriented sectors (notably, Australia and New Zealand) and largest in those that are relatively inefficient and import substituting (notably, Japan, Korea, Norway, and Switzerland). Canada, the European Union, and the United States fell between these two extremes, although support levels in the European Union, at about 35 percent, were significantly higher than in Canada and the United States (about 20 percent).

The nature of agricultural support provided also varied significantly across countries and commodities (Figure 2.7). In Japan and Korea, support was provided almost entirely through policies that alter prices (primarily import tariffs, since both countries import, rather than export, agricultural products). Elsewhere, the levels of price-based support were generally smaller, although still substantial. The European Union is the major user of export subsidies, while other countries, including the United States, tend to use production subsidies, which, as already noted, are somewhat less inefficient. Partly as a result of these countries' efficiency in agricultural production, inefficient price-based support comprises a smaller proportion of total support in Australia, Canada, New Zealand, and the United States, compared with the European Union, Japan, and Korea. Support also varies across commodities, with higher levels of sup-

[20]Throughout this essay, Korea is included in the analysis although it is not in the *World Economic Outlook* definition of industrial countries, as it is wealthy and has high levels of agricultural support.

[21]Organization for Economic Cooperation and Development (2002).

port for dairy and sugar production—sectors that are import competing and where it is easy for producers to organize politically. The somewhat haphazard pattern of support across commodities greatly increases the welfare costs of these policies.

There have been some welcome reductions in the size and desirable changes in the composition of industrial country agricultural support over the past decade or so. The average level of support has declined from 38 percent in 1986–88 to 31 percent in 1999–2001, led by substantial cuts in support by Canada and New Zealand, with more limited progress elsewhere, including the European Union, Japan, and the United States (Figure 2.7). Over the same period, there has also been some shift away from price-based support toward less distorting income support, particularly in the European Union and other European countries (although price-based support still remains higher than in the United States). Recently, the European Commission has proposed a reform of the Common Agricultural Policy (CAP) that, if adopted, would further reduce the share of price-based support. By contrast, the 2002 U.S. Farm Bill moves in the opposite direction, locking in much of the emergency support given to farmers in recent years in the form of inefficient price supports. On a more positive note, the United States recently put forth a proposal that calls for a reduction in the maximum agricultural tariff to 25 percent, elimination of all export subsidies, and a limit on domestic support of no more than 5 percent of agricultural production in all countries.

Industrial countries have in some cases sought to offset the negative effects of agricultural support on the poorest countries by providing preferential access schemes. For example, the European Union has for some time provided preferential access to its markets for some goods (notably beef and sugar) from selected African, Caribbean, and Pacific countries, and the United States allows imports of certain products to enter duty-free from designated countries under the Generalized System of Preferences

Figure 2.7. Changes in Overall Producer Support Estimates (PSE) and Price-based Support, 1986–2001[1]
(PSE in percent of total farm receipts; price-based support in percent of PSE)

Most countries have reduced their use of price-based support.

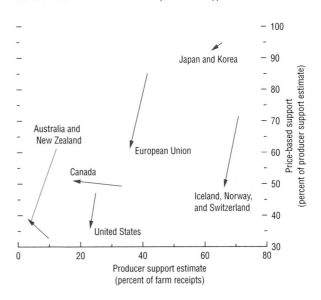

Source: Organization for Economic Cooperation and Development (2002).
[1]The origin of each arrow represents average 1986–88 producer support estimate and percent of producer support estimate composed of price-based support. The head of each arrow represents the average 1999–2001 value.

(GSP).[22] While these preference schemes aim to assist the development of poor countries, and have played a role in the successful development of at least one country (Mauritius), they harm the countries that do not receive the preferences and weaken the incentive that recipient countries have to reform their own policies (and to lobby for reform in industrial countries). They can also lead to significant transitional costs if the preferential scheme is dismantled, as illustrated by tensions over the preferential access granted by the European Union to certain Caribbean producers of bananas.

What Is the Impact of Removing Agricultural Support?

If agricultural support in industrial countries were eliminated tomorrow, there would be significant gains, both for industrial countries themselves and for many countries—particularly commodity producers—in the rest of the world. To assess the size and extent of the static gains from eliminating inefficiencies caused by distorted prices (a widely used if somewhat conservative assessment of the costs), the IMF staff used a general equilibrium model of the world economy (GTAP).[23] The results indicate that agricultural liberalization by industrial countries would increase their own real income by 0.4 percentage points of GDP, almost $92 billion at 1997 prices (Figure 2.8 and Table 2.4). The largest gainers are the major agricultural producers (Australia, Canada, and New Zealand), as a result of higher world prices and greater access to overseas markets, and the countries with most distorted domestic markets (the European

Figure 2.8. Welfare Effects of Agricultural Liberalization: Industrial Versus Developing Countries
(Percent of GDP)

There are aggregate gains from liberalization.

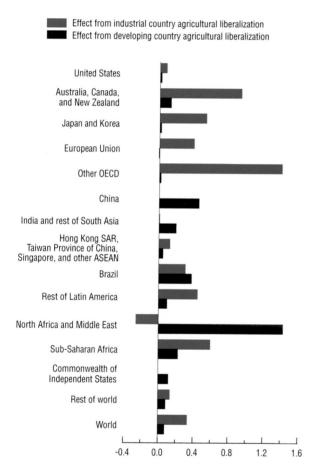

Sources: Simulations with GTAP model; and IMF staff estimates.

[22]These preferences generally apply to tropical products that do not compete with domestically produced goods.

[23]For a description of the GTAP modeling framework, see Hertel (1997). The model uses data on trade flows and agricultural support levels for 1997 and adopts a number of assumptions that influence the results, including full employment. The results also depend on a large number of parameters, whose estimated values are often imprecise.

Table 2.4. Welfare Effects of Industrial, Developing, and Global Agricultural Liberalization

	Industrial Country Liberalization			Developing Country Liberalization			Global Liberalization		
	Change in:			Change in:			Change in:		
	Welfare ($billion)	Welfare (percent of GDP)	Terms of trade (percent)	Welfare ($billion)	Welfare (percent of GDP)	Terms of trade (percent)	Welfare ($billion)	Welfare (percent of GDP)	Terms of trade (percent)
Industrial countries									
United States	. . .	0.08	0.4	. . .	0.02	0.2	. . .	0.10	0.6
Australia, New Zealand, and Canada	. . .	0.94	2.2	. . .	0.13	0.5	. . .	1.11	2.8
Japan and Korea	. . .	0.54	−1.1	. . .	0.02	0.1	. . .	0.56	−1.0
European Union	. . .	0.40	−0.3	. . .	−0.01	0.1	. . .	0.41	−0.2
Other OECD	. . .	1.41	−0.9	. . .	0.02	0.1	. . .	1.46	−0.8
Total industrial	**91.7**	**0.40**	**—**	**2.8**	**0.01**	**—**	**97.8**	**0.43**	**—**
Developing countries									
China	. . .	—	0.4	. . .	0.46	−0.7	. . .	0.42	−0.4
India and rest of South Asia	. . .	0.01	0.4	. . .	0.20	−0.2	. . .	0.20	0.1
Hong Kong SAR, Taiwan Province of China, Singapore, and rest of ASEAN	. . .	0.13	0.2	. . .	0.05	−0.1	. . .	0.17	0.1
Brazil	. . .	0.31	1.4	. . .	0.38	1.0	. . .	0.72	2.6
Rest of Latin America	. . .	0.45	1.7	. . .	0.10	—	. . .	0.54	1.6
North Africa and Middle East	. . .	−0.26	−0.3	. . .	1.43	−1.1	. . .	1.24	−1.6
Sub-Saharan Africa	. . .	0.60	1.6	. . .	0.23	−0.4	. . .	0.81	0.9
Former Soviet Union	. . .	—	0.6	. . .	0.12	−0.2	. . .	0.23	0.2
Rest of world		0.14	0.6	. . .	0.09	−0.2	. . .	0.27	0.4
Total developing	**8.0**	**0.13**	**—**	**21.4**	**0.36**	**—**	**30.4**	**0.51**	**—**
World	**99.7**	**0.34**	**—**	**24.2**	**0.08**	**—**	**128.2**	**0.44**	**—**

Source: Simulations with the GTAP model.

Union, Japan, Korea, Norway, and Switzerland), where domestic food prices fall and generate gains for consumers. In contrast, the gains for the United States are more modest, since its exports of agricultural goods are not particularly large in relation to its economy and the prices paid by consumers are not as distorted as they are in many other industrial countries.

Developing countries also gain from industrial country liberalization, particularly regions that are significant agricultural exporters, with real income increasing by slightly over 0.1 percent of their GDP (equivalent to about one-sixth of aid flows). The gains come largely from tariff removal, consistent with the observation that tariffs reduce world prices of commodities that developing countries export, while, in the case of export subsidies, many developing countries benefit from the resulting lower prices, as they are importers of these goods (Cernat,

Laird, and Turrini, 2002) (Figure 2.9 and Table 2.5).[24] The major exporting regions, such as Latin America and sub-Saharan Africa, gain the most—between 0.3 and 0.6 percent of GDP. Elsewhere, the gains are smaller and are slightly negative in one region that is a particularly large importer of food (North Africa and the Middle East). In general, these results are broadly consistent with the findings from other studies, such as Anderson and others (2001), and from the more specific liberalization scenarios in the Uruguay Round (Harrison, Rutherford, and Tarr, 1997).

The dynamic gains that would arise from agricultural liberalization could far exceed the static gains, including in poor countries with large agricultural sectors. Dynamic gains can arise as countries adopt new technologies, increase investment, accelerate productivity growth, and specialize in accord with their comparative

[24]The costs of export subsidies are often underestimated because the issue of financing these subsidies is usually not considered.

Figure 2.9. Welfare Effects of Removing Industrial Country Tariffs and Subsidies
(Percent of GDP)

Tariff removal benefits all regions, while some regions are hurt by subsidy removal.

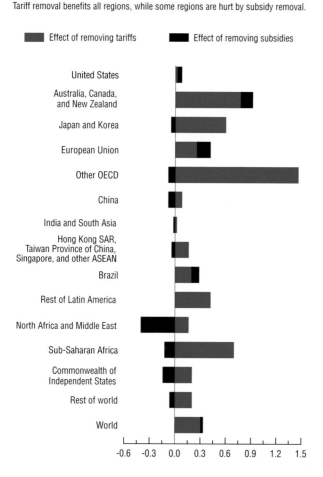

Sources: Simulations with GTAP model; and IMF staff estimates.

advantage. Agricultural liberalization in both industrial and developing countries results in a more efficient allocation of resources, thereby increasing the rate of return on capital and generally inducing an increase in investment.[25] In addition, the reduction in the variability of global commodity prices as a result of liberalization will also lead to an increase in investment in the agricultural sectors of exporting countries. Finally, some of the larger developing country exporters with more capital-intensive production, such as Argentina and South Africa, would probably be able to exploit economies of scale from more open markets.

Several studies have pointed to dynamic gains from liberalization that are much greater than the static gains. For example, Francois, McDonald, and Nordström (1996) report that the dynamic benefits of agricultural liberalization in the Uruguay Round to Africa could be easily double the static effects. In another study, the World Bank (2002) estimates that the static gains to developing countries in 2015 from agricultural liberalization by developed countries would be $31 billion (in 1997 dollars), but this gain would increase over threefold to $99 billion if dynamic effects are considered. Indeed, these estimates may be on the conservative side, given the widespread evidence that increased trade is one of the keys to successful development in poorer countries.[26]

While developing countries benefit from liberalization by industrial countries, even larger gains come from lifting their own restrictions (see also Anderson and others, 2001). The static gains in real income from agricultural liberalization by all developing countries are estimated at 0.4 percentage points of their GDP, several times the gains from industrial country liberalization (Table 2.4). As developing countries generally use tariffs to support domestic agricultural pro-

---

[25]Even if production becomes more efficient, investment could fall, depending on the capital intensity of production in agriculture relative to other sectors.

[26]Krueger and Berg (2002) discuss the importance of trade for rapid development, while Rodriguez and Rodrik (2001) offer a more skeptical view.

Table 2.5. Welfare Effects of Agricultural Liberalization by Industrial Countries

	Tariff Removal			Subsidy Removal			Tariff and Subsidy Removal		
	Change in:			Change in:			Change in:		
	Welfare ($billion)	Welfare (percent of GDP)	Terms of trade (percent)	Welfare ($billion)	Welfare (percent of GDP)	Terms of trade (percent)	Welfare ($billion)	Welfare (percent of GDP)	Terms of trade (percent)
Industrial countries									
United States	. . .	0.03	0.1	. . .	0.50	0.3	. . .	0.08	0.4
Australia, New Zealand, and Canada	. . .	0.78	1.6	. . .	0.14	0.5	. . .	0.94	2.2
Japan and Korea	. . .	0.60	−0.7	. . .	−0.05	−0.3	. . .	0.54	−1.1
European Union	. . .	0.26	−0.3	. . .	0.16	—	. . .	0.40	−0.3
Other OECD	. . .	1.46	−0.8	. . .	−0.08	−0.1	. . .	1.41	−0.9
Total industrial	78.6	0.34	. . .	14.1	0.06	. . .	91.7	0.40	. . .
Developing countries									
China	. . .	0.08	0.4	. . .	−0.08	—	. . .	—	0.4
India and rest of South Asia	. . .	0.02	0.3	. . .	−0.02	−0.2	. . .	0.01	0.4
Hong Kong SAR, Taiwan Province of China, Singapore, and rest of ASEAN	. . .	0.16	0.2	. . .	−0.04	−0.1	. . .	0.13	0.2
Brazil	. . .	0.20	0.9	. . .	0.09	0.4	. . .	0.31	1.4
Rest of Latin America	. . .	0.42	1.4	. . .	—	0.1	. . .	0.45	1.7
North Africa and Middle East	. . .	0.16	0.2	. . .	−0.40	−0.5	. . .	−0.26	−0.3
Sub-Saharan Africa	. . .	0.70	1.7	. . .	−0.12	−0.2	. . .	0.60	1.6
Former Soviet Union	. . .	0.20	0.7	. . .	−0.14	−0.4	. . .	—	0.6
Rest of world	. . .	0.20	0.7	. . .	−0.06	−0.1	. . .	0.14	0.6
Total developing	**12.5**	**0.21**	. . .	**−4.7**	**−0.09**	. . .	**8.0**	**0.13**	. . .
World	**91.1**	**0.31**	. . .	**9.4**	**0.03**	. . .	**99.7**	**0.34**	. . .

Source: Simulations with the GTAP model.

ducers, the largest benefits go to those countries with the higher tariff barriers, including many of the bigger countries, notably China and Brazil, and the Middle East and North Africa (where some countries have tariffs as high as 100 percent on wheat, vegetables, dairy products, meat, and beverages). By contrast, major producing regions such as the rest of Latin America and sub-Saharan Africa have smaller benefits, as local producers generally receive relatively lower levels of protection.

In the case of sub-Saharan Africa, a region that includes some of the world's poorest countries, the benefits from removal of agricultural support by all industrial countries are estimated to be somewhat greater than the benefits from removing agricultural support in all developing countries. This is because the level of agricultural protection applied by industrial countries to sub-Saharan Africa's exports is generally higher than that applied by developing countries, although

the results from the GTAP model may overstate the gains, as the model does not take into account the trade preferences granted to the region by industrial countries. Also, when all developing countries liberalize, the terms of trade deteriorate for sub-Saharan Africa, offsetting some of the efficiency gains from liberalization. This occurs because developing countries export similar products, and liberalization by all these countries depresses the prices of their exports.[27] On the domestic side, countries in sub-Saharan Africa have made progress in liberalizing their trade regimes in the 1990s, with marketing boards largely abolished and tariff rates, while high, coming down (Subramanian and others, 2000). By contrast, sub-Saharan Africa's barriers in other sectors—particularly manufacturing—are much higher than in industrial countries (as is the case in many of the developing country regions; see Chapter III), so that this result generally does not hold outside of

[27]Anderson (2002) finds a similar result.

87

Figure 2.10. Welfare Effects of Global Agricultural Liberalization

(Percent of GDP)

Every country benefits from global liberalization.

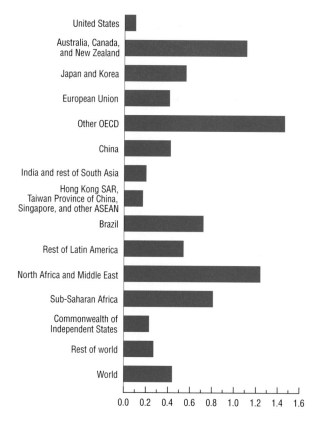

Sources: Simulations with GTAP model; and IMF staff estimates.

agriculture. That said, sub-Saharan Africa could enjoy larger gains from trade liberalization if it were accompanied by more general reforms to improve governance and reduce rent seeking.

In common with numerous other studies, the results from the simulations show that multilateral liberalization generates larger gains than unilateral liberalization by the rich or poor countries alone (Figure 2.10). If all countries removed their agricultural protection, all regions of the world would gain $128 billion (Table 2.4), with about three-fourths of the gains accruing to industrial countries and one-fourth of the gains going to developing countries. The major agricultural exporters benefit the most (Australia, Canada, New Zealand, and much of Latin America and sub-Saharan Africa), largely because their terms of trade improve, along with those countries that have the most distorted domestic markets (the European Union, non-EU European countries, and North Africa and the Middle East), where the benefits to consumers from lower prices and a more efficient allocation of resources outweigh any terms-of-trade losses.

The discussion so far has focused on the aggregate impact of agricultural liberalization across many commodities and major regions. However, it is also of interest to look in more detail at the effects on individual countries and commodities. To do this, the author used a simpler partial equilibrium model to assess the short-run effects of industrial country liberalization on the terms of trade and on net trade flows for six commodities.[28] The main advantage of this approach is that it takes into account the different trade patterns of a wide range of coun-

---

[28]The calculation uses gaps between domestic and world prices for selected commodities from the PSE/CSE database (OECD, 2002) and data on trade flows from FAO (2002) to estimate the impact of removing support on world prices, trade flows, and welfare of 150 countries across six commodities: one highly subsidized raw material (cotton) and a number of foods that are supported through both subsidies and tariffs (wheat, refined sugar, milk, rice, and beef). In contrast to GTAP, the calculation does not include the benefits from switching consumption between goods, moving resources between sectors, or changes in demand due to income effects.

tries, many of which cannot be captured in a general equilibrium model. These partial-equilibrium exercises assume that there are no spillover effects from liberalization of one commodity onto other commodities or countries and that there are no other distortions in place.[29]

In general, when industrial country support to a particular commodity is removed, there are large gains to a relatively small number of major exporters of the commodity, but small losses to developing countries that are food importers, in particular small island states that import a high proportion of their food. The possibility that net food-importing developing countries might be hurt by liberalization arose in the context of the Uruguay Round. To address this concern, ministers adopted an agreement whereby countries experiencing short-term difficulties financing food imports could be eligible for financial assistance from the IMF.[30] Figure 2.11 depicts examples where liberalization benefits many poor countries, as they are net exporters (cotton); hurts a number of poor countries, as they are net importers (wheat); and benefits a mix of rich and poor countries (beef). It should be noted, however, that because this analysis does not take account of substitution between goods, some of the losses may be overstated (for example, as the prices of some of the more expensive types of food rise, such as beef, the poorest consumers can be expected to switch to cheaper alternatives, such as chicken). In addition, it is possible for net-importing countries to benefit from liberalization as the rise in world prices could offset the effects of other distortions in the economy. For a discussion of this issue, see Anderson and Tyers (1993) and Anderson (1998).

For the six specific commodities, the analysis reveals the following points.
- Liberalization of cotton provides large benefits (of as much as 2 percent of exports) to many

poor countries in west Africa and the CIS, as the world price rises by about 4 percent. The United States gains from removing its subsidies on cotton. Losses are universally small (less than ¼ percent of exports).
- Removal of support on rice, refined sugar, and wheat results in an increase in the world prices of these goods in the range of 2 to 8 percent. These are substantial net gains to a few countries, including some poor countries that are major exporters, as well as some relatively rich ones.[31] The major losers are mainly small islands and a number of countries in the Middle East and North Africa that are net importers and some who are currently enjoying preferential access to industrial country markets.
- Liberalization of beef raises the world price by about 7 percent, which would benefit a mix of rich and poor countries, but in this case, the major beneficiaries include a number of middle- to upper-income countries in Latin America (Argentina, Brazil, and Uruguay) while the losers from liberalization include a number of low-income countries.
- Milk (including the highly tradable milk powder) is subject to very high levels of support in industrial countries, so liberalization would lead to an increase in the world price of 23 percent. The gainers from liberalization are predominately middle- and high-income countries, while many other developing countries, including poor ones, generally lose.

Overall, this analysis suggests that while industrial country agricultural liberalization in aggregate is highly beneficial for developing countries in general, there would be gainers and losers within the latter group. That said, three underlying facts should be borne in mind. First, developing countries can also substantially improve on these outcomes by liberalizing their own

[29]These exercises also do not consider the implications of trade preferences.

[30]Eiteljörge and Shiells (1995) examined the sizes of the losses that might be suffered by net food-importing countries as a result of the Uruguay Round and, in general, concluded that the increase in net food import costs would be relatively small.

[31]The net welfare effects from liberalization of sugar depends on how any quota rents (profits from the trade restriction) are allocated. For example, exporters who previously earned rents could lose from liberalization.

Figure 2.11. Welfare Effects of Agricultural Liberalization by Industrial Countries and Per Capita Income
(Change in welfare in percent of GDP)

In specific commodities, large gains for some countries are often offset by small but generalized losses.

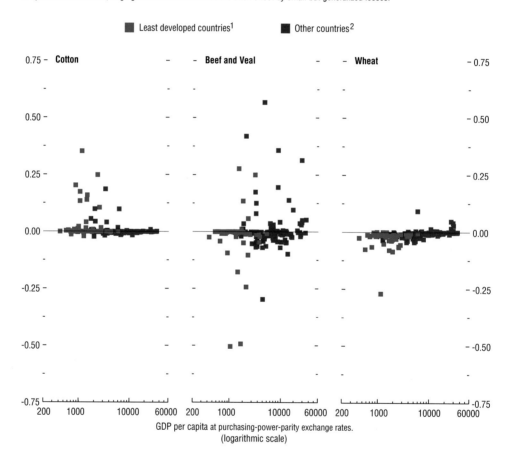

GDP per capita at purchasing-power-parity exchange rates.
(logarithmic scale)

Sources: Simulations with GTAP model; and IMF staff estimates.
[1]Least developed countries are defined in the Statistical Appendix, plus Armenia, Azerbaijan, Moldova, Mongolia, Georgia, Kyrgyz Republic, Tajikistan, and Uzbekistan.
[2]Includes advanced, developing and transition economies as defined in the Statistical Appendix.

regimes; second, any losses, particularly to poor countries, are small compared to the gains to industrial countries; and third, the households in the developing countries that are made worse off are generally relatively affluent city dwellers.

Conclusions and Policy Implications

Overall, the analysis above suggests that there are substantial gains to be had from industrial country agricultural liberalization, both for developed and developing countries, as countries reorient their production in a more efficient manner. Elimination of agricultural support, of course, will involve difficult political decisions, and likely some transitional costs to compensate the losers from reform. Given their wealth and the small size of their agricultural sectors, industrial countries are clearly best placed to take the lead in this area. Furthermore, a bold initiative by the rich countries would provide significant overall benefits to developing countries, as well as sending a strong signal about the importance and urgency of following suit with their own reforms.

The analysis also underscores that reforms are best achieved in a multilateral setting. Multilateral liberalization provides aggregate welfare gains to all regions—about $128 billion in total, with the dynamic gains (from higher investment and faster productivity growth) possibly several times larger—and, by eliminating distortions in a comprehensive manner, ensures a more efficient global agricultural sector. In addition, a multilateral agreement with well-defined rules may well be the best way of neutralizing the political economy constraints that have often successfully delayed or derailed beneficial reforms in individual countries in the past. This should be one of the key objectives of the Doha round of multilateral trade negotiations currently under way.

In the absence of a multilateral agreement, however, unilateral liberalization or appropriately designed regional arrangements can provide significant benefits. If only industrial countries were to liberalize, the aggregate gains would be about $100 billion, with over 90 percent of the gains going to these countries. Likewise, of the $24 billion in aggregate gains from developing country liberalization alone, $21 billion would accrue to developing countries themselves. In both cases, the dynamic gains would raise these estimates further and allow poor countries to accelerate the pace of their development. As demonstrated by these results, the main benefits of trade liberalization almost invariably accrue to those that undertake such reforms. While sub-Saharan Africa benefits relatively more from agricultural liberalization by industrial countries compared with liberalization by developing countries, this result does not hold more generally as relative protection is higher in other sectors. Therefore, countries should continue to work toward liberalizing their own markets. In this respect, the progress made in many major commodity-exporting countries in both the industrial and developing world, most notably New Zealand, is commendable. The recent proposals by both the European Commission and the United States for reform of agricultural support policies are steps in the right direction. However, the 2002 U.S. Farm Bill runs counter to this sentiment.

While removal of industrial country tariffs and subsidies benefits many countries in the developing world, including many poor commodity exporters, a few poor countries that are heavily dependent on imported foodstuffs may lose from the resulting increase in world prices. The value of these losses is small in absolute terms, as these countries are often small, as well as poor, and these losses are dwarfed by the benefits to the finances of industrial countries. As was recognized in the Uruguay Round, consideration should be given to providing assistance to these countries, possibly through building on initiatives to increase and better target aid at the recent summit in Monterrey. One obvious target for aid is agricultural research in developing countries, where relatively modest investments may well convert food-importing nations into food surplus economies.

Capital Structure and Corporate Performance Across Emerging Markets[32]

The 1997–98 Asian financial crisis brought into sharp relief the importance of healthy corporate balance sheets to macroeconomic performance.[33] Given evidence that the combination of high leverage, shorter debt maturities, and decreasing profitability played a key role in that crisis, the evolution of such balance sheet indicators has become a matter of increasing concern to policymakers in recent years. This has been the case particularly in emerging markets, where problems of corporate governance and transparency are often significant and, at times, have had a larger impact on currency and stock market developments than standard macroeconomic variables (Johnson and others, 2000).

Against this background, this essay looks at trends in corporate performance across 18 emerging market economies over the period 1992–2000.[34] In contrast with some previous work on the topic, this essay uses a more updated firm-level data set and considers a broader array of factors that may help explain main differences in corporate capital structure and performance across emerging markets. The two main issues to be addressed are the following.[35]

- How does corporate health vary across emerging market economies and regions? In particular, are east Asian firms financially more vulnerable than their emerging European and Latin American counterparts?

- How are differences in corporate performance related to institutional, macroeconomic, and sector- or firm-specific characteristics of countries or regions? And are these differences diminishing as a result of financial development and greater integration with the world economy?

Assessing Corporate Health in Emerging Markets

In assessing corporate health, three sets of indicators are considered. The first comprises standard leverage measures, such as the ratios of debt to assets, debt to net capital stock, and debt to the market value of equity.[36] Since a highly leveraged corporate sector faces greater bankruptcy risks and higher monitoring costs that induces managers to pass up on otherwise profitable investment projects (Myers, 1977), increasing the risk of deeper recessions and slower recoveries (Bernanke, 1983; Calomiris, Orphanides, and Sharpe, 1994; Sharpe, 1994), it is clearly important to monitor leverage carefully.

The second set of corporate health indicators encompasses the so-called "interest coverage" (the ratio of earnings before interest and taxes to interest expenses)—a yardstick to gauge the risk that the firm will not be able to honor debt payments—together with measures of the firm's liquidity position, such as the ratios of short-term debt to total debt and of liquid assets to total assets, which capture some of the roll-over risk associated with the accumulation of short-term

---

[32]The main authors of this essay are Luis Catão and Hali Edison; Bennett Sutton provided research assistance.

[33]The literature on the links between corporate leverage and the Asian financial crisis is vast, but see Radelet and Sachs (1998); Corsetti, Pesenti, and Roubini (1998); Krugman (1999); and Lane and others (1999) for some of the more representative views.

[34]The data set spans 3,538 publicly traded nonfinancial firms. Altogether these firms account for about 60 percent of the stock market capitalization for this set of countries according to the IFC yearbook. As is usual with firm-level data, the representativeness of the sample varies across countries and is lower in earlier years (1992–94). Coverage peaks at above 80 percent for Argentina, the Czech Republic, Hungary, Korea, and Mexico in 1999, from a low of 36 percent for South Africa and 8 percent for China. Averaging over 1992–2000, no country has less than 50 percent of its stock market capitalization represented in the data, with the exception of China, whose average representation is 20 percent.

[35]Data on nontraded companies are not available. Since the sample of firms under consideration represent traded companies, it is likely that there is a sampling bias. Specifically, it is expected that there is an upward bias in the assessment of corporate health, owing to the fact that nontraded firms tend to be smaller and less subject to monitoring.

[36]The analysis does not distinguish between bank debt and bond debt. In these emerging markets, corporate bond markets are usually thin and hence most of the debt reported tends to be bank debt. Another important dimension of debt leverage in emerging markets is the size of foreign currency–denominated debt and the possibility of significant currency mismatches between assets and liabilities. Unfortunately, however, comprehensive data on the currency denomination of corporate debt is hard to obtain, so this aspect is omitted from the analysis below.

liabilities.[37] In light of the key role that short-term debt and liquidity may play in financial crises, it seems important to examine such indicators carefully. The third set of indicators considered includes two well-known measures of market valuation and profitability—namely, the ratio of market to book value of equity (a proxy for Tobin's q), and the rate of return on assets (ROA).[38]

As can be seen from Figure 2.12, corporate leverage in emerging market economies has, in general, been increasing since the early 1990s, although it declined modestly in emerging markets in Asia following the crisis. More strikingly, the level differs considerably across countries and across regions. While the precise extent of the increase depends on the specific measure considered, leverage is generally largest, and has increased fastest, in Asia, consistent with evidence that high corporate leverage was a major source of macroeconomic vulnerability behind the 1997–98 crisis. Within this, however, there are substantial intraregional differences. This is particularly the case in Asia, where three of the crisis countries (Indonesia, Korea, and Thailand) have been especially leveraged in comparison to other countries in the region, as well as to their eastern European and Latin American counterparts.[39] In

[37]As in other empirical studies, short-term debt and current liabilities are defined here as liabilities with a residual maturity of up to a year. Another widely used measure is the so-called "current ratio," defined as the ratio of current assets to current liabilities. It measures the firm's capacity to match short-term liabilities with short-term assets. For the sample of firms considered in this essay, the current ratio led to results similar to those of other measures and so was omitted to save space. For a more detailed discussion of the pros and cons of these various measures of corporate health, see Brealey and Myers (1998).

[38]Other measures of valuations, such as the price to earnings ratio, the dividend payout, and the rate of return on investment (ROI), were also considered in the background analysis to this essay but the respective trends were very similar to those of the other two measures and so are not reported to save space.

[39]Leverage in east Asia has also been higher than in advanced countries on average, especially if one excludes Japan (Claessens and Djankov, 2000; Begum and Schumacher, 2001). A useful benchmark is the unweighted average of debt to asset ratios in the G-7 countries, which stood at some 18 percent in 1998–99

Figure 2.12. Total Debt to Total Assets[1]
(Percent)

There are substantial inter- and intraregional differences in corporate leverage.

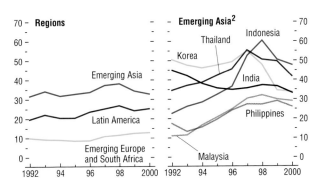

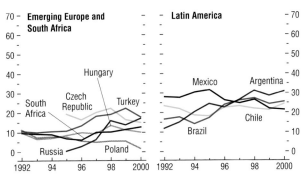

Sources: Thomson Financial Worldscope database; and IMF staff estimates.
[1]Regional and country aggregates represent the median of all firms in the group, excluding outliers greater than plus/minus three standard deviations.
[2]China and Taiwan Province of China not shown.

Figure 2.13. Regional Indicators of Corporate Fragility[1]
(Percent)

Corporate financial indicators vary significantly across regions.

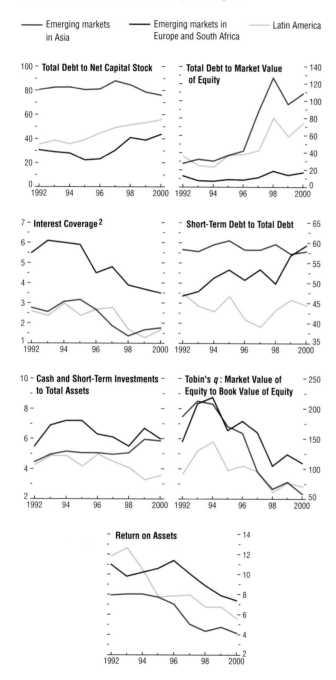

Sources: Thomson Financial Worldscope database; and IMF staff estimates.
[1]Regional aggregates represent the median of all firms in the group, excluding outliers greater than plus/minus three standard deviations.
[2]Interest coverage is presented here as a simple ratio.

comparison with Asia, intraregional differences in emerging markets in Europe and Latin America are much smaller, even though leverage has increased rapidly in some of these countries as well, notably in Argentina (including before the recent crisis) and Turkey.

Turning to the second set of corporate health indicators, Asian corporates have a higher ratio of short-term debt to total debt than do Latin American firms (Figure 2.13), although this is partly offset by a higher ratio of cash and near cash to assets. Interest coverage is very similar in the two regions. The situation in emerging markets in Europe is rather different; corporates there have a far higher interest coverage, a somewhat higher share of liquid assets, and—apart from Turkey—a lower short-term debt ratio.

Market valuation and profitability have declined since the mid-1990s in all regions, with the decline being steeper among Asian emerging market economies. But in contrast to leverage—which still reveals considerable differences across emerging markets, as noted above—there has been some convergence in market valuation and profitability indicators, both inter- and intraregion. This is consistent with the global trend toward that greater capital market integration, and the declining importance of country-specific factors in stock pricing (Baca, Garbe, and Weiss, 2000; Brooks and Catão, 2000).

In sum, the analysis above suggests that the various leverage, solvency, liquidity, and profitability indicators are generally weaker in Asian corporates than in their Latin American and European emerging market counterparts. Even though corporate leverage has declined from its peak during the 1997–98 crisis, reliance on debt and particularly on short-term debt is distinctively high in east Asia relative to other emerging

based on the same (Worldscope) data source. Using debt to market capitalization ratios as a benchmark, the contrast is even greater because of the sharp increase in equity prices in G-7 countries from the mid-1990s. Moreover, in comparison with east Asian economies as well as with other emerging market economies, leverage in advanced countries has been quite stable over time (see Begum and Schumacher, 2001).

markets. Regarding Latin America, while corporates in the region are generally less leveraged than in Asia (and also than in advanced countries for that matter), debt to equity and debt to capital stock ratios have increased considerably in recent years. At the same time, both profitability and interest coverage have declined, reflecting both the cyclical slowdown in earnings and rising borrowing costs faced by the region since 1997. In the cases of eastern Europe (excluding Turkey) and South Africa, both trends have been considerably milder, so overall corporate health in these countries appears somewhat better.

That said, two important considerations should be born in mind when deriving implications from this data to the degree of *macroeconomic* vulnerability of the different countries/regions. One is that financial vulnerability is also a function of macroeconomic circumstances that are heavily influenced by government policies. For instance, the fact that the average publicly traded Latin American corporation relies less on debt—and particularly on short-term debt—than its Asian counterpart possibly reflects a more volatile macroeconomic and policy environment that makes leverage riskier. The other consideration is that the observed international differences in leverage and liquidity are also likely to be a function of institutions, industrial specialization, and average firm size, factors that may increase the desirability of higher leverage and shorter debt maturities in some circumstances. This point is elaborated further below.

What Explains Differences in Corporate Vulnerabilities Across Countries?

From an analytical as well as from a policy perspective, one might expect differences in firms'

financing structures to reflect a variety of factors, including the institutional framework, property rights, and governance issues; the macroeconomic setting, including overall macroeconomic performance and the degree of financial development and integration with the world economy; and sector- or firm-specific factors, such as industrial specialization and average firm size.[40] To assess the relative importance of these factors, the authors have undertaken an econometric analysis relating representative measures from each of the performance categories described above to the various institutional, macroeconomic, and sector-/firm-specific control variables (Box 2.3).

Institutional factors

One of the key determinants of corporate financing choices is the existence of "agency costs," specifically the ability of investors to ensure that management will act in their best interests (Jensen and Meckling, 1976; Myers, 1977). The more difficult this is, the greater will be the cost of raising finance particularly through equity offerings.[41] Recent studies find that the magnitude of agency costs depends importantly on two aspects of a country's institutional framework (La Porta and others, 1997, 1998). The first aspect is the origin of a country's legal system, and in particular whether it is based on civil law versus common law. In general, common law systems feature stricter enforcement of property rights and investors' contracts. Correspondingly, agency costs are expected to be lower than in civil law–based countries, leading to lower leverage and short-term debt ratios. Second, the quality of governance, including corruption, is an important factor.[42] All else being constant, a higher level of

---

[40]Firms' capital structure may also depend on the tax advantages of debt and equity financing. However, Demirgüç-Kunt and Maksimovic (1999) suggest that the implicit of different tax systems for the composition of debt and debt maturity are not clear-cut.

[41]The recent concerns about corporate governance in the United States, and their effects on the stock market, provide a vivid illustration of this point.

[42]The second institutional factor is the extent of corruption in the public administration. A working definition of corruption put forward by the International Country Risk Guide (ICRG) is based, among other things, on the length of time a government remains in power. An alternative corruption variable developed by the World Bank was also considered and it pointed to a similar ranking of countries.

Figure 2.14. Institutional Factors[1]

(Percent)

Institutional factors play an important role in firms' financing patterns. Firms in common law countries and firms in countries with good governance tend to have lower leverage, significantly lower short-term debt ratios, and moderately higher return on assets.

Legal System[2]	Corruption[3]
——— Common law countries	——— Low risk of corruption
——— Civil law countries	——— Moderate risk of corruption
	——— High risk of corruption

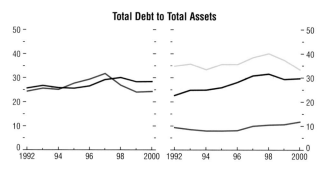

Total Debt to Total Assets

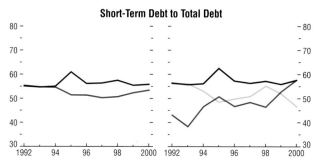

Short-Term Debt to Total Debt

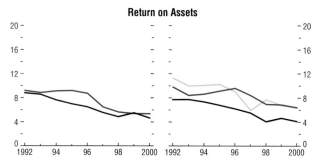

Return on Assets

Sources: International Country Risk Guide (ICRG); La Porta and others (1998); Thomson Finanical Worldscope database; and IMF staff estimates.

[1]Group aggregates represent the median of all firms in the group, excluding outliers greater than plus/minus three standard deviations.

[2]Legal system is defined using La Porta and others (1998). Common law countries include India, Malaysia, South Africa, and Thailand. Civil law countries include Argentina, Brazil, Chile, China, Czech Republic, Hungary, Indonesia, Korea, Mexico, the Philippines, Poland, Russia, Turkey, and Taiwan Province of China.

[3]Corruption is defined using the ICRG definition, which rates the risks of corruption based on the length of time that a government has been in power. The high risk countries include Indonesia, India, Russia, Thailand, and Turkey. The moderate group includes Argentina, Brazil, Chile, China, Korea, Malaysia, Mexico, the Philippines, and Taiwan Province of China. The low risk group includes Czech Republic, Hungary, Poland, and South Africa.

Table 2.6. Institutional Factors and Corporate Vulnerabilities

(Percentage point change from baseline)

	Legal System: Move from Civil to Common	Corruption: Move from High to Low
Debt/total assets	−1.3	−17.1
Short-term debt/total debt	−6.7	−1.4
Return on assets	1.4	1.7

Source: IMF staff estimates.

Note: The baseline is constructed to represent a hypothetical firm with the following characteristics: a small firm, in the general industry sector, in a country with low financial development, low degree of integration, high level of corruption, and a civil-law legal system.

corruption should be expected to result in higher agency costs and thus in a more intensive use of instruments—such as debt and short-term debt—that facilitate outside monitoring and control of managerial performance. Evidence provided in Figure 2.14 is broadly consistent with these associations.

The authors' econometric analysis corroborates the findings by La Porta and others that institutional factors play an important role in firms' financing patterns once one controls for the effects of other variables. Firms in countries with common law systems have modestly lower leverage, significantly lower short-term debt ratios, and a higher return on assets (Table 2.6). Similar results were found for governance, particularly with respect to leverage and the return on assets.

Macroeconomic factors

Corporate financing choices appear to be significantly affected by the level of a country's financial development (Demirgüç-Kunt and Maksimovic, 1999; Levine, 2001). Countries with more developed financial sectors offer more opportunities for firms to tap outside finance, including equity offerings and longer-term debt. Consequently, leverage is likely to be lower, while debt maturity and interest coverage should be higher.[43] Regarding profitability, as rates of

[43]It is important to acknowledge, however, that the impact of higher financial development on the debt to equity ratio is not entirely clear-cut (Harris and Raviv,

Table 2.7. Macroeconomic Factors and Corporate Vulnerabilities

(Percentage point change from baseline)

	Financial Development		Openness
	Move from low to high	Move from moderate to high	Move from closed to open
Debt/total assets	7.5	−1.1	−8.5
Short-term debt/total debt	−6.3	10.2	−4.4
Return on assets	−0.8	−0.6	0.2

Source: IMF staff estimates.

Note: The baseline is constructed to represent a hypothetical firm with the following characteristics: a small firm, in the general industry sector, in a country with low financial development, low degree of integration, high level of corruption, and a civil-law legal system.

return on capital tend to be higher in capital-scarce countries, which are usually the ones with lower levels of financial development, the return on assets should be lower in countries with high levels of financial development. Evidence provided in Figure 2.15 is broadly consistent with these associations.[44]

The authors' econometric analysis confirms that the level of financial development matters, as other studies have also found (Levine, 2001). However, there is evidence that the relationship is nonlinear (Table 2.7). Specifically, the following is found.

• *Leverage increases as countries become moderately financially developed, but then declines.* Firms in more financially developed economies tend to have slightly lower leverage than those in

1991; Rajan and Zingales, 1995). On the one hand, higher market capitalization facilitates equity issuance, thus helping reduce leverage. On the other hand, since countries with highly developed stock markets also tend to have more developed debt markets, long-term debt is cheaper so that firms may prefer long-term debt to equity. Such a preference for debt relative to equity is what the "pecking order" theory of investment financing would predict (Myers, 1984; Fazzari, Hubbard, and Petersen, 1988). Ultimately, which effect predominates will depend on firms' capacity to substitute equity for short-term debt and is largely an empirical issue.

[44]Financial development is measured by the ratio of private credit plus stock market capitalization to GDP, and dividing the sample into three categories, where "high financial development" accounts for the top 25 percent and "low financial development" for the bottom 25 percent of countries.

Figure 2.15. Macroeconomic Factors[1]

(Percent)

Corporate financing choices are significantly affected by the degree of financial development and the degree of integration with world capital markets.

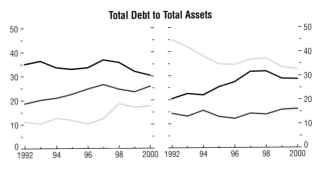

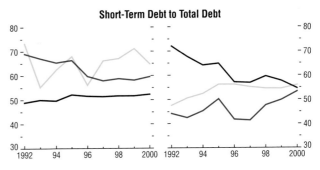

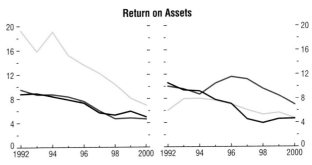

Sources: Edison and Warnock (2001); IMF, *International Financial Statistics;* Standard & Poors Emerging Market Database; and Thomson Financial Worldscope database.

[1]Group aggregates represent the median of all firms in the group, excluding outliers greater than plus/minus three standard deviations.

[2]Financial development is defined using Levine (2001) as the sum of total private credit to GDP and market capitalization to GDP ratios. Low development include Argentina, Hungary, Poland, Russia, and Turkey. The medium group includes Brazil, China, Czech Republic, India, Indonesia, Korea, Mexico, and the Philippines. The high development group includes Chile, Malaysia, South Africa, Taiwan Province of China, and Thailand.

[3]Openness is defined using Edison and Warnock (2001) as one minus the percent of shares that may not be purchased by foreign investors as captured in the ratio of IFC Investable Index to IFC Global Index. The very open category includes Argentina, Mexico, Poland, South Africa, and Turkey. The moderate group includes Brazil, Chile, Czech Republic, Hungary, Indonesia, Malaysia, the Philippines, Russia, and Thailand. The very closed group includes China, India, Korea, and Taiwan Province of China.

Box 2.3. Cross-Country Determinants of Capital Structure

In light of the growing interest in corporate vulnerabilities, a thriving literature has developed to explain cross-country differences in debt leverage and other indicators of firms' capital structure. An earlier but still influential view is that legal systems and differences associated with the enforcement of property rights have a key bearing on countries' financial structure and on the way risk is shared between lenders and borrowers, thus helping shape the financial structure of domestic firms (La Porta and others, 1997, 1998). More recent work, however, suggests that firms can find ways to bypass the deficiencies of a country's legal system and provide investors with firmer contractual guarantees—for instance through the issuing of American Depository Receipts (ADRs) or other evidence of sound accounting practices (Mitton, 2002). Moreover, a variety of other factors not fully captured by differences in legal systems and property rights enforcement have also been found to be important, including the stage of a country's financial development, its macroeconomic performance, and average firm size (Demirgüç-Kunt and Maksimovic, 1999; Claessens and Djankov, 2000). Thus, it seems important to consider a broad set of factors when trying to explain cross-country differences in corporate vulnerabilities.

In light of these considerations, the authors undertook an econometric analysis of the determinants of cross-country differences in firms' capital structure, taking into account a broader set of explanatory variables and a more updated data set than previous studies. As usual in the literature, corporate capital structure is defined in terms of four standard indicators—the ratios of debt to the *market* value of equity, debt to the *book* value of assets, short-term debt to total debt, and the rate of return on assets. Using firm-level data for 18 emerging market economies spanning 3,538 non-financial firms over 1992–2000, the authors' regression analysis includes the various institutional, macroeconomic, and sector- and firm-specific factors featured in the above-mentioned studies, plus two other factors that have been somewhat overlooked in the literature.

The first additional factor is sectoral specialization—that is, the fact that some emerging market economies specialize in sectors that have a distinc-

tive capital structure owing to technological or other structural factors; this is the case, for instance, of the IT firms. Accordingly, an appropriate sectoral breakdown based on the FTSE industrial classification is used to bring to bear those differences in sectoral specialization across economies.

The second additional factor is openness to world capital markets. In this connection, the authors' analysis uses a new measure of openness to world capital markets that takes into account country-specific restrictions on purchase of equities (see the main text). To the extent that such restrictions differ significantly across countries and sectors and influence firms' capacity to tap external finance, one would expect them to be reflected in capital structure.

The results of the respective OLS regressions, reported in the table, are discussed in detail in the main text. All regressions were estimated using time dummies (since the focus is on cross-sectional variations) and the standard White heteroscedasticity correction procedure to produce robust standard errors. As indicated by the R^2 statistics at the bottom of the table, all regressions have a fit that is low relative to those usually obtained with macro data but reasonable for such a large international cross section of individual firm data. More importantly, nearly all the t-statistics underneath each coefficient indicate that the respective explanatory variables are statistically significant, with signs that are generally consistent with the theoretical priors (see the main text for specifics).[1]

Overall, the results clearly support the view that institutions matter (as emphasized by La Porta and others) together with sectoral specialization and firm size. But they also highlight the importance of two other sets of factors. First, financial crises tend to significantly increase debt leverage, over and above their effects on the respective countries'

Note: The main authors of this box are Luis Catão and Hali Edison.

---

[1]As can also be seen from the table, the marginal effects of the various control variables on firms' capital structure vary considerably between the two leverage equations (debt to equity and debt to asset ratios). This is to be expected, since the much higher coefficients and lowered R^2 obtained for the debt to market value of equity regression reflect the fact that, unlike the debt to asset ratio (which is typically bound between zero and one), debt to equity ratios can vary widely (between zero and very large positive numbers) and tend to be far more volatile, as the market value of equity fluctuates with stock prices.

Summary of Empirical Results, 1992–2000[1]

Explanatory Variables	Dependent Variables				Explanatory Variables	Dependent Variables			
	Debt to equity	Debt to assets	Short-term debt to total debt	Return on assets		Debt to equity	Debt to assets	Short-term debt to total debt	Return on assets
Institutions					Size[7]				
Legal system[2]					Small	273.81	6.23	15.41	−7.19
Civil law	33.36	1.28	6.72	−1.36		(13.45)	(11.17)	(19.53)	(−10.33)
	(3.33)	(2.47)	(9.69)	(−5.03)	Moderate/small	135.35	4.44	13.89	−4.69
Corruption[3]						(5.67)	(9.05)	(19.36)	(−9.34)
High	101.71	17.14	1.42	−1.74	Moderate	87.20	2.54	11.97	−3.64
	(7.70)	(30.90)	(1.40)	(−3.49)		(5.87)	(5.64)	(17.43)	(−7.96)
Moderate	113.60	11.08	5.32	−3.85	Moderate/large	46.70	1.55	7.90	−1.85
	(7.00)	(20.99)	(5.34)	(−8.26)		(4.80)	(3.54)	(11.67)	(−4.37)
					Net capital stock to	1.92	0.15	−0.32	−0.07
Macroeconomic factors					total assets	(6.38)	(18.78)	(−28.91)	(−10.87)
Financial development[4]					**Time effects[8]**				
Low	−38.39	−7.47	6.34	0.82	1993	−24.44	1.50	−0.97	3.95
	(−2.52)	(−10.50)	(5.15)	(1.38)		(−2.70)	(2.16)	(−0.84)	(2.04)
Moderate	116.07	1.14	−10.18	0.61	1994	−26.47	1.58	−1.04	−1.10
	(8.01)	(2.80)	(−16.62)	(2.13)		(−3.01)	(2.33)	(−0.92)	(−0.81)
Openness[5]					1995	−11.13	1.20	−0.07	−0.62
Low	124.11	8.48	4.41	−0.20		(−1.32)	(1.85)	(−0.07)	(−0.51)
	(7.17)	(15.96)	(4.83)	(−0.40)	1996	3.71	1.80	−1.95	−0.05
Moderate	62.83	2.74	10.87	−0.16		(0.45)	(2.82)	(−1.84)	(−0.05)
	(5.02)	(6.05)	(12.70)	(−0.36)	1997	156.49	4.07	−1.69	−1.80
						(12.09)	(6.14)	(−1.61)	(−1.42)
Real GDP growth	−16.43	−0.70	−0.06	0.41	1998	116.41	1.44	−1.75	−1.34
	(−11.27)	(−13.92)	(−0.90)	(10.22)		(8.98)	(2.15)	(−1.56)	(−0.95)
					1999	132.91	3.30	−2.17	−1.39
Firm factors						(9.39)	(4.82)	(−2.09)	(−1.08)
Sector affiliation[6]					2000	266.20	4.70	−1.27	−2.20
Utilities	−97.95	−6.53	−19.81	1.07		(8.52)	(6.46)	(−1.21)	(−1.73)
	(−1.57)	(−7.30)	(−15.02)	(1.08)	*Memorandum*				
Information	−94.92	−4.33	−5.86	4.03	R^2	0.062	0.178	0.170	0.208
Technology	(−4.85)	(−5.42)	(−4.99)	(3.45)	Number of observations	18,205	19,441	18,189	16,432

Sources: Edison and Warnock (2001); La Porta and others (1997, 1998); International Finance Corporation; IMF, *International Financial Statistics;* PRS Group; Thomson Financial Worldscope database; and IMF staff calculations.

[1]Countries include Argentina, Brazil, Chile, China, Czech Republic, Hungary, India, Indonesia, Korea, Malaysia, Mexico, the Philippines, Poland, Russia, South Africa, Taiwan Province of China, Thailand, and Turkey. Dependent variable outliers greater than plus/minus three standard deviations removed except for debt to equity for which outliers greater and plus/minus two standard deviations were removed.

[2]Dummy variables based on data from La Porta and others (1997, 1998) results are relative to common law countries.

[3]Dummy variables based on data from PRS Group, results are relative to low corruption countries.

[4]Financial development is measured as the sum of a country's private credit and national market capitalization to GDP. Dummy variables are based on three groups of countries: the 25 percent of countries with the lowest average financial development ratio, the middle 50 percent, and the top 25 percent. Results are relative to the top 25 percent.

[5]Dummy variables based on data from Edison and Warnock (2001); results are relative to countries that are very open to foreign investment.

[6]Dummy variable; results are relative to firms in the general industries sector.

[7]Dummy variable; results are relative to 20 percent of firms that have the highest average market capitalization over the period 1992–2000.

[8]Dummy variable; results are relative to 1992.

macroeconomic performance. This can be seen from the table, which shows that the time dummies for the period 1997 onward are both positive and highly statistically significant, despite the inclusion of a key macroeconomic performance variable

(real GDP growth) in the regressions. Second, openness and financial development do play a major role in the determination of leverage and debt maturity structure, over and above the effects of legal systems and corruption.

moderately developed economies, but firms in economies that are the least financially developed tend to be the least leveraged, presumably reflecting borrowing constraints that force these firms to build equity through retained earnings. Such an inverted U–shaped response of leverage to financial development may reflect the end of financial repression, which allows firms to resort more widely to bank credit in the transition stage from low to moderate levels of financial development, which is then typically followed by more open access to equity markets (in the transition from moderate to high levels of financial development).

- *Differences in short-term debt ratios also vary by level of financial development.* As expected, short-term debt ratios are the highest in financially less developed economies, reflecting the fact that long-term debt instruments require deeper and more sophisticated credit markets. But corporates in countries at intermediate levels of financial development (such as some economies in Latin America) display lower short-term debt ratios than corporates in financially more advanced economies, apparently owing to more intensive use of longer-term bank credit.

- *Rates of return on assets are higher in countries with moderate levels of financial development relative to more financially developed economies,* consistent with the theoretical considerations discussed above.

Corporate financing choices are also likely to be significantly affected by the degree of integration with world capital markets, as such integration helps diversify firms' financing choices (Schmukler and Vesperoni, 2001). Openness is measured by the restrictions on foreign ownership of domestic equity, using the Edison-Warnock measure.[45] It is anticipated that

openness will generally be associated with lower corporate vulnerability and lower returns on assets (Figure 2.15).

The empirical results in Table 2.7 for openness are clear-cut and indicate the following.

- With greater access to longer-term external borrowing and equity financing, *firms in economies that are more open to foreign investors tend to be less leveraged.* For instance, the move from relatively closed economy to relatively open economy would lead to a large decline in leverage, as expected.

- As also expected, *more highly open economies tend to display lower short-term debt ratios,* as a move from closed to open is associated with a decline in this ratio. Regarding the return on assets, the impact is positive but very small and is statistically insignificant (see Box 2.3).

Sector- and firm-specific factors

Although sectoral specialization has been largely overlooked in the recent literature on capital structure, it clearly has an important role. For instance, utilities and basic industries that have heavily capital-intensive technologies, slow but stable sales growth, and long maturity assets rely more on long-term debt, as opposed to short-term debt or equity financing (Morris, 1976; Myers, 1977; Barclay and Smith, 1995). In contrast, IT firms, which have high but less stable demand growth and low ratios of physical capital to assets, are probably better off financing themselves through retained earnings or equity. Thus, countries where the corporate sector is dominated by utility and basic industries will tend to display higher ratios of debt to the market capitalization, a lower rate of short-term debt to equity, and lower profitability, whereas countries with a larger high-tech sector are likely to display a lower rate of tangible capital to assets, higher

---

[45]Specifically, the Edison-Warnock index is constructed as one minus the ratio of the IFC investable index to the IFC global index, where a score of zero means that all shares may be purchased by foreigners so that the market can be considered as completely open, and a score of one implies that the market is completely closed to foreigners. For details, see Edison and Warnock (2001). Using this information, the sample is divided into three subgroups, where the "very open" represents the top 25 percent and "very closed," the bottom 25 percent.

Table 2.8. Sector- and Firm-Specific Factors and Corporate Vulnerabilities
(Percentage point change from baseline)

	Sector		Size	
	Move from general industry to IT	Move from general industry to utilities	Move from small to moderate	Move from moderate to large
Debt/total assets	−4.3	−6.5	−3.7	−2.5
Short-term debt/total debt	−5.9	−19.8	−3.4	−12.0
Return on assets	4.0	1.1	3.5	3.6

Source: IMF staff estimates.
Note: The baseline is constructed to represent a hypothetical firm with the following characteristics: a small firm, in the general industry sector, in a country with low financial development, low degree of integration, high level of corruption, and a civil-law legal system.

stock market capitalization, and higher return on assets.

The empirical evidence confirms some of these prior expectations (Table 2.8). In particular:

- IT firms have lower leverage and a much higher return on assets; and
- utilities have much lower short-term debt ratios, slightly higher returns on assets than general industry (likely reflecting the effects of the various privatization programs in the 1990s on the efficiency of formerly state-owned large firms in the sector), and significantly lower returns than IT.

Correspondingly, corporate vulnerability indicators may be importantly affected by a country's or region's industrial structure. While utility firms account for a substantial share of stock market capitalization in nearly all countries, their weight is clearly highest in Latin America and emerging markets in Europe (Table 2.9); the same applies to resource-based industries.[46] In contrast, the weight of the IT sector is substantially higher in Asia. Asia also has a bigger share of cyclical consumer goods and general industries, which comprise technology-intensive non-IT electronics.

A second important factor is firm size.[47] Since larger firms tend to be financially more resilient, they are less likely to go bankrupt, and consequently can manage higher levels of leverage. On the other hand, however, agency problems are often less binding in larger and well-

established firms, which works in the opposition direction (as discussed above). In addition, the evidence for G-7 countries is mixed, which is consistent with the theoretical ambiguities of these effects (Rajan and Zingales, 1995). Table 2.8 shows that for emerging market economies the results are more clear-cut.

- *Smaller emerging market firms tend to be more highly leveraged.* As the size of the firm increases, the ratio of debt to total assets drops, which is consistent with the hypothesis that small firms have more restricted access to equity markets. Smaller firms also tend to rely proportionately more on short-term debt than larger firms.
- *Smaller emerging market firms tend to have lower returns on assets, relative to larger firms.* While this result appears to be at variance with Fama and French's (1992) well-known finding of higher excess returns for small capitalized firms in the United States, it is consistent with more recent evidence for several countries (Lamont, Polk, and Saa-Requejo, 1997; Brooks and Catão, 2000).

Looking across regions, the average firm size Latin America is far higher than elsewhere (Table 2.10), regardless of whether size is measured by average market capitalization or the book value of assets. This may partly explain the generally lower leverage and reduced reliance on short-term debt observed for Latin American firms relative to Asian firms, since large resource

---

[46]The figure for Mexico should not be considered as representative, in that the large oil company PEMEX is not included in the sample since its shares are not publicly traded.

[47]Firm size is measured as the ratio of its stock market capitalization to global emerging market capitalization.

Table 2.9. Sectoral Composition by Countries
(Percent of country/regional stock market capitalization)[1]

	Basic Industries	Construction	Cyclical Consumer Goods	General Industries	IT Technology	Other Consumer Goods	Resources	Services	Utilities
Emerging markets in Asia									
China	10.5	6.4	9.6	16.3	2.9	1.8	25.2	17.2	10.3
Indonesia	7.4	6.4	31.6	5.2	0.2	15.5	1.7	11.7	20.3
India	10.8	1.4	10.2	5.4	23.9	20.8	11.5	7.3	8.7
Korea	4.1	2.2	8.7	25.3	6.9	3.7	2.5	5.1	41.4
Malaysia	2.9	7.9	6.9	13.5	2.9	7.5	1.3	21.3	35.8
Philippines	1.1	2.3	0.3	21.7	1.4	22.1	3.5	13.7	34.0
Thailand	6.9	14.2	1.6	1.4	11.6	4.7	8.1	20.6	31.0
Taiwan	14.1	2.9	5.8	11.0	58.2	1.8	—	5.0	1.2
Average	**7.2**	**5.5**	**9.3**	**12.5**	**13.5**	**9.7**	**6.7**	**12.7**	**22.9**
Emerging markets in Europe and South Africa									
Czech Republic	2.5	2.5	4.6	0.4	0.1	2.1	4.6	11.4	71.9
Hungary	7.1	0.3	1.7	0.5	0.5	13.9	15.5	4.1	56.5
Poland	9.3	2.2	2.1	6.0	6.0	4.5	12.7	7.1	50.0
Russia	4.0	—	0.2	—	—	0.1	74.4	0.2	21.2
Turkey	12.9	7.7	19.7	12.5	1.7	2.0	19.4	24.3	—
South Africa	33.2	0.9	2.6	8.4	4.8	3.5	8.2	30.9	7.6
Average	**11.5**	**2.2**	**5.1**	**4.6**	**2.2**	**4.3**	**22.5**	**13.0**	**34.5**
Latin America									
Argentina	6.3	3.9	3.0	10.8	—	1.9	35.8	0.8	37.6
Brazil	10.7	1.0	1.6	4.8	0.8	2.8	23.8	12.7	41.7
Chile	8.0	3.8	1.4	1.8	—	12.1	11.2	18.3	43.5
Mexico	6.9	11.2	0.1	6.0	—	15.3	—	25.7	34.8
Average	**8.0**	**5.0**	**1.5**	**5.9**	**0.2**	**8.0**	**17.7**	**14.4**	**39.4**

Sources: Thomson Financial Worldscope database; and IMF staff estimates.
[1]1999–2000 averages. Rows total 100 percent.

and utility firms in Latin America are probably better equipped financially to issue equities and borrow long term from international capital markets. Likewise, the size factor may also account for the marked differences in short-term indebtedness between Latin America and eastern European/South African firms, although the fact that the latter display lower leverage than the former suggests that other factors, besides size, are also at play.

Conclusions and Policy Implications

Trends in corporate health indicators across emerging markets point to the following "stylized facts." First, while leverage has generally increased through the 1990s, some important cross-country differences remain, with east Asian corporates appearing particularly highly leveraged, even though leverage in the region has

declined somewhat since its peak during the 1997/98 Asian crisis. Second, reliance on short-term debt has also been highest (and relatively stable) in Asia, and lowest in Latin America, even though corporate debt maturity in some Latin American countries has been shortening in recent years. Third, interest coverage, profitability, and market valuation indicators have trended downward in all emerging markets. In particular, the ratio of market to book value of equity (a proxy for Tobin's q) has more than halved since the mid-1990s to levels below unity, thus reducing vulnerability to sharp corrections in market valuations, but also pointing to a expected slowdown in earnings growth in the period ahead.

As described above, these trends and cross-country differences in corporate indicators reflect a variety of country-specific institutional and macroeconomic factors, as well as industrial

Table 2.10. Measures of Sample Size, 1999[1]

Country	Total Market Capitalization	Total Assets	Number of Firms	Average Market Capitalization	Average Assets
Emerging markets in Asia					
China	26,984	58,564	115	234.6	509.3
India	85,464	121,519	294	290.7	413.3
Indonesia	36,653	46,556	119	308.0	391.2
Korea	259,022	575,441	573	452.0	1,004.3
Malaysia	81,220	135,156	322	252.2	419.7
Philippines	21,833	36,663	74	295.0	495.4
Taiwan	284,506	182,543	217	1,311.1	841.2
Thailand	33,781	60,963	185	182.6	329.5
Total	**829,462**	**1,217,405**	**1,899**	**436.8**	**641.1**
Emerging markets in Europe and South Africa					
Czech Republic	11,480	24,529	55	208.7	446.0
Hungary	14,112	10,109	38	371.4	266.0
Poland	18,639	18,974	54	345.2	351.4
Russia	29,229	90,368	23	1,270.8	3,929.0
South Africa	93,177	93,639	377	247.2	248.4
Turkey	66,732	43,857	65	1,026.7	674.7
Total	**233,371**	**281,477**	**612**	**381.3**	**459.9**
Latin America					
Argentina	76,822	56,033	51	1,506.3	1,098.7
Brazil	184,058	327,832	255	721.8	1,285.6
Chile	50,216	93,241	124	405.0	751.9
Mexico	144,740	168,216	104	1,391.7	1,617.5
Total	**455,836**	**645,322**	**534**	**853.6**	**1,208.5**

Sources: Thomson Financial Worldscope database; and IMF staff estimates.
[1]Table portrays representative sample of all firms studied. Only firms that had observations for both market capitalization and total assets in 1999 are included.

specialization and firm size, with the following key policy implications. First, policies that promote domestic financial development generally have a positive impact on corporate health. However, the transition from low to intermediary levels of financial development is often accompanied by a substantial increase in leverage, reflecting the fact that greater availability of bank credit tends to find its way into domestic corporate borrowing. For instance, higher financial development in Asia relative to low levels in many Latin American countries explains some of the higher corporate leverage observed in the Asian region. This underscores the need both for careful policy monitoring at that stage—including in the context of IMF surveillance—and concomitant efforts to strengthen financial institutions and supervision.

Second, policies that promote openness to foreign investors have a positive effect on emerging market corporate health in terms of helping reduce their leverage and extend their debt maturity. Again, this point helps to explain some of the differences in the regional groups considered. In particular, lower openness in some Asian emerging market economies appears to be directly related to greater reliance on domestic debt. Although these benefits may come at the cost of potential currency mismatches between assets and liabilities (if the firm has its revenues denominated in domestic currency while borrowing abroad in foreign currency), whether this cost outweighs those other benefits is a question that is not examined here owing to the lack of data on debt currency denomination.

Third, institutions matter, particularly regarding corruption, which tends to increase leverage and reliance on short-term debt, and lower profitability. This finding is not new, but the fact that it holds for a broad sample of emerging market economies and more recent data reinforces the received wisdom. So, policy reforms that help promote institutional transparency are clearly important.

References

Anderson, James E., 1998, "The Uruguay Round and Welfare in Some Distorted Agricultural Economies," *Journal of Development Economics*, Vol. 56 (August), pp. 393–410.

———, and Eric van Wincoop, 2001, "Gravity with Gravitas: A Solution to the Border Puzzle," NBER Working Paper No. 8079 (Cambridge, Massachusetts: National Bureau of Economic Research).

Anderson, Kym, 2002, "Agricultural Trade Liberalization: Implications for Indian Ocean Rim Countries" (Adelaide, Australia: Centre for International Economic Studies, University of Adelaide). Available via the Internet: www.adelaide.edu.au/cies/aglib.pdf.

———, and Rod Tyers, 1993, "More on Welfare Gains to Developing Countries From Liberalizing World Food Trade," *Journal of Agricultural Economics*, Vol. 44 (May), pp. 189–204.

Anderson, Kym, Betina Dimaranan, Joseph Francois, Tom Hertel, Bernard Hoekman, and Will Martin, 2001, "The Cost of Rich (and Poor) Country Protection to Developing Countries," *Journal of African Economies*, Vol. 10, No. 3, pp. 227–57.

Baca, Sean P., Brian Garbe, and Richard A. Weiss, 2000, "The Rise of Sector Effects in Major Equity Markets," *Financial Analysts Journal*, Vol. 56 (September/October), pp. 35–40.

Barclay, Michael J., and Clifford W. Smith Jr., 1995, "The Maturity Structure of Corporate Debt," *Journal of Finance*, Vol. 50 (June), pp. 609–31.

Begum, Jahanara, and Liliana Schumacher, 2001, "International Comparison of Corporate Leverage," IMF MAE Technical Note 01/02 (Washington: International Monetary Fund).

Bernanke, Ben, 1983, "Nonmonetary Effects of the Financial Crisis in the Propagation of the Great Depression," *American Economic Review*, Vol. 73, No. 3, pp. 257–76.

Bertaut, Carol C., 2002, "Equity Prices, Household Wealth, and Consumption Growth in Foreign Industrial Countries: Wealth Effects in the 1990s," International Finance Discussion Paper No. 724 (Washington: Board of Governors of the Federal Reserve System).

Brealey, Richard, and Stewart C. Myers, 1998, *Principles of Corporate Finance* (New York: McGraw-Hill).

Brooks, Robin, and Luis Catão, 2000, "The New Economy and Global Stock Returns," IMF Working Paper 00/216 (Washington: International Monetary Fund).

Calomiris, Charles W., Athanasios Orphanides, and Steven A. Sharpe, 1994, "Leverage as a State Variable for Employment, Inventory Accumulation and Fixed Investment," NBER Working Paper No. 4800 (Cambridge, Massachusetts: National Bureau of Economic Research).

Calvo, Guillermo A., Leonardo Leiderman, and Carmen M. Reinhart, 1993, "Capital Inflows and Real Exchange Rate Appreciation in Latin America: The Role of External Factors," *Staff Papers*, International Monetary Fund, Vol. 40 (March), pp. 108–51.

Cernat, Lucian, Sam Laird, and Alessandro Turrini, 2002, "Back to Basics: Market Access Issues in the Doha Agenda," paper presented at the United Nations Conference on Trade and Development (UNCTAD), Geneva. Available via the Internet: www.unctad.org/p166/modules/mod5/Back%20to%20basics.pdf.

Choudhri, Ehsan, and Dalia Hakura, 2001, "Exchange Rate Pass-Through to Domestic Prices: Does the Inflationary Environment Matter?" IMF Working Paper 01/194 (Washington: International Monetary Fund).

Claessens, Stijn, and Simeon Djankov, 2000, "Publicly Listed East Asian Corporates: Growth, Financing, and Risks," in *Asian Corporate Recovery: Findings From Firm-Level Surveys in Five Countries*, ed. by Dominique Dwor-Frecaut, Francis X. Colaco, and Mary Hallward-Driemeier (Washington: World Bank).

Cooper, Richard N., 2001, "Is the U.S. Current Account Deficit Sustainable? Will It Be Sustained?" *Brookings Papers on Economic Activity: 1*, Brookings Institution, pp. 217–26.

Corsetti, Gian Carlo, Paolo Pesenti, and Nouriel Roubini, 1998, "What Causes the Asian Currency and Financial Crises? Part I: A Macroeconomic Overview," NBER Working Paper No. 6833 (Cambridge, Massachusetts: National Bureau of Economic Research).

Demirgüç-Kunt, Asli, and Vojislav Maksimovic, 1999, "Institutions, Financial Markets, and Firm Debt Maturity," *Journal of Financial Economics*, Vol. 54 (December), pp. 295–336.

Dornbusch, Rudiger, and Jeffrey Frankel, 1987, "Macro-economics and Protection," in *U.S. Trade Policies in a Changing World Economy*, ed. by Robert Mitchell Stern (Cambridge, Massachusetts: MIT Press).

Edison, Hali J., and Francis E. Warnock, 2001, "A Simple Measure of the Intensity of Capital Controls," IMF Working Paper 01/180 (Washington: International Monetary Fund).

Edwards, Sebastian, 1996, "Why Are Latin America's Savings Rates So Low? An International Comparative Analysis," *Journal of Development Economics*, Vol. 51 (October), pp. 5–44.

———, 2001, "Does the Current Account Matter?" NBER Working Paper No. 8275 (Cambridge, Massachusetts: National Bureau of Economic Research).

Eiteljörge, Uwe, and Clinton Shiells, 1995, "The Uruguay Round and Net Food Importers," IMF Working Paper 95/143 (Washington: International Monetary Fund).

Engel, Charles, 2002, "Expenditure Switching and Exchange Rate Policy," in *NBER Macroeconomics Annual 2002*, ed. by Mark Gertler and Kenneth Rogoff (Cambridge, Massachusetts: MIT Press).

Fama, Eugene F., and Kenneth R. French, 1992, "The Cross-Section of Expected Stock Returns," *Journal of Finance*, Vol. 47 (June), pp. 427–65.

Fazzari, Steven M., R. Glenn Hubbard, and Bruce C. Petersen, 1988, "Financing Constraints and Corporate Investment," *Brookings Papers on Economic Activity: 1*, Brookings Institution, pp. 141–95.

Food and Agricultural Organization of the United Nations (FAO), 2002, Database on agriculture and food trade. Available via the Internet: http://apps.fao.org/page/collections.

Francois, Joseph, Bradley McDonald, and Håkan Nordström, 1996, "The Uruguay Round: A Numerically Based Qualitative Assessment," in *The Uruguay Round and the Developing Countries*, ed. by Will Martin and L. Alan Winters (Cambridge: Cambridge University Press).

Freund, Caroline L., 2000, "Current Account Adjustment in Industrialized Countries," International Finance Discussion Paper, No. 692 (Washington: Board of Governors of the Federal Reserve System).

Gagnon, Joseph E., and Jane Ihrig, 2001, "Monetary Policy and Exchange Rate Pass-Through," International Finance Discussion Paper No. 704 (Washington: Board of Governors of the Federal Reserve System).

Goldberger, Arthur, 1991, *A Course in Econometrics* (Cambridge, Massachusetts: Harvard University Press).

Harris, Milton, and Artur Raviv, 1991, "The Theory of Capital Structure," *Journal of Finance*, Vol. 46 (March), pp. 297–355.

Harrison, Glenn, Tom Rutherford, and David Tarr, 1997, "Quantifying the Uruguay Round," in *The Uruguay Round and the Developing Countries*, ed. by Will Martin and L. Alan Winters (Cambridge: Cambridge University Press).

Hertel, Thomas W., ed., 1997, *Global Trade Analysis: Modeling and Applications* (Cambridge: Cambridge University Press).

Hervey, Jack L., and Loula Merkel, 2000, "A Record Current Account Deficit: Causes and Implications," *Economic Perspectives*, Vol. 24, No. 4, pp. 2–13.

Hooper, Peter, Karen Johnson, and Jaime Marquez, 1998, "Trade Elasticities for G-7 Countries," International Finance Discussion Paper No. 609 (Washington: Board of Governors of the Federal Reserve System).

International Monetary Fund, 2001, *Annual Report of the IMF Committee on Balance of Payments Statistics* (Washington: IMF).

Jensen, Michael C., and William H. Meckling, 1976, "Theory of the Firm: Managerial Behavior, Agency Costs, and Ownership Structure," *Journal of Financial Economics*, Vol. 3 (October), pp. 305–60.

Johnson, Simon, Peter Boone, Alasdair Breach, and Eric Friedman, 2000, "Corporate Governance in the Asian Financial Crisis," *Journal of Financial Economics*, Vol. 58 (October/November), pp. 141–86.

Krueger, Anne, and Andrew Berg, 2002, "Trade, Growth, and Poverty: A Selective Survey," paper presented at the Annual World Bank Conference on Development Economics, Washington, April. Draft available via the Internet: www.econ.worldbank.org/files/13377_Berg_and_Krueger.pdf.

Krugman, Paul R., 1989, "Differences in Income Elasticities and Trends in Real Exchange Rates," *European Economic Review*, Vol. 33 (May), pp. 1031–54.

———, 1999, "Balance Sheets, the Transfer Problem, and Financial Crises" (unpublished; Princeton, New Jersey: Economics Department, Princeton University).

Lamont, Owens, Christopher Polk, and Jesus Saa-Requejo, 1997, "Financial Constraints and Stock Returns," NBER Working Paper No. 6210 (Cambridge, Massachusetts: National Bureau of Economic Research).

La Porta, Rafael, Florencio Lopez-de-Silanes, Andrei Shleifer, and Robert W. Vishny, 1997, "Legal Determinants of External Finance," *Journal of Finance*, Vol. 52 (July), pp. 1131–50.

———, 1998, "Law and Finance," *Journal of Political Economy*, Vol. 106 (December), pp. 1113–55.

Lane, Philip R., and Gian Maria Milesi-Ferretti, 2001, "Long-Term Capital Movements," IMF Working Paper 01/107 (Washington: International Monetary Fund).

———, 2002, "External Wealth, the Trade Balance, and the Real Exchange Rate," IMF Working Paper 02/51 (Washington: International Monetary Fund).

Lane, Timothy, Atish Ghosh, Javier Hamann, Steven Phillips, Marianne Schulze-Ghattas, and Tsidi Tsikata, 1999, *IMF-Supported Programs in Indonesia, Korea, and Thailand: A Preliminary Assessment*, IMF Occasional Paper No. 178 (Washington: International Monetary Fund).

Levine, Ross, 2001, "Bank-Based or Market-Based Financial Systems: Which Is Better?" (unpublished; Minneapolis, Minnesota: Carlson School of Management, University of Minnesota). Available via the Internet: www.worldbank.org/research/projects/finstructure/pdf_files/structure.pdf.

Mann, Catherine L., 1999, *Is the U.S. Trade Deficit Sustainable?* (Washington: Institute for International Economics).

———, 2002, "Perspectives on the U.S. Current Account Deficit and Sustainability," *Journal of Economic Perspectives* (forthcoming).

Marquez, Jaime, and Lisa Workman, 2001, "Modeling the IMF's Statistical Discrepancy in the Global Current Account," *IMF Staff Papers*, Vol. 48, No. 3, pp. 499–521.

McCallum, John, 1995, "National Borders Matter: Canada-U.S. Regional Trade Patterns," *American Economic Review*, Vol. 85 (June), pp. 615–23.

McKinnon, Ronald I., 2001, "The International Dollar Standard and the Sustainability of the U.S. Current Account Deficit," *Brookings Papers on Economic Activity: 1*, Brookings Institution, pp. 227–39.

Meese, Richard A., and Kenneth Rogoff, 1983, "Empirical Exchange Rate Models of the Seventies: Do They Fit Out of Sample?" *Journal of International Economics*, Vol. 14 (February), pp. 3–24.

Milesi-Ferretti, Gian Maria, and Assaf Razin, 1998, "Current Account Reversals and Currency Crises: Empirical Regularities," NBER Working Paper No. 6620 (Cambridge, Massachusetts, National Bureau of Economic Research).

Mitton, Todd, 2002, "A Cross-Firm Analysis of the Impact of Corporate Governance on the East Asian Financial Crisis," *Journal of Financial Economics*, Vol. 64 (May), pp. 215–41.

Morris, James R., 1976, "On Corporate Debt Maturity Strategies," *Journal of Finance*, Vol. 31, No. 1, pp. 29–37.

Myers, Stewart C., 1977, "Determinants of Corporate Borrowing," *Journal of Financial Economics*, Vol. 5 (November), pp. 147–75.

———, 1984, "The Capital Structure Puzzle," *Journal of Finance*, Vol. 39 (July), pp. 575–92.

Obstfeld, Maurice, and Kenneth Rogoff, 2000, "Perspectives on OECD Economic Integration: Implications for U.S. Current Account Adjustment," in *Global Economic Integration: Opportunities and Challenges: A Symposium, sponsored by the Federal Reserve Bank of Kansas City, Jackson Hole, Wyoming, August 24–26, 2001* (Kansas City, Missouri: Federal Reserve Bank of Kansas City).

———, 2001, "The Six Major Puzzles in International Macroeconomics: Is There a Common Cause?" in *NBER Macroeconomics Annual 2000*, ed. by Ben S. Bernanke and Kenneth Rogoff (Cambridge, Massachusetts: MIT Press).

Organization for Economic Cooperation and Development, 2002, *Agricultural Policies in OECD Countries: Monitoring and Evaluation* (Paris: OECD).

Radelet, Steven, and Jeffrey D. Sachs, 1998, "The East Asian Financial Crisis: Diagnosis, Remedies, and Prospects," *Brookings Papers on Economic Activity: 1*, Brookings Institution, pp. 1–90.

Rajan, Raghuram G., and Luigi Zingales, 1995, "What Do We Know About Capital Structure? Some Evidence from International Data," *Journal of Finance*, Vol. 50 (December), pp. 1421–60.

Rodriguez, Francisco, and Dani Rodrik, 2001, "Trade Policy and Economic Growth: A Skeptic's Guide to the Cross-National Evidence," in *NBER Macroeconomics Annual 2000*, ed. by Ben S. Bernanke and Kenneth Rogoff (Cambridge, Massachusetts: MIT Press).

Schmukler, Sergio, and Esteban Vesperoni, 2001, "Globalization and Firms' Financing Choices: Evidence from Emerging Economies," IMF Working Paper 01/95 (Washington: International Monetary Fund).

Sharpe, Steven A., 1994, "Financial Market Imperfections, Firm Leverage and the Cyclicality of Employment," *American Economic Review*, Vol. 84 (September), pp. 1060–74.

Skidelsky, Robert, 2001, *John Maynard Keynes: Fighting for Britain, 1937–1946* (London: Macmillan).

Subramanian, Arvind, Enrique Gelbard, Richard Harmsen, Katrin Elborgh-Woytek, and Piroska Nagy, 2000, *Trade and Trade Policies in Eastern and Southern Africa,* IMF Occasional Paper No. 196 (Washington: International Monetary Fund).

Takacs, Wendy E., 1981, "Pressures for Protection: An Empirical Analysis," *Economic Inquiry,* Vol. 19 (October), pp. 687–93.

Taylor, Alan M., 2001, "Potential Pitfalls for the Purchasing-Power-Parity Puzzle? Sampling and Specification Biases in Mean-Reversion Tests of the Law of One Price," *Econometrica,* Vol. 69 (March), pp. 473–98.

Taylor, John B., 2000, "Low Inflation, Pass-Through, and the Pricing Power of Firms," *European Economic Review,* Vol. 44 (June), pp. 1389–1408.

Tyers, Rodney, and Kym Anderson, 1992, *Disarray in World Food Markets: A Quantitative Assessment* (Cambridge and New York: Cambridge University Press).

Ventura, Jaume, 2001, "A Portfolio View of the U.S. Current Account Deficit," *Brookings Papers on Economic Activity: 1,* Brookings Institution, pp. 241–58.

Warnock, Francis E., and Chad Cleaver, 2002, "Financial Centers and the Geography of Capital Flows," International Finance Discussion Paper No. 722 (Washington: Board of Governors of the Federal Reserve System).

White, Eugene N., 1990, "The Stock Market Boom and Crash of 1929 Revisited," *Journal of Economic Perspectives,* Vol. 4, No. 2, pp. 67–83.

World Bank, 2002, *Global Economic Prospects and the Developing Countries* (Washington: World Bank).

CHAPTER III

TRADE AND FINANCIAL INTEGRATION

A crucial and often-overlooked feature of globalization is that trade and financial integration typically go hand in hand (Table 3.1). This is true both over time and across countries, reflecting the inherent linkages between the two—as emphasized by recent theoretical work. The complementarity between trade and finance not only reflects production possibilities—for example, technological improvements in ocean shipping increased both opportunities for world trade and the need to finance these ventures—but also is desirable in order to reap the full benefits of globalization. For example, trade integration is needed to take full advantage of international financial integration, as low trade penetration tends to increase an economy's vulnerability to external financial crises.

An important innovation of this chapter is that it jointly examines the two major pillars of globalization—trade and international financial integration—because of the important links between the two.[1] At a basic level, international trade is accompanied by international financial flows, so greater trade will tend to increase the demand for financial instruments to hedge the riskiness of these flows, and greater financial integration will tend to facilitate international trade. Similarly, "greenfield" foreign direct investment is usually associated with increased capital goods imports during the construction of the project and increased exports after the completion of the project. Also, financial development, which is related to international financial integration, can facilitate specialization and the exploitation of economies of scale, which are

Table 3.1. Rising Global Integration

	Change in the Ratio to GDP from 1981–85 to 1997–2001	
	Trade[1]	External finance[2]
	Percentage points	
Industrial countries	3.9	77.3
Developing countries	15.4	19.9

Sources: IMF staff estimates. See Appendix 3.1 for details.
[1]Sum of exports and imports of goods and services, divided by GDP.
[2]Sum of external assets and liabilities of foreign direct investment and portfolio investment, divided by GDP.

related to trade—for example, by helping firms that rely on external finance to overcome liquidity constraints.

Specifically, this chapter examines three key aspects of the recent increase in trade and international financial integration.

- How does the evolution of trade and international financial integration in the past three decades compare to the experience over the past century and a half? Have the roles of technology and policy differed across historical periods?

- What factors account for the differences in trade integration between developing and industrial countries, and for the unevenness in trade integration across developing countries? How important are trade policies and capital account restrictions?

- What are the consequences of trade integration for the frequency of external financial crises, and of international financial integration for output volatility?

Note: The main authors of this chapter are James Morsink (lead), Thomas Helbling, and Silvia Sgherri. Emily Conover provided able research assistance.

[1]The discussion of globalization has largely treated trade integration and financial integration separately. For example, the May 1997 *World Economic Outlook* addressed trade issues, while the October 2001 *World Economic Outlook* focused on international financial integration. One important exception is the literature on the sequencing of liberalization, which has generally argued that trade liberalization is a precondition for capital account liberalization.

An important theme running through the chapter is that more trade integration is usually associated with more international financial integration, as they respond to many of the same technological and policy factors. The chapter looks at several dimensions of this complementarity. First, openness to trade and capital flows has increased in both industrial and developing countries in recent decades, reflecting the liberalization of trade policies and capital account restrictions. Second, global economic integration in the late nineteenth century was driven mostly by technological developments, while integration since World War II has been driven primarily by the liberalization of policies. Third, an analysis of recent trade patterns suggests that trade remains significantly below expected and that both trade and capital account restrictions play important roles in explaining this finding. Finally, evidence suggests that trade integration tends to reduce the likelihood of external financial crises, while financial integration tends to lower output volatility.

Increasing Integration in Recent Decades

Global economic integration is widely acknowledged to have increased in recent decades, but how should it be measured? How has the increase in trade integration compared with the increase in international financial integration, and are they linked? Are global goods and assets markets now fully integrated, or is there further to go? This section addresses these questions.

Economic integration is not easy to quantify, reflecting difficulties in measuring the nature, extent, intensity, and effectiveness of barriers to transactions involving goods and assets. Notwithstanding these measurement problems, price- and quantity-based indicators of market integration yield similar conclusions (Box 3.1).[2] To capture the experience of as many countries over as long a period as possible, this chapter focuses on quantity-based measures of economic integration (Appendix 3.1). Trade integration is defined as the sum of exports and imports of goods and services, divided by GDP (trade openness). Applying the same principle to measuring asset market integration, financial integration is defined as the sum of external assets and liabilities of foreign direct investment and portfolio investment, divided by GDP (financial openness). Other financial stocks, including bank debt, are excluded from the measure of financial openness because these stocks are much more volatile (see Edison and others, 2002). These measures reflect not only trade policies and capital account restrictions, but also other policies that affect integration (such as labor market policies and institutional frameworks) as well as technological factors (such as transport and other transaction costs) and other fundamentals (like geography, cultural heritage, and language).[3]

Trade openness and financial openness have increased over the past three decades in both industrial and developing countries (upper panels of Figure 3.1). Trade openness rose more than financial openness in developing countries, while financial openness increased much more sharply than trade openness in industrial countries. The rise and then fall in trade openness between the mid-1970s and mid-1980s in both industrial and developing countries reflect mainly the changes in petroleum prices relative to nontraded goods prices over that period. Greater trade openness in developing countries relative to industrial countries mainly reflects the empirical regularity that smaller countries trade more as a share of income than larger countries (average developing country GDP is only one-half of average industrial country GDP), rather than less restrictive policies. Indeed, while trade policies and capital accounts have been liberalized over the past three decades, they remain

---

[2]Neither prices nor quantities provide unambiguous evidence about integration.

[3]An increase in trade openness could even reflect a deterioration in policies, which reduces GDP while leaving trade (say, of a specific mineral product) roughly unchanged.

Figure 3.1.   Complementarity of Trade and Financial Integration
(Percent unless otherwise indicated)

Trade openness and financial openness have largely moved together in industrial and developing countries, reflecting the parallel liberalization of trade and capital controls.

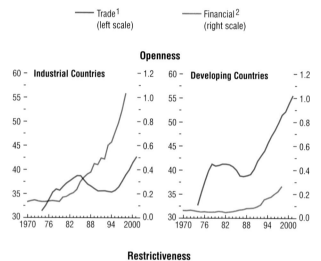

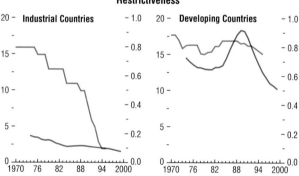

Sources: IMF, *Government Finance Statistics;* IMF, *International Financial Statistics;* IMF, October 2001 *World Economic Outlook;* and IMF staff calculations.
   [1]Trade openness: Sum of exports and imports, divided by GDP (five-year moving average). Trade restrictiveness: Import duties divided by imports (five-year moving average).
   [2]Financial openness: Sum of the stocks of external assets and liabilities of foreign direct investment and portfolio investment, divided by GDP. Financial restrictiveness: Index of capital account restrictions.

considerably more restrictive in developing countries than in industrial countries (lower panels of Figure 3.1). The reversal in trade liberalization in developing countries during the late 1980s primarily reflects increases in import tariffs in two relatively large countries—India and Colombia.

Financial openness in industrial countries increased sharply, especially during the 1980s and 1990s, relative to both the increase in trade openness in industrial countries and the increase in financial openness in developing countries. The rise in financial flows among industrial countries has enabled the United States to become both the world's largest creditor and its largest debtor, while financial flows to developing countries have remained steady at about 4 percent of developing country GDP (Obstfeld and Taylor, 2002). In other words, industrial countries have greatly increased asset swapping among themselves (reflecting hedging and risk sharing) rather than accumulated large one-way positions vis-à-vis developing countries.[4] The contrast between the rise in diversification flows and the steadiness of development flows is consistent with the more rapid capital account liberalization and the greater reduction in investment risk—reflecting the relative stability of the policy and institutional environments—in industrial countries.

The linkage between trade and financial integration is also evident across countries. Trade and financial openness are positively and significantly correlated in both industrial and developing countries (Figure 3.2). This is especially true in developing countries, where the correlation coefficient is 0.66, compared with 0.38 in industrial countries. The linkage is also underscored by the fact that developing countries with higher trade ratios tend to have a lower dependence of investment on domestic saving, suggesting that trade openness improves a country's ability to

---

   [4]This is consistent with Lucas's (1990) observation that flows to capital-poor countries are surprisingly low, given that the marginal product of capital is presumably higher.

Table 3.2. Trade Openness and Saving-Investment Correlations

	Slope Coefficient[1]
Developing countries	0.47
By degree of trade openness:	
Open[2]	0.38
Closed[2]	0.70
By region	
Africa, sub-Saharan	0.49
Asia	
East Asia	0.35
South Asia	0.75
Middle East and North Africa	—
Western Hemisphere	
Caribbean and Central America	0.76
South America	0.78

[1]Slope coefficient from a pooled OLS regression of the saving rate (gross domestic saving divided by GDP) on a constant and the investment rate (gross investment divided by GDP), estimated over 1975–99. "—" indicates that the coefficient is not significantly different from zero at the 5 percent level.

[2]Based on a country's degree of trade openness relative to the median.

borrow from abroad (Table 3.2). In particular, the Western Hemisphere, which has the lowest share of countries that are open to trade (see the section on the consequences of integration for macroeconomic volatility), features the highest correlation between domestic saving and investment rates.

The inverse relationship between trade openness and saving-investment correlations is consistent with the idea that trade frictions can help to explain the segmentation of international financial markets. Obstfeld and Rogoff (2000a) demonstrate theoretically how, even in a world of perfectly integrated international financial markets where global capital should flow to the countries with the highest real rates of return and thus eliminate any dependence of investment on domestic saving, trade frictions can give rise to highly correlated saving and investment rates. The idea is that trade frictions increase the effective real interest rates faced by borrowers, thereby discouraging further saving-investment imbalances. However, the result is also consistent with the idea that, over the long run, trade frictions and international financial frictions tend to go hand in hand, possibly reflecting policy choices.

Notwithstanding the increase in trade integration and financial integration in recent

Figure 3.2. Complementarity of Trade and Financial Integration Across Countries [1]

Trade and financial openness are positively and significantly correlated. The correlation coefficient is 0.38 in industrial countries and 0.66 in developing countries.

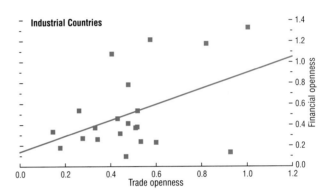

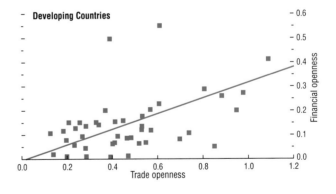

Source: IMF staff estimates.

[1]Trade openness is defined as the sum of imports and exports as a ratio to GDP, averaged over 1975–99. Financial openness is defined as the average gross stock of accumulated FDI and portfolio flows as a ratio to GDP, averaged over 1975–99.

Box 3.1. Using Prices to Measure Goods Market Integration

Goods market integration is traditionally measured using bilateral trade flows, with larger flows implying greater integration. One important reason for the popularity of this approach is that data on bilateral trade flows are readily available, including from the IMF *Direction of Trade Statistics*. The determinants of goods market integration are then typically analyzed using a gravity model, which consistently finds that countries that are closer to each other and more similar (in terms of historical and cultural factors) are more integrated (Box 3.3). One potential limitation of the flows-based approach is that trade flows may not be a good proxy for market integration. For example, across countries with similar production structures, even small trade barriers could make it uneconomic to trade certain goods, leading to low trade flows. To check the robustness of the flows-based approach, it is useful to look at the prices of goods across markets, with smaller price differentials implying greater goods market integration.

In one of the first studies to use price dispersion to measure goods market integration across a large number of countries, Parsley and Wei (2001) analyze data on the prices of 95 tradable goods across 83 cities all over the world from 1990 to 2000.[1] The goods are highly disaggregated and essentially identical, such as frozen chicken, light bulbs, toilet paper, and tonic water, all standardized by weight or volume. The data set was compiled by a single source, the *Economist Intelligence Unit (EIU)*, ensuring comparability of the goods across locations. Using all tradable products, the authors compute the standard deviation of the price differences for every pair of cities for each year, with a smaller standard deviation indicating greater market integra-

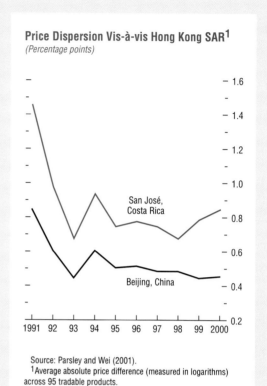

Price Dispersion Vis-à-vis Hong Kong SAR[1]
(Percentage points)

Source: Parsley and Wei (2001).
[1]Average absolute price difference (measured in logarithms) across 95 tradable products.

tion. The standard deviations are then used in an econometric analysis of the factors underlying goods market integration, including transport costs, tariffs, and currency arrangements.

Reassuringly, the price-based approach reaches similar conclusions about the pattern and determinants of goods market integration as the more traditional flows-based approach.[2] Specifically, both approaches suggest the following.

• Goods market integration has increased over the past decade. The figure shows the downward trends in the standard deviation of price differences for two city-pairs: Hong Kong SAR and San Jose, Costa Rica; and Hong Kong SAR and Beijing, China.

Note: The main authors of this box are David Parsley and Shang-Jin Wei.
[1]Engel and Rogers (1996) were the first to use price dispersion to measure goods market integration, but they only considered Canada and the United States. Other recent studies include Engel and Rogers (2001), Rogers (2001), and Hufbauer, Wada, and Warren (2002).

[2]Both approaches take account of the effects of a variety of factors—including tariffs—in a single framework.

- Higher transport costs—proxied by distance—lead to lower market integration. In the flows-based gravity model, bilateral distance always has a negative coefficient, indicating that farther-away countries tend to trade less. In the price-based approach, the distance variable consistently has a positive coefficient, indicating that the price dispersion for identical products (i.e., lack of market integration) increases with distance. For example, the figure shows that price differences are lower between Beijing, China, and Hong Kong SAR than between Hong Kong SAR and San Jose, Costa Rica.

- Some regional preferential trading arrangements have a positive and significant impact on goods market integration. One way to characterize the magnitude of these effects is by their equivalent tariff reductions, i.e., how much tariffs would have to decline to achieve the same effect. The paper finds that the North American Free Trade Area and the European Union both have equivalent tariff reductions of about 5 percent. This effect is large compared with the average external tariff rate of industrial countries of about 4 percent.

- Institutionalized currency arrangements (a union or a board) generally increase goods market integration among their member countries.[3] However, the authors find that the effects of institutionalized currency arrangements are not all the same. For example, the estimate of the equivalent tariff reduction associated with the Communauté Financière Africaine (CFA) is small and not significantly different from zero, while the estimate for the euro area is about 2 percent and significant.

- Finally, border effects are significant, even after taking account of common currencies and free trade areas. The authors find that city-pairs within the United States are the most highly integrated. Relative to the U.S. benchmark, the degree of goods market integration across other city-pairs, including those within common currency and free trade areas, still has further to go.

The similarities in the results from the different approaches imply that the two are complementary, each providing insights into the measurement and determinants of goods market integration.

[3]Reducing nominal exchange rate variability reduces price dispersion and improves goods market integration, but by a smaller order of magnitude than a currency union or currency board.

decades, international markets remain far more segmented than domestic markets, even among advanced economies (Obstfeld and Rogoff, 2000b). Intracountry trade is significantly greater than international trade, after taking account of distance, economic size, and other factors (McCallum, 1995; Wei, 1996; and Anderson and van Wincoop, 2001), and manufactured goods prices adjust only slowly to exchange rate changes—typically, about 50 percent after one year. Evidence regarding the continued segmentation of international financial markets is equally strong, though seg-mentation has decreased in recent years. For example, the share of foreign stocks in U.S. residents' holdings of equities rose from about 4 percent in 1987 to about 11 percent in 2001, but this is still far less than the roughly 50 percent share of non-U.S. stocks in global equity market capitalization. Similarly, global saving-investment correlations (high correlation is suggestive of segmentation) have fallen from about 0.9 to about 0.6 over the past two decades, but remain higher than implied by perfectly integrated international financial markets.[5]

[5]Calvo and Végh (1999) find little evidence that developing countries engage in consumption smoothing through international borrowing and lending.

Comparison with Earlier Historical Periods

Historical evidence on trade integration and financial integration suggests that there are important similarities, but also differences, between the increase in global integration in recent decades and the experience of earlier periods. Trade integration and financial integration have generally moved together over the past one-and-a-half centuries (Figure 3.3). Both increased from the mid-nineteenth century until the outbreak of World War I, then generally declined until the end of World War II, and rose again during the postwar period. What were the primary factors behind these developments and what were the main linkages between trade and international finance?

The increase in trade and financial integration from 1870 to 1914 mostly reflected technological improvements in transport (like railroads, steamships, and the opening of the Suez and Panama Canals) and communications (such as the telegraph, radio telephone, and transatlantic cable). The technological breakthroughs that spurred trade, like steamships and railroads, also created new investment opportunities that required the mobilization of large sums and long waiting periods before investment returns were realized, which stimulated financial development, including international financial integration (Neal, 1990).[6] The gold standard helped foster trade and financial flows.[7] Private international financial transactions remained mostly

Figure 3.3. Global Integration
(Percent)

Trade and financial integration have generally moved together over the past one-and-a-half centuries.

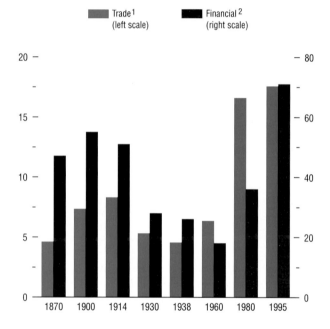

Sources: Maddison (1995); Obstfeld and Taylor (2002); and IMF staff estimates.
[1]Ratio of the sum of exports and imports to GDP.
[2]Ratio of foreign assets to GDP.

---

[6]Rousseau and Sylla (2001) illustrate how trade and financial integration reinforced each other with examples from the early development of what are now advanced economies. Their econometric analysis finds that, for a broad group of industrial countries between 1850 and 1929, financial development had a positive, significant effect on trade integration, and that trade integration had a positive, significant effect on the decline in long-term interest rates.

[7]The gold standard encouraged stabilizing short-term financial flows among the core countries as well as long-term flows from the core to the periphery, as adherence to gold served as evidence that countries were following responsible macroeconomic and financial policies (Eichengreen, 1996; and Bordo and Rockoff, 1996)

free of government control, consistent with the general acceptance of the gold standard and the willingness to subordinate monetary policy to the fixed exchange rate.[8] Trade policy, if anything, tended to restrain integration, as tariffs increased in many countries (Bairoch, 1993).

Between 1914 and 1945, trade integration and financial integration fell sharply, as government controls on both trade and financial flows expanded during the two World Wars and the interwar period. Countries at war had to shift production both toward military goods and away from exports, necessitating controls on trade, and pay for the resulting trade deficit at minimum cost, requiring financial controls to economize on scarce foreign exchange. In the first part of the interwar period, governments increasingly used trade barriers to try to inhibit adjustment to the changing pattern of global production. During the Great Depression, many governments tried to stimulate their economies by imposing quantitative restrictions and other trade barriers, to increase net exports, and reintroducing financial controls, to simultaneously maintain their gold parities and pursue independent monetary policies.[9]

Since World War II, trade and financial integration have increased, reflecting mainly the liberalization of trade and financial flows. Trade barriers have generally been reduced first, reflecting the Bretton Woods consensus that trade was essential to economic prosperity but financial controls were needed to ensure monetary autonomy while maintaining fixed exchange rates.[10] Industrial countries started reducing trade barriers in the 1960s and 1970s, followed by developing countries in the 1980s and 1990s (Krugman, 1995; and Sachs and Warner, 1995).

Rising trade integration permitted the circumvention of financial controls through leads and lags, which in turn allowed pressures from global imbalances to affect—and eventually bring about the downfall of—the system of fixed exchange rates. Following the breakdown of the Bretton Woods system, industrial countries—starting with the major currencies—were able to relax financial controls and retain their monetary autonomy. Developing countries generally liberalized financial controls more gradually during the 1980s and 1990s.[11] By contrast, transport costs have not declined much in the postwar period (Box 3.2).

An important insight from this historical overview is that global economic integration in recent decades has been driven primarily by the liberalization of trade policies and of capital controls, in contrast to the previous episode of globalization in the late nineteenth century, when integration was driven mostly by technological developments. The implication is that policymakers today should pay close attention to the interaction between the different aspects of globalization.

Why Does Trade Integration Differ Across Regions?

While developing countries have generally become more integrated into the world trading system over the past two decades, the degree of integration remains uneven across regions. In particular, artificial barriers to trade—including protectionist trade policies—are preventing greater integration. This section will first develop a measure of expected trade and compare actual trade to expected trade across devel-

---

[8]Central banks occasionally used moral suasion over banks, and intervened to change gold export and import points (Obstfeld and Taylor, 2002). If a central bank could no longer defend the exchange rate through such noncoercive methods, the exchange rate was generally set free to float with no control employed, as sometimes occurred in Latin America.

[9]This was necessary because of the familiar inconsistency between free financial flows, a fixed exchange rate, and monetary policy geared toward domestic objectives—the "impossible trinity" or "trilemma" (Obstfeld and Taylor, 2002).

[10]The sequencing of liberalization is consistent with Lane and Milesi-Ferretti's (2000) finding that financial openness in the 1990s was strongly influenced by trade openness, and Rousseau and Sylla's (2001) result that financial development did not have a significant effect on trade integration in the postwar period, in contrast to the earlier period.

[11]Some countries in Latin America attempted to liberalize during the late 1970s, but these attempts were not adequately supported by fiscal discipline and domestic financial system reform.

Box 3.2. Transport Costs

Transport costs play a central role in explaining trade patterns. Transport costs are still large when compared with tariffs and represent the main impediment to trade in a majority of countries (World Bank, 2002). Transport costs, usually proxied by distance and other geographical variables, are highly significant in the gravity model (Box 3.3) and are important in explaining international vertical specialization—the slicing up of production processes into distinct steps, allowing specialization across countries (Box 3.4). They also help explain the substitution between trade and foreign direct investment (Loungani, Mody, and Razin, 2002).

Transport costs have declined considerably in the past fifty years, but not by as much as during the late nineteenth century, which was also a period of rapid global economic integration. Time series measures of transport costs are difficult to obtain, because no single data set covers all transport costs in a systematic way.[1] The costs of shipping a bushel of wheat from New York to Liverpool declined by about two-thirds between 1854 and 1913, and from New York to Chicago by about three-fourths between 1870 and 1913 (Harley, 1980). The figure shows that sea freight costs have not changed much since 1960, while airfreight costs have been steady since 1980. These trends are broadly consistent with more detailed estimates in Hummels (1999).[2] They are also consistent with Baier and Bergstrand's (2001) finding that the effect of declining transport costs on the growth of industrial country

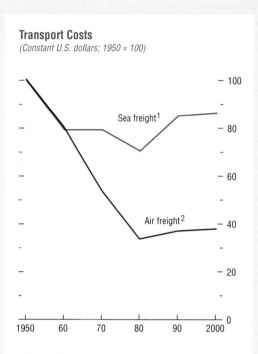

Transport Costs
(Constant U.S. dollars; 1950 = 100)

Sources: *Statistical Abstract of the United States; Review of Maritime Transport* (UNCTAD); and IMF staff calculations.
[1]Average ocean freight and port charges per ton of import and export cargo.
[2]Average air transport revenue per passenger mile.

Note: The main author of this box is Antonio Spilimbergo.
[1]Estimating transport costs is difficult because transport services are not homogenous and available measures are unreliable. A commonly used method is to calculate transport costs as the difference between the value of f.o.b. exports and the value of c.i.f. imports for pairs of countries. However, the original data sources are unreliable and the composition of trade changes over time, making any cross-time comparison problematic (Hummels, 1999).
[2]However, Hummels (1999) reports increasing sea shipping charges between 1970 and 1985.

trade between the late 1950s and the late 1980s was only about one-third of the impact of tariff reductions.

The less rapid decline in transport costs in the recent era reflects three main factors.

• *Innovations in transport technology.* The late nineteenth century saw more dramatic improvements in transport technology, including the introduction of steamships and railroads, as well as the construction of the Suez and Panama Canals. The most important technological breakthroughs of the past fifty years have been the introduction of containers for sea transport in the late 1960s and the introduction of jet engines and large body aircraft for air transport.[3]

[3]The share of U.S. import value transported by air rose from 6.2 percent in 1965 to 24.7 percent in 1998.

- *Competitive environment.* In the late nineteenth century, the disappearance of trading monopolies sharply lowered shipping costs. By contrast, the introduction of containers in the late 1960s raised fixed costs, which increased market concentration, preventing the efficiency gains from being transmitted to users of transport services (Gilman, 1984).[4] Partly in response to this concentration, many developing countries adopted policies to ensure that national flag fleets were granted a large share of shipping, which further stifled competition and increased transport costs, especially for developing countries.

- *Measurement issues.* Comparing the recent decline in transport costs with that in an earlier historical period is complicated by the fact that transport services are not homogenous. Transport services differ along several dimensions, such as speed, reliability, and frequency, and prices are not adjusted for changes in quality. The past fifty years have seen major improvements in quality: Hummels (2000) finds that the decline in shipping time between 1950 and 1998 due to the introduction of air shipping and faster ocean vessels was equivalent to reducing tariffs on manufactured goods from 32 percent to 9 percent. However, because prices are not adjusted for quality, they do not capture this significant improvement in speed.

Notwithstanding the measurement issues, the decline in transport costs—driven by improvements in technology—was likely a more important factor behind the increase in economic integration in the late nineteenth century than globalization in the late twentieth century.

[4]However, the practice of registering ships under flags of convenience reduced shipboard operating costs by 12–27 percent (Hummels, 1999).

For developing countries, an important issue is that the quality of transport infrastructure is a significant determinant of transport costs. Freight costs as a share of import values vary considerably across countries, ranging from about 4.5 percent in industrial countries to 12 percent in Africa (UNCTAD, 2001). These variations in transport costs are mostly due to differences in geography and transport infrastructure. Limão and Venables (2001) find that transport costs in landlocked countries are about 50 percent higher than average. Clark, Dollar, and Micco (2002) find that improving the efficiency of a seaport from below-average to above-average decreases transport costs by more than 12 percent. Low-quality transport infrastructure is especially relevant for poorer countries and substantially limits their trading potential.

Looking forward, the terrorist attacks of September 11, 2001, will likely increase transport costs in the long run. The fact that transport costs remained generally stable in the months after September 11, during a recession and a period of relatively low oil prices (when transport costs usually fall), suggests that underlying transport costs may have increased. Higher transport costs could result, for example, from the need for customs authorities to examine shipping containers on a systematic basis. Costs of security measures could be on the order of 1–3 percent of the value of trade (OECD, 2002). Checking even a small share of containers will imply an explicit cost for governments and a much higher implicit cost for importers and exporters in terms of delays. Hummels (2000) estimates that a one-day delay is equivalent to a loss of 0.8 percent of the value of a manufactured good. In addition, greater uncertainty about delays will force firms to hold higher levels of inventories.

oping regions. The idea is that the difference between actual and expected trade represents a comprehensive measure of artificial barriers to trade, including all aspects of a country's policy and institutional environment, not just trade policies.

The section will then assess the contribution of explicit measures of trade and balance of payments restrictiveness to the shortfall in trade in developing countries. While such policies are generally thought to have important effects on trade, this analysis is one of the first to explicitly include policy-related variables in the gravity model.[12] Illustrative calculations of the trade impact of reducing policy restrictiveness will be presented. Finally, the section will put the role of policies into perspective by comparing it to other key factors—like economic size, level of economic development, and geography—in determining trading patterns in developing countries. The analysis will focus on assessing the role of policies in explaining why developing countries have lower trade volumes than industrial countries, and why east Asia trades more than other developing regions.

Which Regions Undertrade?

To measure the shortfall in actual trade, a benchmark for expected trade is needed. The gravity model of international trade without explicit policy variables is used to derive measures of the expected volume of trade between trading partners (Box 3.3). Just like the force of gravity between two objects is proportional to their mass and inversely proportional to the distance between them, the gravity model of trade postulates that the magnitude of bilateral trade flows between two countries is positively related to the joint size of the two trading economies and negatively related to the distance between them. Over time, the gravity model of trade has been elaborated to incorporate a wide variety of other factors.

A country is said to "undertrade" if its actual trade across trading partners is, on average, sub-

stantially below the level predicted by the gravity model without explicit policy variables. Similarly, a country is said to "overtrade" if its actual bilateral trade is substantially above the average level predicted by the gravity model. As the gravity model accounts for the "natural" causes of trade, under- and overtrading must largely represent above- or below-average "artificial" impediments (Rose, 2002).[13] This approach has the benefit of capturing the overall impact of a country's policy and institutional environment, including a wide variety of artificial impediments and not just trade policies. However, this approach depends on getting the natural causes exactly right—that is, the results are sensitive to the specification of the gravity model.

The analysis of undertrading is based on a conventional gravity model estimated over the period 1995–99, along the lines of Rose (2002). Bilateral merchandise trade data covering 131 industrial and developing countries are taken from the IMF's *Direction of Trade Statistics*. The country coverage reflects the availability of data for the explanatory variables in the gravity model.[14] The data are averaged over 1995–99 to abstract from cyclical developments. The estimated coefficients of the gravity model are similar in sign, magnitude, and statistical significance to the results in the recent literature.

The results suggest that significant undertrading occurs in certain developing country regions, though of course individual countries sometimes diverge from regional averages. Table 3.3 shows the average differences between actual and predicted trade by region, expressed in logarithms following convention.[15] The same rank ordering of regional undertrading is found by Rose (2002). The degree of undertrading is

---

[12]The trade effects of regional trade agreements have received a lot of scrutiny by, among others, Bayoumi and Eichengreen (1997), Frankel (1997), and Soloaga and Winters (2001).

[13]Leamer (1988), Lee (1993), and Spilimbergo, Londoño, and Székely (1999) also use differences between actual and predicted trade as measures of policy-related distortions.

[14]Much of the dataset was kindly provided by Andrew Rose and is available via the Internet at: http://faculty.haas.berkeley.edu/arose/RecRes.htm.

[15]The degree of over- or undertrading in percentage terms implied by an amount x is given by $100\,(e^x - 1)$. For small magnitudes, the numbers can be interpreted as percentage deviations. For large magnitudes, the approximate correspondence between $100x$ and $100(e^x - 1)$ disappears because the term e^x becomes increasingly nonlinear.

Table 3.3. Undertrading in Developing Countries, 1995–99[1]
(Average difference between actual and predicted trade, in logarithms)

Region	All trade[2]	Intraregional trade	Extraregional trade[3] Total	Developing countries[4]	Industrial countries[4]
Africa, sub-Saharan	0.05	0.50	−0.01	−0.04	0.01
Asia					
East Asia	0.45	0.96	0.42	0.40	0.45
South Asia	−0.44	−0.76	−0.43	−0.46	−0.35
Middle East and North Africa	−0.49	−0.74	−0.48	−0.60	−0.24
Western Hemisphere					
Caribbean and Central America	−0.12	0.82	−0.24	−0.41	−0.09
South America	−0.11	0.44	−0.15	−0.34	0.18

Source: IMF staff estimates.
[1]Based on a gravity equation estimated with data averaged over 1995–99.
[2]All bilateral trade flows involving at least one country from this region.
[3]Bilateral trade with other developing and industrial countries.
[4]Extraregional trade flows involving other developing countries or industrial countries.

large in the Middle East and North Africa, in line with the results of Al-Atrash and Yousef (2000), and south Asia, though this assessment does not take account of trade in services, which have grown especially rapidly in that region. The degree of undertrading is smaller in the Western Hemisphere. Countries in sub-Saharan Africa trade slightly more than predicted, consistent with Foroutan and Pritchett (1993), Rodrik (1998), and Coe and Hoffmaister (1999). Countries in east Asia are strong traders relative to other developing countries.

Undertrading is generally less pervasive in intraregional than in extraregional trade. This result is not obvious, because geographical factors that tend to boost intraregional trade are already taken into account in the gravity model. One possible reason for this finding is regional preferential trading arrangements, such as MERCOSUR. If dummy variables representing regional preferential trade agreements are included in the gravity model, the extent of intraregional overtrading in the Western Hemisphere is noticeably reduced, though

intraregional overtrading in other regions is not affected much. Also, extraregional over- or undertrading remains roughly unchanged, suggesting that regional trade agreements do not divert trade in developing country regions.[16]

Over the past twenty years, the degrees of regional undertrading have changed, reflecting developments in artificial barriers to trade (Table 3.4). Two regions became relatively weaker traders: sub-Saharan Africa and—especially—the Middle East and North Africa, which went from slight overtrading to large undertrading. The weakening of sub-Saharan Africa's trade performance (which is only partly related to a secular decline in non-oil commodity prices) is consistent with the concerns noted in the May 2001 *World Economic Outlook* about the marginalization of this region within the world trading system. The other regions—east Asia, south Asia, South America, and especially the Caribbean and central America—became relatively stronger traders. Changes in regional preferential trade agreements cannot account for changes in intraregional overtrading during the

[16]Soloaga and Winters (2001) also find that intraregional trade effects are only significant in Latin American countries (they do not include Caribbean countries) and that evidence of trade diversion due to regional trade agreements is only conclusive in the case of the European Union and the European Free Trade Area (EFTA). Egoumé-Bossogo and Mendis (2002) also find positive intra-Caribbean trade effects.

Table 3.4. Changes in Undertrading Over Time[1]
(Average difference between actual and predicted trade, in logarithms)

Region	Average Difference Between Actual and Predicted[2]				
	1980–84	1985–89	1990–94	1995–99	Change from 1980–84 to 1995–99
Africa, sub-Saharan	0.29	0.32	0.25	0.05	−0.24
Asia					
East Asia	0.27	0.19	0.28	0.45	0.18
South Asia	−0.68	−0.54	−0.65	−0.44	0.24
Middle East and North Africa	0.08	−0.19	−0.29	−0.49	−0.57
Western Hemisphere					
Caribbean and Central America	−0.49	−0.40	−0.30	−0.12	0.37
South America	−0.30	−0.26	−0.17	−0.11	0.19

Source: IMF staff estimates.
[1]Based on a gravity equation estimated with data averaged over the period indicated in the table.
[2]All bilateral trade flows involving at least one country from this region.

1980s and 1990s, except in South America where MERCOSUR led to an increase in intrabloc trade during the 1990s.[17]

In summary, the analysis suggests that undertrading remains a serious problem in many developing countries, especially in the Middle East and North Africa, and south Asia. Undertrading reflects above-average artificial barriers to trade in all aspects of a country's policy and institutional environment.

What Is the Impact of Trade and Balance of Payments Restrictions?

While undertrading is a measure of overall artificial barriers to trade, it is not directly connected to any specific policies. As a result, this measure cannot be used to assess the impact of trade or balance of payments liberalization on trade flows. To answer this type of question, the gravity model was reestimated over 1995–99 with two measures of policy restrictiveness as explanatory variables: (1) the IMF's index of overall trade regime restrictiveness, which is based on average import tariffs and nontariff barriers (IMF, 1998); and (2) an index of balance of payments restrictiveness, which ranks the overall restrictiveness of current and capital account restrictions (Mody and Murshid, 2002).[18]

Both indices suggest that trade and balance of payments policies are generally less restrictive in sub-Saharan Africa, east Asia, and the Western Hemisphere than in other developing country regions, though there are important measurement problems (Table 3.5).[19] In other words, the marginalization of sub-Saharan Africa within the global trading system noted above is not primarily due to measured trade and balance of payments restrictiveness, but rather to other aspects of the region's policy and institutional environment. Similarly, measured trade and balance of payments restrictions are relatively small

[17]Soloaga and Winters (2001) report similar results. From a longer-term historical perspective, the effects of regional preferential trading agreements on intra- and extraregional trade depend on the particular agreement (see, for example, Frankel, 1997).

[18]To characterize bilateral restrictiveness, the indices for each country in a bilateral relationship were summed. The main results are robust to multiplicative or maximum operator-based specifications.

[19]Unweighted average tariff rates are problematic because similar rates can have different economic effects if applied to different commodities. Nontariff barriers are notoriously difficult to measure and their effects depend on other distortions. Moreover, many measures are based on information about whether some regulations are in place rather than on information about their actual enforcement. Also, the difficulties are amplified in the case of bilateral trade flows because the effects of the same policy intervention in one country can differ across trade relations with partner countries. For surveys of measures of trade policy and their shortcomings, see Rodriguez and Rodrik (2000) and Berg and Krueger (2002).

Table 3.5. Bilateral Policy Restrictiveness in Developing Countries, 1997–99[1]

(Deviations from unweighted average of all countries)

Region	Trade Policy Restrictiveness[2] All trade	Trade Policy Restrictiveness[2] Intraregional trade	Balance of Payments Restrictiveness[3] All trade	Balance of Payments Restrictiveness[3] Intraregional trade
Africa, sub-Saharan	0.21	1.52	0.51	2.00
Asia				
East Asia	−0.32	0.37	0.51	1.70
South Asia	2.95	5.07	1.62	3.18
Middle East and North Africa	3.19	6.76	0.70	1.59
Western Hemisphere				
Caribbean and Central America	−0.46	−0.09	−0.66	−0.29
South America	−0.93	−1.48	−0.04	−0.13
Memorandum:				
North-North trade	—	−1.78	—	−2.65
North-South trade	−0.53	—	−0.82	—
South-South trade	—	0.87	—	1.33

Source: IMF staff calculations.

[1]Indices are averaged over 1997–99. Scale varies by index so that only rank comparisons across indices are possible. The indices are averages over bilateral trade relations indices and were constructed under the assumption of additivity.

[2]Index ranging from 2 to 20, based on average tariff rates and nontariff barriers. See IMF (1998).

[3]Index ranging from zero to eight, based on a country's current and financial account openness, the existence of multiple exchange rates for financial account transactions, and the stringency of surrender and repatriation requirements. See Mody and Murshid (2002).

Table 3.6. Gravity Model Estimates[1]

	Without Policy Variables	With Policy Variables
Product of trading partners' GDP[2]	0.91**	0.94**
Product of trading partners' per capita income[2]	0.27**	0.19**
Distance[2]	−1.15**	−1.17**
Number of landlocked countries[3]	−0.34**	−0.41**
Adjacent land border[4]	0.75**	0.70**
Number of islands[3]	0.03	0.06
Product of trading partners' land surface areas[2]	−0.09**	−0.09**
Common language[4]	0.46**	0.45**
Common colonizer[4]	0.69**	0.71**
Past or present colonial relation[4]	1.06**	1.04**
Strict currency union between trading partners[4]	1.23**	1.32**
Trade policy restrictiveness[5]		−0.05**
Balance of payments restrictiveness[6]		−0.05**
Adjusted R^2	0.799	0.803
Number of observations	4,815	4,815

Source: IMF staff calculations.

[1]Estimated with data averaged over 1995–99. Dependent variable: log of bilateral trade volume. One asterisk indicates significance at the 5 percent level; two asterisks, at the 1 percent level. Significance levels based on standard errors that are robust to heteroscedasticity.

[2]Variable in logs.

[3]In bilateral trade relationship.

[4]Dummy variable.

[5]Index ranging from 2 to 20, based on average tariff rates and nontariff barriers. See IMF (1998).

[6]Index ranging from zero to eight, based on a country's current and financial account openness, the existence of multiple exchange rates for financial account transactions, and the stringency of surrender and repatriation requirements. See Mody and Murshid (2002).

in the Western Hemisphere, although the region's undertrading suggests that overall artificial barriers to trade are higher than average.

The two policy variables have significantly negative effects on bilateral trade flows (Table 3.6). The magnitudes of the coefficients measure the effects on trade of changes in policy restrictiveness: one-point increases in both trade and balance of payments restrictiveness reduce trade volumes by about 5 percent. The coefficients on the other variables are generally similar to those obtained for the gravity model without explicit policy measures, and remain comparable in sign, magnitude, and statistical significance to the results reported in the recent literature. Interestingly, the coefficient on the product of per capita incomes becomes somewhat smaller once the policy variables are included, indicating that policy restrictiveness is inversely related to the level of economic development. In other words,

trade and balance of payments policies tend to be more restrictive in poorer countries, which presumably reflects in part the adverse effect of policy restrictiveness on growth.

A striking result is that balance of payments restrictiveness has a significant and large adverse effect on trade, consistent with the idea that *financial* frictions can help to explain the segmentation of global *goods* markets. This idea parallels the view that *trade* frictions are a factor behind the segmentation of international *financial* markets (Obstfeld and Rogoff, 2000a). There is a growing literature on the role of international financial frictions in dampening trade. Tamirisa (1999) finds that exchange and financial controls represent a significant barrier to

Box 3.3. Gravity Model of International Trade

The gravity model has been widely used in empirical trade research during the past four decades. Borrowing from Newtonian physics, the model consists of a single equation postulating that the amount of trade between two countries depends positively on economic mass and negatively on resistance. The key mass variables are the combined size of the trading economies and their combined level of economic development. Including both income and income per capita implies that population is included, which takes account of the empirical regularity that larger countries trade less as a share of income.

Combined size, which is usually measured as the product of gross domestic products, matters for the simple reason that international trade— like virtually any other economic activity— generally increases with the overall size of the economy. The combined level of development, which is usually measured as the product of incomes per capita, is included because bilateral trade tends to rise more than proportionally as economies get richer (see Frankel, 1997; and Boisso and Ferrantino, 1997). In particular, the demand for variety—goods that differ slightly in design, materials, or technology—increases with income, which leads to two-way or intra-industry trade in similar goods because the production of differentiated goods remains specialized, reflecting increasing returns to scale (see Helpman and Krugman, 1985).[1]

The main resistance factor in the gravity model is transport costs, which are usually proxied by geographical variables, for reasons discussed in Box 3.2. The primary geographical variable is the absolute distance between the two trading countries, with closely located country-pairs generally trading more than country-pairs that are far apart.[2] Recently, some theoretical

models of trade have suggested that relative distance (i.e., the distance between two trading partners relative to the distances between them and other trading partners) matters more than absolute distance (e.g., Anderson and van Wincoop, 2001).[3] In line with this insight, some recent empirical studies have included relative distance instead of absolute distance, or added a measure of remoteness like the average distance of each trading partner (see Frankel and Wei; 1998, Soloaga and Winters, 2001; and Mélitz, 2001). The empirical results presented in the main text of this chapter are robust to including remoteness or replacing absolute distance with relative distance.

Other proxies for transport costs are the number of landlocked countries in a bilateral trade relationship, the surface areas in both economies (both associated with higher transport costs), and the existence of adjacent land borders (which lowers transport costs). In particular, being landlocked is associated with large negative trade effects.[4] Historical and cultural similarities, including colonial links and common language, tend to reduce cross-border search and communications costs because of familiarity with customs, institutions, and legal systems, thus facilitating trade.

Besides the "natural" frictions, there are artificial—especially policy-related—frictions. Most obvious among these are trade policies, including tariffs, quotas, and regional preferential trade agreements. Other important policy barriers are exchange and capital controls, which affect trade through a variety of channels, including the

---

Note: The main author of this box is Thomas Helbling.

[1]There is still a vigorous debate about the relative roles of intra-industry trade and trade based on factor endowments (see, for example, Davis and Weinstein, 2001).

[2]The adverse effect of distance on trade flows is consistent with the idea that countries in close proximity

are natural trading partners (see Krugman, 1991). However, the case for the natural trading partner hypothesis may be weaker when other considerations are taken into account (Panagariya, 2000).

[3]This is related to the more general issue about how to properly account for third-country effects in the gravity model.

[4]Limão and Venables (2001) find that the median landlocked economy in their sample faces 42 percent higher transport costs than the median coastal economy, and external trade of the former is only about one-third of the latter.

domestic price of imports and transaction costs. While such policies are generally thought to have important effects on trade, the analysis-presented in this chapter is one of the first to explicitly include policy-related variables in the gravity model (see also Tamirisa, 1999; and Estevadeordal, Frantz, and Taylor, 2002).[5] The results suggest that trade and balance of payments restrictiveness have negative, large, and significant effects on bilateral trade flows.

The gravity model has proven to be highly successful in explaining bilateral trade flows and has provided "some of the clearest and most robust empirical findings in economics" (Leamer and Levinsohn, 1995). Its popularity has been enhanced by research showing that the gravity equation can be derived from some simple theoretical models of trade (see Anderson, 1979, and Deardorff, 1998). Nevertheless, as with any

econometric analysis, the gravity model has some limitations. Most important, the gravity model has the standard econometric problems of endogeneity and multicollinearity, although their effects on the magnitudes and significance of the estimated coefficients tend to be small, as demonstrated by Frankel (1997) or Rose (2000, 2002). In addition, the gravity model is better suited to cross-sectional applications, like the one in this chapter, because it omits relative prices, factor endowments, and the structure of production, which are important in explaining changes in trade patterns over time.[6]

---

[5]An important general exception concerns the trade effects of regional trade agreements. See Bayoumi and Eichengreen (1997), Frankel (1997), and Soloaga and Winters (2001).

[6]Not only do some coefficients change over time, but the direction of change is sometimes difficult to interpret. For example, many studies have found that the adverse effect of distance on bilateral trade flows has either remained roughly constant or increased over time, in contrast to the frequently voiced optimism about the "death of distance" in a globalized world (Leamer and Levinsohn, 1995; Frankel, 1997; and Boisso and Ferrantino, 1997). Recently, Coe and others (forthcoming) have found some evidence of the death of distance.

---

trade. Rose (2000) shows that belonging to a currency union more than triples a country's trade with the other members of the union, with no evidence of trade diversion.[20] Rose and Spiegel (2002) find that sovereign defaults also tend to have adverse trade effects.[21]

Multilateral liberalization of trade and balance of payments restrictiveness would have large effects on trade. Table 3.7 presents illustrative calculations of the impact of policy liberalizations in industrial countries, developing coun-

tries, and all countries, respectively.[22] If industrial countries reduced their trade restrictiveness to the lowest possible level, trade between industrial and developing countries (North-South trade) would increase by about 14 percent. The trade effects of balance of payments liberalization are generally smaller, given the already low levels of restrictiveness in industrial countries. The full liberalization of both trade and balance of payments policies in all countries would increase trade between industrial countries

---

[20]In subsequent research based on pooled time series data, Rose found somewhat smaller but still large effects of currency unions on trade (see Glick and Rose, 2001; and Rose, 2002).

[21]Their results indicate that Paris Club debt renegotiations (a proxy for sovereign default) are associated with a decline in bilateral trade between a debtor and its creditors of about 8 percent a year for a period of about 15 years, after controlling for a host of factors that influence bilateral trade flows.

[22]These calculations capture only first-round effects; second-round income and price effects resulting from trade liberalization are likely to be large. However, the effects are overstated as the positive effects of regional preferential trading arrangements would likely disappear. Also, the results are sensitive to the assumption of additivity in the construction of bilateral restrictiveness.

Table 3.7. Trade Effects of Policy Liberalization[1]
(Reduction in points; trade effects in percent of preliberalization potential trade)

Region	Trade Policy[2]		Balance of Payments Policy[3]		Both Policies
	Liberalization[4]	Trade effect	Liberalization[4]	Trade effect	Trade effects
	Liberalization in industrial countries only				
North-North trade	−5.3	30.5	−1.5	7.3	40.0
North-South trade	−2.7	14.4	−0.6	3.1	17.9
	Liberalization in developing countries only				
North-South trade	−3.9	21.4	−2.7	13.7	38.0
South-South trade	−8.0	49.0	−5.4	29.9	93.6
	Liberalization in all countries				
North-North trade	−5.3	30.5	−1.5	7.3	40.0
North-South trade	−6.5	38.9	−3.3	17.2	62.8
South-South trade	−8.0	49.0	−5.4	29.9	93.6

Source: IMF staff calculations based on gravity model estimates shown in Table 3.5.
[1]Effects of reduction in indicators to lowest possible rank scale. Trade effects are given by the coefficient and the reduction in the indicator. The indicators are averages over bilateral trade relations for the period 1997–99 and were constructed under the assumption of additivity.
[2]Indicator variable ranging from 2 to 20, based on restrictiveness indicated by the average tariff rate and the coverage of nontariff barriers.
[3]Dummy variable ranging from 0 to 8 indicating the degree of openness of a country's current account, capital account, the existence of multiple exchange rates for capital account transactions, and the stringency of surrender and repatriation requirements.
[4]Reduction in average rank index value implied by liberalization.

(North-North trade) by about 40 percent, North-South trade by about 63 percent, and trade between developing countries (South-South trade) by about 94 percent.

How Important Is Policy Relative to Other Factors in Explaining Trade?

To put the role of policies into perspective, this subsection compares the effects of trade and balance of payments restrictiveness on trade with those of other key factors, including economic size, level of economic development, and geography. For this comparison, North-North trade is taken as a benchmark, because industrial countries generally have less restrictive policies, especially for manufactured goods, which account for the bulk of trade between industrial countries.[23] This analysis is based on the gravity model that includes policy variables.

The most important reason why the absolute level of trade between industrial countries is much larger than trade between developing countries is that average industrial country GDP

is twice as large as average developing country GDP. Using the coefficients from the gravity model, differences in economic size account for 80 percent of the difference in average bilateral trade flows. As economic size has such an overwhelming impact on bilateral trade flows, the results below are adjusted for economic size. Even after this adjustment, bilateral trade flows involving developing countries are smaller than those among industrial countries.

Overall, the results suggest that trade and balance of payments restrictiveness play a significant role in explaining why developing countries trade less per unit of GDP than industrial countries, though economic development and geography are even more important (Figure 3.4). Lower income per capita is the single most important reason why adjusted South-South trade is smaller than adjusted North-North trade, and accounts for about one-fifth of the difference between adjusted North-South trade and adjusted North-North trade. Differences in income per capita matter a lot for trade because richer consumers tend to have a higher demand

---

[23]However, industrial countries have generally higher trade barriers vis-à-vis developing countries, even for manufactured goods (see IMF, 2001).

for product variety, while the production of differentiated goods remains specialized, leading to intra-industry trade. Geography, especially distance, is the single most important impediment to North-South trade, and accounts for two-fifths of the shortfall in South-South trade.

More restrictive trade and balance of payments policies account for about 10–20 percent of the shortfall in adjusted bilateral trade flows. Restrictive policies hurt South-South trade more than North-South trade because developing countries have on average greater restrictions than industrial countries, so their adverse effect is doubled as both trading partners have higher restrictions. Other determinants, like linguistic or historical factors, are much less important because the differences between industrial and developing countries are on average small. Finally, unexplained differences account for only a small part of the shortfall in trading involving developing countries.

The gravity model is less successful at explaining why developing countries in east Asia trade more per unit of GDP than countries in other regions (Figure 3.5). In contrast to the results discussed above, unexplained differences account for much of the excess in east Asia's trade relative to other developing country regions. In terms of the explained differences, east Asian countries have on average higher income per capita and less restrictive policies (both of which tend to increase trade) but are relatively distant from their trading partners (which tends to reduce trade).

The large unexplained difference between trade volumes in east Asia and other developing country regions may be related to increasing vertical specialization in global production (Box 3.4). In recent years, the further slicing up of the production chain has accompanied the substantial expansion of trade. With the expansion of international vertical specialization, trade flows per unit of GDP rise even when all other factors remain unchanged. Indeed, the contribution of increased intra-industry trade to total trade growth, which partly reflects greater vertical specialization, has been higher in east Asia

Figure 3.4. Why Do Developing Countries Trade Less Than Industrial Countries?[1]
(Percent)

Trade and balance of payments restrictiveness are significant in explaining why trade per unit of GDP is smaller in developing countries than in industrial countries, but economic development and geography are even more important.

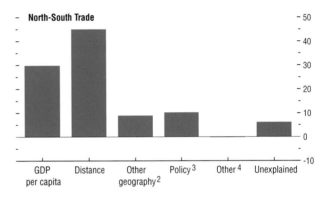

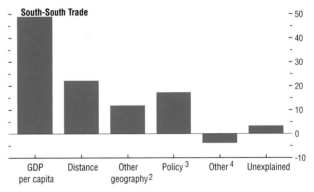

Source: IMF staff calculations.
[1]Contribution to explaining shortfall in North-South trade and in South-South trade, relative to North-North trade, after taking account of economic size.
[2]Other geographical factors include land-locked status, common land, border, and island status.
[3]Policy factors include overall balance of payments restrictions, trade policy restrictiveness, and currency union.
[4]Other factors include former colony, common language, and common colonizer.

Figure 3.5. Why Does East Asia Trade More Than Other Developing Regions?[1]

(Percent)

Developing countries in east Asia trade more per unit of GDP than countries in other regions, partly because of higher income per capita and less restrictive policies, but most of the difference is not explained.

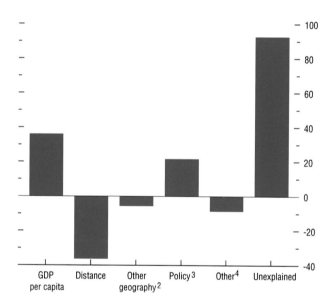

Source: IMF staff calculations.
[1]Contribution to explaining why east Asia trades more than other developing regions, after taking account of economic size.
[2]Other geographical factors include land-locked status, common land, border, and island status.
[3]Policy factors include overall balance of payments restrictions, trade policy restrictiveness, and currency union.
[4]Other factors include former colony, common language, and common colonizer.

Table 3.8. Intra-industry Trade[1]

(Percent)

Region	Shares of Total Trade Growth due to Intra-industry Trade Growth		
	1986–90	1991–95	1996–2000
Africa, sub-Saharan	30.0	30.5	13.0
Asia			
East Asia	42.5	46.9	75.0
South Asia	31.2	21.8	34.4
Middle East and North Africa	6.4	5.8	26.1
Western Hemisphere			
Caribbean and			
Central America	25.9	39.3	34.5
South America	4.6	32.1	34.0

Source: IMF staff calculations based on data from the United Nations Comtrade database.
[1]Average contribution of intra-industry trade growth to total trade growth over five-year periods (at SITC 2-digit level). The methodology is based on Menon and Dixon (1996).

than in other developing country regions (Table 3.8). Also, in the gravity model, the difference between actual and expected trade in east Asia falls once the share of intra-industry trade is taken into account.[24] Thus far, trade flows between industrial countries, and flows with and among east Asian economies, have been most affected by outsourcing, but it is increasingly assuming a global dimension.

The increasing role of vertical specialization in east Asia is consistent with the region's focus on labor-intensive production. Figure 3.6 shows the factor composition of net exports—that is, the embodiment of capital, labor, land, natural resources, and technology—across developing country regions.[25] East Asia is a net exporter of labor-intensive manufactures; sub-Saharan Africa and Latin America are net exporters of agricultural products; and sub-Saharan Africa, Latin

[24]However, more generally, specialization in specific primary commodity products does not help explain over- or undertrading, except for fuel exports. Adding a dummy variable for the fuel exporters reduces undertrading for trade between oil exporters, which affects undertrading for countries in the Middle East and North Africa.
[25]The commodity classification in Figure 3.6 closely follows Leamer (1984). The main difference is that leather manufactures and textile yarns and fabrics were included in the category of labor-intensive products.

America, and the Middle East and North Africa are net exporters of raw materials and fuels. While the share of manufactured goods in total trade has increased over time in many developing countries, the most significant change in the pattern of factor specialization has occurred in east Asia, where net exports of labor-intensive manufacturing products have increased while net exports of agricultural products and raw materials have fallen.

The analysis of developing countries' trading patterns suggests three main points.

- Undertrading, which reflects the overall impact of artificial barriers to trade in a country's policy and institutional environment, remains a serious problem in many developing countries, especially in the Middle East and North Africa, and south Asia.

- Trade and balance of payments restrictiveness are important reasons why developing countries trade less than industrial countries, though economic development and geography matter even more.

- International vertical specialization has played a growing role in east Asia, where less restrictive trade policies helped create a favorable environment. Vertical specialization is likely to become increasingly important for other developing countries with open trading regimes, abundant labor, and flexible economies.

Consequences of Trade and Financial Integration for Macroeconomic Volatility

This section examines how the interaction between trade and financial integration affects macroeconomic volatility. Volatility is undesirable not only in itself, but also because it is strongly and negatively correlated with output growth (Ramey and Ramey, 1995). Trade and financial integration by themselves each tend to increase an economy's exposure to external shocks: trade openness is on the whole associated with somewhat higher output volatility, while financial openness is related to higher volatility of capital flows, especially short-term

Figure 3.6. Factor Content of Net Exports, 1991–2000
(Ratio of GDP; logarithmic scale; 10-year averages)

In line with the increasing role of vertical specialization in the region, east Asia is a large net exporter of labor-intensive manufactures while most other developing country regions continue to export mainly agricultural products or raw materials.

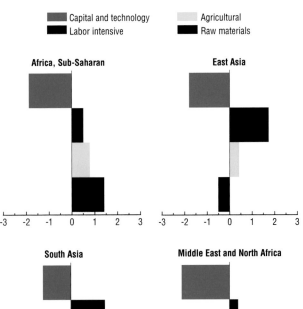
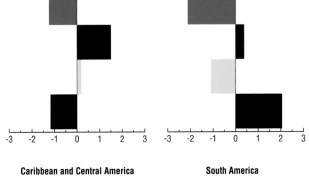
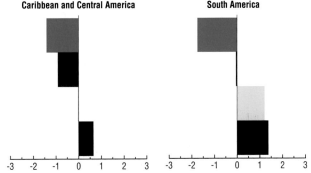

Source: IMF staff calculations following Leamer (1984), based on United Nations, Comtrade data.

Box 3.4. Vertical Specialization in the Global Economy

The growth of world trade has been accompanied by international vertical specialization. Vertical specialization refers to the slicing up of the production process into distinct steps, allowing specialization across locations (locational decentralization) and firms (outsourcing). Historically, international vertical specialization can be traced to the mid-1960s, when electronics components began to be assembled in Hong Kong SAR, Thailand, Malaysia, and Singapore, and apparel and leather goods in the Dominican Republic and the Philippines. Thus, international specialization has become two-dimensional, with countries specializing both vertically in certain stages of the production processes and horizontally in the production of some categories of final goods.

Rising vertical specialization implies an increasing ratio of international trade to value added, as parts and components are shipped back and forth across national borders for further processing along the production chain. The table shows that the ratio of merchandise trade to merchandise value-added rose sharply between 1980 and 2000 in both industrial countries and emerging market economies, especially in Asia and Mexico. While the increase in the trade-to-value added ratio could also be due to greater trade in final goods, other empirical evidence confirms the growing role of international vertical specialization in international trade.[1] Hummels, Ishii, and Yi (2001) find that increased vertical specialization accounted for one-third of world trade growth between 1970 and 1990, after taking account of inter- and intra-industry linkages.[2] Yeats (2001) finds that the share of components and parts in trade in

Ratio of Merchandise Trade to Merchandise Value-Added[1]
(Percent)

Country	1980	1990	2000
Major industrial economies	46.2	51.6	76.3
Canada	63.7	70.6	108.8
France	50.6	62.0	90.0
Germany	52.0	63.7	96.7
Italy	45.7	46.9	76.7
Japan	28.7	20.6	24.2
United Kingdom	52.0	62.4	83.5
United States	30.9	35.1	54.6
Emerging market economies			
Asia	93.8	115.6	168.5
China	12.1	23.7	32.9
India	11.3	12.4	21.6
Newly industrialized economies[2]	216.5	259.3	365.5
Other[3]	39.4	52.4	84.3
Western Hemisphere	37.2	42.6	58.6
Argentina	25.3	13.2	29.7
Brazil	19.4	14.6	34.1
Chile	42.8	55.8	60.9
Mexico	22.8	48.3	102.6
Other[4]	44.4	52.3	63.0

Sources: World Bank, 2002; and U.S. Council of Economic Advisers.

[1]This table is an update and extension of Table 2 in Feenstra (1998). Averages are unweighted.

[2]Hong Kong SAR, Korea, Singapore, and Taiwan Province of China.

[3]Bangladesh, Indonesia, Malaysia, Pakistan, the Philippines, and Thailand.

[4]Bolivia, Colombia, Costa Rica, Panama, Paraguay, Uruguay, and Venezuela.

Note: The main author of this box is Thomas Helbling.

[1]It is often difficult to distinguish between final and intermediate goods in trade data, partly because the distinction sometimes depends on circumstances.

[2]Using a similar methodology, Campa and Goldberg (1997) find that the share of imported intermediate inputs in total manufacturing production increased by about one-fourth in Canada and doubled in the United States between 1974 and 1993.

machinery and transportation equipment among industrial countries rose from 26 percent in 1978 to 30 percent in 1995. Asian exports and imports of components and parts grew even faster than those of most industrial countries between the mid-1980s and the mid-1990s (Ng and Yeats, 1999).

What are the implications of vertical specialization? First, increasing vertical specialization tends to accelerate the global propagation of shocks, as industry-specific shocks are immediately transmitted to countries along the production chain. By contrast, with horizontal specialization, industry-specific shocks tend to initially affect a more limited number of countries. The rising sensitivity of east Asian economies to cyclical developments in the global information technology industry was discussed in Chapter III of the October 2001 *World Economic Outlook*. Second, vertical specialization allows countries to specialize in the stages of production that best fit their relative factor endowments. Specifically, labor-abundant developing countries can increase their role in global manufacturing by specializing in the production of labor-intensive parts and components or labor-intensive assembly processes. Vertical specialization also likely facilitates the convergence of wages for similar types of labor and other factor prices across countries. Finally, vertical specialization underlines the importance of reducing trade barriers further, as the back-and-forth shipping of goods across borders compounds the effects of even relatively low trade barriers.

Vertical specialization is driven by three main factors.

- *Improving service links.* Service links between production locations or producers, including activities like transport, telecommunication, insurance, coordination, and supervision, are critical to the success of vertical specialization. Innovations in transport and communications technology, as well as the deregulation of service provision, have made service links more reliable and less costly (Jones and Kierzkowski, 2001). Economic growth has also helped, as greater demand offsets the fixed set-up costs of services links between locations.
- *Increased customization.* Technological change has increased the scope for the inexpensive customization of generally standardized components and parts, allowing the exploitation of increasing returns to scale in the produc-

tion of parts and components.[3] The greater attractiveness of outsourcing relative to small-scale in-house production has led to the "commoditization" of some manufactures, especially parts and components for electronics and information technology goods (e.g., memory chips and disk drives).

- *Falling trade barriers.* With back-and-forth shipping across borders, the effects of trade barriers are compounded, so reductions in trade barriers have a more than proportional positive impact on vertical specialization. It is not surprising that vertical specialization has sometimes occurred in the context of special tariff or quota provisions for offshore assembly or regional preferential trade agreements.[4]

Looking forward, vertical specialization is likely to become even more important. The negative impact of the September 11, 2001, terrorist attacks on transport costs (Box 3.2) will probably be more than offset by further innovations in telecommunications technology (which will strengthen services links), expansion of inexpensive customization (especially in the electronics and information technology industries), and trade liberalization (which will reduce the adverse effects of trade barriers more than proportionately). Vertical specialization has so far mostly affected trade in industrial countries, east Asia, and the Caribbean and Central America, but it is increasingly assuming a global dimension.

---

[3]See Grossman and Helpman (2002) for a discussion of customization and outsourcing.
[4]See Graziani (2001) on tariff and quota provisions in the context of offshore assembly of textiles and clothing.

flows. But how does *trade* integration affect *financial* vulnerability, and *financial* integration affect *output* volatility? The first part of the section addresses the impact of trade integration on the frequency of external financial crises, and the second part considers the effect of financial integration on output volatility.

The analysis in this section distinguishes between developing countries that are more and less integrated into the world economy. Along both trade and financial dimensions, developing countries are split into two groups, depending on whether a country's openness is above or below the median. Figure 3.7 shows the average

Figure 3.7. Trade and Financial Openness Across Developing Countries, 1995–99[1]
(Deviation from the median, percentage points)

While countries generally tend to be either closed or open on both dimensions, there are also cases in which trade and financial integration diverge.

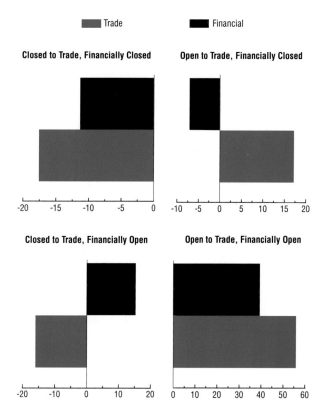

Source: IMF staff calculations.
[1]A country is defined as open if its degree of openness is greater than that of the median country. Average degrees of trade and financial openness in each group are expressed in terms of deviations from the median.

level of trade and financial openness (to foreign direct investment and portfolio investment) relative to the median country in each of the four groups, averaged over the last five years (see Appendix 3.1 for details). Across developing country regions, sub-Saharan Africa and east Asia have the highest proportions of countries that are open to trade, whereas south Asia and South America have the lowest proportions (Figure 3.8). By contrast, the Western Hemisphere has the highest proportion of countries that are financially open, while south Asia has the lowest proportion. The Western Hemisphere is the only region where the proportion of countries that are financially open substantially exceeds the proportion that are open to trade.

While the analysis below is based on simple measures of openness, the results are robust to more sophisticated measures and approaches. Specifically, similar results are obtained if trade integration is defined as the *change* in openness, or if openness is *adjusted* for economic size and level of economic development (larger countries tend to be more closed and richer ones tend to be more open, other things being equal). The effects of trade and financial openness on macroeconomic volatility also remain significant after taking into account other determinants using more sophisticated econometric frameworks.

This section complements the extensive twin literatures on the impact of trade and financial integration on economic growth. The evidence that increasing trade integration has a positive impact on growth is strong (Box 3.5). Trade can foster growth through a variety of channels, including improving the allocation of resources across countries, spreading innovation and technology, reducing rent seeking, and promoting progrowth policy reforms. Similarly, increasing financial integration can support growth by raising domestic investment, creating spillovers through technological transfer, and deepening domestic financial markets, as discussed in Chapter IV of the October 2001 *World Economic Outlook*. However, in the context of inconsistent macroeconomic policies and a weak domestic financial system, increasing financial integration can also lead to excessive and inefficiently allocated financial inflows, possibly resulting in a financial crisis.

A full assessment of the optimal speed and sequencing of trade and capital account liberalization would cover not only the issues discussed in this section and growth effects, but also other structural and institutional reforms.[26] While such an assessment is clearly beyond the scope of this section, the results presented here are consistent with the idea that trade liberalization is essential to reap the full benefits of capital account liberalization. Trade liberalization may lag behind for several reasons: domestic lobbies succeed in impeding reform more than anticipated, returns on investments prove lower than expected due to changing domestic and external factors, and weaknesses exist in the policymaking and institutional environment.

Trade Integration and Vulnerability to Financial Crises

What is the impact of greater trade integration on a country's vulnerability to external financial crises? Two types of external financial crises are considered: debt defaults and currency crashes. A debt default is defined as occurring if there are external arrears to commercial creditors of more than 5 percent of total commercial debt outstanding or if there is a rescheduling or restructuring agreement with commercial creditors, based on Detragiache and Spilimbergo (2001). A currency crisis is defined as an exchange rate depreciation vis-à-vis the U.S. dollar of at least 25 percent and at least double the rate of depreciation in the previous year, as long as the latter is less than 40 percent—to exclude hyperinflationary episodes (Milesi-Ferretti and Razin, 1998).

[26]For discussions of the sequencing of economic liberalization in developing countries, see McKinnon (1973, 1993), Brecher and Diaz-Alejandro (1977), Brecher (1983), Edwards (1984, 2001), Hanson (1995), and Arteta, Eichengreen, and Wyplosz (2001).

Figure 3.8. Trade and Financial Integration Across Developing Regions, 1975–99[1]
(Share of open economies; percent)

The Western Hemisphere region is the only one where a greater proportion of countries are open to finance than to trade. This is especially true in South America.

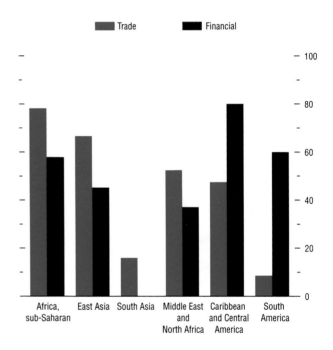

Source: IMF staff calculations.
[1]The average share of countries in each region that are open to trade or financial flows. In each year, a country is classified as open if its degree of integration is greater than the median.

Box 3.5. Trade and Growth

The past two decades have seen a wave of trade liberalization in developing countries. What does this experience show about the relationship between trade openness and growth? The recent literature on trade and growth consists of three main strands: cross-country econometric work, country case studies, and industry- and firm-level analyses. Together, these three types of evidence indicate that trade openness makes an important contribution to higher productivity and income per capita, and that trade liberalization contributes to growth.

Many cross-country econometric studies have concluded that trade openness is a significant explanatory variable for the level or the growth rate of real GDP per capita. One set of studies has found that the large differences across countries in levels of income per capita are systematically and importantly related to openness (see Hall and Jones, 1999; Frankel and Romer, 1999; and Frankel and Rose, 2000). This result remains when a variety of other variables that may explain income are included in the analysis, when the possible feedback from income to openness is taken into account, and across various measures of openness. However, it is difficult to separate the effect of openness on income per capita from that of institutional quality—that is, the rule of law and government effectiveness—because openness and institutional quality are so highly correlated across countries.

Another set of studies has found that the *change* in openness is an important determinant of the *change* in income per capita within countries over time. By focusing on differences over time, this approach avoids the difficulty associated with distinguishing the role of slowly changing institutional factors from that of trade openness. The figure, based on Dollar and Kraay (2001a), shows that developing countries that had the largest increases in trade shares between the late 1970s and the mid-1990s (called "globalizers") experienced on average a much larger increase in income per capita during the 1990s

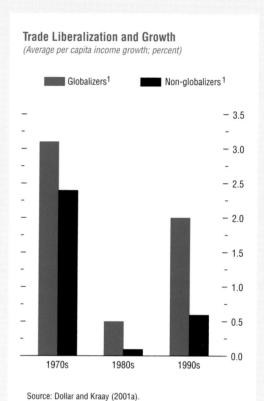

Trade Liberalization and Growth
(Average per capita income growth; percent)

Source: Dollar and Kraay (2001a).
[1] Globalizers consist of those developing countries that had the largest increase in the share of trade in GDP from the late 1970s to the mid-1990s (excluding Chile, Hong Kong SAR, Korea, Singapore, and Taiwan Province of China); non-globalizers are the remaining developing countries.

than did non-globalizers. Dollar and Kraay (2002) find that changes in trade volumes are important determinants of changes in growth, even after taking account of a variety of other determinants of growth and of the possibility that growth could cause the increase in trade (reverse causality).

Country case studies have also found important benefits from trade liberalization. Large, multicountry studies of trade liberalization in the 1970s and 1980s (including Krueger, 1978) drew attention to the highly distortionary nature of the import substituting regimes prior to liberalization. Similarly, Papageorgiou, Michaely, and Choksi (1991) and Sachs and Warner (1995) have found that strong and sustained liberalization episodes result in rapid growth of exports and real GDP.

Note: The main author of this box is Andrew Berg. This box draws on Berg and Krueger (2002).

Industry- and firm-level studies have documented the various channels through which openness contributes to export, productivity, and ultimately income growth (Hallward-Driemeier, 2001, provides a recent survey). Access to imported inputs facilitates the diffusion of knowledge, which contributes to productivity (Coe, Helpman, and Hoffmaister, 1997). Import competition increases not only the exit but also the entry of domestic firms, spurring innovation (Wacziarg, 2001).

Many studies have shown that exporting firms are more productive, and recent work has found unusual increases in productivity after firms begin to export, suggesting that exports lead to higher productivity (Kraay, 1999, and Bigsten and others, 2000). Moreover, Hallward-Driemeier, Iarossi, and Sokoloff (2002) find that firms in east Asia aim at export markets, so that even pre-entry productivity increases are at least in part due to the promise of the export market. Finally, exporting allows highly productive export-oriented firms to grow faster, shifting resources into higher-productivity activities, which increase economy-wide average productivity (Bernard and Jensen, 1999; and Isgut, 2001).

Consistent with the evidence on the benefits of trade for productivity growth, the infant industry argument—the idea that new industries need protection—has consistently failed to find empirical support. Protected industries have tended to grow more slowly than others, reflecting the fact that productivity growth is due not only to learning by doing, which would be helped by protection, but also to active efforts to acquire more sophisticated technologies (Krueger and Tuncer, 1982; and Bell, Ross-Larson, and Westphal, 1984). Also, in developing countries where openness has increased, industrial production has grown relative to agricultural production, in contrast to the prediction of the infant industry argument (Dodzin and Vamvakidis, 1999).

The most important implication of trade openness for poverty reduction is its effect on overall GDP growth, because changes in average income per capita are the main determinant of changes in poverty. The sharp decline in the share of poor people in the world (those with incomes below $2 a day) over the past two decades is almost entirely attributable to growth, not changes in income distribution, because income distribution changes much less over time than does average per capita income. The evidence suggests that growth has no systematic effect on income distribution, regardless of whether growth is trade related or not. Of course, in some countries and in some periods the poor do better than average and sometimes they do worse, but openness itself does not help explain which outcome occurs (Dollar and Kraay, 2001b).

The fact that the effect of trade openness on growth is difficult to separate from that of institutional quality, or from the effects of other reforms that were implemented at the same time, is an econometric problem but a policy opportunity. Specifically, the correlation of trade liberalization with other reforms highlights the advantages of making openness a primary part of the reform package. Trade openness has important positive spillovers on other aspects of reform. For example, competition with foreign firms can expose inefficient industrial policies, and trade raises the marginal product of other reforms (in that better infrastructure, telephones, roads, and ports translate into better performance of the export sector). Trade liberalization also changes the political dynamics of reform by creating constituencies for further reform. Finally, openness seems to encourage institutional reform and reduce corruption (Ades and Di Tella, 1999).

While trade openness is not a "magic bullet" (much else matters for growth and poverty reduction), the evidence clearly suggests that trade openness is a particularly important component of reform. There is little evidence that there are other reforms that must precede an effective trade reform, though there are many reforms that are complementary. The strength of the association between openness and institutional quality should give long pause to any policymaker contemplating the adoption of a novel (or tested and failed) development strategy that does not center around trade openness.

Figure 3.9. Frequency of External Financial Crises in Developing Countries
(Share of countries in crises; percent a year)

External debt defaults and currency crises have been more frequent in those countries that are less integrated into the global trading system.

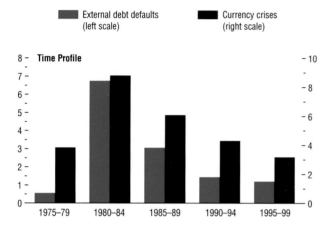

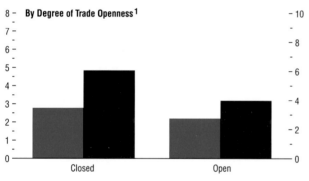

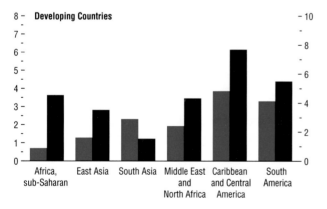

Source: IMF staff calculations.
[1]Based on a country's degree of trade openness relative to the median.

The upper panel of Figure 3.9 shows the frequency of debt defaults and currency crises by five-year periods between 1975 and 1999. The two types of external financial crises have similar time profiles throughout the entire period, including peaks during the early 1980s.

External financial crises have been more frequent in countries that are less integrated into the global trading system (middle panel of Figure 3.9). Over the past quarter century, less integrated countries have been on average about one-fifth more likely to suffer a debt default, and one-third more likely to have a currency crisis than the average developing country. Across developing country regions, the Western Hemisphere has been significantly more vulnerable to episodes of financial turmoil than any other region (lower panel of Figure 3.9), as highlighted in Chapter II of the April 2002 *World Economic Outlook.* The benefits also turn out to be largest for countries that already have open capital markets.

The inverse relationship between trade integration and external financial crises remains statistically significant in a multivariate econometric framework. Sgherri (2002) shows that the relationship is robust to alternative definitions of external financial crises and after taking account of the conventional determinants of crises, including a country's economic fundamentals, its solvency position, foreign exchange reserves, and external macroeconomic conditions. In addition, the result remains significant after incorporating—in a bivariate probit framework—two crucial supplementary relationships: the fact that trade openness may be related to the same factors that affect the frequency of financial crises, and the fact that the frequency of external financial crises and trade openness may both be affected by factors not included in the empirical framework.[27] This result is consistent with other analyses of the determinants of

[27]This result is in line with the empirical literature on the impact of trade openness on the interaction between international financial liberalization and exchange rate instability. Edwards (1989) finds that capital controls are generally intensified before a currency crisis. Alesina,

crisis frequency, including Klein and Marion (1997) and Milesi-Ferretti and Razin (1998), although Detragiache and Spilimbergo (2001) find that recently trade openness has tended to increase the likelihood of financial crises.[28]

Trade integration reduces a country's financial fragility by increasing both the ability and willingness to service external obligations. A higher ratio of exports to GDP implies that exchange rate depreciation will provide a greater boost to a country's ability to earn foreign exchange, which is essential to service foreign currency–denominated debt. In this way, a greater export ratio decreases the likelihood of a sharp reversals of capital flows, as the country is considered to be more able to service its foreign currency–denominated debt. This reassurance is especially important in developing countries, where domestic financial markets are shallow and economic and policy prospects are generally more uncertain than in industrial countries.[29] In addition, trade openness serves as an incentive to meet external obligations by making a country more vulnerable to creditors' sanctions in case of default (Bulow and Rogoff, 1989).[30]

In summary, higher trade integration tends to reduce the frequency of external financial crises. One interpretation of this result is that trade integration provides an important buffer for the inherent volatility associated with financial integration. A possible implication is that countries that are already financially open could see a decline in the frequency of external financial crises by increasing trade openness.

Financial Integration and Output Volatility

What is the impact of openness to foreign direct investment and portfolio investment on output volatility? Output volatility is defined as the unconditional standard deviation of the growth rate of real GDP per capita over the period 1975–99. The upper panel of Figure 3.10 shows that output volatility in developing countries is roughly double that in industrial countries, and that—among developing countries—output volatility in small countries (those with populations between ½ million and 1½ million) is about one-third greater than average. Developing countries that are relatively more integrated into global capital markets tend to have lower output volatility on average than financially closed countries (lower panel of Figure 3.10). This is true for the period as a whole, but not in the early 1980s and late 1990s, when global financial shocks were especially large.

In particular, the output volatility among financially open small developing countries is about one-third lower than among their financially closed counterparts.[31] This result is consistent with the empirical literature on the macroeconomic performance of small econo-

---

Grilli, and Milesi-Ferretti (1994) report evidence that economies that are relatively closed to international trade are more likely to restrict capital flows. Montiel and Reinhart (1999) examine the impact of financial controls on the volume and composition of international financial flows. Glick and Hutchison (2000) analyze the joint causality between the likelihood of a currency crisis and the imposition of financial controls.

[28]In addition, there is an ongoing debate about the role of trade linkages in transmitting financial crises across countries. See Baig and Goldfajn (1998), Masson (1998), Eichengreen and Rose (1999), Glick and Rose (1999), Forbes (2000, 2001), Harrigan (2000), Kaminsky and Reinhart (2000), and Van Wincoop and Yi (2000).

[29]Romer (1993) finds that international openness tends to be associated with lower inflation rates, that in turn may reduce macroeconomic volatility. Catão and Sutton (2002) stress the role of volatility as a key determinant of sovereign debt defaults, while breaking down aggregate volatility into its external and domestic components.

[30]Also, countries that are more open to trade are likely to experience less dramatic drops in real growth and much quicker rebound in the aftermath of a currency crisis (Milesi-Ferretti and Razin, 1998; and Gupta, Deepak, and Sahay, 2000). Rapid export growth helped bring Asian economies out of recession following the 1997–98 crisis, while automatically generating tax revenues needed to meet external debt payments. This did not happen in Latin American markets during the 1980s, despite similarly sharp devaluations. Instead, Latin American countries, partly as a result of such lack of trade openness, witnessed a persistent increase in their ratio of external debt service to export revenues (Catão, 2002).

[31]This result is not obvious, as greater financial integration could lead to greater specialization in production, leading to higher output volatility.

Figure 3.10. Output Volatility, 1975–99[1]
(Percent)

Greater financial openness is associated with lower output volatility, especially among small open economies.

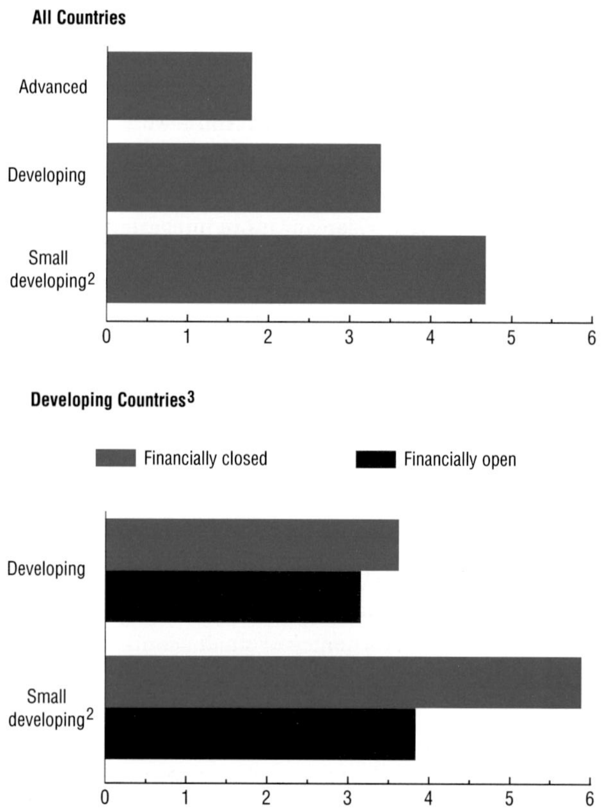

All Countries

Developing Countries[3]

Source: IMF staff calculations.
[1] Standard deviations of the growth rate of real GDP per capita, are calculated for five-year periods and then averaged.
[2] Small developing economies are those with populations between 0.5 and 1.5 million.
[3] Over each five-year period, countries are divided into those that are financially open and those that are not, according to their degree of openness relative to the median country.

Table 3.9. Volatility of Output and Other Macroeconomic Indicators[1]
(Percent, unless otherwise indicated)

	Developing Economies	
	Financially open[2]	Financially closed[2]
Volatility of output	3.2	3.6
Trade openness[3]	67.4	40.9
Volatility of trade flows	6.5	4.4
Volatility of changes in terms of trade	5.7	4.9
Financial openness[3]	28.4	6.4
External debt ratio[3]	62.4	50.6
Volatility of external assets and liabilities	5.0	1.5
Volatility of real exchange rate changes	8.8	10.5
Volatility of inflation rate	6.9	11.8
Volatility of fiscal balance	2.1	1.9

[1] Based on five-year periods over 1975–99.
[2] Based on a country's degree of financial openness relative to the median.
[3] In percent of GDP.

mies, which suggests that the benefits from financial deepening may be substantial (Easterly and Kraay, 2000).

Financial openness appears to be associated with lower output volatility through two channels: the magnitude of inflation and exchange rate shocks is lower, and the impact of all shocks on output is dampened. Financially open countries—which are also more open to trade and have slightly higher debt ratios—experience larger external shocks, as measured by the volatility of the terms of trade, trade flows, and financial flows (Table 3.9). However, financially open countries have somewhat more stable real exchange rates and much more stable inflation rates (the volatility of fiscal balances is similar in financially open and closed countries). The lower volatility of inflation and exchange rates in financially open countries may reflect a disciplining effect of international financial markets or a facilitation of the transfer of international best practices in macroeconomic policymaking.[32]

---

[32] Kim (2000) finds that international financial integration leads to a significant decrease in the fiscal deficit. Rodrik (2000) and Acemoglu and others (2002) study the relationship between international financial liberalization and institutional quality. Wei (2000) looks at the linkages between trade openness and governance.

Table 3.10. Correlations with Output Volatility[1]

	Developing Economies	
	Financially open[2]	Financially closed[2]
Trade openness[3]	—	—
Volatility of trade flows	0.26	0.46
Volatility of changes in terms of trade	0.10	0.45
Financial openness[3]	—	−0.09
External debt ratio[3]	0.14	0.16
Volatility of external assets and liabilities	—	0.09
Volatility of real exchange rate changes	0.15	0.37
Volatility of inflation rate	—	0.28
Volatility of fiscal balance	—	0.39

[1]Based on five-year periods over 1975–99. "—" indicates that the correlation is not significantly different from zero at the 5 percent level.

[2]Based on a country's degree of financial openness relative to the median.

[3]In percent of GDP.

However, it may also reflect causality running in the opposite direction—from sounder macroeconomic policymaking to greater integration.

Financial integration also seems to be associated with lower output volatility because the impact of shocks on output is dampened. Output volatility is significantly correlated with inflation rate volatility and fiscal balance volatility in financially closed economies, but not in financially open countries (Table 3.10). Similarly, the correlations between output volatility and the volatility of external shocks—including terms of trade volatility, trade flow volatility, and real exchange rate volatility—are significantly lower in financially open economies. Strikingly, although financially closed economies experience less volatile capital flows, this lower volatility is significantly correlated with output volatility. Moreover, in countries that are more financially closed than average, greater financial openness is associated with lower output volatility. In other words, it appears that financial integration helps to smooth the effects of shocks on output, not only by comparing financially open to financially closed countries, but also among financially closed countries.

It is important to distinguish the association between greater openness to foreign direct investment and portfolio investment and lower output volatility from that of external debt. Financially open countries have somewhat higher external debt ratios, and external debt ratios are positively correlated with output volatility in both financially open and financially closed countries. External debt may exacerbate output volatility as balance sheet effects magnify the impact of shocks, especially if domestic financial systems are not yet well developed. However, on average, the indirect effect of financial openness in raising output volatility (through a higher external debt ratio) appears to be smaller than the direct impact in lowering output volatility.

The contribution of financial openness to reducing output volatility remains significant in a more sophisticated econometric framework, which accounts for the endogeneity of financial openness and the heteroscedasticity of shocks across countries (Sgherri, 2002). These results are broadly consistent with the theoretical and empirical literatures. Theoretical models of the international business cycle suggest that global financial diversification may be the right response to terms of trade shocks (Razin and Rose, 1994; Heathcote and Perri, 2002; and Kose, Prasad, and Terrones, forthcoming).[33] Empirical work by Bekaert, Harvey, and Lundblad (2002) finds that equity market liberalization is associated with lower volatility of output and consumption. Kim, Kose, and Plummer (forthcoming) show that the amplitude of economic fluctuations in east Asia has fallen over time as countries have become more open. Kraay and Ventura (2001) find that countries use foreign assets as a buffer stock as they try to smooth consumption and investment.

In summary, greater international financial integration is associated with lower output volatility, though this association is generally only realized over the longer term. Output

[33]For a more extensive analysis of the transmission of external shocks to developing countries, see the October 2001 *World Economic Outlook.*

volatility also depends on other factors, including macroeconomic policy stability, domestic financial development, and institutional quality. Greater financial integration appears to be associated with smaller inflation and exchange rate shocks, and a reduced impact of all shocks on output. A possible implication is that economies with less diversified production structures, including small economies, which tend to be very open to trade, could see a decline in output volatility by opening up to financial flows.

Conclusion

Trade integration and international financial integration are largely complementary, both over time and across countries. In recent decades, trade openness and international financial openness have been highly correlated across both industrial and developing countries. Countries that are more open to trade are also more integrated into global financial markets, as evidenced by lower saving-investment correlations. While global economic integration was driven primarily by technological improvements during the previous major episode of globalization (1870–1914), integration since World War II has been driven mostly by policy liberalization. This underlines the importance of paying close attention to the interaction between the trade and financial aspects of globalization.

While developing countries have generally become more integrated into the world trading system over the past two decades, the degree of integration has been uneven across countries. The full, multilateral liberalization of trade and capital account restrictions would have a large, positive effect on trade flows. However, economic development is the single most important factor in accounting for the shortfall in developing countries' trade per unit of GDP relative to that of industrial countries. At the same time, trade openness has a large and significant positive effect on economic development. In other words, globalization is not only a source of growth, it is a natural outcome of it.

The interaction between the trade and financial aspects of globalization is evident in the incidence of external financial crises and the volatility of output. While external financial crises are related to a host of factors, trade openness by itself tends to reduce the likelihood of an external financial crisis, by improving a country's external solvency. Similarly, while low output volatility depends on macroeconomic policy stability, domestic financial development, and institutional quality, it is also associated with openness to foreign direct investment and portfolio investment, as financial openness is related to lower policy volatility and the dampening of shocks. The implications are that countries where trade integration is already high (like small economies) could reduce output volatility through further financial integration, while countries where financial integration is already high (like many countries in Latin America) would reduce the risk of external financial crises by increasing trade integration.

Appendix 3.1. Definitions, Data Sources, and Country Coverage

This appendix defines terms, provides data sources, and specifies country coverage.

Trade openness is defined as the sum of exports and imports of goods and services (from balance of payments statistics), divided by GDP. The source is the WEO database. The country coverage is the same as that for the analysis of bilateral trade patterns listed below.

Trade restrictiveness is defined in two ways, given data limitations. The IMF's index of overall trade regime restrictiveness (IMF, 1998), which is only available for 1997–2001, is used in the analysis of trade patterns. The country coverage is the same as that for the analysis of trade patterns listed below. For Figure 3.1, which shows developments over three decades, trade restrictiveness is defined as the ratio of import duties to imports. Import duties are from the IMF's *Government Finance Statistics* and imports are from the IMF's *International Financial Statistics.* These data are available for a smaller number of countries than the aforementioned index.[34]

Financial openness is defined as the sum of external assets and liabilities of foreign direct investment and portfolio investment, divided by GDP. Other external financial stocks, including bank lending, are not included because these stocks are much more volatile. The source is Chapter IV of the October 2001 *World Economic Outlook*. The data were originally constructed by Lane and Milesi-Ferretti (1999), who accumulated the corresponding flows and made valuation adjustments. The country coverage is the same as that for the analysis of the interaction between trade and financial integration listed below.

Financial restrictiveness is defined as the index of balance of payments restrictions, based on the IMF's *Annual Report on Exchange Arrangements and Exchange Restrictions*. The index does not differentiate across types of restrictions within a category or capture the effectiveness of the restrictions. The data through 1995 are from Chapter IV of the October 2001 *World Economic Outlook* and were originally constructed by Grilli and Milesi-Ferretti (1995), who created a zero-one indicator variable reflecting the existence of various restrictions on international capital flows. The country coverage is the same as that for financial openness. In 1996, a more refined reporting system for balance of payments restrictions was introduced, which is not backwardly compatible with the earlier categories. The new categorization is the basis for the restrictiveness measure constructed by Mody and Murshid (2002) and used in the analysis of trade patterns. The country coverage is the same as that used in the analysis of trade patterns.

The countries that are included in the econometric analyses reported in this chapter are listed below. The analysis of trade patterns covers many more countries than the analysis of the interaction between trade and financial integration, because data on external assets and liabilities are not available for a large number of countries.[35] Conversely, Cambodia and Zimbabwe are not included in the analysis of trade patterns, because data on income per capita are missing for 1995–99. In the list below, countries that are included in only the analysis of trade patterns are not marked at all; countries that are included in both analyses are marked with a star; and countries that are included in only the analysis of the interaction between trade and financial integration are marked with a dagger.

Industrial Countries

Australia,* Austria,* Belgium,* Canada,* Denmark,* Finland,* France,* Germany,* Greece,* Iceland, Ireland,* Italy,* Japan,* Netherlands,* New Zealand,* Norway,* Portugal,* Spain,* Sweden,* Switzerland,* United Kingdom,* and the United States.*

Developing Countries

Africa, Sub-Saharan

Angola, Benin, Botswana,* Burkina Faso, Burundi, Cameroon, Cape Verde, Central African Republic, Chad, Comoros, Congo, Côte d'Ivoire, Equatorial Guinea, Ethiopia, Gabon, Gambia,* Ghana, Guinea, Guinea-Bissau, Kenya,* Lesotho,* Madagascar, Malawi, Mali, Mauritius,* Mozambique, Namibia,* Niger, Nigeria, Rwanda, Senegal, Seychelles, Sierra Leone, South Africa,* Swaziland, Tanzania, Togo, Uganda, Zambia, and Zimbabwe.[†]

---

[34]Austria, the Bahamas, Bahrain, Bangladesh, Botswana, Burundi, Cameroon, Canada, Colombia, Costa Rica, Cyprus, Dominican Republic, Egypt, El Salvador, Ethiopia, Fiji, Finland, France, Greece, Grenada, Guatemala, Iceland, India, Indonesia, Iran, Israel, Italy, Jamaica, Japan, Jordan, Kenya, Korea, Kuwait, Madagascar, Malta, Mauritius, Mexico, Morocco, Myanmar, New Zealand, Nicaragua, Norway, Oman, Pakistan, Panama, Peru, the Philippines, Sierra Leone, South Africa, Spain, Sri Lanka, Swaziland, Sweden, Switzerland, Thailand, Tunisia, the United States, Uruguay, Venezuela, and Zambia.

[35]In addition, the analysis of the interaction between trade and financial integration excludes countries with populations of less than ½ million, highly indebted poor countries, and transition economies, reflecting the country coverage in Chapter IV of the October 2001 *World Economic Outlook*.

Asia, East

Cambodia,[†] China,* Hong Kong SAR, Indonesia,* Korea,* Lao PDR, Malaysia,* Papua New Guinea,* the Philippines,* Samoa, Singapore,* Solomon Islands, Thailand,* Tonga, and Vanuatu.

Asia, South

Bangladesh,* Bhutan, India,* Nepal,* Pakistan,* and Sri Lanka.*

Middle East and North Africa

Algeria, Egypt,* Iran, Israel,* Jordan,* Mauritania, Morocco,* Saudi Arabia, Syrian Arab Republic,* Tunisia,* Turkey,* and Yemen.

Western Hemisphere, Caribbean, and Central America

Antigua and Barbuda, Barbados, Belize, Costa Rica,* Dominica, Dominican Republic,* El Salvador,* Grenada, Guatemala,* Guyana, Haiti,* Honduras, Jamaica,* Mexico,* Nicaragua, Panama,* St. Kitts and Nevis, St. Lucia, Suriname, and Trinidad and Tobago.

Western Hemisphere, South America

Argentina,* Bolivia, Brazil,* Chile,* Colombia,* Ecuador,* Paraguay, Peru,* Uruguay,* and Venezuela.

Countries in Transition

Armenia, Bulgaria, Czech Republic, Estonia, Georgia, Hungary, Kazakhstan, Kyrgyz Republic, Latvia, Lithuania, Moldova, Mongolia, Poland, Slovak Republic, Slovenia, and Ukraine.

References

Acemoglu, Daron, Simon Johnson, James Robinson, and Yunyong Thaicharoen, 2002, "Institutional Causes, Macroeconomic Symptoms: Volatility, Crises and Growth" (unpublished; Cambridge, Massachusetts: Massachusetts Institute of Technology). Available via the Internet: www.world-bank.org/research/conferences/financial_global-ization/institutional_causes.pdf.

Ades, Alberto, and Rafael Di Tella, 1999, "Rents, Competition, and Corruption," *American Economic Review,* Vol. 89 (September), pp. 982–93.

Al-Atrash, Hassan, and Tarik Yousef, 2000, "Intra-Arab Trade: Is It Too Little?" IMF Working Paper 00/10 (Washington: International Monetary Fund).

Alesina, Alberto, Vittorio Grilli, and Gian Maria Milesi-Ferretti, 1994, "The Political Economy of Capital Controls," in *Capital Mobility: The Impact on Consumption, Investment, and Growth,* ed. by Leonardo Leiderman and Assaf Razin (Cambridge: Cambridge University Press), pp. 289–321.

Anderson, James E., 1979, "A Theoretical Foundation for the Gravity Equation," *American Economic Review,* Vol. 69 (March), pp. 106–16.

———, and Eric van Wincoop, 2001, "Gravity with Gravitas: A Solution to the Border Puzzle," NBER Working Paper No. 8079 (Cambridge, Massachusetts: National Bureau of Economic Research).

Arteta, Carlos, Barry Eichengreen, and Charles Wyplosz, 2001, "When Does Capital Account Liberalization Help More Than It Hurts?" NBER Working Paper No. 8414 (Cambridge, Massachusetts: National Bureau of Economic Research).

Baier, Scott L., and Jeffrey H. Bergstrand, 2001, "The Growth of World Trade: Tariffs, Transport Costs, and Income Similarity," *Journal of International Economics,* Vol. 53 (February), pp. 1–27.

Baig, Taimur, and Ilan Goldfajn, 1998, "Financial Market Contagion in the Asian Crisis," IMF Working Paper 98/155 (Washington: International Monetary Fund).

Bairoch, Paul, 1993, *Economics and World History: Myths and Paradoxes* (Chicago, Illinois: University of Chicago Press).

Bayoumi, Tamim A., and Barry Eichengreen, 1997, "Is Regionalism Simply a Diversion? Evidence from the Evolution of the EC and EFTA," in *Regionalism Versus Multilateral Trade Arrangements,* ed. by Takatoshi Ito and Anne O. Krueger, NBER–East Asia Seminar on Economics, Vol. 6 (Chicago and London: University of Chicago Press).

Bekaert, Geert, Campbell R. Harvey, and Christian Lundblad, 2002, "Growth Volatility and Equity Market Liberalization" (unpublished; Durham, North Carolina: Duke University). Available via the Internet: http://faculty.fuqua.duke.edu/~charvey/Research/Working_Papers/W60_Growth_volatility_and.pdf.

Bell, Martin, Bruce Ross-Larson, and Larry Westphal, 1984, "Assessing the Performance of Infant Industries," *Journal of Development Economics,* Vol. 16 (September–October), pp. 101–28.

Berg, Andrew, and Anne O. Krueger, 2002, "Trade, Growth, and Poverty: A Selective Survey," paper presented at the Annual World Bank Conference on Development Economics, Washington, April. Available via the Internet: www.econ.worldbank.org/ files/13377_Berg_and_Krueger.pdf.

Bernard, Andrew B., and J. Bradford Jensen, 1999, "Exceptional Exporter Performance: Cause, Effect, or Both?" *Journal of International Economics,* Vol. 47 (February), pp. 1–25.

Bigsten, Arne, and others, 2000, "Exports and Firm-Level Efficiency in African Manufacturing," Centre for the Study of African Economies Working Paper 2000/16 (Oxford: University of Oxford). Available via the Internet: www.economics.ox.ac.uk/ CSAEadmin/workingpapers/pdfs/20-16text.pdf.

Boisso, Dale, and Michael Ferrantino, 1997, "Economic Distance, Cultural Distance, and Openness in International Trade: Empirical Puzzles," *Journal of Economic Integration,* Vol. 12 (December), pp. 456–84.

Bordo, Michael D., and Hugh Rockoff, 1996, "The Gold Standard as a 'Good Housekeeping Seal of Approval,'" *Journal of Economic History,* Vol. 56 (June), pp. 389–428.

Brecher, Richard A., 1983, "Second-Best Policy for International Trade and Investment," *Journal of International Economics,* Vol. 14 (May), pp. 313–20.

———, and Carlos Diaz-Alejandro, 1977, "Tariffs, Foreign Capital and Immiserizing Growth," *Journal of International Economics,* Vol. 7 (November), pp. 317–22.

Bulow, Jeremy, and Kenneth Rogoff, 1989, "Sovereign Debt: Is to Forgive to Forget?" *American Economic Review,* Vol. 79 (March), pp. 43–50.

Calvo, Guillermo, and Carlos A. Végh, 1999, "Inflation Stabilization and BOP Crises in Developing Countries," in *Handbook of Macroeconomics,* ed. by John B. Taylor and Michael Woodford (New York: North-Holland).

Campa, José, and Linda S. Goldberg, 1997, "The Evolving External Orientation of Manufacturing: A Profile of Four Countries," *Federal Reserve Bank of New York Economic Policy Review,* Vol. 3 (July), pp. 53–81.

Catão, Luis, 2002, "Debt Crises: What's Different About Latin America?" in Chapter II, *World Economic Outlook, April 2002,* World Economic and Financial Surveys (Washington: International Monetary Fund).

———, and Ben Sutton, 2002, "Sovereign Defaults: The Role of Volatility," forthcoming IMF Working Paper (Washington: International Monetary Fund).

Coe, David T., Elhanan Helpman, and Alexander W. Hoffmaister, 1997, "North-South R&D Spillovers," *Economic Journal,* Vol. 107 (January), pp. 134–49.

Coe, David T., and Alexander W. Hoffmaister, 1999, "North-South Trade: Is Africa Unusual?" *Journal of African Economies,* Vol. 8 (July), pp. 228–56.

Coe, David T., Arvind Subramanian, Natalia T. Tamirisa, and Rikhil Bhavnani, forthcoming, "The Missing Globalization Puzzle," IMF Working Paper (Washington: International Monetary Fund).

Clark, Ximena, David Dollar, and Alejandro Micco, 2002, "Maritime Transport Costs and Port Efficiency," World Bank Policy Research Working Paper No. 2781 (Washington: World Bank).

Davis, Donald R., and David E. Weinstein, 2001, "An Account of Global Factor Trade," *American Economic Review,* Vol. 91 (December), pp. 1423–53.

Deardorff, Alan V., 1998, "Determinants of Bilateral Trade: Does Gravity Work in a Neoclassical World?" in *The Regionalization of the World Economy,* ed. by Jeffrey A. Frankel (Chicago: University of Chicago Press).

Detragiache, Enrica, and Antonio Spilimbergo, 2001, "Crises and Liquidity: Evidence and Interpretation," IMF Working Paper 01/02 (Washington: International Monetary Fund).

Dodzin, Sergei, and Athanasios Vamvakidis, 1999, "Trade and Industrialization in Developing Agricultural Economies," IMF Working Paper 99/145 (Washington: International Monetary Fund).

Dollar, David, and Aart Kraay, 2001a, "Trade, Growth and Poverty" (unpublished; Washington: World Bank). Available via the Internet: www.worldbank.org/ research/growth/pdfiles/Trade5.pdf.

———, 2001b, "Growth *Is* Good for the Poor" (unpublished; Washington: World Bank). Available via the Internet: www.worldbank.org/research/ growth/pdfiles/growthgoodforpoor.pdf.

———, 2002, "Institutions, Trade, and Growth" (unpublished; Washington: World Bank). Available via the Internet: www.carnegie-rochester.rochester. edu/April02-pdfs/ITG2.pdf.

Easterly, William, and Aart Kraay, 2000, "Small States, Small Problems? Income, Growth, and Volatility in

Small States," *World Development*, Vol. 28 (November), pp. 2013–27.

Edison, Hali J., Michael Klein, Luca Ricci, and Torsten Slok, 2002, "Capital Account Liberalization and Economic Performance: Survey and Synthesis," IMF Working Paper 02/120 (Washington: International Monetary Fund).

Edwards, Sebastian, 1984, "The Order of Liberalization of the External Sector in Developing Countries," Princeton Essays in International Finance No. 156 (Princeton, New Jersey: International Finance Section, Department of Economics, Princeton University).

———, 1989, *Real Exchange Rates, Devaluation and Adjustment: Exchange Rate Policy in Developing Countries* (Cambridge, Massachusetts: MIT Press).

———, 2001, "Capital Mobility and Economic Performance: Are Emerging Economies Different?" NBER Working Paper No. 8076 (Cambridge, Massachusetts: National Bureau of Economic Research).

Egoumé-Bossogo, Philippe, and Chandima Mendis, 2002, "Trade and Integration in the Caribbean," IMF Working Paper 02/148 (Washington: International Monetary Fund).

Eichengreen, Barry J., 1996, *Globalizing Capital: A History of the International Monetary System* (Princeton, New Jersey: Princeton University Press).

———, 2001, "Capital Account Liberalization: What Do Cross-Country Studies Tell Us?" *World Bank Economic Review*, Vol. 15, No. 3, pp. 341–65.

———, and Andrew K. Rose, 1999, "Contagious Currency Crises: Channels of Conveyance," in *Changes in Exchange Rates in Rapidly Developing Countries: Theory, Practice, and Policy Issues*, ed. by Takatoshi Ito and Anne O. Krueger (Chicago: University of Chicago Press).

Engel, Charles, and John H. Rogers, 1996, "How Wide Is the Border?" *American Economic Review*, Vol. 86 (December), pp. 1112–25.

———, 2001, "Deviations from Purchasing Power Parity: Causes and Welfare Costs," *Journal of International Economics*, Vol. 55 (October), pp. 29–57.

Estevadeordal, Antoni, Brian Frantz, and Alan M. Taylor, 2002, "The Rise and Fall of World Trade, 1870–1939" (unpublished; Washington: Inter-American Development Bank). Available via the Internet: http://emlab.berkeley.edu/users/eichengr/211_f01_nov19.pdf.

Feenstra, Robert C., 1998, "Integration of Trade and Disintegration of Production in the Global Economy," *Journal of Economic Perspectives*, Vol. 12 (Fall), pp. 31–50.

Forbes, Kristin J., 2000, "The Asian Flu and Russian Virus: Firm-Level Evidence on How Crises Are Transmitted Internationally," NBER Working Paper No. 7807 (Cambridge, Massachusetts: National Bureau of Economic Research).

———, 2001, "Are Trade Linkages Important Determinants of Country Vulnerability to Crises?" NBER Working Paper No. 8194 (Cambridge, Massachusetts: National Bureau of Economic Research).

Foroutan, Faezeh, and Lant Pritchett, 1993, "Intra-sub-Saharan African Trade: Is It Too Little?" *Journal of African Economies*, Vol. 2 (May), pp. 74–105.

Frankel, Jeffrey A., 1997, *Regional Trading Blocs in the World Economic System* (Washington: Institute for International Economics).

———, and David Romer, 1999, "Does Trade Cause Growth?" *American Economic Review*, Vol. 89 (June), pp. 379–99.

Frankel, Jeffrey A., and Andrew K. Rose, 2000, "Estimating the Effect of Currency Unions on Trade and Output," NBER Working Paper No. 7857 (Cambridge, Massachusetts: National Bureau of Economic Research).

Frankel, Jeffrey A., and Shang-Jin Wei, 1998, "Regionalization of World Trade and Currencies," in *The Regionalization of the World Economy*, ed. by Jeffrey A. Frankel (Chicago: University of Chicago Press).

Gilman, Sidney, 1984, *The Competitive Dynamics of Container Shipping* (Aldershot, Hampshire: Ashgate Publishing Company).

Glick, Reuven, and Andrew K. Rose, 1999, "Contagion and Trade: Why Are Currency Crises Regional?" *Journal of International Money and Finance*, Vol. 18 (August), pp. 603–17.

———, 2001, "Does a Currency Union Affect Trade? The Time Series Evidence," NBER Working Paper No. 8396 (Cambridge, Massachusetts: National Bureau of Economic Research).

Glick, Reuven, and Michael M. Hutchison, 2000, "Capital Controls and Exchange Rate Instability in Developing Economies," Pacific Basin Working Paper Series No. PB00–05 (San Francisco, California: Federal Reserve Bank of San Francisco).

Graziani, Giovanni, 2001, "International Subcontracting in the Textile and Clothing

Industry," in *Fragmentation: New Production Patterns in the World Economy,* ed. by Sven W. Arndt and Henryk Kierzkowski (Oxford and New York: Oxford University Press).

Grilli, Vittorio, and Gian Maria Milesi-Ferretti, 1995, "Economic Effects and Structural Determinants of Capital Controls," *Staff Papers,* International Monetary Fund, Vol. 42 (September), pp. 517–51.

Grossman, Gene M., and Elhanan Helpman, 2002, "Outsourcing in a Global Economy," NBER Working Paper No. 8728 (Cambridge, Massachusetts: National Bureau of Economic Research).

Gupta, Poonam, Deepak Mishra, and Ratna Sahay, 2000, "Output Response During Currency Crises" (unpublished; Washington: International Monetary Fund). Available via the Internet: http://sccie.uscs.edu/papers/epapers/gsahay.pdf.

Hall, Robert E., and Charles I. Jones, 1999, "Why Do Some Countries Produce So Much More Output Per Worker Than Others?" *Quarterly Journal of Economics,* Vol. 114 (February), pp. 83–116.

Hallward-Driemeier, Mary, 2001, "Openness, Firms, and Competition," paper prepared for the Globalization, Growth, and Poverty Policy Research Report (Washington: World Bank). Available via the Internet: http://econ.worldbank.org/files/2868_Openness,_Firms_and_Competition.pdf.

———, Giuseppe Iarossi, and Kenneth L. Sokoloff, 2002, "Exports and Manufacturing Productivity in East Asia: A Comparative Analysis with Firm-Level Data," NBER Working Paper No. 8894 (Cambridge, Massachusetts: National Bureau of Economic Research).

Hanson, James A., 1995, "Opening the Capital Account: Costs, Benefits, and Sequencing," in *Capital Controls, Exchange Rates, and Monetary Policy in the World Economy,* ed. by Sebastian Edwards (Cambridge: Cambridge University Press).

Harley, Knick C., 1980, "Transportation, the World Wheat Trade and the Kuznets Cycle, 1850–1913," *Explorations in Economic History,* Vol. 17 (July), pp. 218–50.

Harrigan, James, 2000, "The Impact of the Asia Crisis on U.S. Industry: An Almost-Free Lunch?" *Federal Reserve Bank of New York Economic Policy Review,* Vol. 6 (September), pp. 71–81.

Heathcote, Jonathan, and Fabrizio Perri, 2002, "Financial Globalization and Real Regionalization," CEPR Discussion Paper No. 3268 (London: Center for Economic Policy Research).

Helpman, Elhanan, and Paul R. Krugman, 1985, *Market Structure and Foreign Trade: Increasing Returns, Imperfect Competition, and the International Economy* (Cambridge, Massachusetts: MIT Press).

Hufbauer, Gary C., Erika Wada, and Tony Warren, 2002, *The Benefits of Price Convergence: Speculative Calculations,* Policy Analyses in International Economics, No. 65 (Washington: Institute for International Economics).

Hummels, David, 1999, "Have International Transportation Costs Declined?" (unpublished; West Lafayette, Indiana: Purdue University). Available via the Internet: www.mgmt.purdue.edu/faculty/hummelsd/research/decline/declined.pdf.

———, 2000, "Time as a Trade Barrier," CIBER Working Paper No. 2000–007 (West Lafayette, Indiana: Purdue University, Center for International Business Education and Research). Available via the Internet: www.mgmt.purdue.edu/centers/ciber/eiit/ConfInfo/2000Papers/hummels.pdf.

———, Jun Ishii, and Kei-Mu Yi, 2001, "The Nature and Growth of Vertical Specialization in World Trade," *Journal of International Economics,* Vol. 54 (June), pp. 75–96.

International Monetary Fund, 1998, *Trade Liberalization in Fund-Supported Programs,* World Economic and Financial Surveys (Washington: International Monetary Fund).

———, 2001, *Market Access for Developing Countries' Exports* (Washington). Available via the Internet: www.imf.org/external/np/madc/eng/042701.htm.

Isgut, Alberto E., 2001, "What's Different About Exporters? Evidence from Colombian Manufacturing," *Journal of Development Studies,* Vol. 37 (June), pp. 57–82.

Jones, Ronald W., and Henryk Kierzkowski, 2001, "A Framework for Fragmentation," in *Fragmentation: New Production Patterns in the World Economy,* ed. by Sven W. Arndt and Henryk Kierzkowski (Oxford and New York: Oxford University Press).

Kaminsky, Graciela L., and Carmen M. Reinhart, 2000, "On Crises, Contagion, and Confusion," *Journal of International Economics,* Vol. 51 (June), pp. 145–68.

Kim, Sunghyun H., M. Ayhan Kose, and Michael G. Plummer, forthcoming, "Dynamics of Business Cycles in Asia: Differences and Similarities," *Review of Development Economics.*

Kim, Woochan, 2000, "Does Capital Account Liberalization Discipline Budget Deficit," KDI School Working Paper No. 00–04 (Seoul: Korea

Development Institute). Available via the Internet: www.kdischool.ac.kr/library/data/w00–04.PDF.

Klein, Michael W., and Nancy P. Marion, 1997, "Explaining the Duration of Exchange-Rate Pegs," *Journal of Development Economics,* Vol. 54 (December), pp. 387–404.

Kose, Ayhan, Eswar Prasad, and Marco Terrones, forthcoming, "The Effects of Globalization on International Business Cycles," IMF Working Paper (Washington: International Monetary Fund).

Kraay, Aart, 1999, "Exportations et Performances Économiques: Étude d'un Panel d'entreprises Chinoises (Exports and Economic Performance: Evidence from a Panel of Chinese Enterprises, with English Summary)," *Revue d'Economie du Developpement,* Vol. 7 (June), pp. 183–207.

———, and Jaume Ventura, 2001, "Comparative Advantage and the Cross-Section of Business Cycles," NBER Working Paper No. 8104 (Cambridge, Massachusetts: National Bureau of Economic Research).

Krueger, Anne O., 1978, *Liberalization Attempts and Consequences* (Cambridge, Massachusetts: Ballinger Publishing Company).

———, and Baran Tuncer, 1982, "An Empirical Test of the Infant Industry Argument," *American Economic Review,* Vol. 72 (December), pp. 1142–52.

Krugman, Paul, 1991, "The Move to Free Trade Zones," in *Policy Implications of Trade and Currency Zones: A Symposium, sponsored by the Federal Reserve Bank of Kansas City, Jackson Hole, Wyoming, August 22–24, 1991* (Kansas City: Federal Reserve Bank of Kansas City).

———, 1995, "Growing World Trade: Causes and Consequences," *Brookings Papers on Economic Activity: 1,* Brookings Institution, pp. 327–77.

Lane, Philip R., and Gian Maria Milesi-Ferretti, 1999, "The External Wealth of Nations: Measures of Foreign Assets and Liabilities for Industrial and Developing Countries," CEPR Discussion Paper No. 2231 (London: Center for Economic Policy Research).

———, 2000, "External Capital Structure: Theory and Evidence," IMF Working Paper 00/152 (Washington: International Monetary Fund).

Leamer, Edward E., 1984, *Sources of International Comparative Advantage: Theory and Evidence* (Cambridge, Massachusetts: MIT Press).

———, 1988, "Measures of Openness," in *Trade Policy Issues and Empirical Analysis,* ed. by Robert E. Baldwin (Chicago and London: University of Chicago Press).

———, and James Levinsohn, 1995, "International Trade Theory: The Evidence," in *Handbook of International Economics,* Vol. 3, ed. by Gene M. Grossman and Kenneth Rogoff (Amsterdam: Elsevier).

Lee, Jong-Wha, 1993, "International Trade, Distortions, and Long-Run Economic Growth," *Staff Papers,* International Monetary Fund, Vol. 40 (June), pp. 299–328.

Limão, Nuno, and Anthony J. Venables, 2001, "Infrastructure, Geographical Disadvantage, Transport Costs, and Trade," *World Bank Economic Review,* Vol. 15 (October), pp. 451–79.

Loungani, Prakash, Ashoka Mody, and Assaf Razin, 2002, "The Global Disconnect: Transactional Distance and Scale Economies" (unpublished; Washington: International Monetary Fund, Research Department).

Lucas, Robert E., Jr., 1990, "Why Doesn't Capital Flow from Rich to Poor Countries?" *American Economic Review, Papers and Proceedings,* Vol. 80 (May), pp. 92–6.

Maddison, Angus, 1995, *Monitoring the World Economy: 1820–1992* (Paris: Development Center of the Organization for Economic Cooperation and Development).

Masson, Paul R., 1998, "Contagion: Monsoonal Effects, Spillovers, and Jumps Between Multiple Equilibria," IMF Working Paper 98/142 (Washington: International Monetary Fund).

McCallum, John, 1995, "National Borders Matter: Canada-U.S. Regional Trade Patterns," *American Economic Review,* Vol. 85 (June), pp. 615–23.

McKinnon, Ronald I., 1973, *Money and Capital in Economic Development* (Washington: Brookings Institution).

———, 1993, *The Order of Economic Liberalization: Financial Control in the Transition to a Market Economy* (Baltimore, Maryland: Johns Hopkins University Press).

Mélitz, Jacques, 2001, "Geography, Trade, and Currency Union," CEPR Discussion Paper No. 2987 (London: Center for Economic Policy Research).

Menon, Jayant, and Peter B. Dixon, 1996, "How Important Is Intra-industry Trade in Trade Growth?" *Open Economies Review,* Vol. 7 (April), pp. 161–75.

Milesi-Ferretti, Gian Maria, and Assaf Razin, 1998, "Current Account Reversals and Currency Crises: Empirical Regularities," IMF Working Paper 98/89 (Washington: International Monetary Fund).

Mody, Ashoka, and Antu Panini Murshid, 2002, "Growing Up with Capital Flows," IMF Working Paper 02/75 (Washington: International Monetary Fund).

Montiel, Peter, and Carmen M. Reinhart, 1999, "Do Capital Controls and Macroeconomic Policies Influence the Volume and Composition of Capital Flows? Evidence from the 1990s," *Journal of International Money and Finance*, Vol. 18 (August), pp. 619–35.

Neal, Larry, 1990, *The Rise of Financial Capitalism: International Capital Markets in the Age of Reason* (Cambridge: Cambridge University Press).

Ng, Francis, and Alexander J. Yeats, 1999, "Production Sharing in East Asia: Who Does What for Whom, and Why?" Policy Research Working Paper No. 2197 (Washington: World Bank).

Obstfeld, Maurice, and Kenneth Rogoff, 2000a, "The Six Major Puzzles in International Macroeconomics: Is There a Common Cause?" in *NBER Macroeconomics Annual 2000*, ed. by Ben S. Bernanke and Kenneth Rogoff (Cambridge, Massachusetts: MIT Press).

———, 2000b, "Perspectives and OECD Economic Integration: Implications for U.S. Current Account Adjustment," in *Global Economic Integration: Opportunities and Challenges: A Symposium, sponsored by the Federal Reserve Bank of Kansas City, Jackson Hole, Wyoming, August 24–26, 2000* (Kansas City: Federal Reserve Bank of Kansas City).

Obstfeld, Maurice, and Alan M. Taylor, 2002, "Globalization and Capital Markets," NBER Working Paper No. 8846 (Cambridge, Massachusetts: National Bureau of Economic Research).

Organization for Economic Cooperation and Development, 2002, *OECD Economic Outlook*, No. 71 (Paris: June).

Panagariya, Arvind, 2000, "Preferential Trade Liberalization: The Traditional Theory and New Developments," *Journal of Economic Literature*, Vol. 38 (June), pp. 287–331.

Papageorgiou, Demetris, Michael Michaely, and Armeane M. Choksi, 1991, *Liberalizing Foreign Trade: Lessons of Experience in the Developing World*, Vol. 7 (New York: Blackwell).

Parsley, David C., and Shang-Jin Wei, 2001, "Limiting Currency Volatility to Stimulate Goods Market Integration: A Price-Based Approach," NBER Working Paper No. 8468 (Cambridge, Massachusetts: National Bureau of Economic Research).

Ramey, Garey, and Valerie A. Ramey, 1995, "Cross-Country Evidence on the Link Between Volatility and Growth," *American Economic Review*, Vol. 85 (December), pp. 1138–51.

Razin, Assaf, and Andrew K. Rose, 1994, "Business-Cycle Volatility and Openness: An Exploratory Cross-Sectional Analysis," in *Capital Mobility: The Impact on Consumption, Investment and Growth*, ed. by Leonardo Leiderman and Assaf Razin (Cambridge: Cambridge University Press).

Rodriguez, Francisco, and Dani Rodrik, 2000, "Trade Policy and Economic Growth: A Skeptic's Guide to Cross-National Evidence," in *NBER Macroeconomics Annual 2000*, ed. by Ben S. Bernanke and Kenneth Rogoff (Cambridge, Massachusetts: MIT Press).

Rodrik, Dani, 1998, "Trade Policy and Economic Performance in Sub-Saharan Africa," NBER Working Paper No. 6562 (Cambridge, Massachusetts: National Bureau of Economic Research).

———, 2000, "Institutions for High-Quality Growth: What They Are and How to Acquire Them," *Studies in Comparative International Development*, Vol. 35 (Fall), pp. 3–31.

Rogers, John H., 2001, "Price Level Convergence, Relative Prices, and Inflation in Europe," International Finance Discussion Paper No. 699 (Washington: Board of Governors of the Federal Reserve System).

Romer, David, 1993, "Openness and Inflation: Theory and Evidence," *Quarterly Journal of Economics*, Vol. 108 (November), pp. 869–903.

Rose, Andrew K., 2000, "One Money, One Market: The Effect of Common Currencies on Trade," *Economic Policy*, No. 30 (April), pp. 9–45.

———, 2002, "Estimating Protectionism from the Gravity Model" (unpublished; Washington: International Monetary Fund, Research Department).

———, and Mark M. Spiegel, 2002, "A Gravity Model of International Lending: Trade, Default, and Credit" (unpublished; Berkeley, California: University of California, Hass School of Business). Available via the Internet: http://faculty.haas.berkeley.edu/arose/Spiegel.pdf.

Rousseau, Peter L., and Richard Eugene Sylla, 2001, "Financial Systems, Economic Growth, and Globalization," NBER Working Paper No. 8323 (Cambridge, Massachusetts: National Bureau of Economic Research).

Sachs, Jeffrey D., and Andrew Warner, 1995, "Economic Reform and the Process of Global

Integration," *Brookings Papers on Economic Activity: 1*, Brookings Institution, pp. 1–118.

Sgherri, Silvia, 2002, "Trade, Financial Openness, and Volatility: Some Interactions," forthcoming IMF Working Paper (Washington: International Monetary Fund).

Soloaga, Isidro, and L. Alan Winters, 2001, "Regionalism in the Nineties: What Effect on Trade?" *North American Journal of Economics and Finance*, Vol. 12 (March), pp. 1–29.

Spilimbergo, Antonio, Juan Luis Londoño, and Miguel Székely, 1999, "Income Distribution, Factor Endowments, and Trade Openness," *Journal of Development Economics*, Vol. 59 (June), pp. 77–101.

Tamirisa, Natalia, 1999, "Exchange and Capital Controls as Barriers to Trade," *IMF Staff Papers*, Vol. 46 (March), pp. 69–88.

United Nations Conference on Trade and Development, 2001, *Review of Maritime Transport* (New York).

U.S. Council of Economic Advisors, various issues, *Economic Report of the President* (Washington: U.S. Government Printing Office). Available via the Internet: http://w3.access.gpo.gov/eop.

Van Wincoop, Eric, and Kei-Mu Yi, 2000, "Asia Crisis Postmortem: Where Did the Money Go and Did the United States Benefit?" *Federal Reserve Bank of New York Economic Policy Review*, Vol. 6 (September), pp. 51–70.

Wacziarg, Romain, 2001, "Measuring the Dynamic Gains from Trade," *World Bank Economic Review*, Vol. 15, No. 3, pp. 393–429.

Wei, Shang-Jin, 1996, "Intra-National Versus International Trade: How Stubborn Are Nations in Global Integration?" NBER Working Paper No. 5531 (Cambridge, Massachusetts: National Bureau of Economic Research).

———, 2000, "Natural Openness and Good Government," NBER Working Paper No. 7765 (Cambridge, Massachusetts: National Bureau of Economic Research).

World Bank, 2002, *World Development Report 2002: Building Institutions for Markets* (Washington).

Yeats, Alexander J., 2001, "Just How Big Is Global Production Sharing?" in *Fragmentation: New Production Patterns in the World Economy*, ed. by Sven W. Arndt and Henryk Kierzkowski (Oxford and New York: Oxford University Press).

SUMMING UP BY THE CHAIRMAN

The following remarks by the Chairman were made at the conclusion of the Executive Board's discussion of the World Economic Outlook. They were made on September 4, 2002.

Executive Directors noted that from the second quarter of 2002, economic and financial market developments have been mixed. They pointed to the negative developments on several fronts, including the sharp decline in global equity markets since end-March; the deterioration in financing conditions facing most emerging market borrowers—notably in Latin America; and weaknesses in a number of current and forward-looking indicators for the United States, Europe, and several other regions. These developments were especially disappointing against the backdrop of the strengthening of global economic indicators, including trade and industrial production, seen since end-2001, as well as first quarter growth that exceeded expectations in several regions.

Directors noted that the world economy and the financial markets have shown considerable resilience in the face of multiple recent shocks and that, going forward, several factors should support a steady strengthening in global growth—including the continuing stimulus from earlier macroeconomic easing in many regions, the winding down of inventory corrections, and the recent signs of greater stability returning to global financial markets. Nonetheless, Directors expressed concern that recent developments have raised questions about the strength and sustainability of the recovery, and agreed with the assessment that, overall, the outlook for the remainder of 2002 and for 2003 is likely to be weaker than had been anticipated in the April *World Economic Outlook*.

Directors assessed the risks to the short-term outlook as being predominantly on the downside. In particular, they noted that recent, and possibly further, equity price falls could have a more marked impact on domestic demand than currently expected—especially in the United States, which has led the global recovery to date. Directors noted that recent movements in major exchange rates are appropriate from a medium-term perspective, although in the short term some negative impact on the recovery in Japan and the euro area, which has so far been led by external demand, should not be ruled out. Many Directors also saw the persistently high U.S. current account deficit and the still high U.S. dollar value as posing some risk of an abrupt and disruptive adjustment. Directors were also concerned that tight emerging market financing conditions could further weaken growth prospects and increase vulnerabilities in a number of countries. They also noted the potential for further volatility in oil prices in the event of a deterioration in the security situation in the Middle East.

Against the backdrop of heightened uncertainty about the strength of the recovery, Directors agreed that macroeconomic policies in most industrial countries will need to remain accommodative for longer than had been expected earlier in the year. Should the outlook weaken further, some further easing in monetary policy will likely be needed in the United States and in the euro area, provided inflationary pressures remain subdued in the United States and come down as expected in Europe. Directors noted that among emerging market economies, policy priorities necessarily vary widely. Where there is room for policy maneuver, they felt that the macroeconomic stance should, in general, remain accommodative, but in countries facing external financing difficulties, the restoration of financial market confidence through appropriate policies should be the priority. Looking ahead, Directors concurred that, in most industrial and emerging countries, fiscal restraint and progress with ongoing structural reforms will remain the essential priorities needed to strengthen and broaden the sources of growth over the medium term, to reduce global imbalances, and to improve resilience to future economic shocks.

Major Currency Areas

Turning to the prospects for the major currency areas, Directors agreed that recent indicators still generally point to the continued moderate recovery in the *United States*, supported by the further fall in long-term interest rates, the lower dollar, and the macroeconomic stimulus still in the pipeline. They noted that, nevertheless, important uncertainties to the outlook remain. These uncertainties relate to the extent to which equity market developments and corporate accounting scandals will affect consumption growth and investment recovery, the extent of overcapacity in a number of industries, and the outlook for productivity growth. Against this backdrop, Directors recommended that the Federal Reserve should wait to withdraw monetary stimulus until the recovery is firmly established, and that it consider further easing if incoming data remain weak. While fiscal policy has provided welcome support to activity during the economic slowdown, Directors noted that following its recent deterioration, the medium-term fiscal outlook will need to be strengthened. Many Directors recommended that the U.S. authorities adopt a medium-term budgetary framework directed at attaining budget balance over the business cycle, both to increase domestic saving and to better prepare for the fiscal pressures from population aging. Noting that restoration of confidence will be key to underpinning the recovery, Directors welcomed the U.S. authorities' swift actions to strengthen corporate governance and auditing, and considered that their vigorous implementation and enforcement, as well as their possible further strength-

ening if needed, will be crucial to ensuring that they have the necessary impact.

Directors were encouraged by recent indicators in *Japan*, suggesting that activity is stabilizing. They were concerned, however, that economic signals still remain mixed. With the outlook for domestic demand remaining weak, the modest rebound projected for the rest of 2002 and for 2003 is subject to downside risks, particularly if, in an uncertain external environment, the global recovery turns out to be weaker than expected or if the yen appreciates further. Directors agreed that strong implementation of structural reforms to improve the financial health and profitability of the banking sector, accelerate corporate restructuring, and increase investment opportunities remain key to strengthen Japan's growth prospects durably. To support activity in the short term, most Directors recommended a more aggressive monetary stimulus, combined with a public commitment to end deflation in the near future. In view of the high level of public debt, Directors agreed that the focus of fiscal policy will need to turn toward gradual consolidation. They suggested that in the context of an acceleration in structural reforms, the authorities should consider maintaining a neutral fiscal stance in the short run to mitigate any initial negative impact on growth of the reforms.

Directors noted that recovery is not yet well established in the *euro area*, with domestic demand still weak—especially in Germany and Italy—and the resilience of export-led growth possibly at risk should the global recovery falter. Several factors should, however, support a steady—albeit moderate—pickup in activity in late 2002 and in 2003, including growth in household and corporate earnings, lower inflation—partly as a result of a stronger euro—and improvements in labor market performance over recent years. Given the hesitant recovery, and with risks to price stability having become more balanced, Directors concurred that monetary policy should remain on hold for the time being, and that the ECB should stand ready to consider interest rate cuts if activity weakens and inflation declines as expected. With budgetary positions in several countries having become more difficult, most Directors saw little room for maneuver on the fiscal front. Directors generally were of the view that in most euro-area countries, a further strengthening of fiscal positions over the medium term will still be needed to prepare for the effects of population aging and to provide scope for reductions in high tax burdens. In addition, building on the significant progress achieved in recent years, Europe should press ahead with the sustained implementation of structural reforms, especially in its labor and product markets, as these will boost productivity and growth potential. Some Directors encouraged deeper analysis of the impact of the structural reforms in Europe on potential output.

Directors welcomed the staff's analysis of external imbalances in the industrial countries during the 1990s as providing a useful framework for discussing policy responses in a multilateral setting. They noted that the significant expansion in current account imbalances among deficit countries reflects faster growth combined with buoyant expectations about future economic prospects associated with the IT revolution, which has supported real demand and fostered autonomous capital inflows. Directors agreed that existing current account imbalances are unlikely to be viable over the medium term, and that an adjustment will be needed over the coming years, with its speed likely to reflect in part underlying differences in growth prospects across countries. To enhance prospects for a smooth rotation of demand from countries in deficit to those in surplus, Directors reiterated the importance of fiscal consolidation in deficit countries, which should be combined with accelerated structural reforms in surplus countries designed to make these economies more flexible, and enhance their medium-term growth potential and demand.

Emerging Markets

Directors noted that developments and prospects among *emerging markets* are being shaped by the hesitant recovery in industrialized economies, adverse developments—including heightened risk aversion—in international financial markets, and significant economic and political uncertainties in some major economies with large external financing requirements. In particular, Directors expressed concern about the sharp deterioration of economic conditions in *Latin America,* although some countries continue to resist the region's difficulties reasonably well. They noted that this deterioration partly reflects the turmoil in Argentina and its spillover effects on some neighboring countries, notably Uruguay. The difficulties being faced by a number of Latin American economies are, however, also largely the result of interactions between domestic political uncertainties and underlying economic vulnerabilities, particularly high debt levels, large external financing requirements, and—in some countries—fragile banking systems. To reduce these vulnerabilities, Directors urged these countries to make further determined efforts to achieve sustainable improvements in fiscal positions, maintain firm monetary policies, and push ahead with wide-ranging structural reforms—including measures to strengthen banking systems and liberalize external trade.

In contrast to most other regions, activity in *emerging markets in Asia* has picked up markedly, led by strong growth in China and India and improvements among countries most oriented to the information technology sector. To reduce remaining vulnerabilities, Directors agreed that in general policy priorities across the region will need to include creating the conditions for a sustainable strengthening of domestic demand and improving the region's resilience to shocks, including through further bank and corporate restructuring, strengthening medium-term fiscal sustainability, and ensuring appropriate flexibility in exchange rate regimes. Noting the increasing contribution of intra-Asian trade to regional stability and growth, Directors also highlighted the importance of ensuring that the Asian economies remain sufficiently flexible and dynamic to take advantage of prospective changes in intraregional trade opportunities—including as a result of China's rapid growth and entry into the World Trade Organization.

Growth among most of the *European Union accession candidates in central and eastern Europe* has been relatively well sustained, aided by strong domestic demand and export growth. Although the high current account deficits in many of these countries have been readily financed, especially through direct investment, Directors suggested continued vigilance to ensure that these investment inflows are sustained. Fiscal restraint, together with structural reforms, will help underpin market confidence and support economic adjustment. Noting the recent increases in economic and political uncertainties in *Turkey*, Directors urged the authorities to maintain their commitment to macroeconomic stability and structural reforms, including improvements in bank supervision and public financial management.

Directors noted that growth in the *CIS*—especially *Russia and other countries relatively advanced with economic reforms*—has remained reasonably strong, mainly on account of robust domestic demand. The key medium-term challenge remaining for the region is to accelerate the reform process, especially among the less advanced reformers whose growth performance continues to be hampered by macroeconomic instability, lack of corporate restructuring, and an unfavorable investment climate. Directors looked forward to improved prospects for the lowest-income CIS countries, with technical and financial assistance provided under the CIS-7 Initiative supporting their reform efforts.

Directors noted that growth in *Africa* has weakened in 2002 as a result of commodity price developments, the severe drought in southern Africa, and the remaining conflicts in some countries. The expected strengthening of external demand and improvement in commodity prices are, however, expected to support a pickup in growth in 2003. Welcoming the substantial progress that many African economies have made since the mid-1990s toward macroeconomic stability, Directors agreed that the pressing

need now is to improve the overall environment for investment and growth—particularly by strengthening the economic infrastructure and the main market institutions, as well as the quality of governance. In this context, Directors looked forward to the sustained implementation, with appropriate external support, of the New Partnership for African Development (NEPAD), which embraces these key priorities. They also noted the positive contribution of the HIPC Initiative in reinforcing growth prospects and development efforts in the region.

Directors noted that, following the recent slowdown, growth in the *Middle East* is expected to pick up in the near term, assuming the global recovery gains momentum, oil prices remain firm, and the regional security situation improves. In several countries, sustaining stronger and broader-based growth will also importantly require strengthening the fiscal situation and accelerating structural reforms, especially as regards trade and price liberalization.

Agricultural Policies

Directors welcomed the essay on agricultural policies as an important contribution to the increasing body of Fund analysis demonstrating the benefits of trade liberalization for both industrial and developing countries. They noted that the extremely high level of support provided to farmers in industrial countries affects developing countries in various ways—including by depressing the world prices of commodities of interest to poor farmers and by increasing world price variability. Directors strongly encouraged industrial countries to use the opportunity provided by the Doha round of multilateral trade negotiations to reduce agricultural support and/or shift to less distorting forms of support—moves that would bring aggregate gains by increasing efficiency and real incomes in both industrial and developing countries. Directors also saw a need for food-importing poor countries to receive appropriately targeted assistance to mitigate the effects of higher food prices resulting from liberalization.

Capital Structure and Corporate Performance

Directors welcomed the essay on capital structure and corporate performance with its focus on differences in corporate structures and financial vulnerabilities across emerging market countries. Directors underscored the importance of close monitoring of the health of the corporate sector and of strengthening financial sector supervision, in particular to take account of the significant increase in corporate leverage that normally occurs as countries move from low to moderate levels of financial development. They generally agreed with the main thrust of the staff's findings that greater openness to foreign investment tends to reduce leverage and reliance on short-term debt, thus helping strengthen corporate performance—but cautioned that care should be taken to avoid currency mismatches in balance sheets.

Trade and Financial Integration

Directors welcomed the analysis of trade and financial integration. They noted the observed complementarity of trade integration and financial integration, both over time and across countries, with policy liberalization being the driving force of the integration process in the current episode of globalization. Despite the overall historical trend toward progressive liberalization, today's trade and capital account restrictions across the world continue to restrain global trade flows. Full liberalization around the globe will surely increase international trade flows significantly. Directors also agreed that trade and financial integration tend to reinforce each other. Increased trade integration is naturally accompanied by rising international financial flows, which in turn fosters financial integration. At the same time, increased financial integration fosters trade integration, as financial frictions partly explain the segmentation of global goods markets. Based on this analysis, Directors were of the view that balanced trade and financial integration is essential, since recent experience reemphasizes that an uneven pattern of integration can pose risks to macroeconomic stability. Directors also discussed, and many endorsed, the finding that—along with macroeconomic stability and domestic financial and institutional development—international financial openness reduces output volatility. A number of Directors, however, stressed that financial openness could be risky, especially if the domestic financial sector is insufficiently robust. They also noted that, while greater openness to FDI and portfolio flows is associated with lower output volatility, higher external debt ratios lead to higher output volatility in both financially open and closed economies.

STATISTICAL APPENDIX

The statistical appendix presents historical data, as well as projections. It comprises four sections: Assumptions, Data and Conventions, Classification of Countries, and Statistical Tables.

The assumptions underlying the estimates and projections for 2002–03 and the medium-term scenario for 2004–07 are summarized in the first section. The second section provides a general description of the data, and of the conventions used for calculating country group composites. The classification of countries in the various groups presented in the *World Economic Outlook* is summarized in the third section.

The last, and main, section comprises the statistical tables. Data in these tables have been compiled on the basis of information available through early September 2002. The figures for 2002 and beyond are shown with the same degree of precision as the historical figures solely for convenience; since they are projections, the same degree of accuracy is not to be inferred.

Assumptions

Real effective *exchange rates* for the advanced economies are assumed to remain constant at their average levels during the period July 19–August 16, 2002. For 2002 and 2003, these assumptions imply average U.S. dollar/SDR conversion rates of 1.293 and 1.324, U.S. dollar/euro conversion rates of 0.94 and 0.98, and U.S. dollar/yen conversion rates of 124.0 and 117.2.

Established *policies* of national authorities are assumed to be maintained. The more specific policy assumptions underlying the projections for selected advanced economies are described in Box A1.

It is assumed that the *price of oil* will average $24.40 a barrel in 2002 and $24.20 a barrel in 2003.

With regard to *interest rates*, it is assumed that the London interbank offered rate (LIBOR) on six-month U.S. dollar deposits will average 2.1 percent in 2002 and 3.2 percent in 2003; that the three-month certificate of deposit rate in Japan will average 0.1 percent in 2002 and in 2003; and that the three-month interbank deposit rate for the euro will average 3.4 percent in 2002 and 3.8 percent in 2003.

With respect to *introduction of the euro*, on December 31, 1998 the Council of the European Union decided that, effective January 1, 1999, the irrevocably fixed conversion rates between the euro and currencies of the member states adopting the euro are:

1 euro =	13.7603	Austrian schillings
=	40.3399	Belgian francs
=	1.95583	Deutsche mark
=	5.94573	Finnish markkaa
=	6.55957	French francs
=	340.750	Greek drachma[1]
=	0.787564	Irish pound
=	1,936.27	Italian lire
=	40.3399	Luxembourg francs
=	2.20371	Netherlands guilders
=	200.482	Portuguese escudos
=	166.386	Spanish pesetas

See Box 5.4 in the October 1998 *World Economic Outlook* for details on how the conversion rates were established.

Data and Conventions

Data and projections for 182 countries form the statistical basis for the *World Economic Outlook*

---

[1]The conversion rate for Greece was established prior to inclusion in the euro area on January 1, 2001.

Box A1. Economic Policy Assumptions Underlying the Projections for Selected Advanced Economies

The short-term *fiscal policy assumptions* used in the *World Economic Outlook* are based on officially announced budgets, adjusted for differences between the national authorities and the IMF staff regarding macroeconomic assumptions and projected fiscal outturns. The medium-term fiscal projections incorporate policy measures that are judged likely to be implemented. In cases where the IMF staff has insufficient information to assess the authorities' budget intentions and prospects for policy implementation, an unchanged structural primary balance is assumed, unless otherwise indicated. Specific assumptions used in some of the advanced economies follow (see also Tables 14–16 in the Statistical Appendix for data on fiscal and structural balances).[1]

United States. The fiscal projections are based on the 2003 mid-session review of the Administration's budget (July 2002), adjusted for Congressional Budget Office's baseline revisions (August 2002) and the IMF staff's macroeconomic and budget assumptions.

Japan. The projections take into account the initial FY2002 budget, the first supplementary budget of November 2001 which included additional measures of about ¥3 trillion, and the second supplementary budget of February 2002 with measures of ¥4 trillion, of which ¥2.5 trillion is central government spending and ¥1.5 trillion is local government spending.

Germany. Fiscal projections for 2002–05 are based on the national authorities' updated Stability Program of December 2001, as adjusted for (i) the IMF staff's updated macroeconomic scenario; (ii) differences between the Stability Program's estimates for fiscal developments in 2001 and the outcome in 2001; (iii) the new expenditure paths agreed under the national stability pact between the federal and local governments in May 2002, as reflected in the updated medium-term fiscal projections prepared by the *Finanzplanungsrat*—the advisory intergovernmental council that coordinates fiscal policy between the Bund and Länder—in June 2002; and (iv) recently announced changes to expenditure and taxes that are related to flood damage repair.

France. The IMF staff has assumed that, other than the tax cuts already embodied in the 2002 supplementary budget, the government's intention to reduce the tax burden by €30 billion will result in cuts spread over the 2004–07 period. Expenditures are assumed to grow at an annual real rate of 1.3 percent, as set in the latest available Stability Program (2003–05) except in 2003, when overruns in health care spending are projected to result in faster overall expenditure growth. Projections are based on the staff's macroeconomic assumptions.

Italy. Fiscal projections for 2003 and beyond are based on the authorities' targets as published in their medium term economic program released in July 2002, adjusted for differences in macroeconomic assumptions.

United Kingdom. The fiscal projections are based on the April 2002 budget report. Additionally, the projections incorporate the most recent statistical releases from the Office for National Statistics, including provisional budgetary outturns throughout May 2002. The main difference with respect to the official budgetary projections is that the staff projections are based on potential growth of 2.6 percent rather than the 2.5 percent underlying official projections. They also include an adjustment for the proceeds of the recent UMTS license auction (about 2.4 percent of GDP)

[1]The output gap is actual less potential output, as a percent of potential output. Structural balances are expressed as a percent of potential output. The structural budget balance is the budgetary position that would be observed if the level of actual output coincided with potential output. Changes in the structural budget balance consequently include effects of temporary fiscal measures, the impact of fluctuations in interest rates and debt-service costs, and other non-cyclical fluctuations in the budget balance. The computations of structural budget balances are based on IMF staff estimates of potential GDP and revenue and expenditure elasticities (see the October 1993 *World Economic Outlook*, Annex I). Net debt is defined as gross debt less financial assets of the general government, which include assets held by the social security insurance system. Estimates of the output gap and of the structural balance are subject to significant margins of uncertainty.

received in fiscal year 2000/01 to conform to the Eurostat accounting guidelines. These proceeds are not included in the computation of the structural balance.

Canada. The fiscal outlook assumes tax and expenditure policies in line with those outlined in the government's 2001 budget, announced in December 2001, adjusted for the staff's economic projections. Over the medium term, the staff assumes that the federal government budget will be in surplus by an amount equivalent to the contingency reserve in the budget. The staff assumes that the contingency reserve is restored to its pre-2001 budget level of Can$3 billion after FY 2003/04. The consolidated fiscal position for the provinces is assumed to evolve in line with their stated medium-term targets.

Australia. The fiscal projections through the fiscal year 2005/06 are based on the 2002/03 budget, which was published by the Australian Treasury in May 2002. For the remainder of the projection period, the IMF staff assumes unchanged policies.

Netherlands. Projections for 2002 reflect the 2002 budget adjusted for the IMF staff's macroeconomic projections. For 2003–06, the forecasts are based on the authorities' multiyear framework as laid out in the new cabinet's coalition agreement adjusted for the staff's macroeconomic projections. The framework in based on a binding multiyear ceiling on real expenditure.

Portugal. The fiscal projections for 2002 take into account the authorities' revised estimates for 2001, assume that 2002 fiscal measures yield the effects estimated by the authorities, and adjust revenue projections for differences between the authorities' and staff's macroeconomic framework. Fiscal projections for 2003–07 assume a constant structural primary balance.

Spain. Fiscal projections through 2005 are based on the policies outlined in the national authorities' updated Stability Program of December 2001. Projections for subsequent years assume no significant changes in those policies.

Sweden. Projections for 2002 are based on the central government budget outturn for the first quarter of 2002, and the policies and projections (for general government) underlying the Spring Budget Bill published in April 2002. The projections also take account of the authorities' medium-term fiscal objective of a general government surplus of 2 percent of GDP over the economic cycle, the Ministry of Finance's medium-term fiscal projections for 2003–04, and the nominal ceilings on central government expenditures for the same period.

Switzerland. Projections for 2002 are based on the official budget plans, including supplementary budgets, and preliminary figures on the budget outturn. The projections for 2003–05 are based on official budget plans that include measures to strengthen the finances of social security. Beyond 2005, the general government's structural balance is assumed to remain unchanged.

Monetary policy assumptions are based on the established policy framework in each country. In most cases, this implies a nonaccommodative stance over the business cycle: official interest rates will therefore increase when economic indicators suggest that prospective inflation will rise above its acceptable rate or range; and they will decrease when indicators suggest that prospective inflation will not exceed the acceptable rate or range, that prospective output growth is below its potential rate, and that the margin of slack in the economy is significant. On this basis, the projected path for the London interbank offered rate (LIBOR) on six-month U.S. dollar deposits—2.1 percent on average in 2002 and 3.2 percent in 2003—and the federal funds target rate are broadly consistent with market expectations as of early September 2002. The interest rate on six-month Japanese yen deposits is assumed to average 0.1 percent in 2002 and 0.1 percent in 2003, with the current monetary policy framework being maintained. The rate on six-month euro deposits is assumed to average 3.4 percent in 2002 and 3.8 in 2003. Changes in interest rate assumptions compared with the April 2002 *World Economic Outlook* are summarized in Table 1.1.

(the World Economic Outlook database). The data are maintained jointly by the IMF's Research Department and area departments, with the latter regularly updating country projections based on consistent global assumptions.

Although national statistical agencies are the ultimate providers of historical data and definitions, international organizations are also involved in statistical issues, with the objective of harmonizing methodologies for the national compilation of statistics, including the analytical frameworks, concepts, definitions, classifications, and valuation procedures used in the production of economic statistics. The *World Economic Outlook* database reflects information from both national source agencies and international organizations.

The completion in 1993 of the comprehensive revision of the standardized *System of National Accounts 1993* (*SNA*) and the IMF's *Balance of Payments Manual* (*BPM*) represented important improvements in the standards of economic statistics and analysis.[2] The IMF was actively involved in both projects, particularly the new *Balance of Payments Manual*, which reflects the IMF's special interest in countries' external positions. Key changes introduced with the new *Manual* were summarized in Box 13 of the May 1994 *World Economic Outlook*. The process of adapting country balance of payments data to the definitions of the new *BPM* began with the May 1995 *World Economic Outlook*. However, full concordance with the *BPM* is ultimately dependent on the provision by national statistical compilers of revised country data, and hence the *World Economic Outlook* estimates are still only partially adapted to the *BPM*.

The members of the European Union have recently adopted a harmonized system for the compilation of the national accounts, referred to as ESA 1995. All national accounts data from 1995 onward are now presented on the basis of the new system. Revision by national authorities of data prior to 1995 to conform to the new system has progressed, but has in some cases not been completed. In such cases, historical *World Economic Outlook* data have been carefully adjusted to avoid breaks in the series. Users of EU national accounts data prior to 1995 should nevertheless exercise caution until such time as the revision of historical data by national statistical agencies has been fully completed. See Box 1.2, *Revisions in National Accounts Methodologies,* in the May 2000 *World Economic Outlook*.

Composite data for country groups in the *World Economic Outlook* are either sums or weighted averages of data for individual countries. Unless otherwise indicated, multiyear averages of growth rates are expressed as compound annual rates of change. Arithmetically weighted averages are used for all data except inflation and money growth for the developing and transition country groups, for which geometric averages are used. The following conventions apply.

- Country group composites for exchange rates, interest rates, and the growth rates of monetary aggregates are weighted by GDP converted to U.S. dollars at market exchange rates (averaged over the preceding three years) as a share of group GDP.
- Composites for other data relating to the domestic economy, whether growth rates or ratios, are weighted by GDP valued at purchasing power parities (PPPs) as a share of total world or group GDP.[3]
- Composites for data relating to the domestic economy for the euro area (12 member countries throughout the entire period unless oth-

[2]Commission of the European Communities, International Monetary Fund, Organization for Economic Cooperation and Development, United Nations, and World Bank, *System of National Accounts 1993* (Brussels/Luxembourg, New York, Paris, and Washington, 1993); and International Monetary Fund, *Balance of Payments Manual, Fifth Edition* (Washington: IMF, 1993).

[3]See Box A1 of the May 2000 *World Economic Outlook* for a summary of the revised PPP-based weights and Annex IV of the May 1993 *World Economic Outlook*. See also Anne Marie Gulde and Marianne Schulze-Ghattas, "Purchasing Power Parity Based Weights for the *World Economic Outlook,*" in *Staff Studies for the World Economic Outlook* (International Monetary Fund, December 1993), pp. 106–23.

erwise noted) are aggregates of national source data using weights based on 1995 ECU exchange rates.

- Composite unemployment rates and employment growth are weighted by labor force as a share of group labor force.
- Composites relating to the external economy are sums of individual country data after conversion to U.S. dollars at the average market exchange rates in the years indicated for balance of payments data and at end-of-year market exchange rates for debt denominated in currencies other than U.S. dollars. Composites of changes in foreign trade volumes and prices, however, are arithmetic averages of percentage changes for individual countries weighted by the U.S. dollar value of exports or imports as a share of total world or group exports or imports (in the preceding year).

For central and eastern European countries, external transactions in nonconvertible currencies (through 1990) are converted to U.S. dollars at the implicit U.S. dollar/ruble conversion rates obtained from each country's national currency exchange rate for the U.S. dollar and for the ruble.

Classification of Countries

Summary of the Country Classification

The country classification in the *World Economic Outlook* divides the world into three major groups: advanced economies, developing countries, and countries in transition.[4] Rather than being based on strict criteria, economic or otherwise, this classification has evolved over time with the objective of facilitating analysis by providing a reasonably meaningful organization of data. A few countries are presently not included in these groups, either because they are not IMF members, and their economies are not monitored by the IMF, or because databases

have not yet been compiled. Cuba and the Democratic People's Republic of Korea are examples of countries that are not IMF members, whereas San Marino, among the advanced economies, is an example of an economy for which a database has not been completed. It should also be noted that, owing to a lack of data, only three of the former republics of the dissolved Socialist Federal Republic of Yugoslavia (Croatia, the former Yugoslav Republic of Macedonia, and Slovenia) are included in the group composites for countries in transition.

Each of the three main country groups is further divided into a number of subgroups. Among the advanced economies, the seven largest in terms of GDP, collectively referred to as the major advanced countries, are distinguished as a subgroup, and so are the 15 current members of the European Union, the 12 members of the euro area, and the four newly industrialized Asian economies. The developing countries are classified by region, as well as into a number of analytical and other groups. A regional breakdown is also used for the classification of the countries in transition. Table A provides an overview of these standard groups in the *World Economic Outlook*, showing the number of countries in each group and the average 2001 shares of groups in aggregate PPP-valued GDP, total exports of goods and services, and population.

General Features and Compositions of Groups in the *World Economic Outlook* Classification

Advanced Economies

The 29 advanced economies are listed in Table B. The seven largest in terms of GDP—the United States, Japan, Germany, France, Italy, the United Kingdom, and Canada—constitute the subgroup of *major advanced economies*, often

---

[4]As used here, the term "country" does not in all cases refer to a territorial entity that is a state as understood by international law and practice. It also covers some territorial entities that are not states, but for which statistical data are maintained on a separate and independent basis.

Table A. Classification by *World Economic Outlook* Groups and Their Shares in Aggregate GDP, Exports of Goods and Services, and Population, 2001[1]

(Percent of total for group or world)

	Number of Countries	GDP		Exports of Goods and Services		Population	
		Share of total for					
		Advanced economies	World	Advanced economies	World	Advanced economies	World
Advanced Economies	**29**	**100.0**	**56.3**	**100.0**	**75.1**	**100.0**	**15.4**
Major advanced economies	7	79.4	44.7	61.9	46.5	74.3	11.5
United States		38.0	21.4	18.1	13.6	29.7	4.6
Japan		13.0	7.3	8.0	6.0	13.6	2.1
Germany		8.0	4.5	11.6	8.7	8.8	1.4
France		5.7	3.2	6.6	5.0	6.4	1.0
Italy		5.5	3.1	5.3	4.0	6.2	0.9
United Kingdom		5.6	3.1	6.8	5.1	6.4	1.0
Canada		3.5	2.0	5.4	4.1	3.3	0.5
Other advanced economies	22	20.6	11.6	38.1	28.6	25.7	4.0
Memorandum							
European Union	15	35.4	19.9	50.2	37.7	40.3	6.2
Euro area	12	28.3	15.9	40.3	30.3	32.4	5.0
Newly industrialized Asian countries	4	5.9	3.3	12.5	9.4	8.6	1.3
		Developing countries	World	Developing countries	World	Developing countries	World
Developing countries	**125**	**100.0**	**37.6**	**100.0**	**20.3**	**100.0**	**78.0**
Regional groups							
Africa	51	8.5	3.2	9.9	2.0	16.0	12.5
Sub-Sahara	48	6.6	2.5	7.2	1.5	14.5	11.3
Excluding Nigeria and South Africa	46	3.8	1.4	3.5	0.7	10.8	8.4
Developing Asia	25	59.1	22.2	46.1	9.3	66.9	52.2
China		32.2	12.1	19.7	4.0	26.9	21.0
India		12.5	4.7	4.4	0.9	21.4	16.7
Other developing Asia	23	14.4	5.4	22.1	4.5	18.6	14.5
Middle East and Turkey	16	10.6	4.0	20.7	4.2	6.4	5.0
Western Hemisphere	33	21.8	8.2	23.3	4.7	10.7	8.4
Analytical groups							
By source of export earnings							
Fuel	18	9.3	3.5	20.4	4.1	7.0	5.5
Nonfuel	109	90.7	34.1	79.6	16.1	93.0	72.5
Of which, primary products	42	6.3	2.4	6.0	1.2	11.1	8.6
By external financing source							
Net debtor countries	113	97.3	36.5	88.8	18.0	99.3	77.4
Of which, official financing	43	5.6	2.1	5.4	1.1	13.9	10.8
Net debtor countries by debt-servicing experience							
Countries with arrears and/or rescheduling during 1994–98	55	24.6	9.2	24.0	4.9	29.2	22.8
Other groups							
Heavily indebted poor countries	40	5.1	1.9	4.6	0.9	14.0	10.9
Middle East and north Africa	21	10.5	3.9	19.8	4.0	7.5	5.9
		Countries in transition	World	Countries in transition	World	Countries in transition	World
Countries in transition	**29**	**100.0**	**6.2**	**100.0**	**4.7**	**100.0**	**6.6**
Central and eastern Europe	16	37.6	2.3	52.5	2.4	28.8	1.9
CIS and Mongolia	13	62.4	3.8	47.5	2.2	71.2	4.7
Russia		42.8	2.6	32.2	1.5	36.4	2.4
Excluding Russia	11	19.6	1.2	15.3	0.7	34.7	2.3

[1]The GDP shares are based on the purchasing-power-parity (PPP) valuation of country GDPs.

Table B. Advanced Economies by Subgroup

	European Union		Euro Area	Newly Industrialized Asian Economies	Other Countries
Major advanced economies	France Germany Italy United Kingdom		France Germany Italy		Canada Japan United States
Other advanced economies	Austria Belgium Denmark Finland Greece Ireland	Luxembourg Netherlands Portugal Spain Sweden	Austria Belgium Finland Greece Ireland Luxembourg Netherlands Portugal Spain	Hong Kong SAR[1] Korea Singapore Taiwan Province of China	Australia Cyprus Iceland Israel New Zealand Norway Switzerland

[1]On July 1, 1997, Hong Kong was returned to the People's Republic of China and became a Special Administrative Region of China.

referred to as the Group of Seven (G-7) countries. The current members of the *European Union* (15 countries), the euro area (12 countries), and the *newly industrialized Asian economies* are also distinguished as subgroups. Composite data shown in the tables for the European Union and the euro area cover the current members for all years, even though the membership has increased over time.

In 1991 and subsequent years, data for *Germany* refer to west Germany *and* the eastern Länder (i.e., the former German Democratic Republic). Before 1991, economic data are not available on a unified basis or in a consistent manner. Hence, in tables featuring data expressed as annual percent change, these apply to west Germany in years up to and including 1991, but to unified Germany from 1992 onward. In general, data on national accounts and domestic economic and financial activity through 1990 cover west Germany only, whereas data for the central government and balance of payments apply to west Germany through June 1990 and to unified Germany thereafter.

Developing Countries

The group of developing countries (125 countries) includes all countries that are not classified as advanced economies or as countries in

transition, together with a few dependent territories for which adequate statistics are available.

The *regional breakdowns* of developing countries in the *World Economic Outlook* conform to the IMF's *International Financial Statistics (IFS)* classification—*Africa, Asia, Europe, Middle East,* and *Western Hemisphere*—with one important exception. Because all of the non-advanced countries in Europe except Malta and Turkey are included in the group of countries in transition, the *World Economic Outlook* classification places these two countries in a combined *Middle East and Turkey* region. In both classifications, Egypt and the Libyan Arab Jamahiriya are included in this region, not in Africa. Three additional regional groupings—two of them constituting part of Africa and one a subgroup of Asia—are included in the *World Economic Outlook* because of their analytical significance. These are *sub-Sahara, sub-Sahara excluding Nigeria and South Africa,* and *Asia excluding China and India.*

The developing countries are also classified according to *analytical criteria* and into *other groups.* The analytical criteria reflect countries' composition of export earnings and other income from abroad, a distinction between net creditor and net debtor countries, and, for the net debtor countries, financial criteria based on external financing source and experience with external debt servicing. Included as

Table C. Developing Countries by Region and Main Source of Export Earnings

	Fuel	Nonfuel, Of Which Primary Products		Fuel	Nonfuel, Of Which Primary Products
Africa **Sub-Sahara**	Angola Congo, Rep. of Equatorial Guinea Gabon Nigeria	Benin Botswana Burkina Faso Burundi Central African Rep. Chad Congo, Democratic Rep. of Côte d'Ivoire Gambia, The Ghana Guinea Guinea-Bissau Liberia Madagascar Malawi Mali Mauritania Namibia Niger Somalia Sudan Swaziland Tanzania Togo Zambia Zimbabwe	**Developing Asia**	Brunei Darussalam	Bhutan Cambodia Myanmar Papua New Guinea Solomon Islands Vanuatu Vietnam
			Middle East, and Turkey	Bahrain Iran, Islamic Rep. of Iraq Kuwait Libya Oman Qatar Saudi Arabia United Arab Emirates	
			Western Hemisphere	Trinidad and Tobago Venezuela	Belize Bolivia Chile Guyana Honduras Nicaragua Paraguay Peru Suriname
North Africa	Algeria				

"other groups" are currently the heavily indebted poor countries (HIPCs), and Middle East and north Africa (MENA). The detailed composition of developing countries in the regional, analytical, and other groups is shown in Tables C through E.

The first analytical criterion, by *source of export earnings*, distinguishes between categories: *fuel* (Standard International Trade Classification— SITC 3) and nonfuel and then focuses on *nonfuel primary products* (SITC 0, 1, 2, 4, and 68).

The financial criteria focus on *net creditor* and *net debtor countries* which are differentiated on the basis of two additional financial criteria: by

official external financing and by *experience with debt servicing.*[5]

The *other groups* of developing countries (see Table E) constitute the HIPCs and MENA countries. The first group comprises 40 of the countries (all except Nigeria) considered by the IMF and the World Bank for their debt initiative, known as the HIPC Initiative.[6] Middle East and north Africa, also referred to as the MENA countries, is a *World Economic Outlook* group, whose composition straddles the Africa and Middle East and Europe regions. It is defined as the Arab League countries plus the Islamic Republic of Iran.

[5]During 1994–98, 55 countries incurred external payments arrears or entered into official or commercial bank debt-rescheduling agreements. This group of countries is referred to as *countries with arrears and/or rescheduling during 1994–98.*

[6]See David Andrews, Anthony R. Boote, Syed S. Rizavi, and Sukwinder Singh, *Debt Relief for Low-Income Countries: The Enhanced HIPC Initiative,* IMF Pamphlet Series, No. 51 (Washington: International Monetary Fund, November 1999)

Table D. Developing Countries by Region and Main External Financing Source

Countries	Net Debtor Countries		Countries	Net Debtor Countries	
	By main external financing source			By main external financing source	
	Net debtor countries	Of which official financing		Net debtor countries	Of which official financing
Africa			**Developing Asia**		
Sub-Sahara			Afghanistan, Islamic State of	•	
Angola	•		Bangladesh	•	•
Benin	•	•	Bhutan	•	•
Burkina Faso	•	•	Cambodia	•	•
Burundi	•	•	China	•	
Cameroon	•	•	Fiji	•	
Cape Verde	•	•	India	•	
Central African Rep.	•	•	Indonesia	•	
Chad	•	•	Kiribati	•	
Comoros	•	•	Lao People's Democratic Rep.	•	•
Congo, Democratic Rep. of	•	•	Malaysia	•	
Congo, Rep. of	•		Maldives	•	
Côte d'Ivoire	•		Myanmar	•	
Djibouti	•		Nepal	•	•
Equatorial Guinea	•		Pakistan	•	
Eritrea	•		Papua New Guinea	•	
Ethiopia	•	•	Philippines	•	
Gabon	•	•	Samoa	•	•
Gambia, The	•	•	Solomon Islands	•	
Ghana	•		Sri Lanka	•	•
Guinea	•	•	Thailand	•	
Guinea-Bissau	•	•	Tonga	•	•
Kenya	•		Vanuatu	•	
Lesotho	•		Vietnam	•	
Liberia	•	•			
Madagascar	•	•	**Middle East and Turkey**		
Malawi	•	•	Bahrain	•	
Mali	•	•	Egypt	•	
Mauritania	•	•	Iran, Islamic Rep. of	•	
Mauritius	•		Iraq	•	
Mozambique, Rep. of	•	•	Jordan	•	
Namibia	•		Lebanon	•	•
Niger	•	•	Malta	•	
Nigeria	•		Oman	•	•
Rwanda	•	•	Syrian Arab Rep.	•	
São Tomé and Príncipe	•	•	Turkey	•	
Senegal	•	•	Yemen, Rep. of	•	
Seychelles	•				
Sierra Leone	•		**Western Hemisphere**		
Somalia	•		Antigua and Barbuda	•	•
South Africa	•		Argentina	•	•
Sudan	•		Bahamas, The	•	•
Tanzania	•	•	Barbados	•	
Togo	•	•	Belize	•	•
Uganda	•	•	Bolivia	•	
Zambia	•	•	Brazil	•	•
Zimbabwe	•		Chile	•	•
North Africa			Colombia	•	•
Algeria	•	•	Costa Rica	•	•
Morocco	•		Dominica	•	
Tunisia	•		Dominican Rep.	•	•
			Ecuador	•	•
			El Salvador	•	
			Grenada	•	

Table D (concluded)

| Countries | Net Debtor Countries | | Countries | Net Debtor Countries | |
| | By main external financing source | | | By main external financing source | |
	Net debtor countries	Of which official financing		Net debtor countries	Of which official financing
Guatemala	•	•	Paraguay	•	
Guyana	•	•	Peru	•	
Haiti	•	•	St. Kitts and Nevis	•	
Honduras	•	•	St. Lucia	•	
Jamaica	•		St. Vincent and the Grenadines	•	
Mexico	•	•	Suriname	•	
Netherlands Antilles	•	•	Trinidad and Tobago	•	
Nicaragua	•	•	Uruguay	•	
Panama	•		Venezuela	•	

Table E. Other Developing Country Groups

Countries	Heavily Indebted Poor Countries	Middle East and North Africa	Countries	Heavily Indebted Poor Countries	Middle East and North Africa
Africa			Tanzania	•	
Sub-Sahara			Togo	•	
Angola	•		Uganda	•	
Benin	•		Zambia	•	
Burkina Faso	•		**North Africa**		
Burundi	•		Algeria		•
Cameroon	•		Morocco		•
Central African Rep.	•		Tunisia		•
Chad	•		**Developing Asia**		
Congo, Democratic Rep. of	•		Lao People's Democratic Rep.	•	
Congo, Rep. of	•		Myanmar	•	
Côte d'Ivoire	•		Vietnam	•	
Djibouti		•	**Middle East and Turkey**		
Ethiopia	•		Bahrain		•
Gambia, The	•		Egypt		•
Ghana	•		Iran, Islamic Rep. of		•
Guinea	•		Iraq		•
Guinea-Bissau	•		Jordan		•
Kenya	•		Kuwait		•
Liberia	•		Lebanon		•
Madagascar	•		Liberia	•	
Malawi	•		Libya		•
Mali	•		Oman		•
Mauritania	•	•	Qatar		•
Mozambique, Rep. of	•		Saudi Arabia		•
Niger	•		Syrian Arab Rep.		•
Rwanda	•		United Arab Emirates		•
São Tomé and Príncipe	•		Yemen, Rep. of	•	•
Senegal	•		**Western Hemisphere**		
Sierra Leone	•		Bolivia	•	
Somalia	•	•	Guyana	•	
Sudan	•	•	Honduras	•	
			Nicaragua	•	

Table F. Countries in Transition by Region

Central and Eastern Europe		Commonwealth of Independent States and Mongolia
Albania	Lithuania	Armenia
Bosnia and Herzegovina	Macedonia, former Yugoslav Republic of	Azerbaijan
Bulgaria	Poland	Belarus
Croatia	Romania	Georgia
Czech Republic	Slovak Republic	Kazakhstan
Estonia	Slovenia	Kyrgyz Republic
Hungary	Yugoslavia, Federal Republic of (Serbia/Montenegro)	Moldova
Latvia		Mongolia
		Russia
		Tajikistan
		Turkmenistan
		Ukraine
		Uzbekistan

Countries in Transition

The group of countries in transition (29 countries) is divided into two regional subgroups: *central and eastern Europe, and the Commonwealth of Independent States and Mongolia.* The detailed country composition is shown in Table F.

One common characteristic of these countries is the transitional state of their economies from a centrally administered system to one based on market principles. Another is that this transition involves the transformation of sizable industrial sectors whose capital stocks have proven largely obsolete. Although several other countries are also "in transition" from partially command-based economic systems toward market-based systems (including China, Cambodia, the Lao People's Democratic Republic, Vietnam, and a number of African countries), most of these are largely rural, low-income economies for whom the principal challenge is one of economic development. These countries are therefore classified in the developing country group rather than in the group of countries in transition.

List of Tables

Table 1. Summary of World Output[1]
(Annual percent change)

	Ten-Year Averages 1984–93	Ten-Year Averages 1994–2003	1994	1995	1996	1997	1998	1999	2000	2001	2002	2003
World	**3.3**	**3.5**	**3.7**	**3.7**	**4.0**	**4.2**	**2.8**	**3.6**	**4.7**	**2.2**	**2.8**	**3.7**
Advanced economies	**3.2**	**2.7**	**3.4**	**2.7**	**3.0**	**3.4**	**2.7**	**3.4**	**3.8**	**0.8**	**1.7**	**2.5**
United States	3.2	3.2	4.0	2.7	3.6	4.4	4.3	4.1	3.8	0.3	2.2	2.6
European Union	2.4	2.4	2.8	2.4	1.7	2.6	2.9	2.8	3.5	1.6	1.1	2.3
Japan	3.7	1.0	0.9	1.7	3.6	1.8	−1.2	0.8	2.4	−0.3	−0.5	1.1
Other advanced economies	4.7	4.1	5.9	5.0	4.3	4.6	1.2	5.9	6.0	1.3	3.6	3.9
Developing countries	**5.1**	**5.2**	**6.7**	**6.2**	**6.5**	**5.9**	**3.5**	**4.0**	**5.7**	**3.9**	**4.2**	**5.2**
Regional groups												
Africa	2.0	3.4	2.3	3.0	5.6	3.1	3.4	2.8	3.0	3.5	3.1	4.2
Developing Asia	7.6	6.8	9.7	9.0	8.3	6.6	4.0	6.1	6.7	5.6	6.1	6.3
Middle East and Turkey[2]	3.5	3.6	0.5	4.4	4.7	6.2	3.6	1.2	6.1	1.5	3.6	4.7
Western Hemisphere	2.9	2.5	5.0	1.8	3.6	5.2	2.3	0.2	4.0	0.6	−0.6	3.0
Analytical groups												
By source of export earnings												
Fuel	2.6	3.2	0.4	3.3	3.4	5.4	2.8	1.5	5.2	4.1	2.2	4.3
Nonfuel	5.4	5.4	7.4	6.5	6.8	5.9	3.6	4.2	5.8	3.9	4.4	5.3
of which, primary products	3.1	4.3	5.3	6.5	5.6	5.5	3.0	2.6	3.6	2.8	3.2	4.7
By external financing source												
Net debtor countries	5.2	5.3	6.9	6.3	6.7	5.9	3.5	4.1	5.7	3.9	4.3	5.3
of which, official financing	2.4	4.2	2.5	5.3	5.3	4.3	3.9	4.0	3.9	4.3	3.8	4.8
Net debtor countries by debt-servicing experience												
Countries with arrears and/or rescheduling during 1994–98	3.0	3.7	4.7	5.2	5.0	4.6	−0.6	2.3	4.6	3.3	3.4	4.3
Countries in transition	**−1.4**	**1.3**	**−8.5**	**−1.6**	**−0.5**	**1.6**	**−0.7**	**3.7**	**6.6**	**5.0**	**3.9**	**4.5**
Central and eastern Europe	...	3.3	3.2	5.2	4.1	2.6	2.4	2.2	3.8	3.0	2.7	3.8
Commonwealth of Independent States and Mongolia	...	0.1	−14.5	−5.5	−3.3	1.1	−2.8	4.6	8.4	6.3	4.6	4.9
Russia	...	0.2	−13.5	−4.2	−3.4	0.9	−4.9	5.4	9.0	5.0	4.4	4.9
Excluding Russia	...	0.1	−16.6	−8.6	−3.1	1.5	1.6	2.8	6.9	8.9	5.2	4.9
Memorandum												
Median growth rate												
Advanced economies	3.1	3.1	4.1	2.9	3.6	3.7	3.5	3.6	4.0	1.4	1.6	2.5
Developing countries	3.5	3.9	3.9	4.5	4.6	4.8	3.7	3.5	4.0	2.8	3.0	4.0
Countries in transition	−1.3	3.0	−2.7	−0.8	3.1	3.7	3.9	3.3	5.3	5.0	4.3	4.8
Output per capita												
Advanced economies	2.5	2.2	2.7	2.1	2.3	2.8	2.1	2.9	3.3	0.3	1.2	2.1
Developing countries	3.1	3.5	5.0	4.4	4.8	4.2	1.9	2.4	4.1	2.3	2.6	3.7
Countries in transition	−2.0	1.5	−8.5	−1.6	−0.4	1.7	−0.6	3.8	6.9	5.3	4.2	4.8
World growth based on market exchange rates	**2.9**	**2.7**	**2.9**	**2.8**	**3.3**	**3.5**	**2.2**	**3.1**	**3.9**	**1.1**	**1.7**	**2.8**
Value of world output in billions of U.S. dollars												
At market exchange rates	19,214	30,357	26,261	29,120	29,861	29,728	29,527	30,593	31,374	30,995	32,059	34,049
At purchasing power parities	24,205	41,420	32,170	33,996	36,032	38,241	39,729	41,691	44,631	46,742	48,853	52,114

[1]Real GDP.
[2]Includes Malta.

167

Table 2. Advanced Economies: Real GDP and Total Domestic Demand

(Annual percent change)

	Ten-Year Averages		1994	1995	1996	1997	1998	1999	2000	2001	2002	2003	Fourth Quarter[1]		
	1984–93	1994–2003											2001	2002	2003
Real GDP															
Advanced economies	**3.2**	**2.7**	**3.4**	**2.7**	**3.0**	**3.4**	**2.7**	**3.4**	**3.8**	**0.8**	**1.7**	**2.5**	. . .	. . .	. . .
Major advanced economies	3.0	2.5	3.1	2.4	2.8	3.2	2.8	3.0	3.4	0.6	1.4	2.3	−0.3	2.3	2.4
United States	3.2	3.2	4.0	2.7	3.6	4.4	4.3	4.1	3.8	0.3	2.2	2.6	0.1	2.6	3.1
Japan	3.7	1.0	0.9	1.7	3.6	1.8	−1.2	0.8	2.4	−0.3	−0.5	1.1	−3.2	1.6	0.7
Germany	2.8	1.6	2.3	1.7	0.8	1.4	2.0	2.0	2.9	0.0	0.5	2.0	0.1	1.6	2.0
France	2.0	2.3	1.9	1.8	1.1	1.9	3.5	3.2	4.2	1.8	1.2	2.3	0.2	2.4	2.2
Italy	2.1	1.9	2.2	2.9	1.1	2.0	1.8	1.6	2.9	1.8	0.7	2.3	0.6	1.8	2.1
United Kingdom	2.4	2.8	4.7	2.9	2.6	3.4	2.9	2.4	3.1	1.9	1.7	2.4	1.5	2.6	1.9
Canada	2.6	3.6	4.8	2.8	1.6	4.2	4.1	5.4	4.5	1.5	3.4	3.4	0.8	4.2	3.3
Other advanced economies	3.8	3.7	4.6	4.3	3.8	4.3	2.2	5.0	5.3	1.6	2.6	3.3	. . .	. . .	. . .
Spain	2.9	3.2	2.4	2.8	2.4	4.0	4.3	4.2	4.2	2.7	2.0	2.7	2.3	2.1	3.2
Netherlands	2.7	2.8	3.2	2.3	3.0	3.9	4.3	4.0	3.4	1.2	0.4	2.0	0.2	1.0	2.4
Belgium	2.2	2.4	3.2	2.5	1.2	3.6	2.2	3.0	4.0	1.0	0.6	2.2	. . .	. . .	. . .
Sweden	1.6	2.8	4.1	3.7	1.1	2.1	3.6	4.5	3.6	1.2	1.6	2.5	0.7	2.0	2.9
Austria	2.3	2.1	2.6	1.6	2.0	1.6	3.5	2.8	3.0	1.0	0.9	2.3	. . .	. . .	. . .
Denmark	1.6	2.6	5.5	2.8	2.5	3.0	2.5	2.3	3.0	1.0	1.5	2.2	0.3	2.1	2.0
Finland	1.2	3.8	4.0	3.8	4.0	6.3	5.3	4.1	5.6	0.7	1.1	3.0	−1.2	3.5	2.5
Greece[2]	1.8	3.2	2.0	2.1	2.4	3.6	3.4	3.6	4.1	4.1	3.7	3.2	. . .	. . .	. . .
Portugal	2.9	2.8	2.4	2.9	3.7	3.8	4.7	3.4	3.2	1.7	0.4	1.5	1.0	0.1	1.5
Ireland	3.4	8.0	5.8	10.0	7.8	10.8	8.6	10.9	11.5	5.9	3.8	5.3	. . .	. . .	. . .
Luxembourg	6.2	5.1	4.1	3.5	3.6	9.0	5.8	6.0	7.5	3.5	2.7	5.1	. . .	. . .	. . .
Switzerland	1.8	1.3	0.5	0.5	0.3	1.7	2.4	1.6	3.0	0.9	—	1.9	−0.2	0.7	2.3
Norway	2.9	3.2	5.3	4.6	5.3	5.2	2.6	2.1	2.4	1.4	1.7	1.9	. . .	. . .	. . .
Israel	4.5	3.6	8.6	6.8	4.7	3.3	3.0	2.6	7.4	−0.9	−1.5	1.8	. . .	. . .	. . .
Iceland	2.1	3.2	4.5	0.1	5.2	4.6	5.0	3.6	5.5	3.1	−0.5	1.7	. . .	. . .	. . .
Cyprus	5.8	4.1	5.9	6.1	1.9	2.5	5.0	4.5	5.1	4.0	2.5	4.0	. . .	. . .	. . .
Korea	8.2	5.7	8.3	8.9	6.8	5.0	−6.7	10.9	9.3	3.0	6.3	5.9	3.7	6.5	5.3
Australia	3.7	4.0	4.8	3.5	4.3	3.7	5.2	4.8	3.1	2.6	4.0	3.8	4.2	4.2	3.7
Taiwan Province of China	8.3	4.7	7.1	6.4	6.1	6.7	4.6	5.4	5.9	−1.9	3.3	4.0	−1.6	4.0	3.7
Hong Kong SAR	6.5	3.1	5.4	3.9	4.5	5.0	−5.3	3.0	10.4	0.2	1.5	3.4	−1.7	3.8	2.4
Singapore	7.5	5.8	11.4	8.0	7.7	8.5	−0.1	6.9	10.3	−2.0	3.6	4.2	−6.6	6.1	3.0
New Zealand	2.3	3.2	5.8	4.3	3.6	2.2	−0.2	3.9	3.8	2.5	3.0	2.9	3.1	3.4	2.1
Memorandum															
European Union	2.4	2.4	2.8	2.4	1.7	2.6	2.9	2.8	3.5	1.6	1.1	2.3	. . .	. . .	. . .
Euro area	2.4	2.2	2.4	2.2	1.4	2.3	2.9	2.8	3.5	1.5	0.9	2.3	0.4	1.9	2.3
Newly industrialized Asian economies	8.0	5.1	7.7	7.5	6.3	5.8	−2.4	8.0	8.5	0.8	4.7	4.9	1.0	5.7	4.5
Real total domestic demand															
Advanced economies	**3.2**	**2.8**	**3.4**	**2.7**	**3.0**	**3.2**	**3.0**	**4.0**	**3.8**	**0.7**	**1.8**	**2.6**	. . .	. . .	. . .
Major advanced economies	3.0	2.7	3.1	2.2	2.8	3.1	3.5	3.8	3.6	0.6	1.5	2.4	−0.4	2.4	2.5
United States	3.2	3.6	4.4	2.5	3.7	4.7	5.4	5.0	4.4	0.4	2.7	2.7	0.1	3.0	3.3
Japan	3.8	1.0	1.1	2.3	4.1	0.9	−1.5	1.0	1.9	0.4	−1.3	1.0	−2.7	0.6	0.8
Germany	2.7	1.3	2.3	1.7	0.3	0.6	2.4	2.8	1.8	−0.8	−0.7	2.3	−1.6	1.3	1.5
France	2.0	2.3	1.8	1.7	0.7	0.6	4.1	3.7	4.3	1.6	1.3	2.7	−0.1	2.7	2.6
Italy	2.1	2.0	1.7	2.0	0.9	2.7	3.1	3.0	2.1	1.6	0.9	2.1	0.3	1.9	2.5
United Kingdom	2.6	3.2	3.7	2.0	3.1	3.9	5.0	3.7	4.0	2.3	2.4	2.4	1.8	2.6	2.2
Canada	2.6	3.0	2.3	1.2	0.9	5.7	2.4	4.4	5.0	1.3	3.2	3.7	0.1	5.5	3.0
Other advanced economies	4.0	3.4	4.7	4.6	3.8	3.6	1.1	5.1	4.5	0.8	2.7	3.3	. . .	. . .	. . .
Memorandum															
European Union	2.5	2.4	2.4	2.2	1.4	2.3	4.0	3.4	3.2	1.2	1.0	2.4	. . .	. . .	. . .
Euro area	2.4	2.1	2.1	2.1	1.0	1.8	3.6	3.4	2.9	0.9	0.5	2.5	−0.1	1.9	2.2
Newly industrialized Asian economies	8.3	4.0	8.5	7.8	6.9	3.9	−9.2	7.6	7.3	−0.9	4.7	4.8	. . .	. . .	. . .

[1]From fourth quarter of preceding year.
[2]Based on revised national accounts for 1988 onward.

Table 3. Advanced Economies: Components of Real GDP
(Annual percent change)

	Ten-Year Averages		1994	1995	1996	1997	1998	1999	2000	2001	2002	2003
	1984–93	1994–2003										
Private consumer expenditure												
Advanced economies	**3.2**	**2.9**	**3.1**	**2.6**	**2.8**	**2.8**	**3.0**	**4.0**	**3.6**	**2.4**	**2.2**	**2.7**
Private consumer expenditure												
Advanced economies	**3.2**	**2.9**	**3.1**	**2.6**	**2.8**	**2.8**	**3.0**	**4.1**	**3.5**	**2.3**	**2.2**	**2.3**
Major advanced economies	3.1	2.7	2.8	2.3	2.5	2.6	3.3	3.8	3.2	2.2	2.0	2.1
United States	3.2	3.5	3.8	3.0	3.2	3.6	4.8	4.9	4.3	2.5	2.9	2.3
Japan	3.5	1.2	2.5	1.5	2.3	0.9	−0.1	1.2	0.6	1.4	1.0	1.0
Germany	3.0	1.5	1.1	2.1	1.0	0.6	1.8	3.7	1.4	1.5	−0.3	2.3
France	1.8	2.1	0.9	1.3	1.3	0.1	3.6	3.5	2.8	2.8	1.9	2.3
Italy	2.5	2.0	1.5	1.7	1.2	3.2	3.2	2.4	2.7	1.1	0.3	2.3
United Kingdom	3.1	3.6	3.3	1.9	3.8	3.8	3.8	4.5	5.2	4.1	3.5	2.4
Canada	2.8	3.2	3.0	2.1	2.6	4.6	2.8	3.9	3.7	2.6	2.8	3.6
Other advanced economies	3.8	3.5	4.1	3.8	4.0	3.6	1.6	5.0	4.4	2.3	2.9	3.1
Memorandum												
European Union	2.6	2.4	1.8	1.8	2.0	2.1	3.3	3.7	3.0	2.2	1.4	2.4
Euro area	2.5	2.0	1.3	1.9	1.6	1.6	3.1	3.5	2.5	1.8	0.8	2.3
Newly industrialized Asian economies	8.1	4.8	8.0	6.9	6.7	5.1	−4.8	7.7	6.9	2.8	4.8	4.5
Public consumption												
Advanced economies	**2.5**	**2.0**	**0.9**	**1.1**	**1.7**	**1.4**	**1.7**	**2.6**	**2.7**	**2.7**	**3.0**	**2.1**
Major advanced economies	2.2	1.9	0.9	0.8	1.2	1.2	1.5	2.7	2.8	3.0	3.1	2.2
United States	2.2	2.1	0.2	—	0.5	1.8	1.4	2.9	2.8	3.7	4.4	3.3
Japan	2.9	2.8	3.0	4.2	2.9	1.0	2.1	4.4	4.5	2.9	2.0	1.3
Germany	1.7	1.2	2.4	1.5	1.8	0.3	1.9	1.0	1.2	0.8	0.9	0.5
France	2.7	1.6	0.5	—	2.2	2.1	—	1.5	2.9	2.4	2.8	1.9
Italy	2.1	0.7	−0.8	−2.1	1.1	0.3	0.3	1.4	1.7	2.3	2.1	0.6
United Kingdom	0.9	1.7	1.0	1.7	1.2	0.1	1.5	3.1	2.1	2.2	2.9	1.7
Canada	2.3	1.0	−1.2	−0.6	−1.2	−1.0	3.2	1.9	2.3	3.3	1.6	1.6
Other advanced economies	3.7	2.2	1.3	2.1	3.7	2.4	2.6	2.2	2.3	1.7	2.5	1.6
Memorandum												
European Union	2.1	1.6	1.0	0.8	1.5	1.0	1.6	2.1	2.2	2.0	2.0	1.3
Euro area	2.2	1.5	1.2	0.7	1.7	1.3	1.4	1.9	1.9	1.9	1.8	1.3
Newly industrialized Asian economies	6.3	2.2	0.8	2.6	8.0	3.3	1.8	−0.6	1.5	0.6	3.4	1.1
Gross fixed capital formation												
Advanced economies	**3.7**	**3.5**	**4.6**	**4.0**	**5.8**	**5.6**	**5.5**	**5.2**	**5.1**	**−1.8**	**−1.4**	**3.1**
Major advanced economies	3.5	3.4	4.2	3.2	5.9	5.5	6.2	5.5	4.8	−1.8	−2.2	2.8
United States	3.6	5.2	7.3	5.4	8.4	8.8	10.2	7.9	5.5	−2.7	−2.0	3.6
Japan	4.9	−0.1	−1.8	0.6	7.4	0.9	−4.1	−0.2	3.2	−2.3	−5.2	0.8
Germany	2.9	0.3	4.0	−0.6	−0.8	0.6	3.0	4.1	2.5	−5.3	−4.8	1.4
France	2.1	3.1	1.5	2.2	0.1	−0.2	7.3	8.3	8.3	2.7	0.1	1.5
Italy	1.3	3.3	0.1	6.0	3.6	2.1	4.0	5.7	6.5	2.4	—	2.8
United Kingdom	3.2	3.5	4.7	3.1	4.7	6.9	12.8	0.6	1.9	−0.4	−1.9	3.3
Canada	2.6	5.1	7.5	−2.1	4.4	15.2	2.4	7.8	6.5	1.7	3.6	4.9
Other advanced economies	4.7	4.2	6.2	7.2	5.4	6.1	2.8	4.0	5.9	−1.7	1.9	4.3
Memorandum												
European Union	2.7	3.0	2.6	3.5	2.4	3.4	6.8	5.2	4.7	—	−1.3	2.4
Euro area	2.6	2.4	2.3	2.4	1.3	2.4	5.2	5.9	4.8	−0.6	−1.6	2.1
Newly industrialized Asian economies	10.0	3.4	10.3	10.4	7.2	4.4	−9.0	—	10.0	−6.4	4.0	5.3

Table 3 *(concluded)*

	Ten-Year Averages		1994	1995	1996	1997	1998	1999	2000	2001	2002	2003
	1984–93	1994–2003										
Final domestic demand												
Advanced economies	**3.2**	**2.8**	**2.9**	**2.6**	**3.2**	**3.1**	**3.1**	**4.0**	**3.7**	**1.4**	**1.6**	**2.4**
Major advanced economies	3.0	2.7	2.6	2.2	3.0	2.9	3.5	3.9	3.5	1.5	1.3	2.2
United States	3.1	3.6	3.8	3.0	3.7	4.3	5.3	5.2	4.3	1.6	2.2	2.6
Japan	3.8	1.1	1.3	1.7	3.8	0.9	−0.9	1.3	1.9	0.6	−0.5	1.0
Germany	2.7	1.2	2.0	1.3	0.7	0.5	2.1	3.3	1.6	−0.2	−1.1	1.8
France	2.0	2.2	0.9	1.2	1.3	0.5	3.4	3.9	3.9	2.7	1.7	2.1
Italy	2.2	2.0	0.8	1.7	1.7	2.4	2.8	2.9	3.3	1.6	0.6	2.1
United Kingdom	2.6	3.2	3.0	2.1	3.5	3.6	4.9	3.5	4.0	3.0	2.5	2.4
Canada	2.6	3.1	2.8	0.7	2.1	5.4	2.8	4.3	4.0	2.5	2.7	3.5
Other advanced economies	3.9	3.4	4.1	4.3	4.2	3.9	1.7	4.2	4.5	1.2	2.6	3.2
Memorandum												
European Union	2.5	2.3	1.8	1.9	2.0	2.2	3.6	3.7	3.2	1.7	0.9	2.2
Euro area	2.5	2.0	1.5	1.7	1.6	1.7	3.2	3.7	2.9	1.3	0.5	2.1
Newly industrialized Asian economies	8.3	4.1	7.8	7.6	7.2	4.5	−5.7	4.1	7.1	—	4.3	4.4
Stock building[1]												
Advanced economies	**—**	**—**	**0.5**	**0.1**	**−0.2**	**0.2**	**−0.1**	**—**	**—**	**−0.8**	**0.2**	**0.1**
Major advanced economies	—	—	0.5	0.1	−0.2	0.3	0.1	−0.2	—	−0.9	0.2	0.2
United States	0.1	—	0.6	−0.4	—	0.4	0.2	−0.2	0.1	−1.2	0.5	0.1
Japan	—	−0.1	−0.2	0.6	0.3	−0.1	−0.6	−0.4	—	−0.2	−0.7	0.1
Germany	—	0.1	0.3	0.3	−0.5	—	0.3	−0.4	0.2	−0.6	0.4	0.5
France	−0.1	0.1	0.9	0.6	−0.6	0.1	0.7	−0.3	0.4	−1.0	−0.4	0.6
Italy	—	—	0.8	0.2	−0.7	0.3	0.3	0.1	−1.1	—	0.4	—
United Kingdom	—	—	0.7	—	−0.4	0.3	0.1	0.2	—	−0.7	−0.1	−0.1
Canada	0.2	0.2	0.6	1.1	−0.7	0.7	−0.3	0.1	0.5	−1.5	1.3	0.3
Other advanced economies	0.1	—	0.6	0.3	−0.4	−0.2	−0.6	0.7	—	−0.4	—	0.1
Memorandum												
European Union	—	—	0.6	0.3	−0.5	0.1	0.3	−0.2	—	−0.5	—	0.3
Euro area	—	0.1	0.6	0.3	−0.5	0.1	0.4	−0.2	—	−0.4	−0.1	0.4
Newly industrialized Asian economies	—	−0.1	0.7	0.3	−0.3	−0.6	−3.3	2.7	0.1	−0.9	0.2	0.3
Foreign balance[1]												
Advanced economies	**—**	**−0.1**	**−0.1**	**0.1**	**—**	**0.2**	**−0.4**	**−0.5**	**0.1**	**0.1**	**−0.1**	**−0.1**
Major advanced economies	—	−0.2	−0.1	0.2	−0.1	0.1	−0.8	−0.7	−0.2	—	−0.1	−0.2
United States	—	−0.5	−0.4	0.1	−0.2	−0.3	−1.2	−1.0	−0.8	−0.2	−0.6	−0.4
Japan	—	0.1	−0.2	−0.5	−0.4	1.0	0.3	−0.1	0.5	−0.7	0.7	0.1
Germany	—	0.4	0.1	0.1	0.5	0.8	−0.4	−0.7	1.0	1.4	1.1	−0.2
France	—	0.1	0.1	0.1	0.4	1.2	−0.5	−0.4	−0.1	0.2	—	−0.3
Italy	—	—	0.6	1.0	0.2	−0.6	−1.2	−1.3	0.8	0.2	−0.3	0.2
United Kingdom	−0.3	−0.5	0.8	0.9	−0.4	−0.5	−2.2	−1.4	−1.1	−0.6	−0.8	−0.1
Canada	−0.1	0.4	1.4	1.0	0.3	−1.7	1.7	1.1	0.2	0.6	0.1	−0.3
Other advanced economies	−0.1	0.5	−0.1	−0.1	0.1	0.8	1.2	0.3	1.2	0.8	0.1	0.3
Memorandum												
European Union	−0.1	—	0.4	0.4	0.2	0.3	−0.9	−0.6	0.3	0.4	0.1	−0.1
Euro area	—	0.2	0.3	0.2	0.4	0.6	−0.6	−0.6	0.6	0.6	0.4	−0.1
Newly industrialized Asian economies	0.1	1.5	−0.8	0.1	−0.3	1.9	6.5	1.6	2.6	1.8	0.7	1.0

[1]Changes expressed as percent of GDP in the preceding period.

Table 4. Advanced Economies: Unemployment, Employment, and Real Per Capita GDP
(Percent)

	Ten-Year Averages[1]		1994	1995	1996	1997	1998	1999	2000	2001	2002	2003
	1984–93	1994–2003										
Unemployment rate												
Advanced economies	**6.9**	**6.6**	**7.4**	**7.1**	**7.1**	**6.9**	**6.8**	**6.4**	**5.9**	**5.9**	**6.4**	**6.5**
Major advanced economies	6.7	6.5	7.0	6.7	6.8	6.6	6.3	6.1	5.7	6.0	6.6	6.7
United States[2]	6.5	5.2	6.1	5.6	5.4	4.9	4.5	4.2	4.0	4.8	5.9	6.3
Japan	2.5	4.2	2.9	3.2	3.4	3.4	4.1	4.7	4.7	5.0	5.5	5.6
Germany	6.5	8.4	8.2	8.0	8.7	9.6	9.1	8.4	7.8	7.8	8.3	8.3
France	10.0	10.6	12.1	11.4	12.1	12.1	11.5	10.8	9.5	8.6	9.0	8.9
Italy	10.8	10.8	11.1	11.6	11.6	11.7	11.8	11.4	10.6	9.5	9.3	8.9
United Kingdom	9.2	6.7	9.7	8.7	8.2	7.1	6.3	6.0	5.5	5.1	5.2	5.3
Canada	9.7	8.3	10.3	9.4	9.6	9.1	8.3	7.6	6.8	7.2	7.6	6.7
Other advanced economies	7.3	7.2	8.7	8.2	8.1	7.8	8.1	7.3	6.2	5.7	5.8	5.7
Spain	19.4	16.8	24.2	22.9	22.2	20.8	18.7	15.7	13.9	10.5	10.7	9.9
Netherlands	7.4	4.5	7.6	7.1	6.6	5.5	4.2	3.2	2.6	2.0	2.9	3.2
Belgium	8.5	8.4	9.8	9.7	9.5	9.2	9.3	8.6	6.9	6.6	6.9	7.1
Sweden	3.1	6.1	8.0	7.7	8.1	8.0	6.5	5.6	4.7	4.0	4.2	4.2
Austria	3.3	4.0	3.8	3.9	4.3	4.4	4.5	3.9	3.7	3.6	4.3	3.8
Denmark	9.5	7.0	11.9	10.1	8.6	7.8	6.5	5.6	5.2	5.0	5.1	5.1
Finland	6.5	11.8	16.6	15.4	14.6	12.6	11.4	10.2	9.8	9.1	9.4	9.3
Greece	7.9	10.5	9.6	10.0	10.3	9.8	11.1	12.0	11.2	10.4	10.2	10.3
Portugal	6.5	5.5	6.8	7.2	7.3	6.7	5.0	4.4	4.0	4.1	4.7	5.1
Ireland	15.6	7.7	14.1	12.1	11.5	9.8	7.4	5.6	4.3	3.9	4.5	4.7
Luxembourg	1.6	2.9	2.7	3.0	3.3	3.3	3.1	2.9	2.6	2.6	2.9	2.8
Switzerland	1.3	3.5	4.7	4.2	4.7	5.2	3.9	2.7	2.0	1.9	2.7	2.7
Norway	4.1	4.0	5.5	5.0	4.9	4.1	3.2	3.2	3.4	3.6	3.6	3.6
Israel	8.2	8.6	7.8	6.8	6.6	7.6	8.5	8.9	8.8	9.3	10.7	10.9
Iceland	1.6	3.1	4.8	5.0	4.4	3.9	2.8	1.9	1.3	1.7	2.3	2.6
Cyprus	2.8	3.4	2.7	2.6	3.1	3.4	3.4	3.6	3.4	3.6	3.8	4.0
Korea	3.0	3.6	2.4	2.0	2.0	2.6	6.8	6.3	4.1	3.7	3.0	3.0
Australia	8.4	7.4	9.4	8.2	8.2	8.3	7.7	7.0	6.3	6.7	6.3	6.0
Taiwan Province of China	1.9	3.2	1.6	1.8	2.6	2.7	2.7	2.9	3.0	4.6	5.0	4.9
Hong Kong SAR	2.1	4.5	1.9	3.2	2.8	2.2	4.7	6.2	4.9	5.0	7.5	7.1
Singapore	3.2	2.8	2.6	2.7	2.0	1.8	3.2	3.5	3.1	3.3	3.0	2.3
New Zealand	6.9	6.4	8.2	6.3	6.1	6.7	7.5	6.8	6.0	5.3	5.4	5.6
Memorandum												
European Union	9.5	9.3	11.1	10.6	10.8	10.6	9.9	9.1	8.2	7.4	7.7	7.6
Euro area	9.6	9.9	11.3	11.1	11.3	11.3	10.7	9.8	8.8	8.0	8.4	8.2
Newly industrialized Asian economies	2.6	3.5	2.2	2.1	2.2	2.6	5.4	5.2	3.8	4.0	4.0	3.8
Growth in employment												
Advanced economies	**1.5**	**1.1**	**1.1**	**1.2**	**1.2**	**1.5**	**1.1**	**1.4**	**1.6**	**0.6**	**0.2**	**1.0**
Major advanced economies	1.6	0.8	1.0	0.8	0.8	1.4	1.0	1.1	1.2	0.3	−0.1	0.8
United States	1.8	1.3	2.3	1.5	1.5	2.3	1.5	1.5	1.3	−0.1	−0.2	1.1
Japan	1.2	−0.1	0.1	0.1	0.4	1.1	−0.6	−0.8	−0.2	−0.5	−0.9	0.2
Germany	3.6	0.4	−0.2	0.1	−0.3	−0.2	1.1	1.2	1.8	0.4	−0.4	0.2
France	0.2	1.1	0.1	0.5	0.4	0.3	1.5	1.9	2.4	2.1	1.0	0.8
Italy	−0.1	0.6	−1.6	−0.6	0.5	0.4	1.1	1.3	1.9	2.1	0.7	0.9
United Kingdom	0.6	1.0	1.0	1.4	1.1	2.0	1.2	1.5	1.3	0.4	−0.3	0.2
Canada	1.6	2.2	2.0	1.9	0.8	2.3	2.7	2.8	2.6	1.1	2.1	3.9
Other advanced economies	1.4	1.8	1.3	2.2	2.3	1.6	1.2	2.3	2.9	1.5	1.1	1.3
Memorandum												
European Union	1.2	1.1	−0.1	0.7	1.1	0.9	2.0	1.9	2.1	1.4	0.3	0.7
Euro area	1.2	0.9	−0.4	0.5	0.5	0.8	1.7	1.7	2.0	1.4	0.4	0.8
Newly industrialized Asian economies	2.6	1.5	2.8	2.5	2.1	1.6	−2.7	1.5	3.2	1.0	1.5	1.6

Table 4 *(concluded)*

	Ten-Year Averages[1]		1994	1995	1996	1997	1998	1999	2000	2001	2002	2003
	1984–93	1994–2003										
Growth in real per capita GDP												
Advanced economies	**2.5**	**2.2**	**2.7**	**2.1**	**2.3**	**2.8**	**2.1**	**2.9**	**3.3**	**0.3**	**1.2**	**2.1**
Major advanced economies	2.4	1.9	2.4	1.7	2.1	2.6	2.2	2.5	2.9	0.1	1.0	1.8
United States	2.3	2.0	3.0	1.7	2.6	3.4	3.3	3.2	0.9	−1.3	1.2	1.5
Japan	3.2	0.8	0.7	1.4	3.2	1.6	−1.4	0.6	2.2	−0.5	−0.7	1.0
Germany	2.2	1.5	2.0	1.4	0.5	1.2	2.0	2.0	2.7	0.4	0.5	2.0
France	1.5	1.9	1.5	1.5	0.7	1.5	3.2	2.8	3.7	1.3	0.8	1.9
Italy	2.1	1.8	1.9	2.7	1.0	1.8	1.8	1.6	2.9	1.6	0.5	2.1
United Kingdom	2.1	2.4	4.3	2.5	2.3	3.1	2.5	2.0	2.7	1.6	1.3	2.0
Canada	1.3	2.4	3.6	1.7	0.5	3.1	3.2	4.5	3.6	0.5	2.2	0.6
Other advanced economies	3.1	3.2	3.9	3.6	3.2	3.7	1.6	4.5	4.8	1.2	2.2	2.9
Memorandum												
European Union	2.1	2.2	2.4	2.1	1.4	2.4	2.8	2.6	3.3	1.5	1.0	2.2
Euro area	2.1	2.0	2.0	2.0	1.2	2.1	2.7	2.6	3.2	1.0	0.7	2.1
Newly industrialized Asian economies	6.8	4.1	6.6	6.3	5.2	4.6	−3.5	6.9	7.5	−0.1	3.8	4.1

[1]Compound annual rate of change for employment and per capita GDP; arithmetic average for unemployment rate.
[2]The projections for unemployment have been adjusted to reflect the new survey techniques adopted by the U.S. Bureau of Labor Statistics in January 1994.

Table 5. Developing Countries: Real GDP

(Annual percent change)

| | Ten-Year Averages | | 1994 | 1995 | 1996 | 1997 | 1998 | 1999 | 2000 | 2001 | 2002 | 2003 |
	1984–93	1994–2003										
Developing countries	**5.1**	**5.2**	**6.7**	**6.2**	**6.5**	**5.9**	**3.5**	**4.0**	**5.7**	**3.9**	**4.2**	**5.2**
Regional groups												
Africa	2.0	3.4	2.3	3.0	5.6	3.1	3.4	2.8	3.0	3.5	3.1	4.2
Sub-Sahara	1.9	3.4	1.8	3.8	5.1	3.7	2.7	2.9	3.2	3.3	3.0	4.2
Excluding Nigeria and South Africa	1.8	3.9	1.5	4.5	5.3	4.5	3.9	3.6	2.9	4.0	4.4	4.9
Developing Asia	7.6	6.8	9.7	9.0	8.3	6.6	4.0	6.1	6.7	5.6	6.1	6.3
China	10.5	8.6	12.6	10.5	9.6	8.8	7.8	7.1	8.0	7.3	7.5	7.2
India	5.2	5.9	6.8	7.6	7.5	5.0	5.8	6.7	5.4	4.1	5.0	5.7
Other developing Asia	5.5	4.0	7.0	7.6	6.7	3.8	−5.1	3.7	5.1	3.0	3.9	4.5
Middle East and Turkey	3.5	3.6	0.5	4.4	4.7	6.2	3.6	1.2	6.1	1.5	3.6	4.7
Western Hemisphere	2.9	2.5	5.0	1.8	3.6	5.2	2.3	0.2	4.0	0.6	−0.6	3.0
Analytical groups												
By source of export earnings												
Fuel	2.6	3.2	0.4	3.3	3.4	5.4	2.8	1.5	5.2	4.1	2.2	4.3
Nonfuel	5.4	5.4	7.4	6.5	6.8	5.9	3.6	4.2	5.8	3.9	4.4	5.3
of which, primary products	3.1	4.3	5.3	6.5	5.6	5.5	3.0	2.6	3.6	2.8	3.2	4.7
By external financing source												
Net debtor countries	5.2	5.3	6.9	6.3	6.7	5.9	3.5	4.1	5.7	3.9	4.3	5.3
of which, official financing	2.4	4.2	2.5	5.3	5.3	4.3	3.9	4.0	3.9	4.3	3.8	4.8
Net debtor countries by debt-servicing experience												
Countries with arrears and/or rescheduling during 1994–98	3.0	3.7	4.7	5.2	5.0	4.6	−0.6	2.3	4.6	3.3	3.4	4.3
Other groups												
Heavily indebted poor countries	2.2	4.6	2.9	5.8	5.8	5.3	4.0	4.3	3.9	4.2	4.7	5.3
Middle East and north Africa	2.8	4.0	2.6	2.9	4.6	4.9	4.2	3.2	5.2	4.3	3.5	4.5
Memorandum												
Real per capita GDP												
Developing countries	3.1	3.5	5.0	4.4	4.8	4.2	1.9	2.4	4.1	2.3	2.6	3.7
Regional groups												
Africa	−0.8	0.9	−0.3	0.4	3.0	0.5	0.9	0.3	0.6	1.1	0.7	1.8
Developing Asia	5.8	5.4	8.1	7.5	6.8	5.1	2.6	4.8	5.4	4.3	4.8	5.0
Middle East and Turkey	0.6	1.5	−1.6	2.3	2.5	4.0	1.4	−0.9	4.0	−0.5	1.6	2.7
Western Hemisphere	1.0	0.9	3.3	0.1	1.9	3.6	0.7	−1.4	2.4	−0.9	−2.1	1.5

Table 6. Developing Countries—by Country: Real GDP[1]
(Annual percent change)

	Average 1984–93	1994	1995	1996	1997	1998	1999	2000	2001	2002	2003
Africa	**2.0**	**2.3**	**3.0**	**5.6**	**3.1**	**3.4**	**2.8**	**3.0**	**3.5**	**3.1**	**4.2**
Algeria	1.2	−0.9	3.8	3.8	1.1	5.1	3.2	2.5	2.8	2.1	2.9
Angola	−1.1	1.3	10.4	11.2	7.9	6.8	3.3	3.0	3.2	17.1	4.8
Benin	2.1	4.4	4.6	5.5	5.7	4.6	4.7	5.8	5.0	5.3	6.0
Botswana	8.6	3.5	4.5	5.7	6.7	5.9	6.3	8.6	4.9	2.6	3.7
Burkina Faso	4.3	1.4	4.5	7.5	4.8	6.4	6.3	2.2	5.7	5.7	5.4
Burundi	2.9	−3.7	−7.3	−8.4	0.4	4.8	−1.0	−0.1	2.4	3.4	5.0
Cameroon	−0.7	−2.5	3.3	5.0	5.1	5.0	4.4	4.2	5.3	4.4	4.7
Cape Verde	4.3	6.9	7.5	6.7	7.6	7.4	8.6	6.8	2.9	3.0	3.5
Central African Republic	2.0	5.6	5.2	−7.5	7.7	3.9	3.6	1.8	1.0	4.5	4.3
Chad	4.6	5.5	0.4	3.1	4.2	7.7	2.3	1.0	8.5	11.2	9.2
Comoros	1.2	−5.4	8.9	−1.3	4.2	1.2	1.9	−1.1	1.9	3.5	3.0
Congo, Dem. Rep. of	−2.9	−3.9	0.7	−1.0	−5.6	−1.6	−4.3	−6.2	−4.4	3.0	5.5
Congo, Rep. of	5.5	−5.5	4.0	4.3	−0.6	3.7	−3.0	8.2	2.9	3.9	−1.0
Côte d'Ivoire	0.8	2.0	7.1	7.7	5.7	4.8	1.6	−2.3	0.1	3.0	4.5
Djibouti	−0.7	−0.9	−3.5	−5.0	−0.7	0.1	2.2	0.7	1.9	2.6	3.5
Equatorial Guinea	2.5	5.1	14.3	29.1	71.2	22.0	41.4	16.1	45.5	30.4	16.4
Eritrea	...	23.4	2.5	9.2	8.0	3.1	0.6	−12.1	9.7	8.8	7.1
Ethiopia	0.6	1.6	6.2	10.6	4.7	−1.4	6.0	5.4	7.7	5.0	6.0
Gabon	2.1	3.7	5.0	3.6	5.7	3.5	−8.9	−1.9	2.4	1.0	−0.5
Gambia, The	2.5	3.8	−3.4	6.1	4.9	3.5	6.4	5.6	5.5	6.0	6.0
Ghana	4.6	3.3	4.0	4.6	4.2	4.7	4.4	3.7	4.2	4.5	5.0
Guinea	3.8	4.0	4.7	5.1	5.0	4.8	4.6	2.1	3.6	4.2	4.9
Guinea-Bissau	3.2	3.2	4.4	4.6	5.5	−28.1	8.0	9.5	0.2	3.9	4.4
Kenya	3.3	2.7	4.4	4.2	2.1	1.6	1.3	−0.1	1.2	1.4	2.8
Lesotho	5.3	−0.4	12.6	9.5	4.8	−3.0	2.4	3.5	4.0	4.0	4.3
Liberia	...	...	...	...	...	...	...	...	...	...	...
Madagascar	1.3	—	1.7	2.1	3.7	3.9	4.7	4.8	6.7	−10.0	10.0
Malawi	3.2	−10.3	16.7	7.3	3.8	3.3	4.0	1.7	−1.5	1.8	4.5
Mali	2.4	2.6	7.0	4.3	6.7	4.9	6.7	3.7	1.5	9.3	5.3
Mauritania	4.8	4.6	4.6	5.5	3.2	3.7	4.1	5.0	4.6	5.1	5.5
Mauritius	6.8	4.4	3.5	5.2	6.0	6.0	5.3	2.6	7.2	5.3	4.9
Morocco	3.4	10.4	−6.6	12.2	−2.2	7.7	−0.1	1.0	6.5	4.4	4.1
Mozambique, Rep. of	2.6	7.5	4.3	7.1	11.1	12.6	7.5	1.6	13.9	9.0	5.6
Namibia	2.6	6.8	4.2	3.0	4.2	3.4	3.6	3.4	2.5	3.1	3.8
Niger	−0.1	4.0	2.6	3.4	2.8	10.4	−0.6	−1.4	7.6	2.7	3.9
Nigeria	4.6	−0.6	2.6	6.4	2.9	1.8	1.0	4.3	2.8	−2.3	3.7
Rwanda	1.0	−50.2	35.2	12.7	13.8	8.9	7.6	6.0	6.7	6.5	6.2
São Tomé and Príncipe	—	2.2	2.0	1.5	1.0	2.5	2.5	3.0	4.0	5.0	5.0
Senegal	1.2	2.9	5.2	5.1	5.0	5.7	5.1	5.6	5.6	5.0	5.1
Seychelles	6.0	−2.4	0.5	10.0	12.2	5.7	−2.8	−5.4	−8.1	−2.4	−0.6
Sierra Leone	−1.3	3.5	−10.0	−24.8	−17.6	−0.8	−8.1	3.8	5.4	6.6	7.0
Somalia	...	...	...	...	...	...	...	...	...	...	...
South Africa	1.0	3.2	3.1	4.3	2.6	0.8	2.1	3.4	2.2	2.5	3.0
Sudan	2.5	2.0	3.0	4.9	10.0	6.0	7.7	9.7	5.3	5.2	6.3
Swaziland	6.8	3.4	3.8	3.9	3.8	3.2	3.5	2.2	1.6	1.8	2.3
Tanzania	3.7	1.6	3.6	4.5	3.5	3.7	3.5	5.1	5.6	5.8	6.0
Togo	—	17.5	6.9	9.7	4.3	−2.1	2.9	−1.9	2.7	3.0	4.0
Tunisia	4.0	3.2	2.4	7.1	5.4	4.8	6.1	4.7	5.0	3.8	6.4
Uganda	3.8	6.4	11.9	8.6	5.1	4.7	7.6	5.0	5.6	5.7	6.5
Zambia	0.9	−13.3	−2.5	6.5	3.4	−1.9	2.2	3.6	4.9	3.7	4.0
Zimbabwe	2.8	5.8	0.2	10.4	2.7	2.9	−0.7	−5.1	−8.5	−10.6	−2.8

Table 6 *(continued)*

	Average 1984–93	1994	1995	1996	1997	1998	1999	2000	2001	2002	2003
Developing Asia	**7.6**	**9.7**	**9.0**	**8.3**	**6.6**	**4.0**	**6.1**	**6.7**	**5.6**	**6.1**	**6.3**
Afghanistan, Islamic State of	...	...	...	...	...	...	...	...	...	...	...
Bangladesh	4.4	4.5	4.8	5.0	5.3	5.0	5.4	5.6	4.7	4.0	4.0
Bhutan	6.4	6.4	7.4	6.1	7.3	5.5	5.9	6.1	5.9	6.0	5.7
Brunei Darussalam	...	1.8	3.1	1.1	2.6	−4.0	2.6	2.8	−0.4	3.0	2.9
Cambodia	...	7.7	5.9	4.6	4.3	2.1	6.9	7.7	6.3	4.5	6.0
China	10.5	12.6	10.5	9.6	8.8	7.8	7.1	8.0	7.3	7.5	7.2
Fiji	3.1	5.1	2.5	3.1	−0.9	1.4	9.7	−2.8	2.6	3.7	5.2
India	5.2	6.8	7.6	7.5	5.0	5.8	6.7	5.4	4.1	5.0	5.7
Indonesia	6.7	7.5	8.2	8.0	4.5	−13.1	0.8	4.8	3.3	3.5	4.5
Kiribati	0.4	7.9	5.9	4.1	1.6	6.6	2.1	−1.7	1.5	2.7	2.5
Lao P.D. Republic	5.0	8.2	7.0	6.9	6.9	4.0	7.3	5.8	5.2	5.5	6.0
Malaysia	6.9	9.2	9.8	10.0	7.3	−7.4	6.1	8.3	0.5	3.5	5.3
Maldives	10.2	6.6	7.2	8.8	11.2	7.9	8.5	5.6	4.9	1.2	7.0
Myanmar	1.1	6.8	7.2	6.4	5.7	5.8	10.9	5.5	4.8	4.2	4.8
Nepal	5.3	8.6	3.3	5.3	5.3	2.9	4.5	6.2	4.8	0.8	3.8
Pakistan	5.5	4.4	4.9	2.9	1.8	3.1	4.1	4.3	3.6	4.6	5.0
Papua New Guinea	4.9	5.9	−3.3	7.7	−3.9	−3.8	7.6	−0.8	−3.4	1.2	2.8
Philippines	1.0	4.4	4.7	5.8	5.2	−0.6	3.4	4.4	3.2	4.0	3.8
Samoa	1.8	6.5	6.4	7.3	0.8	2.4	2.6	6.9	6.5	4.5	4.0
Solomon Islands	3.5	9.2	10.5	3.5	−2.3	1.1	−1.3	−14.0	−3.0	−0.5	1.5
Sri Lanka	4.3	5.6	5.5	3.8	6.4	4.7	4.3	6.0	−1.4	3.7	5.5
Thailand	8.7	9.0	9.2	5.9	−1.4	−10.5	4.4	4.6	1.8	3.5	3.5
Tonga	2.0	5.0	3.2	−0.2	−0.1	1.6	3.1	6.2	3.0	2.9	3.3
Vanuatu	3.0	1.3	2.3	0.4	0.6	6.0	−2.5	3.7	−0.5	2.0	3.0
Vietnam	6.0	8.8	9.5	9.3	8.2	3.5	4.2	5.5	5.0	5.3	6.5
Middle East and Turkey	**3.5**	**0.5**	**4.4**	**4.7**	**6.2**	**3.6**	**1.2**	**6.1**	**1.5**	**3.6**	**4.7**
Bahrain	4.1	−0.2	3.9	4.1	3.1	4.8	4.3	5.3	4.8	4.1	4.1
Egypt	3.9	3.9	4.7	5.0	5.3	5.7	6.0	5.1	3.3	2.0	3.7
Iran, Islamic Republic of	1.7	2.3	3.3	5.7	5.0	1.8	3.6	5.7	4.8	5.8	5.5
Iraq	...	...	...	...	...	...	...	...	...	...	...
Jordan	3.2	5.0	6.2	2.1	3.3	3.0	3.1	4.0	4.2	5.1	6.0
Kuwait	1.5	−7.1	20.1	−2.7	1.2	3.2	−1.7	3.8	−1.0	−1.0	1.7
Lebanon	0.8	8.0	6.5	4.0	4.0	3.0	1.0	−0.5	2.0	1.5	1.0
Libya	−0.5	−1.3	−0.3	3.3	5.2	−3.6	0.7	4.4	0.6	−0.6	2.5
Malta	4.9	5.7	6.2	4.0	4.9	3.4	4.1	5.2	−1.0	2.0	4.9
Oman	6.3	3.8	4.8	2.9	6.2	2.7	−0.2	5.1	7.3	3.3	3.8
Qatar	0.7	2.3	2.9	4.8	25.4	6.2	5.3	11.6	7.2	3.0	4.0
Saudi Arabia	2.7	0.5	0.5	1.4	2.6	2.8	−0.8	4.9	1.2	0.7	3.3
Syrian Arab Republic	3.1	7.7	5.8	4.4	1.8	7.6	−2.0	2.5	2.8	3.9	3.4
Turkey	5.4	−5.0	6.9	6.9	7.6	3.1	−4.7	7.4	−7.4	3.9	5.0
United Arab Emirates	2.0	8.5	7.9	6.2	6.7	4.3	3.9	5.0	5.1	0.3	3.1
Yemen, Republic of	...	2.2	10.9	5.9	8.1	4.9	3.7	5.1	3.3	4.1	3.7

Table 6 *(concluded)*

	Average 1984–93	1994	1995	1996	1997	1998	1999	2000	2001	2002	2003
Western Hemisphere	**2.9**	**5.0**	**1.8**	**3.6**	**5.2**	**2.3**	**0.2**	**4.0**	**0.6**	**−0.6**	**3.0**
Antigua and Barbuda	6.4	6.2	−5.0	6.1	5.6	3.9	3.2	2.5	−0.6	−3.7	1.0
Argentina	2.0	5.8	−2.8	5.5	8.1	3.8	−3.4	−0.8	−4.4	−16.0	1.0
Bahamas, The	1.5	0.9	0.3	4.2	3.3	3.0	5.9	5.0	−0.5	—	2.9
Barbados	0.7	4.0	3.1	1.7	6.4	4.1	1.3	3.1	−2.1	−4.1	3.6
Belize	6.7	1.8	3.3	1.5	3.7	2.6	3.7	9.7	2.5	—	3.0
Bolivia	2.1	4.7	4.7	4.4	5.0	5.2	0.4	2.4	1.2	1.5	2.5
Brazil	2.8	5.9	4.2	2.7	3.3	0.2	0.8	4.4	1.5	1.5	3.0
Chile	7.0	5.7	10.8	7.4	6.6	3.2	−1.0	4.4	2.8	2.2	4.2
Colombia	4.1	5.8	5.2	2.1	3.4	0.6	−4.2	2.7	1.4	1.2	2.0
Costa Rica	4.8	4.7	3.9	0.9	5.6	8.4	9.4	2.2	0.9	2.4	2.0
Dominica	4.1	2.1	1.6	3.1	2.0	2.4	0.9	0.5	1.0	1.0	1.0
Dominican Republic	2.5	4.3	4.7	7.2	8.3	7.3	8.0	7.2	2.8	3.5	5.3
Ecuador	2.9	4.4	2.3	2.0	3.4	0.4	−7.3	2.3	5.6	3.5	3.5
El Salvador	3.3	6.0	6.4	1.8	4.3	3.8	3.4	2.2	1.8	3.0	3.0
Grenada	3.2	3.3	3.1	3.1	4.0	7.3	7.5	6.4	3.5	−1.8	5.0
Guatemala	2.7	4.0	4.9	3.0	4.1	5.1	3.8	3.6	1.8	2.3	3.5
Guyana	1.7	8.5	5.0	7.9	6.2	−1.7	3.0	−1.3	1.4	1.8	2.7
Haiti	−1.0	−11.9	9.9	4.1	2.7	2.2	2.7	0.9	−1.7	—	2.5
Honduras	3.9	−1.3	4.1	3.6	5.0	2.9	−1.9	4.9	2.6	2.5	4.0
Jamaica	2.4	1.0	0.2	−1.5	−1.5	−0.4	−0.1	1.1	3.0	2.5	3.0
Mexico	2.4	4.4	−6.2	5.2	6.8	5.0	3.6	6.6	−0.3	1.5	4.0
Netherlands Antilles	1.2	6.0	1.1	2.1	0.9	−0.7	−1.5	−1.9	−0.6	0.7	1.5
Nicaragua	−2.2	3.3	4.2	4.7	5.1	4.1	7.4	5.8	3.0	1.5	3.5
Panama	2.7	2.9	1.8	2.4	4.4	4.0	3.2	2.5	0.3	1.2	2.8
Paraguay	3.5	3.1	4.7	1.3	2.6	−0.4	0.5	−0.4	0.8	2.6	3.6
Peru	0.7	12.8	8.6	2.5	6.7	−0.5	1.0	3.1	0.2	3.5	3.0
St. Kitts and Nevis	5.8	5.1	3.5	5.9	7.3	1.0	3.7	7.5	1.8	−2.5	4.5
St. Lucia	6.8	2.1	4.1	1.4	0.6	3.1	3.5	0.7	0.5	−4.0	2.0
St. Vincent and the Grenadines	5.7	−2.0	6.8	1.4	3.9	6.0	4.1	1.8	1.7	1.0	2.0
Suriname	−2.5	−4.1	7.2	12.3	7.0	4.1	−4.8	−5.7	1.3	1.2	3.0
Trinidad and Tobago	−2.2	3.6	4.0	3.8	3.1	4.8	6.8	4.8	4.5	5.2	5.5
Uruguay	3.4	7.3	−1.4	5.6	5.0	4.8	−2.8	−1.4	−3.1	−11.1	−4.5
Venezuela	3.0	−2.3	4.0	−0.2	6.4	0.2	−6.1	3.2	2.8	−6.2	2.2

[1]For many countries, figures for recent years are IMF staff estimates. Data for some countries are for fiscal years.

Table 7. Countries in Transition: Real GDP[1]

(Annual percent change)

	Average 1984–93	1994	1995	1996	1997	1998	1999	2000	2001	2002	2003
Central and eastern Europe	. . .	**3.2**	**5.2**	**4.1**	**2.6**	**2.4**	**2.2**	**3.8**	**3.0**	**2.7**	**3.8**
Albania	−2.8	9.4	−0.9	19.8	−7.0	8.0	7.3	7.8	6.5	6.0	7.0
Bosnia and Herzegovina	. . .	. . .	32.4	85.8	39.9	10.0	10.0	4.5	2.3	2.3	4.1
Bulgaria	−2.4	−3.5	−1.8	−8.0	−5.6	4.0	2.3	5.4	4.0	4.0	5.0
Croatia	. . .	5.9	6.8	6.0	6.6	2.5	−0.4	3.7	4.1	3.5	4.0
Czech Republic	. . .	2.2	5.9	4.3	−0.8	−1.0	0.5	3.3	3.3	2.7	3.2
Estonia	. . .	−2.0	4.3	3.9	9.8	4.6	−0.6	7.1	5.0	4.5	5.0
Hungary	−1.1	2.9	1.5	1.3	4.6	4.9	4.2	5.2	3.8	3.5	4.0
Latvia	. . .	0.6	−0.8	3.3	8.6	3.9	1.1	6.8	7.6	5.0	6.0
Lithuania	. . .	−9.8	3.3	4.7	7.3	5.1	−3.9	3.8	5.9	4.4	4.8
Macedonia, former Yugoslav Rep. of	. . .	−1.8	−1.1	1.2	1.4	3.4	4.3	4.5	−4.1	2.5	4.0
Poland	0.8	5.2	6.8	6.0	6.8	4.8	4.1	4.0	1.0	1.0	3.0
Romania	−2.2	3.9	7.3	3.9	−6.1	−4.8	−1.2	1.8	5.3	4.3	4.9
Slovak Republic	. . .	5.2	6.5	5.8	5.6	4.0	1.3	2.2	3.3	4.0	3.7
Slovenia	. . .	5.3	4.1	3.5	4.6	3.8	5.2	4.6	3.0	2.5	3.2
Commonwealth of Independent States and Mongolia	. . .	**−14.5**	**−5.5**	**−3.3**	**1.1**	**−2.8**	**4.6**	**8.4**	**6.3**	**4.6**	**4.9**
Russia	. . .	−13.5	−4.2	−3.4	0.9	−4.9	5.4	9.0	5.0	4.4	4.9
Excluding Russia	. . .	−16.6	−8.6	−3.1	1.5	1.6	2.8	6.9	8.9	5.2	4.9
Armenia	. . .	5.4	6.9	5.9	3.3	7.3	3.3	6.0	9.6	7.5	6.0
Azerbaijan	. . .	−19.7	−11.8	1.3	5.8	10.0	7.4	11.1	9.0	7.9	7.3
Belarus	. . .	−9.0	−10.4	2.8	11.4	8.3	3.4	5.8	4.1	3.5	3.8
Georgia	. . .	−10.4	2.6	10.5	10.6	2.9	3.0	1.9	4.5	3.5	4.0
Kazakhstan	. . .	−12.6	−8.3	0.5	1.6	−1.9	2.7	9.8	13.2	8.0	7.0
Kyrgyz Republic	. . .	−19.8	−5.4	7.0	9.9	2.1	3.7	5.4	5.3	4.4	3.8
Moldova	. . .	−30.9	−1.4	−5.9	1.6	−6.5	−3.4	2.1	6.1	4.8	5.0
Mongolia	0.8	2.3	6.3	2.4	4.0	3.5	3.2	1.1	1.1	3.9	5.0
Tajikistan	. . .	−21.4	−12.5	−4.4	1.7	5.3	3.7	8.3	10.2	7.0	6.0
Turkmenistan	. . .	−17.3	−7.2	−6.7	−11.3	7.0	16.5	18.0	20.5	. . .	. . .
Ukraine	. . .	−22.9	−12.2	−10.0	−3.0	−1.9	−0.2	5.9	9.1	4.8	5.0
Uzbekistan	. . .	−4.2	−0.9	1.6	2.5	4.3	4.3	3.8	4.5	2.7	3.0
Memorandum EU accession candidates	. . .	0.8	5.8	4.8	4.1	2.6	0.2	4.9	—	3.0	4.1

[1]Data for some countries refer to real net material product (NMP) or are estimates based on NMP. For many countries, figures for recent years are IMF staff estimates. The figures should be interpreted only as indicative of broad orders of magnitude because reliable, comparable data are not generally available. In particular, the growth of output of new private enterprises of the informal economy is not fully reflected in the recent figures.

Table 8. Summary of Inflation

(Percent)

	Ten-Year Averages		1994	1995	1996	1997	1998	1999	2000	2001	2002	2003
	1984–93	1994–2003										
GDP deflators												
Advanced economies	**4.1**	**1.6**	**2.2**	**2.3**	**1.9**	**1.7**	**1.3**	**0.9**	**1.3**	**1.8**	**1.2**	**1.5**
United States	3.2	1.8	2.1	2.2	1.9	1.9	1.2	1.4	2.1	2.4	1.2	1.9
European Union	5.0	2.2	2.7	3.1	2.6	1.9	2.0	1.5	1.6	2.3	2.3	1.9
Japan	1.7	−0.8	0.2	−0.5	−0.8	0.3	−0.1	−1.4	−2.0	−1.2	−1.4	−1.2
Other advanced economies	7.1	1.9	3.3	3.4	2.9	2.2	1.5	—	1.7	1.4	0.9	1.8
Consumer prices												
Advanced economies	**4.2**	**2.0**	**2.6**	**2.6**	**2.4**	**2.1**	**1.5**	**1.4**	**2.3**	**2.2**	**1.4**	**1.7**
United States	3.8	2.4	2.6	2.8	2.9	2.3	1.5	2.2	3.4	2.8	1.5	2.3
European Union	4.5	2.2	3.0	2.9	2.5	1.8	1.5	1.4	2.3	2.6	2.1	1.8
Japan	1.7	−0.1	0.7	−0.1	—	1.7	0.6	−0.3	−0.8	−0.7	−1.0	−0.6
Other advanced economies	7.1	2.5	3.3	3.8	3.2	2.4	2.6	1.0	2.2	2.4	1.8	2.2
Developing countries	**48.5**	**13.7**	**55.4**	**23.2**	**15.4**	**10.0**	**10.5**	**6.9**	**6.1**	**5.7**	**5.6**	**6.0**
Regional groups												
Africa	24.3	19.7	54.7	35.3	30.2	14.6	10.9	12.3	14.3	13.1	9.6	9.5
Developing Asia	10.2	6.1	16.0	13.2	8.3	4.8	7.7	2.5	1.9	2.6	2.1	3.2
Middle East and Turkey	24.2	25.0	37.8	39.1	29.6	28.3	27.6	23.6	19.6	17.2	17.1	13.3
Western Hemisphere	184.3	24.7	200.4	36.0	21.2	12.9	9.8	8.9	8.1	6.4	8.6	9.3
Analytical groups												
By source of export earnings												
Fuel	16.9	21.7	36.2	42.6	35.1	20.1	17.5	17.1	13.8	11.9	13.8	13.0
Nonfuel	53.6	12.9	57.8	21.3	13.5	9.0	9.8	5.9	5.3	5.1	4.8	5.3
of which, primary products	75.5	19.5	63.0	29.8	27.0	16.1	14.0	12.6	13.4	12.2	7.5	8.9
By external financing source												
Net debtor countries	50.6	14.1	57.5	23.8	15.8	10.2	10.8	7.1	6.3	6.0	5.7	6.1
of which, official financing	38.8	16.8	64.2	30.2	22.7	11.4	10.7	11.2	10.4	8.8	4.8	4.3
Net debtor countries by debt-servicing experience												
Countries with arrears and/or rescheduling during 1994–98	125.1	28.3	221.6	40.1	21.1	12.2	18.4	13.8	11.4	11.4	9.5	7.8
Countries in transition	**72.8**	**47.0**	**274.2**	**133.8**	**42.5**	**27.4**	**22.1**	**44.1**	**20.2**	**15.9**	**11.3**	**8.8**
Central and eastern Europe	...	19.0	45.6	24.7	23.3	41.8	17.2	11.0	12.8	9.6	6.1	5.6
Commonwealth of Independent States and Mongolia	...	65.5	508.1	235.7	55.9	19.1	25.5	70.5	25.0	19.8	14.5	10.7
Russia	...	57.1	307.5	198.0	47.9	14.7	27.8	85.7	20.8	20.7	15.8	11.0
Excluding Russia	...	85.4	1,334.5	338.9	75.5	29.7	20.8	41.7	34.7	17.9	11.9	10.1
Memorandum												
Median inflation rate												
Advanced economies	4.2	2.2	2.4	2.5	2.2	1.8	1.7	1.5	2.7	2.6	2.2	2.1
Developing countries	9.5	6.0	10.8	10.0	7.3	6.2	5.8	3.9	4.0	4.4	4.0	4.0
Countries in transition	123.8	25.8	131.6	41.5	24.1	14.8	9.9	8.0	10.0	7.4	5.4	5.0

Table 9. Advanced Economies: GDP Deflators and Consumer Prices
(Annual percent change)

	Ten-Year Averages		1994	1995	1996	1997	1998	1999	2000	2001	2002	2003	Fourth Quarter[1]		
	1984–93	1994–2003											2001	2002	2003
GDP deflators															
Advanced economies	**4.1**	**1.6**	**2.2**	**2.3**	**1.9**	**1.7**	**1.3**	**0.9**	**1.3**	**1.8**	**1.2**	**1.5**	. . .	. . .	. . .
Major advanced economies	3.4	1.4	1.8	1.9	1.6	1.5	1.1	0.9	1.2	1.5	1.0	1.3	1.5	1.0	1.7
United States	3.2	1.8	2.1	2.2	1.9	1.9	1.2	1.4	2.1	2.4	1.2	1.9	1.9	1.4	2.1
Japan	1.7	−0.8	0.2	−0.5	−0.8	0.3	−0.1	−1.4	−2.0	−1.2	−1.4	−1.2	−0.6	−2.2	−0.3
Germany	2.9	1.2	2.5	2.0	1.0	0.7	1.1	0.5	−0.3	1.4	1.7	1.5	2.4	1.0	1.9
France	3.7	1.3	1.8	1.7	1.4	1.3	0.9	0.5	0.5	1.4	1.8	1.2	1.7	1.8	1.2
Italy	7.2	3.0	3.5	5.0	5.3	2.4	2.7	1.7	2.1	2.6	2.4	1.9	3.3	2.3	1.8
United Kingdom	5.3	2.4	1.4	2.6	3.3	2.9	2.9	2.5	2.2	2.0	2.6	2.1	2.2	1.4	3.1
Canada	3.2	1.6	1.1	2.3	1.6	1.2	−0.4	1.7	3.9	1.0	1.1	2.4	−1.2	3.8	1.9
Other advanced economies	7.3	2.5	3.8	3.9	2.9	2.5	2.3	0.8	2.0	2.6	1.9	1.9	. . .	. . .	. . .
Spain	7.4	3.4	3.9	4.9	3.5	2.3	2.4	2.7	3.5	4.2	3.5	2.6	4.1	3.1	2.6
Netherlands	1.4	2.6	2.3	1.8	1.2	2.0	1.7	1.5	4.1	5.3	3.4	2.5	4.0	3.3	2.1
Belgium	3.5	1.5	2.1	1.2	1.2	1.3	1.6	1.2	1.4	2.3	1.8	1.0	. . .	. . .	. . .
Sweden	5.7	1.8	2.4	3.5	1.4	1.7	0.9	0.7	1.0	2.0	1.8	2.2	2.8	1.8	1.8
Austria	3.1	1.4	2.7	2.5	1.3	0.9	0.5	0.7	1.2	1.8	1.0	1.6	. . .	. . .	. . .
Denmark	3.8	2.2	1.7	1.8	2.5	2.2	1.0	2.7	3.7	2.7	2.4	1.9	2.0	2.8	1.9
Finland	4.7	1.9	2.0	4.1	−0.2	2.1	3.0	−0.2	3.2	2.2	1.9	1.4	. . .	. . .	. . .
Greece	16.9	5.8	11.2	11.2	7.4	6.8	5.2	3.0	3.4	3.2	3.6	3.2	. . .	. . .	. . .
Portugal	14.0	4.2	6.1	7.4	3.8	3.1	4.3	3.4	2.8	4.4	3.8	2.9	. . .	. . .	. . .
Ireland	3.8	3.7	1.7	3.0	2.2	4.1	5.9	4.2	4.3	5.4	3.5	3.1	. . .	. . .	. . .
Luxembourg	2.6	2.6	4.9	4.3	1.9	2.8	2.6	2.2	3.5	0.2	2.0	1.9	. . .	. . .	. . .
Switzerland	3.3	0.8	1.6	1.2	0.3	−0.2	—	0.6	1.1	1.7	0.8	1.0	2.0	0.6	1.2
Norway	3.6	2.9	−0.1	2.6	4.0	2.9	−0.7	6.7	16.0	1.7	−3.1	0.6	. . .	. . .	. . .
Israel	55.6	6.7	11.9	9.8	10.9	9.0	6.9	6.4	1.3	2.1	6.2	3.0	2.0	11.3	0.2
Iceland	17.3	3.8	1.7	2.8	2.0	3.3	4.2	3.4	3.0	9.0	5.5	3.2	. . .	. . .	. . .
Cyprus	5.0	2.9	5.1	3.6	1.9	2.5	2.3	2.3	4.0	2.8	2.5	2.2	. . .	. . .	. . .
Korea	7.0	2.8	7.7	7.1	3.9	3.1	5.1	−2.0	−1.1	1.3	1.4	2.0	. . .	. . .	. . .
Australia	4.8	1.9	0.9	2.0	2.1	1.6	0.4	0.6	4.3	3.3	2.3	2.0	2.2	2.5	2.3
Taiwan Province of China	2.4	1.0	2.0	2.0	3.1	1.7	2.6	−1.4	−1.7	0.7	−0.4	1.4	0.5	−0.3	2.0
Hong Kong SAR	8.6	0.5	7.0	2.5	5.7	5.8	0.5	−5.5	−6.3	−0.9	−2.4	−0.5	0.6	−4.2	2.6
Singapore	2.1	0.3	2.9	2.2	1.2	0.8	−1.8	−4.8	3.5	−2.0	—	1.0	−5.3	0.9	0.1
New Zealand	6.7	1.6	1.4	2.1	1.9	1.0	0.9	—	2.3	3.9	0.9	1.1	3.6	−0.2	3.3
Memorandum															
European Union	5.0	2.2	2.7	3.1	2.6	1.9	2.0	1.5	1.6	2.3	2.3	1.9	. . .	. . .	. . .
Euro area	4.8	2.0	2.8	2.9	2.2	1.6	1.7	1.2	1.3	2.3	2.2	1.8	2.8	2.0	1.8
Newly industrialized Asian economies	5.6	1.8	5.5	4.7	3.7	2.9	3.2	−2.5	−1.6	0.6	0.3	1.5	. . .	. . .	. . .
Consumer prices															
Advanced economies	**4.2**	**2.0**	**2.6**	**2.6**	**2.4**	**2.1**	**1.5**	**1.4**	**2.3**	**2.2**	**1.4**	**1.7**	. . .	. . .	. . .
Major advanced economies	3.6	1.9	2.2	2.2	2.2	2.0	1.3	1.4	2.3	2.1	1.2	1.6	1.4	1.5	1.8
United States	3.8	2.4	2.6	2.8	2.9	2.3	1.5	2.2	3.4	2.8	1.5	2.3	1.9	2.1	2.5
Japan	1.7	−0.1	0.7	−0.1	—	1.7	0.6	−0.3	−0.8	−0.7	−1.0	−0.6	−1.0	−0.7	−0.4
Germany[2]	2.4	1.5	2.7	1.7	1.2	1.5	0.6	0.7	2.1	2.4	1.4	1.1	1.7	1.5	1.2
France[2]	3.6	1.5	1.7	1.8	2.1	1.3	0.7	0.6	1.8	1.8	1.8	1.4	1.5	1.5	1.9
Italy[2]	6.4	2.8	4.1	5.2	4.1	1.9	2.0	1.7	2.6	2.7	2.4	1.8	2.3	2.4	1.8
United Kingdom[3]	5.0	2.4	2.4	2.8	3.0	2.8	2.7	2.3	2.1	2.1	1.9	2.1	2.0	1.5	2.6
Canada	3.9	1.7	0.2	1.9	1.6	1.6	1.0	1.8	2.7	2.5	1.8	2.1	1.1	2.7	2.0
Other advanced economies	6.7	2.7	4.1	3.8	3.2	2.3	2.4	1.3	2.4	2.9	2.3	2.2	. . .	. . .	. . .
Memorandum															
European Union[2]	4.5	2.2	3.0	2.9	2.5	1.8	1.5	1.4	2.3	2.6	2.1	1.8	. . .	. . .	. . .
Euro area[2]	4.2	2.1	3.0	2.7	2.3	1.6	1.2	1.1	2.4	2.6	2.1	1.6	2.2	2.1	1.6
Newly industrialized Asian economies	4.2	2.9	5.7	4.6	4.3	3.4	4.4	—	1.1	1.9	1.1	2.2	. . .	. . .	. . .

[1]From fourth quarter of preceding year.
[2]Based on Eurostat's harmonized index of consumer prices.
[3]Retail price index excluding mortgage interest.

Table 10. Advanced Economies: Hourly Earnings, Productivity, and Unit Labor Costs in Manufacturing
(Annual percent change)

	Ten-Year Averages		1994	1995	1996	1997	1998	1999	2000	2001	2002	2003
	1984–93	1994–2003										
Hourly earnings												
Advanced economies	**5.8**	**3.2**	**3.3**	**3.3**	**3.1**	**2.6**	**3.2**	**3.0**	**4.5**	**2.5**	**3.2**	**3.3**
Major advanced economies	4.9	2.8	2.7	2.8	2.4	2.2	3.2	2.7	4.5	2.1	3.0	3.0
United States	4.1	3.4	2.8	2.1	1.4	1.9	5.4	4.0	7.4	1.6	4.0	3.8
Japan	3.9	1.0	2.1	2.3	1.8	3.1	0.8	−0.8	−0.2	0.9	−0.1	−0.2
Germany	5.4	3.0	2.3	4.5	4.5	1.8	2.0	2.7	2.8	3.4	3.0	3.0
France	5.1	1.9	1.7	2.4	2.3	−1.5	0.8	1.4	2.3	3.1	2.8	3.4
Italy	8.5	2.9	3.1	4.7	5.8	4.2	−1.4	2.5	2.7	2.7	2.4	2.6
United Kingdom	8.0	4.3	5.0	4.4	4.3	4.2	4.5	4.0	4.6	4.3	3.2	4.1
Canada	4.5	2.0	1.6	2.2	1.0	2.2	0.8	1.6	1.3	3.5	3.0	3.0
Other advanced economies	9.9	4.6	5.8	5.2	6.0	4.5	3.1	4.5	4.5	4.1	4.2	4.4
Memorandum												
European Union	6.9	3.3	3.3	4.2	4.3	2.7	2.2	2.9	3.3	3.6	3.2	3.4
Euro area	7.6	3.3	3.1	4.3	4.3	2.4	1.8	2.8	3.0	3.8	3.5	3.5
Newly industrialized Asian economies	13.4	6.5	11.4	7.9	10.2	5.6	0.8	7.2	6.7	4.2	5.4	6.2
Productivity												
Advanced economies	**3.1**	**3.3**	**4.8**	**3.8**	**3.2**	**4.4**	**2.3**	**4.3**	**4.8**	**0.6**	**2.4**	**2.4**
Major advanced economies	3.0	3.2	4.4	3.8	3.1	4.3	2.4	4.1	4.9	0.5	2.5	2.4
United States	2.9	3.7	3.0	3.9	3.5	4.2	4.9	5.1	4.0	0.9	4.4	2.9
Japan	2.5	1.9	3.1	4.5	3.8	4.7	−4.2	3.4	6.6	−4.5	0.5	1.5
Germany	3.7	5.2	8.9	4.9	5.8	7.7	4.7	3.0	6.6	4.1	3.2	3.0
France	3.1	3.7	6.8	6.0	1.0	5.6	5.5	2.9	6.7	0.6	0.2	2.1
Italy	2.8	2.4	6.0	3.6	3.7	2.3	−1.7	2.2	4.0	3.2	−0.5	1.4
United Kingdom	4.4	1.8	4.5	−0.5	−0.6	0.9	0.9	3.8	5.5	2.0	−0.5	2.0
Canada	2.5	1.3	4.8	1.4	−2.4	3.4	−0.4	2.6	2.1	−2.0	2.0	2.0
Other advanced economies	3.3	3.6	6.6	4.0	3.4	4.6	1.8	5.3	4.4	1.2	1.7	2.6
Memorandum												
European Union	3.3	3.4	7.3	3.7	2.6	4.5	2.7	2.9	5.0	2.2	0.9	2.2
Euro area	4.4	4.0	7.9	4.9	3.7	5.6	3.5	3.0	5.1	2.6	1.5	2.5
Newly industrialized Asian economies	7.2	5.9	7.1	7.9	7.0	6.1	−1.1	13.2	9.5	1.8	3.1	4.7
Unit labor costs												
Advanced economies	**2.7**	**−0.1**	**−1.4**	**−0.6**	**−0.1**	**−1.7**	**1.0**	**−1.2**	**−0.2**	**1.9**	**0.9**	**0.8**
Major advanced economies	1.9	−0.3	−1.6	−1.0	−0.7	−2.0	0.8	−1.3	−0.3	1.7	0.4	0.5
United States	1.2	−0.2	−0.2	−1.7	−2.1	−2.2	0.4	−1.1	3.2	0.6	−0.3	0.9
Japan	1.4	−0.9	−0.9	−2.1	−1.9	−1.6	5.3	−4.0	−6.3	5.6	−0.5	−1.6
Germany	1.7	−2.1	−6.1	−0.4	−1.2	−5.5	−2.6	−0.3	−3.5	−0.7	−0.2	—
France	1.9	−1.8	−4.8	−3.4	1.2	−6.7	−4.5	−1.5	−4.1	2.5	2.6	1.3
Italy	5.6	0.5	−2.7	1.0	2.0	1.9	0.3	0.3	−1.2	−0.5	2.9	1.2
United Kingdom	3.4	2.5	0.5	4.9	5.0	3.3	3.6	0.3	−0.9	2.3	3.7	2.0
Canada	1.9	0.7	−3.0	0.9	3.4	−1.2	1.1	−0.9	−0.7	5.5	1.0	0.9
Other advanced economies	6.1	1.0	−0.8	0.9	2.2	−0.2	1.4	−0.5	0.1	2.8	2.5	1.7
Memorandum												
European Union	3.4	—	−3.6	0.6	1.7	−1.7	−0.5	—	−1.6	1.4	2.3	1.2
Euro area	3.1	−0.7	−4.4	−0.6	0.6	−3.0	−1.6	−0.2	−2.0	1.2	1.9	1.0
Newly industrialized Asian economies	4.9	0.3	2.6	−1.0	1.9	−0.7	2.3	−4.5	−2.6	2.1	2.0	1.3

Table 11. Developing Countries: Consumer Prices
(Annual percent change)

| | Ten-Year Averages | | 1994 | 1995 | 1996 | 1997 | 1998 | 1999 | 2000 | 2001 | 2002 | 2003 |
	1984–93	1994–2003										
Developing countries	**48.5**	**13.7**	**55.4**	**23.2**	**15.4**	**10.0**	**10.5**	**6.9**	**6.1**	**5.7**	**5.6**	**6.0**
Regional groups												
Africa	24.3	19.7	54.7	35.3	30.2	14.6	10.9	12.3	14.3	13.1	9.6	9.5
Sub-Sahara	28.8	24.0	68.5	40.9	36.6	17.9	13.0	15.6	18.4	16.4	11.6	11.6
Excluding Nigeria and South Africa	38.7	35.2	121.6	57.5	58.8	25.5	17.2	23.5	28.7	22.2	12.7	14.4
Developing Asia	10.2	6.1	16.0	13.2	8.3	4.8	7.7	2.5	1.9	2.6	2.1	3.2
China	8.9	4.9	24.1	17.1	8.3	2.8	-0.8	-1.4	0.4	0.7	-0.4	1.5
India	8.8	7.1	10.2	10.2	9.0	7.2	13.2	4.7	4.0	3.8	4.5	5.1
Other developing Asia	12.9	8.2	8.1	9.1	7.7	6.8	22.0	9.1	3.3	5.9	6.0	5.6
Middle East and Turkey	24.2	25.0	37.8	39.1	29.6	28.3	27.6	23.6	19.6	17.2	17.1	13.3
Western Hemisphere	184.3	24.7	200.4	36.0	21.2	12.9	9.8	8.9	8.1	6.4	8.6	9.3
Analytical groups												
By source of export earnings												
Fuel	16.9	21.7	36.2	42.6	35.1	20.1	17.5	17.1	13.8	11.9	13.8	13.0
Nonfuel	53.6	12.9	57.8	21.3	13.5	9.0	9.8	5.9	5.3	5.1	4.8	5.3
of which, primary products	75.5	19.5	63.0	29.8	27.0	16.1	14.0	12.6	13.4	12.2	7.5	8.9
By external financing source												
Net debtor countries	50.6	14.1	57.5	23.8	15.8	10.2	10.8	7.1	6.3	6.0	5.7	6.1
of which, official financing	38.8	16.8	64.2	30.2	22.7	11.4	10.7	11.2	10.4	8.8	4.8	4.3
Net debtor countries by debt-servicing experience												
Countries with arrears and/or rescheduling during 1994–98	125.1	28.3	221.6	40.1	21.1	12.2	18.4	13.8	11.4	11.4	9.5	7.8
Other groups												
Heavily indebted poor countries	53.9	27.8	92.0	49.6	46.6	21.7	17.6	18.2	20.1	15.6	9.0	7.5
Middle East and north Africa	16.2	12.6	22.3	24.2	16.8	11.7	10.7	10.6	8.1	6.9	8.2	7.8
Memorandum												
Median												
Developing countries	9.5	6.0	10.8	10.0	7.3	6.2	5.8	3.9	4.0	4.4	4.0	4.0
Regional groups												
Africa	9.5	8.2	24.7	12.3	7.8	7.8	5.8	4.2	5.3	5.0	4.2	4.4
Developing Asia	8.2	5.9	8.4	7.9	7.6	6.4	8.4	4.4	3.6	3.9	4.3	4.2
Middle East and Turkey	6.8	3.7	7.0	6.4	6.8	3.4	3.0	2.2	1.5	1.4	2.5	3.1
Western Hemisphere	14.7	5.7	8.3	10.2	7.4	7.0	5.1	3.5	4.8	2.7	4.3	3.9

Table 12. Developing Countries—by Country: Consumer Prices[1]

(Annual percent change)

	Average 1984–93	1994	1995	1996	1997	1998	1999	2000	2001	2002	2003
Africa	**24.3**	**54.7**	**35.3**	**30.2**	**14.6**	**10.9**	**12.3**	**14.3**	**13.1**	**9.6**	**9.5**
Algeria	13.6	29.0	29.8	18.7	5.7	5.0	2.6	0.3	4.2	4.0	3.0
Angola	62.0	949.8	2,672.2	4,146.0	221.5	107.4	248.2	325.0	152.6	108.5	74.9
Benin	2.3	38.5	14.5	4.9	3.8	5.8	0.3	4.2	4.0	3.3	3.0
Botswana	12.6	12.3	10.5	10.3	9.4	7.6	6.9	7.9	7.2	5.5	4.7
Burkina Faso	—	24.7	7.8	6.1	2.3	5.0	−1.1	−0.3	4.9	2.0	2.0
Burundi	7.3	14.7	19.4	26.4	31.1	12.5	3.4	24.3	9.3	8.0	8.0
Cameroon	2.5	12.7	25.8	6.6	5.1	—	2.9	0.8	2.8	4.0	3.0
Cape Verde	7.6	3.3	8.4	6.0	8.6	4.4	4.4	−2.4	3.7	2.9	2.5
Central African Republic	−0.3	24.5	19.2	3.7	1.6	−1.9	−1.4	3.2	3.8	1.5	2.7
Chad	0.5	41.3	5.4	11.3	5.6	4.3	−8.4	3.7	12.4	4.0	4.0
Comoros	0.4	25.3	7.1	2.0	3.0	3.5	3.5	4.5	5.0	3.0	3.0
Congo, Dem. Rep. of	282.8	23,760.5	541.8	617.0	199.0	107.0	270.0	553.7	357.9	27.7	9.1
Congo, Rep. of	−1.1	42.9	8.6	10.2	13.2	1.8	3.1	0.4	−0.5	4.0	3.0
Côte d'Ivoire	3.5	26.0	14.1	2.7	4.2	4.5	0.7	2.5	4.4	3.0	3.0
Djibouti	5.7	6.5	4.9	2.6	2.5	2.2	2.0	2.4	1.8	1.5	2.0
Equatorial Guinea	8.0	38.9	11.4	6.0	3.0	3.0	6.5	6.0	12.0	9.0	5.0
Eritrea	…	13.1	12.0	10.3	3.7	9.5	8.4	19.9	14.6	8.9	6.3
Ethiopia	7.9	1.2	13.4	0.9	−6.4	3.6	3.9	4.2	−7.1	−7.2	4.5
Gabon	1.2	36.1	10.0	4.5	4.1	2.3	−0.7	0.4	2.1	2.0	2.0
Gambia, The	17.3	4.0	4.0	4.8	3.1	1.1	3.8	0.9	4.0	3.0	2.5
Ghana	25.7	24.9	59.5	46.6	27.9	14.6	12.4	25.2	32.9	14.6	10.8
Guinea	25.7	4.2	5.6	3.0	1.9	5.1	4.6	6.8	5.4	3.6	3.5
Guinea-Bissau	64.9	15.2	45.4	50.7	49.1	8.0	−2.1	8.6	3.3	3.0	3.0
Kenya	16.7	28.8	1.6	8.9	11.9	6.7	5.8	10.0	5.8	2.0	4.7
Lesotho	14.0	7.2	10.0	9.1	8.5	7.8	8.6	6.1	6.9	10.3	3.4
Liberia	…	…	…	…	…	…	…	…	…	…	…
Madagascar	12.9	39.0	49.0	19.8	4.5	6.2	9.9	11.9	5.0	15.0	5.0
Malawi	18.0	34.7	83.1	37.7	9.1	29.8	44.8	29.6	27.2	9.4	5.0
Mali	0.1	24.8	12.4	6.5	−0.7	4.1	−1.2	−0.7	5.2	2.4	2.0
Mauritania	8.5	4.1	6.5	4.7	4.5	8.0	4.1	3.3	4.7	4.0	3.8
Mauritius	7.1	9.4	6.0	5.9	7.9	5.4	7.9	5.3	4.4	6.0	5.8
Morocco	6.3	5.1	6.1	3.0	1.0	2.7	0.7	1.9	0.6	2.1	2.1
Mozambique, Rep. of	49.6	63.1	54.4	44.6	6.4	0.6	2.9	12.7	9.0	16.7	6.8
Namibia	12.5	10.8	10.0	8.0	8.8	6.2	8.6	9.3	13.4	10.2	7.0
Niger	−1.1	24.8	21.9	5.3	2.9	4.5	−2.3	2.9	4.0	2.7	2.0
Nigeria	25.3	57.0	72.8	29.3	8.5	10.0	6.6	6.9	18.9	15.9	13.2
Rwanda	6.1	47.3	48.2	13.4	11.7	6.8	−2.4	3.9	3.4	2.4	4.5
São Tomé and Príncipe	26.6	51.2	36.8	42.0	69.0	42.1	16.3	11.0	9.5	9.2	8.0
Senegal	2.2	32.0	8.1	2.8	1.7	1.1	0.8	0.7	3.0	3.5	2.0
Seychelles	2.2	1.8	−0.3	−1.1	0.6	2.7	3.5	−0.1	−0.1	6.0	6.0
Sierra Leone	75.5	24.2	26.0	23.1	14.6	36.0	34.1	−0.9	2.2	5.0	5.0
Somalia	…	…	…	…	…	…	…	…	…	…	…
South Africa	14.4	8.8	8.7	7.3	8.6	6.9	5.2	5.4	5.7	7.9	6.0
Sudan	67.3	115.5	68.4	132.8	46.7	17.1	16.0	8.0	5.0	5.5	5.0
Swaziland	13.0	13.8	12.3	6.4	7.9	7.5	5.9	9.9	7.5	10.9	7.0
Tanzania	29.3	37.1	26.5	21.0	16.1	9.8	9.0	6.2	5.2	4.4	3.9
Togo	1.0	48.5	6.4	2.5	5.5	−1.4	4.5	−2.5	6.8	4.8	4.3
Tunisia	6.9	4.5	6.3	4.6	3.7	3.1	2.7	3.0	1.9	3.4	3.0
Uganda	80.1	6.5	6.1	7.5	7.8	5.8	−0.2	6.3	4.6	−1.8	1.0
Zambia	82.6	54.6	34.9	43.1	24.4	24.5	26.8	26.1	21.7	20.0	9.8
Zimbabwe	18.2	22.2	22.6	21.5	18.8	31.7	58.5	55.9	76.7	137.2	522.2

Table 12 *(continued)*

	Average 1984–93	1994	1995	1996	1997	1998	1999	2000	2001	2002	2003
Developing Asia	**10.2**	**16.0**	**13.2**	**8.3**	**4.8**	**7.7**	**2.5**	**1.9**	**2.6**	**2.1**	**3.2**
Afghanistan, Islamic State of	...	...	...	...	...	...	...	...	...	...	...
Bangladesh	8.5	6.1	7.7	3.9	5.1	8.5	6.4	2.3	1.9	4.8	6.2
Bhutan	9.3	7.0	9.5	8.8	6.5	10.6	6.8	4.8	5.0	5.0	5.0
Brunei Darussalam	...	2.4	6.0	2.0	1.7	−0.4	—	1.2	1.1	1.4	1.6
Cambodia	...	9.4	1.3	7.1	8.0	14.8	4.0	−0.8	0.2	1.8	3.0
China	8.9	24.1	17.1	8.3	2.8	−0.8	−1.4	0.4	0.7	−0.4	1.5
Fiji	5.8	1.2	2.2	2.4	2.9	8.3	0.2	3.0	2.3	2.5	2.5
India	8.8	10.2	10.2	9.0	7.2	13.2	4.7	4.0	3.8	4.5	5.1
Indonesia	7.9	8.5	9.4	7.9	6.2	58.0	20.7	3.8	11.5	11.9	8.7
Kiribati	2.8	4.0	4.1	−1.5	2.2	4.7	0.4	1.0	7.7	2.7	2.7
Lao P.D. Republic	21.4	7.7	19.1	19.1	19.5	90.1	128.4	23.2	8.0	7.2	5.0
Malaysia	2.6	4.1	3.5	3.5	2.6	5.1	2.8	1.6	1.4	1.8	2.5
Maldives	7.6	3.4	5.5	6.2	7.6	−1.4	3.0	−1.1	3.7	5.7	4.3
Myanmar	19.5	22.4	28.9	20.0	33.9	49.1	11.4	10.3	15.0	15.0	15.0
Nepal	10.8	8.9	7.7	7.2	8.1	8.3	11.4	3.4	2.4	3.0	4.0
Pakistan	7.7	12.4	12.3	10.4	11.4	6.2	4.1	4.4	3.1	3.4	4.0
Papua New Guinea	5.3	2.9	17.3	11.6	3.9	13.6	14.9	15.6	10.2	7.5	4.7
Philippines	13.7	8.4	8.0	9.0	5.8	9.7	6.7	4.3	6.1	4.0	5.0
Samoa	1.7	12.1	−2.9	5.4	6.9	2.2	0.3	1.0	4.0	5.0	3.0
Solomon Islands	12.0	13.3	9.6	11.8	8.1	12.4	8.3	6.0	7.0	9.3	8.1
Sri Lanka	11.5	8.4	7.7	15.9	9.6	9.4	4.7	6.2	14.2	8.8	6.6
Thailand	3.6	5.1	5.8	5.9	5.6	8.1	0.3	1.6	1.7	0.7	1.9
Tonga	9.4	2.4	−0.5	2.7	2.0	3.0	3.9	5.3	7.0	3.5	3.1
Vanuatu	6.3	2.3	2.2	0.9	2.9	3.2	2.0	2.0	2.0	2.0	2.0
Vietnam	117.5	9.5	17.4	5.7	3.2	7.3	4.1	−1.7	0.1	4.1	3.8
Middle East and Turkey	**24.2**	**37.8**	**39.1**	**29.6**	**28.3**	**27.6**	**23.6**	**19.6**	**17.2**	**17.1**	**13.3**
Bahrain	−0.2	0.4	3.1	−0.1	4.6	−0.4	−1.3	−0.7	−1.2	−1.0	−1.3
Egypt	18.1	9.0	9.4	7.1	6.2	4.7	3.8	2.8	2.4	2.5	3.4
Iran, Islamic Republic of	18.9	35.2	49.4	23.2	17.3	18.1	20.1	12.6	11.4	15.0	15.0
Iraq	...	...	...	...	...	...	...	...	...	...	...
Jordan	4.9	3.6	2.3	6.5	3.0	3.1	0.6	0.7	1.8	3.2	2.1
Kuwait	1.2	2.6	2.7	3.6	0.7	0.1	3.0	1.7	2.5	2.5	2.5
Lebanon	92.8	8.2	10.3	8.9	7.7	4.5	0.2	−0.4	−0.4	5.0	3.4
Libya	7.4	10.7	8.3	4.0	3.6	3.7	2.6	−2.9	−8.5	5.9	2.8
Malta	1.5	4.1	4.0	2.0	3.1	2.4	2.1	2.4	2.9	2.0	2.0
Oman	1.8	−0.7	−1.1	0.5	−0.5	−0.5	0.5	−1.2	−1.1	2.4	4.3
Qatar	2.6	1.4	3.0	7.1	2.7	2.9	2.2	1.7	−0.7	1.5	2.6
Saudi Arabia	−0.4	0.6	5.0	0.9	−0.4	−0.2	−1.3	−0.6	−0.8	—	1.1
Syrian Arab Republic	21.2	15.3	7.7	8.9	1.9	−0.4	−2.1	−0.6	1.0	2.5	3.5
Turkey	56.1	106.2	93.6	82.3	85.7	84.6	64.9	54.9	54.4	47.1	28.6
United Arab Emirates	4.0	5.7	4.4	3.0	2.9	2.0	2.1	1.4	0.9	1.9	2.5
Yemen, Republic of	...	71.3	62.5	40.0	4.6	11.5	8.0	10.9	11.9	15.8	9.0

Table 12 *(concluded)*

	Average 1984–93	1994	1995	1996	1997	1998	1999	2000	2001	2002	2003
Western Hemisphere	**184.3**	**200.4**	**36.0**	**21.2**	**12.9**	9.8	8.9	**8.1**	**6.4**	**8.6**	**9.3**
Antigua and Barbuda	3.7	6.5	2.7	3.0	0.3	3.3	1.1	0.7	1.0	1.0	1.0
Argentina	346.5	4.2	3.4	0.2	0.5	0.9	−1.2	−0.9	−1.1	29.0	48.0
Bahamas, The	5.0	1.3	2.1	1.4	0.5	1.3	1.3	1.6	2.0	1.9	1.2
Barbados	4.1	−0.1	1.9	2.4	7.7	−1.3	1.6	2.5	2.2	1.5	1.6
Belize	2.5	2.5	2.9	6.4	1.0	−0.8	−1.2	0.6	1.2	1.5	1.5
Bolivia	163.8	7.9	10.2	12.4	4.7	7.7	2.2	4.6	1.6	0.9	4.4
Brazil	614.2	2,075.8	66.0	15.8	6.9	3.2	4.9	7.0	6.8	6.5	4.3
Chile	19.7	11.4	8.2	7.4	6.1	5.1	3.3	3.8	3.6	2.1	2.8
Colombia	24.5	22.8	20.9	20.8	18.5	18.7	10.9	9.2	8.0	5.7	5.0
Costa Rica	17.1	13.5	23.2	17.6	13.3	11.7	10.0	11.0	11.3	11.0	11.3
Dominica	3.7	—	1.3	1.7	2.4	0.9	1.6	1.9	1.8	1.7	1.6
Dominican Republic	26.5	8.3	12.5	5.4	8.3	4.8	6.5	7.7	8.9	4.8	4.5
Ecuador	43.4	27.3	22.9	24.4	30.6	36.1	52.2	96.2	37.7	12.7	8.9
El Salvador	19.5	10.6	10.1	9.8	4.5	0.1	0.1	0.1	0.1	0.1	0.1
Grenada	2.9	2.6	2.2	2.8	1.3	1.4	0.5	2.2	2.5	1.5	1.5
Guatemala	16.2	12.5	8.4	11.0	9.2	6.6	4.9	5.1	8.7	5.0	3.9
Guyana	38.0	12.4	12.2	7.1	3.6	4.6	7.5	6.1	2.7	4.3	4.5
Haiti	11.0	37.4	30.2	21.9	16.2	12.7	8.1	11.5	16.7	11.6	11.0
Honduras	10.4	21.7	29.5	23.8	20.2	13.7	11.6	11.0	9.7	7.8	7.2
Jamaica	28.4	33.2	21.7	21.5	8.8	6.0	8.4	6.4	5.0	4.5	4.0
Mexico	49.9	7.0	35.0	34.4	20.6	15.9	16.6	9.5	6.4	4.8	3.7
Netherlands Antilles	2.4	1.9	2.8	3.4	3.1	1.2	0.8	3.1	0.7	1.4	2.4
Nicaragua	901.7	7.7	11.2	11.6	9.2	13.0	11.2	7.4	7.4	5.3	4.5
Panama	0.8	1.3	0.9	1.3	1.3	0.6	1.5	0.7	—	0.8	1.6
Paraguay	24.2	20.6	13.4	9.8	7.0	11.6	6.8	9.0	7.7	8.7	6.0
Peru	367.0	23.7	11.1	11.5	8.5	7.3	3.5	3.8	2.0	0.4	2.0
St. Kitts and Nevis	2.5	1.4	3.0	2.0	8.7	3.7	3.4	2.1	2.1	1.9	2.0
St. Lucia	3.0	2.7	5.9	1.2	0.3	2.8	3.5	3.6	2.5	2.3	2.3
St. Vincent and the Grenadines	3.3	1.0	1.7	4.4	0.5	2.1	1.0	0.2	0.8	0.1	2.4
Suriname	28.4	368.5	235.5	−0.8	7.3	19.0	98.8	58.9	42.3	11.4	14.6
Trinidad and Tobago	9.3	3.7	5.3	3.3	3.6	5.6	3.4	5.6	2.5	3.8	3.5
Uruguay	73.9	45.0	42.6	28.6	19.8	9.6	5.7	4.8	4.4	24.2	49.9
Venezuela	30.8	60.8	59.9	99.9	50.0	35.8	23.6	16.2	12.5	22.7	25.2

[1]For many countries, figures for recent years are IMF staff estimates. Data for some countries are for fiscal years.

Table 13. Countries in Transition: Consumer Prices[1]
(Annual percent change)

	Average 1984–93	1994	1995	1996	1997	1998	1999	2000	2001	2002	2003
Central and eastern Europe	...	**45.6**	**24.7**	**23.3**	**41.8**	**17.2**	**11.0**	**12.8**	**9.6**	**6.1**	**5.6**
Albania	23.4	22.6	7.8	12.7	32.1	20.9	0.4	—	3.1	5.3	3.0
Bosnia and Herzegovina	...	...	0.2	−13.7	9.5	0.6	3.2	5.6	3.3	2.3	1.8
Bulgaria	35.3	96.0	62.1	123.0	1,061.2	18.8	2.6	10.4	7.5	6.4	4.3
Croatia	...	97.5	2.0	3.5	3.6	5.7	4.1	6.2	4.9	3.5	3.5
Czech Republic	...	10.0	9.1	8.8	8.5	10.6	2.1	3.9	4.7	2.7	3.0
Estonia	...	47.7	29.0	23.1	11.2	8.2	3.3	4.0	5.8	3.7	3.0
Hungary	16.7	18.8	28.3	23.5	18.3	14.3	10.0	9.8	9.2	5.5	5.2
Latvia	...	35.8	25.1	17.6	8.4	4.6	2.4	2.6	2.5	3.0	3.0
Lithuania	...	72.1	39.5	24.7	8.8	5.1	0.8	1.0	1.3	1.1	2.5
Macedonia, former Yugoslav Rep. of	...	126.4	15.8	2.3	2.6	−0.1	−0.7	5.8	5.3	3.5	3.0
Poland	73.6	32.2	27.9	19.9	14.9	11.8	7.3	10.1	5.5	2.1	2.3
Romania	52.7	136.7	32.3	38.8	154.8	59.1	45.8	45.7	34.5	24.2	19.1
Slovak Republic	...	13.4	9.9	5.8	6.1	6.7	10.7	12.0	7.3	4.2	7.1
Slovenia	...	21.5	13.5	9.9	8.4	8.0	6.1	8.9	8.4	7.7	5.5
Commonwealth of Independent States and Mongolia	...	**508.1**	**235.7**	**55.9**	**19.1**	**25.5**	**70.5**	**25.0**	**19.8**	**14.5**	**10.7**
Russia	...	307.5	198.0	47.9	14.7	27.8	85.7	20.8	20.7	15.8	11.0
Excluding Russia	...	1,334.5	338.9	75.5	29.7	20.8	41.7	34.7	17.9	11.9	10.1
Armenia	...	5,273.4	176.7	18.7	14.0	8.7	0.7	−0.8	3.2	2.8	2.8
Azerbaijan	...	1,664.0	411.8	19.8	3.7	−0.8	−8.5	1.8	1.5	2.4	3.3
Belarus	...	2,434.1	709.3	52.7	63.9	73.2	293.8	168.9	61.3	43.1	22.5
Georgia	...	15,606.5	162.7	39.3	7.0	3.6	19.1	4.0	4.7	5.9	5.0
Kazakhstan	...	1,879.9	176.3	39.1	17.4	7.3	8.4	13.3	8.3	5.8	6.2
Kyrgyz Republic	...	190.1	43.5	32.0	23.5	10.5	35.9	18.7	7.0	4.1	4.5
Moldova	...	329.6	30.2	23.5	11.8	7.7	39.3	31.3	9.8	6.6	8.4
Mongolia	29.6	87.6	56.8	46.8	36.6	9.4	7.6	11.6	8.0	6.0	5.0
Tajikistan	...	350.4	610.0	418.2	88.0	43.2	27.5	32.9	38.6	10.7	7.6
Turkmenistan	...	1,748.3	1,005.2	992.4	83.7	16.8	23.5	8.0	11.3	...	...
Ukraine	...	891.2	376.4	80.2	15.9	14.5	22.7	28.2	12.0	5.1	9.1
Uzbekistan	...	1,568.3	304.6	54.0	70.9	29.0	29.1	25.0	27.2	23.2	13.5
Memorandum											
EU accession candidates	...	59.1	42.7	39.4	55.4	35.6	25.3	24.7	21.2	16.8	11.9

[1]For many countries, inflation for the earlier years is measured on the basis of a retail price index. Consumer price indices with a broader and more up-to-date coverage are typically used for more recent years.

Table 14. Summary Financial Indicators
(Percent)

	1994	1995	1996	1997	1998	1999	2000	2001	2002	2003
Advanced economies										
Central government fiscal balance[1]										
Advanced economies	−3.7	−3.4	−2.7	−1.6	−1.3	−0.8	0.3	−0.9	−2.0	−1.9
United States	−3.0	−2.6	−1.8	−0.6	0.5	1.3	2.2	0.6	−1.8	−2.0
Japan	−3.5	−4.1	4.4	−4.0	−5.8	−6.7	−6.5	−6.4	−6.1	−5.3
European Union	−5.3	−4.7	−4.0	−2.4	−1.8	−1.0	0.3	−0.9	−1.5	−1.4
Euro area	−4.5	−4.1	−3.8	−2.6	−2.4	−1.6	−0.4	−1.5	−1.8	−1.5
Other advanced economies	−1.5	−1.0	−0.2	0.6	−0.1	—	1.7	0.3	0.1	0.5
General government fiscal balance[1]										
Advanced economies	−4.3	−4.1	−3.4	−1.9	−1.5	−1.0	0.1	−1.4	−2.5	−2.3
United States	−3.8	−3.3	−2.4	−1.3	−0.1	0.6	1.5	−0.2	−2.6	−2.8
Japan	−2.8	−4.2	−4.9	−3.7	−5.5	−7.0	−7.3	−7.1	−7.2	−6.1
European Union	−5.6	−5.3	−4.3	−2.4	−1.7	−0.7	0.9	−1.0	−1.5	−1.2
Euro area	−5.1	−5.0	−4.2	−2.6	−2.3	−1.3	0.1	−1.6	−1.9	−1.5
Other advanced economies	−3.2	−2.5	−1.4	0.3	−0.5	—	1.5	−0.1	—	0.5
General government structural balance[2]										
Advanced economies	−3.8	−3.6	−2.9	−1.6	−1.2	−0.9	−0.7	−1.1	−1.8	−1.5
Growth of broad money[3]										
Advanced economies	2.6	5.0	4.8	5.0	6.7	5.8	5.1	8.7	. . .	. . .
United States	0.6	3.8	4.5	5.6	8.5	6.3	6.1	10.3	. . .	. . .
Japan	2.9	3.2	2.9	3.8	4.4	2.6	2.0	3.4	. . .	. . .
Euro area[4]	2.3	5.5	4.0	4.6	4.8	5.5	4.1	11.0	. . .	. . .
Other advanced economies	9.5	8.8	8.7	6.4	10.2	10.9	8.2	7.4	. . .	. . .
Short-term interest rates[5]										
United States	3.1	4.4	5.7	5.1	4.9	4.8	6.0	3.5	1.8	2.7
Japan	1.9	0.8	0.3	0.3	0.2	0.0	0.2	0.0	0.0	0.0
Euro area[4]	6.4	6.1	4.8	4.3	4.1	3.1	4.5	4.2	3.3	3.7
LIBOR	5.1	6.1	5.6	5.8	5.5	5.5	6.6	3.7	2.1	3.2
Developing countries										
Central government fiscal balance[1]										
Weighted average	−2.8	−2.6	−2.1	−2.5	−3.8	−4.1	−3.2	−3.9	−4.0	−3.2
Median	−3.6	−3.3	−2.2	−2.4	−3.1	−3.3	−3.3	−3.5	−4.0	−2.8
General government fiscal balance[1]										
Weighted average	−3.8	−3.2	−3.0	−3.5	−4.8	−5.3	−4.2	−4.9	−5.0	−4.0
Median	−3.4	−3.3	−2.6	−2.4	−3.2	−3.5	−3.3	−3.5	−3.5	−2.6
Growth of broad money										
Weighted average	68.4	24.6	23.0	22.7	17.1	15.1	11.3	12.3	9.3	12.1
Median	18.7	16.3	13.7	15.1	10.5	12.5	12.3	11.6	9.1	9.3
Countries in transition										
Central government fiscal balance[1]	−7.4	−4.6	−4.6	−4.7	−3.5	−2.1	—	−0.1	−0.8	−0.9
General government fiscal balance[1]	−7.5	−4.7	−5.8	−5.4	−4.9	−2.1	0.2	−0.4	−1.5	−1.5
Growth of broad money	215.0	75.8	32.2	33.2	20.3	38.7	37.1	26.8	16.5	14.6

[1]Percent of GDP.

[2]Percent of potential GDP.

[3]M2, defined as M1 plus quasi-money, except for Japan, for which the data are based on M2 plus certificates of deposit (CDs). Quasi-money is essentially private term deposits and other notice deposits. The United States also includes money market mutual fund balances, money market deposit accounts, overnight repurchase agreements, and overnight Eurodollars issued to U.S. residents by foreign branches of U.S. banks. For Japan, M2 plus CDs is currency in circulation plus total private and public sector deposits and installments of Sogo Bank plus CDs. For the euro area, M3 is composed of M2 plus marketable instruments held by euro area residents, which comprise repurchase agreements, money market fund shares/units, money market paper, and debt securities up to two years.

[4]Excludes Greece prior to 2001.

[5]For the United States, three-month treasury bills; for Japan, three-month certificates of deposit; for the euro area, a weighted average of national three-month money market interest rates through 1998 and three-month EURIBOR thereafter; for LIBOR, London interbank offered rate on six-month U.S. dollar deposits.

Table 15. Advanced Economies: General and Central Government Fiscal Balances and Balances Excluding Social Security Transactions[1]

(Percent of GDP)

	1994	1995	1996	1997	1998	1999	2000	2001	2002	2003
General government fiscal balance										
Advanced economies	**−4.3**	**−4.1**	**−3.4**	**−1.9**	**−1.5**	**−1.0**	**0.1**	**−1.4**	**−2.5**	**−2.3**
Major advanced economies	−4.3	−4.2	−3.6	−2.1	−1.6	−1.1	−0.1	−1.7	−3.0	−2.8
United States	−3.8	−3.3	−2.4	−1.3	−0.1	0.6	1.5	−0.2	−2.6	−2.8
Japan	−2.8	−4.2	−4.9	−3.7	−5.5	−7.0	−7.3	−7.1	−7.2	−6.1
Germany	−2.4	−3.3	−3.4	−2.7	−2.2	−1.5	1.1	−2.8	−2.9	−2.2
France[2]	−5.5	−5.5	−4.1	−3.0	−2.7	−1.6	−1.3	−1.4	−2.5	−2.1
Italy	−9.3	−7.6	−7.1	−2.7	−2.8	−1.8	−0.5	−2.2	−2.0	−1.5
United Kingdom	−6.8	−5.4	−4.2	−1.6	0.2	1.4	4.0	0.2	−0.8	−1.1
Canada	−6.7	−5.3	−2.8	0.2	0.1	1.7	3.1	1.8	1.1	1.2
Other advanced economies	−4.0	−3.8	−2.5	−1.1	−0.9	−0.5	0.8	—	−0.2	0.1
Spain	−6.1	−7.0	−4.9	−3.2	−2.6	−1.1	−0.3	−0.1	—	—
Netherlands	−3.6	−4.2	−1.7	−1.6	−0.9	0.3	2.0	0.1	−0.8	−0.7
Belgium	−5.0	−4.3	−3.8	−2.0	−0.7	−0.5	0.1	0.4	−0.1	−0.3
Sweden	−10.8	−7.9	−3.4	−1.6	1.8	1.9	4.0	4.8	1.8	1.8
Austria[3]	−5.0	−5.2	−3.8	−2.0	−2.5	−2.4	−1.7	−0.1	−0.5	−0.3
Denmark	−2.4	−2.3	−1.0	0.4	1.1	3.1	2.5	2.8	2.0	2.2
Finland	−5.7	−3.7	−3.2	−1.5	1.3	1.9	7.0	4.9	3.1	2.0
Greece	−10.0	−10.2	−7.4	−4.0	−2.4	−1.7	−0.8	0.1	0.8	0.7
Portugal	−6.0	−4.6	−4.0	−2.6	−1.9	−2.9	−2.7	−4.1	−3.6	−3.2
Ireland	−1.7	−2.1	−0.3	1.2	2.3	4.1	4.5	1.7	−0.4	−1.0
Luxembourg	2.9	2.7	2.0	2.9	3.2	3.8	5.8	5.2	1.0	0.7
Switzerland	−2.8	−1.9	−2.0	−2.4	−0.4	−0.2	2.4	−0.3	0.1	−0.3
Norway	0.4	3.4	6.5	7.8	3.5	5.6	14.7	14.0	12.1	10.9
Israel	−3.2	−4.5	−5.8	−4.3	−3.8	−4.8	−2.2	−6.1	−6.0	−4.5
Iceland	−4.7	−3.0	−1.6	—	0.5	2.4	2.4	−0.1	3.7	0.6
Cyprus	−1.4	−1.0	−3.4	−5.3	−5.5	−4.0	−2.7	−2.8	−2.6	−2.4
Korea[4]	0.1	0.3	—	−1.7	−4.3	−3.3	1.3	0.7	0.9	1.1
Australia[5]	−3.5	−2.1	−0.9	−0.1	0.3	0.9	0.9	0.2	0.1	0.4
Taiwan Province of China	−3.7	−4.5	−5.1	−3.8	−3.4	−6.0	−4.5	−6.5	−4.4	−2.5
Hong Kong SAR	1.0	−0.3	2.1	6.5	−1.8	0.8	−0.6	−5.1	−3.6	−3.0
Singapore	13.9	12.2	9.3	9.3	3.6	4.5	7.6	6.4	4.1	6.7
New Zealand[6]	2.2	3.6	2.7	1.6	0.9	0.4	0.8	1.4	1.5	1.5
Memorandum										
European Union	−5.6	−5.3	−4.3	−2.4	−1.7	−0.7	0.9	−1.0	−1.5	−1.2
Euro area	−5.1	−5.0	−4.2	−2.6	−2.3	−1.3	0.1	−1.6	−1.9	−1.5
Newly industrialized Asian economies	—	−1.1	−1.2	0.7	−2.0	−2.9	−1.8	−4.3	−2.9	−1.3
Fiscal balance excluding social security transactions										
United States	−4.2	−3.7	−2.7	−1.7	−0.7	−0.4	−0.1	−1.1	−2.6	−2.7
Japan	−5.1	−6.5	−7.0	−5.8	−7.1	−8.5	−8.4	−7.4	−7.1	−5.9
Germany	−2.5	−2.9	−3.1	−2.8	−2.4	−1.8	1.2	−2.7	−2.9	−2.2
France	−5.0	−4.8	−3.6	−2.6	−2.5	−1.9	−1.9	−1.8	−2.4	−2.3
Italy	−7.1	−5.6	−5.3	−0.7	1.3	2.6	3.5	1.8	2.4	2.8
Canada	−3.9	−2.7	—	3.0	2.7	4.0	4.9	3.5	2.9	2.7

Table 15 *(concluded)*

	1994	1995	1996	1997	1998	1999	2000	2001	2002	2003
Central government fiscal balance										
Advanced economies	**−3.7**	**−3.4**	**−2.7**	**−1.6**	**−1.3**	**−0.8**	**0.3**	**−0.9**	**−2.0**	**−1.9**
Major advanced economies	−3.9	−3.5	−3.0	−1.7	−1.3	−0.8	0.2	−1.2	−2.4	−2.3
United States[7]	−3.0	−2.6	−1.8	−0.6	0.5	1.3	2.2	0.6	−1.8	−2.0
Japan[8]	−3.5	−4.1	−4.4	−4.0	−5.8	−6.7	−6.5	−6.4	−6.1	−5.3
Germany[9]	−1.5	−1.4	−2.2	−1.7	−1.5	−1.3	1.3	−1.1	−1.2	−0.8
France	−4.8	−4.1	−3.7	−3.6	−3.9	−2.5	−2.4	−2.2	−3.1	−2.7
Italy	−9.1	−8.0	−7.0	−2.9	−2.7	−1.6	−1.0	−2.8	−2.7	−2.4
United Kingdom	−6.8	−5.4	−4.3	−1.6	0.3	1.4	4.0	0.2	−0.7	−1.0
Canada	−4.6	−3.9	−2.0	0.7	0.8	0.8	1.7	1.0	0.6	0.6
Other advanced economies	−3.2	−2.8	−1.7	−1.0	−1.1	−0.5	0.7	0.2	−0.5	−0.2
Memorandum										
European Union	−5.3	−4.7	−4.0	−2.4	−1.8	−1.0	0.3	−0.9	−1.5	−1.4
Euro area	−4.5	−4.1	−3.8	−2.6	−2.4	−1.6	−0.4	−1.5	−1.8	−1.5
Newly industrialized Asian economies	1.0	1.0	1.0	0.8	−1.3	−1.2	1.0	−0.6	−1.0	−0.1

[1]On a national income accounts basis except as indicated in footnotes. See Box A1 for a summary of the policy assumptions underlying the projections.
[2]Adjusted for valuation changes of the foreign exchange stabilization fund.
[3]Based on ESA95 methodology, according to which swap income is not included. Data on swap income are not yet available for other countries in the European Union.
[4]Data cover the consolidated central government including the social security funds but excluding privatization.
[5]Data exclude net advances (primarily privatization receipts and net policy-related lending).
[6]Data from 1992 onward are on an accrual basis and are not strictly comparable with previous cash-based data.
[7]Data are on a budget basis.
[8]Data are on a national income basis and exclude social security transactions.
[9]Data are on an administrative basis and exclude social security transactions.

Table 16. Advanced Economies: General Government Structural Balances[1]

(Percent of potential GDP)

	1994	1995	1996	1997	1998	1999	2000	2001	2002	2003
Structural balance										
Advanced economies	**−3.8**	**−3.6**	**−2.9**	**−1.6**	**−1.2**	**−0.9**	**−0.7**	**−1.1**	**−1.8**	**−1.5**
Major advanced economies	−3.7	−3.6	−3.0	−1.7	−1.3	−1.0	−0.8	−1.3	−2.2	−1.9
United States	−3.2	−2.7	−1.9	−1.1	−0.2	0.3	0.9	0.1	−1.9	−1.9
Japan	−2.5	−3.8	−5.2	−4.1	−4.9	−6.1	−6.8	−6.1	−5.7	−4.6
Germany[2,3]	−2.5	−3.5	−2.8	−1.7	−1.4	−1.0	−1.5	−2.2	−1.6	−0.9
France[3]	−3.5	−3.7	−1.9	−1.0	−1.5	−0.9	−1.6	−1.6	−1.9	−1.4
Italy[3]	−8.1	−7.0	−6.2	−1.9	−2.0	−0.9	−1.3	−1.8	−1.7	−1.2
United Kingdom[3]	−5.7	−4.6	−3.4	−1.0	0.3	1.2	1.3	−0.1	−0.6	−0.5
Canada	−6.7	−5.4	−2.0	0.8	0.5	1.6	2.5	2.2	1.6	1.2
Other advanced economies	−4.3	−3.8	−2.2	−1.3	−0.8	−0.3	0.3	0.3	0.4	0.6
Spain[3]	−5.2	−5.1	−3.0	−1.7	−1.8	−0.9	−0.8	−0.4	0.5	0.7
Netherlands[3]	−2.7	−3.1	−0.8	−1.3	−1.4	−1.0	−0.1	−0.6	−0.4	—
Belgium[3]	−3.2	−2.6	−1.6	−0.7	0.6	0.3	−0.2	0.5	1.2	1.1
Sweden	−11.8	−8.8	−4.9	−3.7	0.6	1.8	4.6	4.3	1.8	2.0
Austria[3]	−4.7	−5.0	−3.7	−1.7	−2.3	−2.5	−2.3	0.3	1.0	1.0
Denmark	−1.4	−2.0	−1.0	0.1	0.8	2.8	1.9	3.2	2.3	2.3
Finland	−0.7	0.3	0.3	0.1	2.0	2.3	7.1	6.0	5.1	4.1
Greece	−9.4	−9.5	−6.9	−3.9	−2.5	−1.9	−1.3	−0.6	0.1	0.2
Portugal[3]	−5.0	−3.4	−3.2	−2.3	−2.3	−3.4	−3.7	−4.3	−2.9	−2.1
Ireland[3]	0.7	−1.3	0.5	0.9	1.8	2.8	2.1	−0.1	−1.3	−1.4
Norway[4]	−6.6	−4.4	−3.5	−2.7	−3.8	−2.9	−1.9	−2.4	−3.0	−2.4
Australia[5]	−3.0	−2.0	−0.8	0.1	0.2	0.6	0.8	0.3	0.2	0.5
New Zealand[6]	0.9	1.7	1.3	1.6	1.7	0.9	1.1	1.6	1.7	2.0
Memorandum										
European Union[3,7]	−4.7	−4.5	−3.3	−1.5	−1.1	−0.4	−0.5	−1.0	−0.9	−0.5
Euro area[3,7]	−4.1	−4.2	−3.1	−1.5	−1.5	−0.8	−1.1	−1.4	−1.1	−0.6

[1]On a national income accounts basis. The structural budget position is defined as the actual budget deficit (or surplus) less the effects of cyclical deviations of output from potential output. Because of the margin of uncertainty that attaches to estimates of cyclical gaps and to tax and expenditure elasticities with respect to national income, indicators of structural budget positions should be interpreted as broad orders of magnitude. Moreover, it is important to note that changes in structural budget balances are not necessarily attributable to policy changes but may reflect the built-in momentum of existing expenditure programs. In the period beyond that for which specific consolidation programs exist, it is assumed that the structural deficit remains unchanged.

[2]The estimate of the fiscal impulse for 1995 is affected by the assumption by the federal government of the debt of the Treuhandanstalt and various other agencies, which were formerly held outside the general government sector. At the public sector level, there would be an estimated withdrawal of fiscal impulse amounting to just over 1 percent of GDP.

[3]Excludes one-off receipts from the sale of mobile telephone licenses equivalent to 2.5 percent of GDP in 2000 for Germany, 0.1 percent of GDP in 2001 and 2002 for France, 1.2 percent of GDP in 2000 for Italy, 2.4 percent of GDP in 2000 for the United Kingdom, 0.1 percent of GDP in 2000 for Spain, 0.7 percent of GDP in 2000 for Netherlands, 0.2 percent of GDP in 2001 for Belgium, and 0.4 percent of GDP in 2000 for Austria, 0.3 percent of GDP in 2000 for Portugal, and 0.2 percent of GDP in 2002 for Ireland. Also excludes one-off receipts from sizable asset transactions.

[4]Excludes oil.

[5]Excludes commonwealth government privatization receipts.

[6]Excludes privatization proceeds.

[7]Excludes Luxembourg.

Table 17. Advanced Economies: Monetary Aggregates
(Annual percent change)[1]

	1994	1995	1996	1997	1998	1999	2000	2001
Narrow money[2]								
Advanced economies	**4.4**	**5.1**	**4.7**	**4.7**	**6.0**	**8.2**	**2.6**	**8.5**
United States	2.5	−1.6	−4.4	−1.2	2.1	1.9	−1.7	6.8
Japan	4.9	12.8	10.0	8.9	6.1	11.8	4.1	13.6
Euro area[3]	4.2	5.8	8.0	7.5	10.8	11.0	5.1	6.2
United Kingdom	6.8	5.6	6.7	6.4	5.3	11.6	4.3	8.0
Canada	8.4	7.6	18.9	10.9	8.0	7.8	14.4	15.0
Memorandum								
Newly industrialized Asian economies	9.3	10.5	5.8	−3.8	0.9	19.7	4.5	7.3
Broad money[4]								
Advanced economies	**2.6**	**5.0**	**4.8**	**5.0**	**6.7**	**5.8**	**5.1**	**8.7**
United States	0.6	3.8	4.5	5.6	8.5	6.3	6.1	10.3
Japan	2.9	3.2	2.9	3.8	4.4	2.6	2.0	3.4
Euro area[3]	2.3	5.5	4.0	4.6	4.8	5.5	4.1	11.0
United Kingdom	4.2	9.9	9.6	5.6	8.5	4.2	8.5	6.5
Canada	2.8	4.1	2.1	−1.4	0.8	5.1	6.4	5.8
Memorandum								
Newly industrialized Asian economies	16.5	13.0	11.4	11.5	19.7	17.0	14.0	6.4

[1]Based on end-of-period data except for Japan, which is based on monthly averages.

[2]M1 except for the United Kingdom, where M0 is used here as a measure of narrow money; it comprises notes in circulation plus bankers' operational deposits. M1 is generally currency in circulation plus private demand deposits. In addition, the United States includes traveler's checks of nonbank issues and other checkable deposits and excludes private sector float and demand deposits of banks. Japan includes government demand deposits and excludes float. Canada excludes private sector float.

[3]Excludes Greece prior to 2001.

[4]M2, defined as M1 plus quasi-money, except for Japan, and the United Kingdom, for which the data are based on M2 plus certificates of deposit (CDs), and M4, respectively. Quasi-money is essentially private term deposits and other notice deposits. The United States also includes money market mutual fund balances, money market deposit accounts, overnight repurchase agreements, and overnight Eurodollars issued to U.S. residents by foreign branches of U.S. banks. For Japan, M2 plus CDs is currency in circulation plus total private and public sector deposits and installments of Sogo Bank plus CDs. For the United Kingdom, M4 is composed of non-interest-bearing M1, private sector interest-bearing sterling sight bank deposits, private sector sterling time bank deposits, private sector holdings of sterling bank CDs, private sector holdings of building society shares and deposits, and sterling CDs less building society holdings of bank deposits and bank CDs and notes and coins. For the euro area, M3 is composed of M2 plus marketable instruments held by euro area residents, which comprise repurchase agreements, money market fund shares/units, money market paper, and debt securities up to two years.

Table 18. Advanced Economies: Interest Rates
(Percent a year)

	1994	1995	1996	1997	1998	1999	2000	2001	August 2002
Policy-related interest rate[1]									
United States	5.5	5.6	5.3	5.5	4.7	5.3	6.4	1.8	1.8
Japan	2.2	0.4	0.4	0.4	0.3	0.0	0.2	0.0	0.0
Euro area[2]	...	...	...	...	...	3.0	4.8	3.3	3.3
United Kingdom	6.1	6.4	5.9	7.3	6.3	5.5	6.0	4.0	4.0
Canada	5.7	5.8	3.0	4.3	5.0	4.8	5.8	2.3	2.8
Short-term interest rate[3]									
Advanced economies	**4.5**	**4.6**	**4.3**	**4.0**	**4.0**	**3.5**	**4.5**	**3.2**	**2.3**
United States	3.1	4.4	5.7	5.1	4.9	4.8	6.0	3.5	1.7
Japan	1.9	0.8	0.3	0.3	0.2	0.0	0.2	0.0	0.0
Euro area[2]	6.4	6.1	4.8	4.3	4.1	3.1	4.5	4.2	3.4
United Kingdom	5.6	6.8	6.1	6.9	7.4	5.5	6.1	5.0	4.0
Canada	5.4	7.0	4.3	3.2	4.7	4.7	5.5	3.9	3.0
Memorandum									
Newly industrialized Asian economies	9.1	9.2	8.7	9.2	9.8	4.8	5.0	3.5	3.5
Long-term interest rate[4]									
Advanced economies	**7.1**	**6.8**	**6.1**	**5.5**	**4.5**	**4.6**	**5.0**	**4.4**	**4.2**
United States	7.1	6.6	6.4	6.4	5.3	5.6	6.0	5.0	4.3
Japan	4.2	3.3	3.0	2.1	1.3	1.7	1.7	1.3	1.2
Euro area[2]	8.3	8.5	7.2	6.0	4.8	4.6	5.4	4.9	4.8
United Kingdom	8.4	8.4	8.1	7.4	5.4	5.4	5.4	5.1	5.0
Canada	8.4	8.1	7.2	6.1	5.3	5.6	5.9	5.5	5.6
Memorandum									
Newly industrialized Asian economies	9.4	9.4	8.5	9.2	9.4	6.6	6.6	5.2	5.9

[1]Annual data are end of period. For the United States, federal funds rate; for Japan, overnight call rate; for the euro area, main refinancing rate; for the United Kingdom, base lending rate; and for Canada, overnight money market financing rate.

[2]Excludes Greece prior to 2001.

[3]Annual data are period average. For the United States, three-month treasury bill market bid yield at constant maturity; for Japan, three-month bond yield with repurchase agreement; for the euro area, a weighted average of national three-month money market interest rates through 1998 and three-month EURIBOR thereafter; for the United Kingdom, three-month London interbank offered rate; and for Canada, three-month treasury bill yield.

[4]Annual data are period average. For the United States, 10-year treasury bond yield at constant maturity; for Japan, 10-year government bond yield; for euro area, a weighted average of national 10-year government bond yields through 1998 and 10-year euro bond yield thereafter; for the United Kingdom, 10-year government bond yield; and for Canada, government bond yield of 10 years and over.

Table 19. Advanced Economies: Exchange Rates

	1994	1995	1996	1997	1998	1999	2000	2001	Exchange Rate Assumption[1] 2002
					U.S. dollars per national currency unit				
U.S. dollar nominal exchange rates									
Euro	...	...	...	...	...	1.067	0.924	0.896	0.939
ECU	1.188	1.308	1.269	1.134	1.120	...	...	...	...
Pound sterling	1.532	1.578	1.562	1.638	1.656	1.618	1.516	1.440	1.493
Irish pound	1.498	1.604	1.601	1.518	1.426	1.355	1.173	1.137	...
					National currency units per U.S. dollar				
Deutsche mark	1.623	1.433	1.505	1.734	1.760	1.833	2.117	2.184	...
French franc	5.552	4.991	5.116	5.837	5.900	6.149	7.101	7.324	...
Italian lira	1,612.4	1,628.9	1,542.9	1,703.1	1,736.2	1,815.0	2,096.2	2,161.8	...
Spanish peseta	134.0	124.7	126.7	146.4	149.4	156.0	180.1	185.8	...
Netherlands guilder	1.820	1.606	1.686	1.951	1.984	2.066	2.386	2.460	...
Belgian franc	33.456	29.480	30.962	35.774	36.299	37.813	43.671	45.039	...
Austrian schilling	11.422	10.081	10.587	12.204	12.379	12.898	14.897	15.363	...
Finnish markka	5.224	4.367	4.594	5.191	5.344	5.573	6.437	6.638	...
Greek drachma	242.6	231.7	240.7	273.1	295.5	305.1	360.9	380.4	...
Portuguese escudo	166.0	151.1	154.2	175.3	180.1	187.9	217.0	223.8	...
Japanese yen	102.2	94.1	108.8	121.0	130.9	113.9	107.8	121.5	124.0
Canadian dollar	1.366	1.372	1.363	1.385	1.483	1.486	1.485	1.549	1.573
Swedish krona	7.716	7.133	6.706	7.635	7.950	8.262	9.162	10.329	9.865
Danish krone	6.361	5.602	5.799	6.604	6.701	6.976	8.083	8.323	7.931
Swiss franc	1.368	1.182	1.236	1.451	1.450	1.502	1.689	1.688	1.562
Norwegian krone	7.058	6.335	6.450	7.073	7.545	7.799	8.802	8.992	8.062
Israeli new sheqel	3.011	3.011	3.192	3.449	3.800	4.140	4.077	4.206	4.727
Icelandic krona	69.94	64.69	66.50	70.90	70.96	72.34	78.62	97.42	91.57
Cyprus pound	0.492	0.452	0.466	0.514	0.518	0.543	0.622	0.643	0.613
Korean won	803.4	771.3	804.5	951.3	1,401.4	1,188.8	1,131.0	1,291.0	1,245.0
Australian dollar	1.367	1.349	1.277	1.344	1.589	1.550	1.717	1.932	1.860
New Taiwan dollar	26.456	26.486	27.458	28.703	33.456	32.270	31.234	33.813	34.294
Hong Kong dollar	7.728	7.736	7.734	7.742	7.745	7.757	7.767	7.800	7.800
Singapore dollar	1.527	1.417	1.410	1.485	1.674	1.695	1.724	1.792	1.787
					Index, 1990 = 100				*Percent change from previous assumption[2]*
Real effective exchange rates[3]									
United States	93.7	86.4	89.5	94.5	100.7	99.2	106.7	116.7	0.7
Japan	139.0	146.4	125.2	119.6	111.7	127.0	136.5	120.8	0.1
Euro[4]	97.2	101.5	102.1	91.9	88.7	84.3	75.1	74.9	−1.0
Germany	113.6	122.0	120.5	113.3	110.4	107.1	100.9	100.0	−0.4
France	96.5	97.4	94.4	90.5	90.1	89.4	85.9	85.0	−0.3
United Kingdom	96.0	92.6	96.0	114.4	121.7	123.8	130.6	130.3	1.1
Italy	80.1	73.7	84.4	86.3	84.5	84.2	81.3	80.8	−0.3
Canada	88.7	88.0	88.7	91.1	85.4	84.4	84.5	81.1	−2.9
Spain	94.9	94.0	96.5	94.1	96.0	96.2	95.1	97.2	−0.3
Netherlands	102.4	104.9	101.8	97.2	98.5	97.9	95.7	97.6	−0.4
Belgium	100.8	103.8	99.4	95.9	95.3	91.7	88.8	89.8	−0.3
Sweden	79.9	80.4	90.7	88.4	87.0	84.3	83.8	76.1	−2.1
Austria	95.4	91.9	87.5	83.2	82.0	80.3	78.8	78.5	−0.2
Denmark	99.3	102.3	100.5	98.0	99.6	99.5	96.4	97.7	−1.1
Finland	67.4	74.3	68.7	64.8	63.9	61.6	58.7	59.2	−1.1
Greece	100.3	106.4	109.3	113.3	109.6	110.4	106.9	107.5	−0.3
Portugal	115.0	119.8	120.3	119.8	121.4	122.1	121.3	124.4	−0.4
Ireland	75.0	70.1	66.6	62.4	56.4	52.7	47.6	47.2	−0.6
Switzerland	104.8	111.5	111.7	108.3	114.6	114.2	113.9	119.6	−0.1
Norway	97.5	103.0	105.4	110.1	111.4	116.7	118.9	125.7	−3.4
Australia	93.5	92.5	108.4	112.8	101.0	102.6	96.5	91.2	−3.8
New Zealand	96.5	102.4	114.4	118.6	102.7	100.0	88.3	85.8	−4.1

[1]Average exchange rates for the period July 19–August 16, 2002. See "Assumptions" in the Introduction to the Statistical Appendix.
[2]In nominal effective terms. Average July 1–16, 2002 rates compared with July 19–August 16, 2002 rates.
[3]Defined as the ratio, in common currency, of the normalized unit labor costs in the manufacturing sector to the weighted average of those of its industrial country trading partners, using 1989–91 trade weights.
[4]A synthetic euro for the period prior to January 1, 1999 is used in the calculation of real effective exchange rates for the euro. See Box 5.5 in the *World Economic Outlook*, October 1998.

Table 20. Developing Countries: Central Government Fiscal Balances
(Percent of GDP)

	1994	1995	1996	1997	1998	1999	2000	2001	2002	2003
Developing countries	**−2.8**	**−2.6**	**−2.1**	**−2.5**	**−3.8**	**−4.1**	**−3.2**	**−3.9**	**−4.0**	**−3.2**
Regional groups										
Africa	−5.2	−4.0	−2.3	−3.0	−3.9	−3.6	−1.6	−2.0	−3.0	−2.3
Sub-Sahara	−5.7	−4.3	−2.9	−3.7	−3.9	−4.3	−2.7	−2.4	−3.4	−2.8
Excluding Nigeria and South Africa	−6.0	−5.3	−3.0	−4.2	−3.7	−4.9	−4.0	−3.0	−3.3	−3.2
Developing Asia	−2.6	−2.5	−2.0	−2.5	−3.6	−4.2	−4.3	−4.1	−4.1	−3.6
China	−1.6	−2.1	−1.6	−1.9	−3.0	−4.0	−3.6	−3.2	−3.3	−2.7
India	−5.5	−4.6	−4.2	−4.7	−5.3	−5.5	−5.7	−6.1	−6.4	−6.3
Other developing Asia	−2.1	−1.4	−1.0	−2.1	−3.2	−3.3	−4.4	−4.4	−4.1	−3.3
Middle East and Turkey	−5.5	−3.6	−3.1	−3.4	−5.7	−3.6	−0.3	−5.7	−5.0	−3.6
Western Hemisphere	−1.1	−1.9	−1.7	−1.7	−3.3	−4.3	−2.7	−3.2	−3.3	−2.2
Analytical groups										
By source of export earnings										
Fuel	−6.6	−3.3	—	−0.9	−5.6	−1.7	5.5	—	−0.9	−0.2
Nonfuel	−2.4	−2.5	−2.3	−2.7	−3.6	−4.4	−4.1	−4.3	−4.3	−3.5
of which, primary products	−3.9	−1.8	−0.6	−1.8	−1.6	−2.7	−3.2	−3.3	−3.7	−3.2
By external financing source										
Net debtor countries	−2.7	−2.6	−2.2	−2.6	−3.7	−4.2	−3.5	−4.0	−4.1	−3.3
of which, official financing	−5.1	−3.5	−1.6	−2.7	−3.6	−3.3	−2.2	−2.7	−3.6	−3.1
Net debtor countries by debt-servicing experience										
Countries with arrears and/or rescheduling during 1994–98	−2.2	−1.8	−1.0	−2.0	−4.0	−3.8	−1.1	−2.5	−3.4	−2.1
Other groups										
Heavily indebted poor countries	−5.7	−3.7	−1.9	−3.5	−2.5	−3.6	−3.1	−3.3	−3.7	−3.5
Middle East and north Africa	−5.5	−3.4	−1.0	−1.6	−4.7	−1.1	3.5	−0.8	−1.8	−1.4
Memorandum										
Median										
Developing countries	−3.6	−3.3	−2.2	−2.4	−3.1	−3.3	−3.3	−3.5	−4.0	−2.8
Regional groups										
Africa	−4.7	−3.8	−3.8	−3.0	−3.4	−3.6	−3.2	−3.2	−4.0	−3.1
Developing Asia	−3.4	−3.4	−2.1	−2.4	−2.7	−3.4	−4.6	−4.6	−4.9	−4.3
Middle East and Turkey	−4.7	−4.3	−2.2	−2.5	−5.8	−2.0	1.9	−0.7	−1.2	−1.6
Western Hemisphere	−1.5	−1.5	−1.7	−1.6	−2.4	−3.2	−2.8	−3.3	−3.5	−2.6

Table 21. Developing Countries: Broad Money Aggregates
(Annual percent change)

	1994	1995	1996	1997	1998	1999	2000	2001	2002	2003
Developing countries	**68.4**	**24.6**	**23.0**	**22.7**	**17.1**	**15.1**	**11.3**	**12.3**	**9.3**	**12.1**
Regional groups										
Africa	43.5	23.8	18.1	21.5	15.2	18.2	19.7	22.1	15.1	15.0
Sub-Sahara	53.5	28.8	20.4	23.8	16.2	19.6	22.4	23.2	16.4	16.7
Developing Asia	25.2	22.6	20.4	17.9	18.4	14.4	12.2	12.8	13.2	13.0
China	34.9	29.5	25.3	19.6	14.8	14.7	12.3	14.4	14.0	13.0
India	20.2	13.7	16.9	17.6	20.2	18.6	16.2	13.9	15.2	15.0
Other developing Asia	18.9	20.8	17.5	16.5	21.3	11.5	9.7	9.4	10.3	11.5
Middle East and Turkey	43.8	33.0	36.8	27.4	26.8	29.7	19.0	24.4	15.0	10.9
Western Hemisphere	155.4	23.4	21.8	26.2	12.9	10.3	5.9	5.3	1.7	10.8
Analytical groups										
By source of export earnings										
Fuel	25.8	17.0	22.0	17.4	12.3	15.9	17.7	16.4	13.0	11.3
Nonfuel	76.3	25.7	23.1	23.4	17.7	15.0	10.5	11.7	8.8	12.2
of which, primary products	61.7	32.6	23.1	24.8	12.6	21.0	18.3	17.7	15.3	16.8
By external financing source										
Net debtor countries	73.7	26.0	24.1	23.7	18.0	15.6	11.6	12.4	9.6	12.5
of which, official financing	45.6	22.8	12.0	21.0	15.2	20.4	23.1	20.2	15.7	12.2
Net debtor countries by debt-servicing experience										
Countries with arrears and/or rescheduling during 1994–98	230.0	28.1	17.0	23.9	18.2	14.1	11.5	15.5	12.9	11.7
Other groups										
Heavily indebted poor countries	91.6	39.6	29.0	28.4	18.6	31.0	31.2	24.7	20.4	14.8
Middle East and north Africa	14.5	12.5	13.0	10.2	10.2	11.2	12.4	15.3	11.1	9.4
Memorandum										
Median										
Developing countries	18.7	16.3	13.7	15.1	10.5	12.5	12.3	11.6	9.1	9.3
Regional groups										
Africa	31.0	16.2	15.0	14.3	9.6	13.5	14.4	13.3	9.6	9.4
Developing Asia	19.4	16.7	15.0	16.8	12.4	14.9	12.6	11.4	10.5	10.6
Middle East and Turkey	13.2	9.4	9.0	9.7	8.5	11.4	10.2	11.7	7.9	6.5
Western Hemisphere	17.2	19.9	16.7	17.3	11.5	12.2	9.0	9.1	8.4	8.8

Table 22. Summary of World Trade Volumes and Prices

(Annual percent change)

	Ten-Year Averages		1994	1995	1996	1997	1998	1999	2000	2001	2002	2003
	1984–93	1994–2003										
Trade in goods and services												
World trade[1]												
Volume	5.6	6.5	8.9	8.7	6.9	10.6	4.3	5.5	12.6	−0.1	2.1	6.1
Price deflator												
In U.S. dollars	2.3	−0.4	2.6	9.3	−1.4	−6.1	−5.3	−1.7	−0.9	−3.3	1.3	2.7
In SDRs	−0.4	0.2	0.1	3.2	3.0	−0.9	−4.0	−2.5	2.8	0.1	−0.2	0.3
Volume of trade												
Exports												
Advanced economies	6.0	6.0	8.8	8.6	6.1	10.6	4.1	5.4	12.0	−1.1	1.2	5.4
Developing countries	6.7	7.9	11.5	7.9	9.6	14.0	4.8	4.4	15.0	2.6	3.2	6.5
Imports												
Advanced economies	6.3	6.6	9.6	8.6	6.5	9.3	6.0	8.1	11.8	−1.3	1.7	6.2
Developing countries	4.4	6.6	6.3	9.8	9.9	11.9	−0.7	1.1	15.9	1.6	3.8	7.1
Terms of trade												
Advanced economies	1.0	−0.1	0.1	—	−0.2	−0.6	1.5	−0.2	−2.5	0.3	0.2	0.4
Developing countries	−2.8	0.4	0.7	2.6	2.8	−0.7	−6.6	4.3	6.3	−3.0	−0.6	−1.0
Trade in goods												
World trade[1]												
Volume	5.7	6.7	10.1	9.3	6.4	10.8	4.7	5.7	12.9	−0.6	2.2	6.2
Price deflator												
In U.S. dollars	2.0	−0.4	2.6	9.8	−1.2	−6.4	−6.2	−1.5	—	−3.6	0.7	2.5
In SDRs	−0.6	0.1	0.1	3.6	3.2	−1.3	−4.9	−2.3	3.7	−0.1	−0.9	0.1
World trade prices in U.S. dollars[2]												
Manufactures	4.4	−0.3	3.1	10.3	−3.1	−8.0	−1.8	−2.0	−5.2	−2.3	2.6	4.2
Oil	−5.5	3.7	−5.0	7.9	18.4	−5.4	−32.1	37.5	57.0	−14.0	0.5	−0.8
Nonfuel primary commodities	0.3	−0.1	13.4	8.4	−1.3	−3.0	−14.7	−7.0	1.8	−5.4	4.2	5.7
World trade prices in SDRs[2]												
Manufactures	1.6	0.2	0.6	4.1	1.2	−3.0	−0.4	−2.8	−1.7	1.2	1.1	1.8
Oil	−8.0	4.3	−7.3	1.8	23.7	−0.2	−31.2	36.5	62.8	−10.9	−1.0	−3.1
Nonfuel primary commodities	−2.4	0.4	10.6	2.3	3.1	2.3	−13.5	−7.8	5.5	−2.0	2.6	3.2
World trade prices in euros[2]												
Manufactures	1.5	1.5	1.7	0.2	−0.2	2.9	−0.6	2.9	9.4	0.8	−2.1	—
Oil	−8.1	5.6	−6.3	−2.0	22.0	5.8	−31.3	44.5	81.4	−11.3	−4.2	−4.8
Nonfuel primary commodities	−2.4	1.7	11.9	−1.5	1.7	8.6	−13.7	−2.3	17.6	−2.4	−0.7	1.4

Table 22 *(concluded)*

	Ten-Year Averages		1994	1995	1996	1997	1998	1999	2000	2001	2002	2003
	1984–93	1994–2003										
Trade in goods												
Volume of trade												
Exports												
Advanced economies	6.1	6.2	9.6	9.1	5.7	11.0	4.4	5.4	12.2	−1.7	1.3	5.5
Developing countries	6.9	7.9	12.1	8.2	9.0	13.3	4.9	4.4	15.3	2.4	3.8	6.7
Fuel exporters	5.9	2.5	3.8	−0.9	7.1	7.0	2.0	−1.8	5.6	1.6	−2.9	4.2
Nonfuel exporters	7.5	9.5	15.0	11.0	9.5	15.3	5.7	5.7	17.8	2.7	5.8	7.4
Imports												
Advanced economies	6.6	6.9	11.2	9.4	5.9	10.0	6.0	8.8	12.1	−1.8	1.7	6.3
Developing countries	4.5	7.0	8.1	9.9	9.3	10.7	0.5	0.8	16.8	1.9	4.9	7.9
Fuel exporters	−2.8	4.8	−11.4	5.4	6.3	16.7	2.0	−0.8	12.2	11.0	4.4	4.9
Nonfuel exporters	7.4	7.4	12.6	10.8	9.8	9.7	0.2	1.1	17.6	0.5	5.0	8.4
Price deflators in SDRs												
Exports												
Advanced economies	0.1	−0.3	0.3	3.5	1.8	−2.3	−3.4	−3.4	0.6	0.1	−0.8	1.1
Developing countries	−3.2	1.4	0.2	5.3	7.8	0.8	−10.8	5.5	13.7	−2.1	−2.5	−2.2
Fuel exporters	−8.1	3.9	−3.5	8.9	18.3	−0.1	−26.8	30.3	48.7	−8.2	−4.0	−5.3
Nonfuel exporters	−0.7	0.7	1.6	4.2	4.9	1.1	−6.2	0.2	4.6	−0.1	−1.6	−1.0
Imports												
Advanced economies	−1.1	−0.2	−0.3	3.1	2.5	−1.7	−5.0	−3.4	3.5	−0.5	−0.7	0.4
Developing countries	0.2	0.7	−0.9	2.0	4.8	1.7	−4.6	0.2	6.1	0.9	−1.8	−1.2
Fuel exporters	0.2	−0.3	−2.0	1.3	2.0	−1.4	−0.3	−2.5	1.9	2.3	−0.5	−3.7
Nonfuel exporters	—	0.8	−0.6	2.2	5.3	2.2	−5.2	0.7	6.7	0.6	−2.1	−0.8
Terms of trade												
Advanced economies	1.2	—	0.6	0.4	−0.7	−0.6	1.7	−0.1	−2.8	0.6	−0.1	0.7
Developing countries	−3.4	0.7	1.1	3.2	2.9	−0.8	−6.6	5.3	7.2	−2.9	−0.7	−1.0
Fuel exporters	−8.4	4.3	−1.5	7.5	16.0	1.4	−26.5	33.6	45.9	−10.3	−3.5	−1.7
Nonfuel exporters	−0.7	−0.1	2.2	2.0	−0.4	−1.0	−1.1	−0.5	−2.0	−0.7	0.5	−0.3
Memorandum												
World exports in billions of U.S. dollars												
Goods and services	3,565	7,008	5,284	6,268	6,595	6,860	6,750	6,977	7,759	7,487	7,720	8,385
Goods	2,849	5,601	4,204	5,044	5,280	5,482	5,364	5,559	6,254	5,993	6,152	6,681

[1]Average of annual percent change for world exports and imports. The estimates of world trade comprise, in addition to trade of advanced economies and developing countries (which is summarized in the table), trade of countries in transition.

[2]As represented, respectively, by the export unit value index for the manufactures of the advanced economies; the average of U.K. Brent, Dubai, and West Texas Intermediate crude oil spot prices; and the average of world market prices for nonfuel primary commodities weighted by their 1987–89 shares in world commodity exports.

Table 23. Nonfuel Commodity Prices[1]
(Annual percent change; U.S. dollar terms)

| | Ten-Year Averages | | | | | | | | | | | |
	1984–93	1994–2003	1994	1995	1996	1997	1998	1999	2000	2001	2002	2003
Nonfuel primary commodities	**0.3**	**−0.1**	**13.4**	**8.4**	**−1.3**	**−3.0**	**−14.7**	**−7.0**	**1.8**	**−5.4**	**4.2**	**5.7**
Food	−1.0	−0.7	5.1	8.1	12.2	−10.7	−12.6	−15.6	−0.5	3.1	3.2	4.7
Beverages	−6.0	0.1	74.9	0.9	−17.4	32.6	−15.2	−21.3	−16.6	−19.1	11.0	3.9
Agricultural raw materials	4.6	−0.5	9.5	4.3	−3.1	−6.1	−16.2	2.3	2.0	−6.9	6.4	6.2
Metals	−1.1	1.3	16.7	19.7	−12.0	3.0	−16.4	−1.4	12.2	−9.6	0.6	7.0
Fertilizers	−1.4	2.1	8.0	10.6	13.7	1.1	2.8	−4.0	−5.3	−5.8	−0.1	1.7
Advanced economies	**−0.3**	**—**	**13.4**	**11.2**	**−2.4**	**−3.9**	**−15.7**	**−6.8**	**4.1**	**−5.9**	**3.8**	**6.1**
Developing countries	**−0.4**	**−0.3**	**15.9**	**9.6**	**−2.7**	**−1.4**	**−16.2**	**−9.2**	**1.8**	**−6.9**	**4.3**	**6.0**
Regional groups												
Africa	−0.3	−0.3	16.6	8.1	−5.3	−1.0	−14.7	−8.3	0.7	−7.2	6.1	5.6
Sub-Sahara	−0.3	−0.4	16.9	8.1	−6.0	−0.7	−14.7	−8.2	0.7	−7.5	6.3	5.6
Developing Asia	0.1	−0.4	13.6	8.2	−1.4	−3.4	−14.3	−8.0	0.3	−6.8	4.9	5.8
Excluding China and India	0.1	−0.7	14.0	7.5	−1.5	−3.9	−13.7	−9.3	−1.4	−6.7	5.7	5.7
Middle East and Turkey	−0.6	0.1	15.2	12.5	−3.5	−2.7	−15.4	−7.8	4.2	−6.2	2.8	6.4
Western Hemisphere	−1.1	−0.2	17.8	11.0	−2.9	0.4	−18.3	−10.6	3.3	−7.2	3.3	6.3
Analytical groups												
By source of export earnings												
Fuel	0.3	−0.2	10.7	11.7	−7.3	−0.4	−17.0	−3.4	7.4	−8.4	2.2	6.6
Nonfuel	−0.5	−0.3	16.0	9.5	−2.5	−1.5	−16.1	−9.3	1.6	−6.9	4.3	6.0
of which, primary products	−0.6	−0.1	18.9	14.1	−8.8	−1.0	−16.2	−11.4	3.1	−7.5	7.3	6.2
By external financing source												
Net debtor countries	−0.5	−0.3	15.8	9.6	−2.6	−1.5	−16.2	−9.2	1.8	−7.0	4.3	6.0
of which, official financing	−0.4	−1.0	21.1	9.2	−8.2	−0.3	−13.9	−12.0	−2.5	−10.0	5.5	6.6
Net debtor countries by debt-servicing experience												
Countries with arrears and/or rescheduling during 1994–98	−1.1	−0.3	18.6	9.3	−4.3	0.5	−15.9	−10.6	1.2	−7.6	4.8	5.7
Other groups												
Heavily indebted poor countries	−1.9	−0.3	24.9	7.8	−7.0	2.0	−12.1	−14.6	−4.5	−8.1	9.7	4.6
Middle East and north Africa	−0.6	—	15.3	11.4	−2.8	−2.8	−15.0	−8.5	3.2	−6.1	3.0	6.3
Memorandum												
Average oil spot price[2]	−5.5	3.7	−5.0	7.9	18.4	−5.4	−32.1	37.5	57.0	−14.0	0.5	−0.8
In U.S. dollars a barrel	19.91	20.50	15.95	17.20	20.37	19.27	13.07	17.98	28.24	24.28	24.40	24.20
Export unit value of manufactures[3]	4.4	−0.3	3.1	10.3	−3.1	−8.0	−1.8	−2.0	−5.2	−2.3	2.6	4.2

[1]Averages of world market prices for individual commodities weighted by 1987–89 exports as a share of world commodity exports and total commodity exports for the indicated country group, respectively.
[2]Average of U.K. Brent, Dubai, and West Texas Intermediate crude oil spot prices.
[3]For the manufactures exported by the advanced economies.

Table 24. Advanced Economies: Export Volumes, Import Volumes, and Terms of Trade in Goods and Services
(Annual percent change)

	Ten-Year Averages		1994	1995	1996	1997	1998	1999	2000	2001	2002	2003
	1984–93	1994–2003										
Export volume												
Advanced economies	**6.0**	**6.0**	**8.8**	**8.6**	**6.1**	**10.6**	**4.1**	**5.4**	**12.0**	**−1.1**	**1.2**	**5.4**
Major advanced economies	5.6	5.5	8.0	8.0	5.8	10.6	3.8	4.1	11.4	−1.7	0.6	4.9
United States	8.2	4.9	8.9	10.3	8.2	12.3	2.1	3.4	9.7	−5.4	−2.7	4.0
Japan	4.3	4.2	3.5	4.0	6.4	11.4	−2.4	1.3	12.6	−7.0	7.1	6.5
Germany	4.7	6.7	7.6	5.7	5.1	11.2	7.0	5.6	13.7	5.0	1.9	4.3
France	4.7	6.3	7.7	7.7	3.5	11.8	8.3	4.2	13.6	1.5	0.5	5.5
Italy	5.2	5.1	9.8	12.6	0.6	6.4	3.4	0.3	11.7	0.8	0.7	5.6
United Kingdom	4.2	5.8	9.2	9.0	8.2	8.3	3.0	5.3	10.1	1.4	−0.8	4.4
Canada	6.4	6.5	12.8	8.5	5.6	8.3	9.1	10.1	8.0	−3.8	1.1	6.3
Other advanced economies	6.8	7.0	10.1	9.4	6.5	10.5	4.6	7.6	13.1	−0.1	2.3	6.2
Memorandum												
European Union	4.7	6.3	8.8	7.8	5.0	10.2	6.4	5.3	11.9	2.4	0.8	5.0
Euro area	4.9	6.4	8.6	7.5	4.5	10.6	7.1	5.1	12.4	2.7	0.9	5.2
Newly industrialized Asian economies	12.0	8.4	12.4	15.1	7.9	11.0	1.0	9.7	17.6	−3.1	5.6	8.1
Import volume												
Advanced economies	**6.3**	**6.6**	**9.6**	**8.6**	**6.5**	**9.3**	**6.0**	**8.1**	**11.8**	**−1.3**	**1.7**	**6.2**
Major advanced economies	5.9	6.6	8.9	7.9	6.5	9.5	7.9	8.2	11.6	−1.0	1.1	6.0
United States	7.0	8.3	12.0	8.2	8.6	13.7	11.8	10.9	13.2	−2.9	2.6	6.0
Japan	5.9	4.5	8.0	12.4	13.2	1.0	−6.6	3.3	9.2	−0.8	0.3	7.2
Germany	4.8	5.7	7.4	5.6	3.1	8.3	9.1	8.5	10.5	1.0	−1.5	5.7
France	4.5	6.5	8.2	8.0	1.6	6.9	11.6	6.2	15.0	0.8	0.6	7.1
Italy	5.7	5.8	8.1	9.7	−0.3	10.1	8.9	5.3	9.4	0.2	1.7	5.4
United Kingdom	5.2	6.8	5.7	5.4	9.6	9.7	9.6	8.7	11.7	2.7	1.3	3.9
Canada	7.3	5.6	8.1	5.8	5.1	14.3	5.1	7.8	8.2	−5.7	1.0	7.8
Other advanced economies	7.1	6.6	10.8	9.9	6.3	9.1	2.8	7.8	12.2	−1.7	2.7	6.5
Memorandum												
European Union	5.1	6.3	7.9	6.9	4.1	9.3	9.9	7.5	11.3	1.3	0.3	5.5
Euro area	5.3	6.3	8.0	7.1	3.3	9.1	9.9	7.5	11.3	1.2	−0.1	5.8
Newly industrialized Asian economies	13.0	6.8	13.8	15.0	8.5	8.0	−8.6	8.8	16.5	−6.0	6.7	8.7
Terms of trade												
Advanced economies	**1.0**	**−0.1**	**0.1**	**—**	**−0.2**	**−0.6**	**1.5**	**−0.2**	**−2.5**	**0.3**	**0.2**	**0.4**
Major advanced economies	1.0	—	0.1	−0.1	−0.3	−0.5	2.2	−0.1	−3.2	0.6	0.3	0.6
United States	−0.1	0.3	—	−0.5	0.6	1.6	3.5	−0.7	−3.1	2.4	−0.9	0.3
Japan	3.1	−1.0	1.5	−0.3	−5.4	−3.9	3.6	−0.3	−5.0	−1.4	0.1	1.4
Germany	−0.3	—	0.2	0.8	−0.7	−1.9	2.2	0.4	−4.4	0.8	1.4	1.3
France	0.7	−0.3	0.2	0.1	−1.2	—	1.6	−0.4	−3.4	0.6	0.2	−0.4
Italy	1.9	−0.3	−0.9	−2.3	4.3	−1.5	2.1	−0.2	−6.9	1.8	0.5	0.1
United Kingdom	1.8	0.5	−2.0	−2.5	1.2	3.3	2.2	0.7	1.0	−0.1	2.6	−1.7
Canada	−0.5	0.2	−0.7	2.9	1.7	−0.7	−3.8	1.3	4.1	−1.4	−2.2	1.4
Other advanced economies	0.8	−0.3	—	—	0.1	−0.7	0.3	−0.5	−1.3	−0.2	−0.3	−0.1
Memorandum												
European Union	0.9	—	−0.5	−0.3	0.2	−0.4	1.6	−0.1	−2.5	0.7	0.9	0.1
Euro area	0.8	−0.1	−0.2	—	0.1	−0.9	1.7	−0.3	−3.4	0.9	0.6	0.3
Newly industrialized Asian economies	0.9	−1.0	−0.3	−1.7	−0.1	−1.0	0.1	−1.9	−4.3	−1.0	0.1	—
Memorandum												
Trade in goods												
Advanced economies												
Export volume	6.1	6.2	9.6	9.1	5.7	11.0	4.4	5.4	12.2	−1.7	1.3	5.5
Import volume	6.6	6.9	11.2	9.4	5.9	10.0	6.0	8.8	12.1	−1.8	1.7	6.3
Terms of trade	1.2	—	0.6	0.4	−0.7	−0.6	1.7	−0.1	−2.8	0.6	0.3	0.5

Table 25. Developing Countries—by Region: Total Trade in Goods

(Annual percent change)

| | Ten-Year Averages | | 1994 | 1995 | 1996 | 1997 | 1998 | 1999 | 2000 | 2001 | 2002 | 2003 |
	1984–93	1994–2003										
Developing countries												
Value in U.S. dollars												
Exports	5.0	8.5	15.1	20.4	11.9	8.1	−7.8	9.7	25.2	−3.2	3.2	7.1
Imports	6.6	6.9	9.8	18.8	9.3	6.5	−5.3	0.7	19.2	−1.0	4.6	9.1
Volume												
Exports	6.9	7.9	12.1	8.2	9.0	13.3	4.9	4.4	15.3	2.4	3.8	6.7
Imports	4.5	7.0	8.1	9.9	9.3	10.7	0.5	0.8	16.8	1.9	4.9	7.9
Unit value in U.S. dollars												
Exports	−0.6	0.9	2.8	11.6	3.2	−4.4	−12.0	6.3	9.7	−5.5	−0.6	0.4
Imports	2.9	0.1	1.6	8.1	0.3	−3.6	−5.9	1.0	2.3	−2.6	−0.3	1.2
Terms of trade	−3.4	0.8	1.1	3.2	2.8	−0.8	−6.5	5.2	7.2	−2.9	−0.3	−0.7
Memorandum												
Real GDP growth in developing country trading partners	4.0	3.1	4.3	3.6	3.9	4.1	1.7	3.4	4.6	0.8	1.8	2.9
Market prices of nonfuel commodities exported by developing countries	−0.4	−0.3	15.9	9.6	−2.7	−1.4	−16.2	−9.2	1.8	−6.9	4.3	6.0
Regional groups												
Africa												
Value in U.S. dollars												
Exports	1.8	4.9	3.7	17.6	11.1	2.8	−13.7	6.9	25.9	−5.6	−0.2	5.9
Imports	2.0	4.3	5.2	19.8	1.1	4.1	−0.9	−1.8	5.7	1.5	4.5	5.7
Volume												
Exports	2.7	4.0	3.0	8.0	8.0	6.8	−0.2	3.8	6.5	1.0	0.1	3.3
Imports	1.6	4.9	4.2	11.3	3.1	7.8	5.4	0.1	4.2	4.6	4.6	3.9
Unit value in U.S. dollars												
Exports	−0.1	1.0	1.0	9.1	3.1	−3.7	−13.8	3.4	18.3	−6.5	−0.3	2.7
Imports	1.4	−0.2	1.8	7.8	−1.6	−3.1	−5.7	−1.6	2.4	−2.9	0.2	1.7
Terms of trade	−1.6	1.2	−0.7	1.2	4.8	−0.6	−8.6	5.1	15.6	−3.7	−0.5	0.9
Sub-Sahara												
Value in U.S. dollars												
Exports	2.0	4.4	4.8	17.4	10.4	2.7	−13.9	5.5	22.7	−5.4	—	4.9
Imports	1.6	4.1	3.2	20.9	3.5	6.7	−3.0	−3.6	6.3	0.9	3.5	4.9
Volume												
Exports	3.1	3.9	3.3	8.8	9.6	6.8	−1.2	2.3	6.3	1.1	−0.3	3.0
Imports	2.1	4.9	2.2	13.0	7.3	9.0	3.6	−1.3	4.4	4.3	4.2	3.4
Unit value in U.S. dollars												
Exports	−0.1	0.7	2.1	8.0	1.0	−3.8	−13.3	3.5	15.7	−6.4	0.3	2.1
Imports	0.7	−0.4	1.7	7.2	−3.4	−1.6	−6.0	−1.9	3.0	−3.1	−0.4	1.5
Terms of trade	−0.8	1.0	0.4	0.8	4.6	−2.2	−7.7	5.6	12.4	−3.4	0.6	0.6

Table 25 *(concluded)*

	Ten-Year Averages		1994	1995	1996	1997	1998	1999	2000	2001	2002	2003
	1984–93	1994–2003										
Developing Asia												
Value in U.S. dollars												
Exports	11.8	10.8	23.9	23.2	10.1	12.1	−2.3	8.4	22.2	−1.7	7.4	8.7
Imports	10.9	8.8	17.8	23.7	10.4	1.1	−13.6	9.0	27.2	−0.9	8.3	11.3
Volume												
Exports	9.6	10.9	20.6	11.5	9.2	18.4	6.2	5.6	22.7	1.6	7.2	7.6
Imports	8.3	8.7	16.2	13.0	10.0	6.2	−6.5	6.6	23.3	2.5	9.1	9.2
Unit value in U.S. dollars												
Exports	2.3	0.3	2.8	10.5	1.2	−5.0	−7.8	4.6	−0.2	−3.3	0.2	1.1
Imports	2.8	0.5	1.6	9.5	0.8	−4.7	−8.0	5.4	3.7	−3.0	−0.7	2.0
Terms of trade	−0.4	−0.2	1.2	0.9	0.4	−0.4	0.2	−0.7	−3.7	−0.2	0.9	−0.9
Excluding China and India												
Value in U.S. dollars												
Exports	11.4	7.7	18.9	22.3	5.7	7.3	−3.9	10.3	18.6	−9.2	3.5	7.9
Imports	10.1	5.8	20.3	26.9	5.6	−0.7	−23.1	6.2	22.6	−7.0	5.5	11.8
Volume												
Exports	10.5	7.0	16.5	10.4	2.1	11.3	8.4	3.4	15.5	−5.8	4.2	5.4
Imports	8.5	4.7	19.7	16.5	4.0	1.9	−14.2	−0.1	17.6	−6.1	6.1	6.9
Unit value in U.S. dollars												
Exports	1.2	1.1	2.1	10.8	3.8	−3.4	−11.2	10.1	2.8	−3.7	−0.7	2.4
Imports	1.8	1.6	0.6	9.0	2.1	−2.6	−10.6	11.9	4.5	−0.8	−0.6	4.6
Terms of trade	−0.6	−0.5	1.5	1.7	1.8	−0.8	−0.6	−1.6	−1.7	−2.9	−0.1	−2.1
Middle East and Turkey												
Value in U.S. dollars												
Exports	0.5	5.8	6.4	14.3	17.0	1.1	−21.6	22.4	39.4	−5.9	−3.5	1.1
Imports	1.7	3.9	−10.6	17.5	10.9	6.7	−1.6	−4.6	14.4	−2.3	6.9	5.0
Volume												
Exports	6.7	3.7	6.3	−0.6	8.1	7.6	2.4	−1.5	7.0	3.8	−0.3	4.4
Imports	−0.8	5.1	−12.5	9.2	13.3	14.5	3.2	−2.2	14.7	—	7.5	6.4
Unit value in U.S. dollars												
Exports	−5.3	2.5	0.3	16.0	9.6	−6.1	−23.2	24.4	31.6	−9.2	−3.0	−3.2
Imports	3.0	−1.1	1.4	7.6	−1.8	−6.7	−4.5	−2.3	−0.3	−1.9	−0.8	−1.1
Terms of trade	−8.0	3.7	−1.1	7.8	11.6	0.7	−19.6	27.3	32.0	−7.4	−2.3	−2.1
Western Hemisphere												
Value in U.S. dollars												
Exports	4.8	8.4	15.4	22.2	11.2	9.8	−3.7	4.3	19.4	−2.8	2.0	9.4
Imports	9.8	6.9	17.2	10.7	9.7	18.1	4.5	−6.6	14.5	−1.1	−3.6	9.0
Volume												
Exports	7.1	7.9	8.6	10.5	9.8	12.6	6.7	6.4	11.3	3.3	2.2	8.2
Imports	7.8	6.4	15.0	4.4	8.1	17.8	8.2	−4.8	12.6	1.2	−4.2	8.0
Unit value in U.S. dollars												
Exports	0.4	0.6	6.3	10.7	1.3	−2.2	−9.7	−1.7	7.8	−6.0	−0.1	1.1
Imports	3.6	0.5	2.0	6.1	1.8	0.4	−3.4	−2.0	1.7	−2.3	0.4	0.9
Terms of trade	−3.1	—	4.2	4.3	−0.6	−2.6	−6.5	0.3	5.9	−3.7	−0.5	0.2

Table 26. Developing Countries—by Source of Export Earnings: Total Trade in Goods
(Annual percent change)

	Ten-Year Averages		1994	1995	1996	1997	1998	1999	2000	2001	2002	2003
	1984–93	1994–2003										
Fuel												
Value in U.S. dollars												
Exports	−0.6	5.6	2.5	13.4	20.3	1.2	−26.6	28.9	50.7	−10.2	−5.6	0.9
Imports	−0.2	3.8	−10.9	12.7	3.3	9.2	0.2	−2.6	10.0	9.7	5.5	3.1
Volume												
Exports	5.9	2.5	3.8	−0.9	7.1	7.0	2.0	−1.8	5.6	1.6	−2.9	4.2
Imports	−2.8	4.8	−11.4	5.4	6.3	16.7	2.0	−0.8	12.2	11.0	4.4	4.9
Unit value in U.S. dollars												
Exports	−5.7	3.4	−1.1	15.4	13.2	−5.3	−27.8	31.3	43.5	−11.4	−2.5	−3.1
Imports	2.9	−0.8	0.4	7.3	−2.4	−6.6	−1.7	−1.7	−1.7	−1.2	1.0	−1.4
Terms of trade	−8.4	4.3	−1.5	7.5	16.0	1.4	−26.5	33.6	45.9	−10.3	−3.5	−1.7
Nonfuel												
Value in U.S. dollars												
Exports	8.2	9.4	19.6	22.5	9.5	10.2	−2.5	5.6	18.6	−1.0	5.8	8.7
Imports	9.2	7.5	14.6	19.9	10.3	6.1	−6.1	1.2	20.7	−2.6	4.5	10.1
Volume												
Exports	7.5	9.5	15.0	11.0	9.5	15.3	5.7	5.7	17.8	2.7	5.8	7.4
Imports	7.4	7.4	12.6	10.8	9.8	9.7	0.2	1.1	17.6	0.5	5.0	8.4
Unit value in U.S. dollars												
Exports	2.0	0.2	4.2	10.4	0.4	−4.2	−7.6	1.0	0.9	−3.6	—	1.3
Imports	2.7	0.3	1.9	8.2	0.8	−3.2	−6.6	1.5	3.0	−2.9	−0.6	1.6
Terms of trade	−0.7	−0.1	2.2	2.0	−0.4	−1.0	−1.1	−0.5	−2.0	−0.7	0.5	−0.3
Primary products												
Value in U.S. dollars												
Exports	5.3	7.7	17.9	25.2	6.2	6.2	−5.1	4.0	10.9	0.5	4.9	9.7
Imports	6.0	6.7	11.7	25.4	10.7	7.3	−1.7	−8.6	9.2	0.6	5.5	10.0
Volume												
Exports	4.1	7.3	8.0	9.6	7.6	9.6	5.0	7.6	7.4	6.4	5.2	6.6
Imports	4.4	7.1	9.5	18.3	7.6	10.9	8.3	−7.2	6.9	4.5	6.2	8.0
Unit value in U.S. dollars												
Exports	1.9	0.5	10.2	14.5	−1.2	−2.7	−9.7	−3.5	3.0	−5.7	−0.3	3.0
Imports	2.5	−0.3	2.7	6.1	3.0	−3.4	−9.7	−1.5	2.8	−3.5	−0.6	2.0
Terms of trade	−0.6	0.8	7.3	7.9	−4.1	0.7	—	−2.1	0.3	−2.2	0.3	0.9

Table 27. Summary of Payments Balances on Current Account
(Billions of U.S. dollars)

	1994	1995	1996	1997	1998	1999	2000	2001	2002	2003
Advanced economies	**21.2**	**50.9**	**34.0**	**93.3**	**47.2**	**−96.0**	**−227.1**	**−188.4**	**−210.3**	**−242.2**
United States	−118.2	−105.8	−117.8	−128.4	−203.8	−292.9	−410.3	−393.4	−479.6	−514.9
European Union	10.1	48.3	79.0	108.6	68.5	13.7	−35.1	3.2	50.7	48.2
Euro area[1]	17.0	55.9	82.9	103.8	71.3	33.9	−16.2	21.8	70.6	70.9
Japan	130.6	111.4	65.7	96.6	119.1	114.5	119.6	87.8	119.3	122.1
Other advanced economies	−1.2	−3.0	7.0	16.5	63.4	68.6	98.7	114.0	99.4	102.3
Memorandum										
Newly industrialized Asian										
economies	12.9	2.8	−3.5	10.8	67.4	60.9	45.5	57.1	57.9	60.4
Developing countries	**−84.6**	**−95.5**	**−74.7**	**−58.0**	**−85.1**	**−10.2**	**66.7**	**39.6**	**18.9**	**0.9**
Regional groups										
Africa	−11.1	−16.8	−6.4	−7.4	−20.1	−14.3	5.4	1.3	−7.2	−7.1
Developing Asia	−19.0	−42.5	−38.9	8.9	47.3	46.0	45.4	39.4	33.5	18.0
Excluding China and India	−25.0	−38.6	−40.0	−25.0	22.7	33.5	29.3	22.1	14.1	5.0
Middle East and Turkey	−2.3	0.2	10.6	7.7	−21.5	14.9	63.7	51.8	25.2	18.2
Western Hemisphere	−52.2	−36.5	−40.0	−67.2	−90.8	−56.7	−47.8	−52.9	−32.6	−28.1
Analytical groups										
By source of export earnings										
Fuel	−2.5	2.6	30.4	21.5	−27.6	19.9	104.2	63.8	37.9	33.6
Nonfuel	−82.1	−98.2	−105.1	−79.5	−57.4	−30.1	−37.5	−24.2	−18.9	−32.6
of which, primary products	−11.3	−14.3	−16.4	−18.6	−18.7	−9.6	−9.8	−9.2	−11.5	−13.3
By external financing source										
Net debtor countries	−77.7	−98.0	−87.9	−70.2	−71.3	−23.8	6.6	−4.3	−5.9	−19.6
of which, official financing	−9.7	−12.1	−9.1	−5.1	−10.4	−7.2	3.1	0.2	−5.4	−6.1
Net debtor countries by debt-servicing experience										
Countries with arrears and/or										
rescheduling during 1994–98	−18.1	−46.1	−42.8	−49.3	−58.5	−22.5	10.5	−8.6	−20.8	−27.8
Countries in transition	**2.4**	**−2.3**	**−16.8**	**−24.1**	**−29.4**	**−1.9**	**27.1**	**11.8**	**1.4**	**−1.4**
Central and eastern Europe	−3.3	−3.2	−14.9	−17.3	−20.2	−23.0	−19.7	−18.7	−20.8	−23.1
Commonwealth of Independent										
States and Mongolia	5.6	0.9	−1.9	−6.8	−9.2	21.1	46.8	30.6	22.2	21.7
Russia	8.2	4.9	3.8	−0.4	−1.6	22.7	45.3	31.9	24.1	24.5
Excluding Russia	−2.6	−3.9	−5.7	−6.4	−7.6	−1.6	1.5	−1.3	−1.9	−2.8
Total[1]	**−61.1**	**−46.9**	**−57.6**	**11.2**	**−67.3**	**−108.0**	**−133.4**	**−136.9**	**−189.9**	**−242.7**
In percent of total world current										
account transactions	−0.6	−0.4	−0.4	0.1	−0.5	−0.8	−0.9	−0.9	−1.2	−1.4
In percent of world GDP	−0.2	−0.2	−0.2	—	−0.2	−0.4	−0.4	−0.4	−0.6	−0.7
Memorandum										
Emerging market countries, excluding										
Asian countries in surplus[2]	−73.5	−75.5	−76.0	−105.7	−171.3	−60.1	46.9	16.1	−11.9	−20.5

[1]Reflects errors, omissions, and asymmetries in balance of payments statistics on current account, as well as the exclusion of data for international organizations and a limited number of countries. Calculated as the sum of the balance of individual euro area countries. See "Classification of Countries" in the introduction to this Statistical Appendix.
[2]All developing and transition countries excluding China, Hong Kong SAR, Korea, Malaysia, the Philippines, Singapore, Taiwan Province of China, and Thailand.

Table 28. Advanced Economies: Balance of Payments on Current Account

	1994	1995	1996	1997	1998	1999	2000	2001	2002	2003
					Billions of U.S. dollars					
Advanced economies	**21.2**	**50.9**	**34.0**	**93.3**	**47.2**	**−96.0**	**−227.1**	**−188.4**	**−210.3**	**−242.2**
Major advanced economies	−14.4	2.2	−9.7	26.3	−46.5	−177.9	−308.3	−287.7	−312.2	−344.6
United States	−118.2	−105.8	−117.8	−128.4	−203.8	−292.9	−410.3	−393.4	−479.6	−514.9
Japan	130.6	111.4	65.7	96.6	119.1	114.5	119.6	87.8	119.3	122.1
Germany	−24.0	−20.7	−7.9	−2.7	−6.2	−19.1	−20.9	2.4	38.7	45.5
France	7.4	10.9	20.5	39.5	40.1	42.0	19.4	24.0	26.6	22.0
Italy	13.2	25.1	40.0	32.4	20.0	8.1	−5.7	1.6	2.8	3.2
United Kingdom	−10.4	−14.2	−13.6	−2.8	−8.0	−31.9	−29.1	−29.5	−32.2	−37.1
Canada	−13.0	−4.4	3.4	−8.2	−7.7	1.3	18.7	19.4	12.2	14.5
Other advanced economies	35.6	48.7	43.7	67.1	93.7	81.9	81.2	99.3	102.0	102.4
Spain	−6.6	0.2	0.4	2.5	−2.9	−14.0	−19.4	−15.2	−11.3	−12.8
Netherlands	17.3	25.8	21.4	25.1	13.6	15.7	14.1	10.6	13.5	13.5
Belgium-Luxembourg	12.6	16.5	15.0	15.1	15.3	14.6	11.3	13.0	12.7	12.9
Sweden	0.8	4.9	6.5	7.0	6.8	8.8	7.6	6.7	7.2	7.9
Austria	−3.3	−6.1	−5.4	−6.5	−5.2	−6.8	−4.7	−4.1	−4.6	−5.0
Denmark	2.7	1.8	3.2	0.7	−1.5	2.9	2.5	4.2	5.0	6.5
Finland	1.1	5.3	5.1	6.8	7.3	7.8	8.9	7.8	9.4	10.4
Greece	−0.1	−2.9	−4.6	−4.8	−3.6	−5.1	−7.7	−7.2	−6.7	−7.9
Portugal	−2.2	−0.1	−4.1	−6.1	−7.9	−9.7	−11.1	−10.0	−9.6	−9.8
Ireland	1.6	1.9	2.4	2.5	0.8	0.4	−0.6	−1.0	−0.8	−1.2
Switzerland	17.3	21.0	21.9	25.5	26.1	28.4	30.9	24.7	28.0	31.3
Norway	3.7	5.2	11.0	10.0	0.1	8.5	25.0	26.0	20.6	17.8
Israel	−3.4	−5.2	−5.4	−4.0	−1.3	−3.3	−2.0	−1.9	−2.0	−2.0
Iceland	0.1	0.1	−0.1	−0.1	−0.6	−0.6	−0.9	−0.3	−0.2	—
Cyprus	0.1	−0.2	−0.5	−0.3	−0.6	−0.2	−0.5	−0.4	−0.5	−0.4
Korea	−3.9	−8.5	−23.0	−8.2	40.4	24.5	12.2	8.6	7.1	5.0
Australia	−16.9	−19.3	−15.8	−12.7	−17.9	−22.9	−15.3	−9.1	−14.6	−16.8
Taiwan Province of China	6.5	5.5	10.9	7.1	3.4	8.4	8.9	19.0	16.6	17.9
Hong Kong SAR	−1.1	−9.1	−4.0	−6.2	3.9	11.5	8.9	12.0	14.9	16.2
Singapore	11.4	14.9	12.6	18.1	19.7	16.5	15.5	17.5	19.3	21.2
New Zealand	−2.0	−3.1	−3.9	−4.3	−2.1	−3.5	−2.8	−1.4	−2.0	−2.6
Memorandum										
European Union	10.1	48.3	79.0	108.6	68.5	13.7	−35.1	3.2	50.7	48.2
Euro area[1]	17.0	55.9	82.9	103.8	71.3	33.9	−16.2	21.8	70.6	70.9
Newly industrialized Asian economies	12.9	2.8	−3.5	10.8	67.4	60.9	45.5	57.1	57.9	60.4
					Percent of GDP					
United States	−1.7	−1.4	−1.5	−1.5	−2.3	−3.2	−4.2	−3.9	−4.6	−4.7
Japan	2.7	2.1	1.4	2.2	3.0	2.5	2.5	2.1	3.0	2.9
Germany	−1.1	−0.8	−0.3	−0.1	−0.3	−0.9	−1.1	0.1	1.9	2.1
France	0.5	0.7	1.3	2.8	2.8	2.9	1.5	1.8	1.9	1.4
Italy	1.3	2.3	3.2	2.8	1.7	0.7	−0.5	0.1	0.2	0.2
United Kingdom	−1.0	−1.3	−1.1	−0.2	−0.6	−2.2	−2.0	−2.1	−2.1	−2.3
Canada	−2.3	−0.8	0.5	−1.3	−1.2	0.2	2.6	2.8	1.7	1.9
Spain	−1.3	—	0.1	0.5	−0.5	−2.3	−3.4	−2.6	−1.7	−1.8
Netherlands	4.9	6.2	5.2	6.6	3.5	3.9	3.8	2.8	3.2	3.0
Belgium-Luxembourg	5.0	5.6	5.2	5.7	5.7	5.4	4.5	5.2	4.7	4.5
Sweden	0.4	2.1	2.5	2.9	2.8	3.6	3.3	3.2	3.2	3.2
Austria	−1.6	−2.6	−2.3	−3.2	−2.5	−3.2	−2.5	−2.2	−2.3	−2.3
Denmark	1.8	1.0	1.8	0.4	−0.9	1.7	1.6	2.6	2.8	3.4
Finland	1.1	4.1	4.0	5.6	5.6	6.0	7.4	6.5	7.3	7.6
Greece	−0.1	−2.4	−3.7	−4.0	−3.0	−4.0	−6.8	−6.2	−5.1	−5.4
Portugal	−2.5	−0.1	−3.6	−5.7	−7.0	−8.4	−10.4	−9.2	−8.0	−7.5
Ireland	2.9	2.8	3.3	3.1	0.9	0.4	−0.6	−1.0	−0.7	−0.9
Switzerland	6.6	6.8	7.4	9.9	10.0	11.0	12.9	10.0	10.5	11.0
Norway	3.0	3.5	6.9	6.3	—	5.4	15.0	15.4	11.4	9.5
Israel	−4.4	−5.7	−5.5	−3.9	−1.3	−3.2	−1.7	−1.7	−1.9	−1.8
Iceland	1.9	0.8	−1.8	−1.6	−7.0	−6.9	−10.1	−4.4	−2.0	0.1
Cyprus	1.2	−1.8	−5.2	−4.0	−6.7	−2.4	−5.2	−4.4	−5.5	−3.6
Korea	−1.0	−1.7	−4.4	−1.7	12.7	6.0	2.7	2.0	1.5	0.9
Australia	−5.0	−5.3	−3.9	−3.1	−4.9	−5.9	−4.0	−2.6	−3.6	−3.9
Taiwan Province of China	2.7	2.1	3.9	2.4	1.3	2.9	2.9	6.7	5.8	5.9
Hong Kong SAR	−0.8	−6.4	−2.6	−3.5	2.4	7.2	5.4	7.3	9.2	9.7
Singapore	16.3	17.9	13.8	19.2	24.0	20.0	16.7	20.4	21.7	22.3
New Zealand	−4.0	−5.2	−5.9	−6.5	−3.9	−6.3	−5.5	−2.9	−3.5	−4.1

[1]Calculated as the sum of the balances of individual euro area countries.

Table 29. Advanced Economies: Current Account Transactions
(Billions of U.S. dollars)

	1994	1995	1996	1997	1998	1999	2000	2001	2002	2003
Exports	3,318.6	3,965.9	4,084.1	4,196.7	4,169.3	4,276.6	4,650.6	4,421.1	4,528.9	4,936.8
Imports	3,245.2	3,875.2	4,025.4	4,126.5	4,106.0	4,352.6	4,874.0	4,600.3	4,716.7	5,153.0
Trade balance	73.4	90.7	58.7	70.2	63.3	−76.0	−223.4	−179.2	−187.9	−216.2
Services, credits	894.5	1,006.2	1,067.7	1,102.4	1,121.1	1,164.6	1,224.3	1,201.7	1,272.4	1,383.7
Services, debits	831.3	942.1	991.0	1,006.2	1,044.1	1,092.6	1,151.7	1,136.8	1,215.6	1,333.6
Balance on services	63.2	64.1	76.7	96.2	77.0	72.0	72.6	64.9	56.8	50.1
Balance on goods and services	136.5	154.8	135.4	166.4	140.3	−4.0	−150.8	−114.3	−131.1	−166.1
Income, net	−26.5	−21.9	−8.7	14.0	−3.6	12.5	25.2	27.2	24.9	33.8
Current transfers, net	−88.9	−82.0	−92.8	−87.1	−89.5	−104.5	−101.5	−101.2	−104.1	−109.9
Current account balance	**21.2**	**50.9**	**34.0**	**93.3**	**47.2**	**−96.0**	**−227.1**	**−188.4**	**−210.3**	**−242.2**
Balance on goods and services										
Advanced economies	**136.5**	**154.8**	**135.4**	**166.4**	**140.3**	**−4.0**	**−150.8**	**−114.3**	**−131.1**	**−166.1**
Major advanced economies	70.8	83.4	56.0	74.5	19.2	−117.4	−263.5	−249.8	−260.1	−297.9
United States	−96.7	−96.4	−101.8	−107.8	−166.9	−262.2	−378.7	−358.3	−428.0	−474.8
Japan	96.4	74.7	21.2	47.3	73.2	69.2	69.0	26.5	54.8	63.7
Germany	10.1	18.1	25.2	29.1	31.7	17.9	7.3	37.6	71.6	78.8
France	25.0	28.9	31.2	45.8	44.8	36.3	19.4	23.1	25.2	20.1
Italy	37.0	45.3	62.2	47.6	39.8	24.5	10.7	17.8	17.4	20.3
United Kingdom	−7.3	−5.6	−6.4	0.3	−15.2	−25.2	−28.0	−32.3	−30.8	−37.7
Canada	6.3	18.4	24.4	12.1	11.8	22.3	36.9	35.9	29.7	31.7
Other advanced economies	65.7	71.4	79.4	91.9	121.1	113.4	112.7	135.4	129.0	131.8
Memorandum										
European Union	110.8	147.0	176.5	187.0	154.7	97.7	42.7	90.0	135.9	138.1
Euro area	99.9	128.2	156.2	162.4	151.9	100.7	48.6	100.9	143.6	151.2
Newly industrialized Asian economies	8.7	1.0	−3.4	7.0	63.3	59.8	45.4	53.5	49.8	50.8
Income, net										
Advanced economies	**−26.5**	**−21.9**	**−8.7**	**14.0**	**−3.6**	**12.5**	**25.2**	**27.2**	**24.9**	**33.8**
Major advanced economies	6.2	1.2	23.1	34.8	20.9	34.7	45.5	50.4	38.7	48.2
United States	16.7	24.6	24.1	20.2	7.6	18.1	21.8	14.4	0.4	9.0
Japan	40.3	44.4	53.5	58.1	54.7	57.4	60.4	69.2	69.3	68.0
Germany	3.0	0.1	0.9	−1.4	−7.6	−9.6	−3.1	−11.3	−7.1	−5.9
France	−6.9	−9.0	−2.7	2.6	4.9	19.0	13.8	14.2	15.8	17.5
Italy	−16.7	−15.6	−15.0	−11.2	−12.3	−11.1	−12.0	−10.9	−9.0	−10.9
United Kingdom	−11.3	−20.6	−16.2	−12.6	−6.4	−17.5	−16.3	−7.4	−12.4	−11.6
Canada	−19.0	−22.7	−21.6	−20.9	−19.9	−21.7	−19.1	−17.8	−18.3	−17.9
Other advanced economies	−32.6	−23.1	−31.8	−20.8	−24.5	−22.2	−20.3	−23.2	−13.7	−14.4
Memorandum										
European Union	−56.9	−62.5	−55.7	−43.3	−49.6	−42.6	−42.0	−47.1	−43.8	−45.3
Euro area	−33.2	−28.2	−26.8	−18.6	−35.4	−21.0	−20.4	−35.4	−26.9	−29.3
Newly industrialized Asian economies	5.1	5.4	3.5	8.2	5.1	4.2	5.0	9.7	15.3	17.3

Table 30. Developing Countries: Payments Balances on Current Account

	1994	1995	1996	1997	1998	1999	2000	2001	2002	2003
					Billions of U.S. dollars					
Developing countries	**−84.6**	**−95.5**	**−74.7**	**−58.0**	**−85.1**	**−10.2**	**66.7**	**39.6**	**18.9**	**0.9**
Regional groups										
Africa	−11.1	−16.8	−6.4	−7.4	−20.1	−14.3	5.4	1.3	−7.2	−7.1
Sub-Sahara	−7.9	−12.6	−7.2	−10.2	−18.4	−13.7	−2.5	−6.3	−11.2	−11.8
Excluding Nigeria and South Africa	−6.4	−8.7	−7.8	−10.2	−13.2	−11.6	−6.9	−8.6	−9.7	−11.7
Developing Asia	−19.0	−42.5	−38.9	8.9	47.3	46.0	45.4	39.4	33.5	18.0
China	7.7	1.6	7.2	37.0	31.5	15.7	20.5	17.4	19.0	13.1
India	−1.7	−5.6	−6.0	−3.0	−6.9	−3.2	−4.3	−0.1	0.4	−0.1
Other developing Asia	−25.0	−38.6	−40.0	−25.0	22.7	33.5	29.3	22.1	14.1	5.0
Middle East and Turkey	−2.3	0.2	10.6	7.7	−21.5	14.9	63.7	51.8	25.2	18.2
Western Hemisphere	−52.2	−36.5	−40.0	−67.2	−90.8	−56.7	−47.8	−52.9	−32.6	−28.1
Analytical groups										
By source of export earnings										
Fuel	−2.5	2.6	30.4	21.5	−27.6	19.9	104.2	63.8	37.9	33.6
Nonfuel	−82.1	−98.2	−105.1	−79.5	−57.4	−30.1	−37.5	−24.2	−18.9	−32.6
of which, primary products	−11.3	−14.3	−16.4	−18.6	−18.7	−9.6	−9.8	−9.2	−11.5	−13.3
By external financing source										
Net debtor countries	−77.7	−98.0	−87.9	−70.2	−71.3	−23.8	6.6	−4.3	−5.9	−19.6
of which, official financing	−9.7	−12.1	−9.1	−5.1	−10.4	−7.2	3.1	0.2	−5.4	−6.1
Net debtor countries by debt-servicing experience										
Countries with arrears and/or rescheduling during 1994–98	−18.1	−46.1	−42.8	−49.3	−58.5	−22.5	10.5	−8.6	−20.8	−27.8
Other groups										
Heavily indebted poor countries	−9.6	−12.5	−13.1	−14.3	−16.0	−12.9	−7.7	−8.8	−12.1	−14.9
Middle East and north Africa	−10.9	−4.5	12.5	11.6	−27.1	14.2	80.2	54.6	29.4	23.2

Table 30 *(concluded)*

	Ten-Year Averages		1994	1995	1996	1997	1998	1999	2000	2001	2002	2003
	1984–93	1994–2003										
					Percent of exports of goods and services							
Developing countries	**−15.6**	**0.1**	**−9.7**	**−9.2**	**−6.4**	**−4.6**	**−7.3**	**−0.8**	**4.3**	**2.6**	**1.2**	**0.1**
Regional groups												
Africa	−10.9	−4.5	−10.9	−14.0	−4.9	−5.5	−16.7	−11.2	3.5	0.9	−4.8	−4.5
Sub-Sahara	−13.0	−10.4	−10.2	−13.7	−7.2	−9.9	−20.2	−14.4	−2.2	−5.8	−10.3	−10.4
Excluding Nigeria and South Africa	−24.8	−19.5	−16.9	−19.3	−15.7	−20.1	−28.6	−23.6	−12.6	−15.9	−16.9	−19.5
Developing Asia	−11.1	2.2	−5.1	−9.3	−7.7	1.6	8.8	8.0	6.5	5.7	4.5	2.2
China	−13.8	3.7	6.4	1.1	4.2	17.8	15.2	7.2	7.3	5.8	5.8	3.7
India	−6.1	−0.2	−5.3	−14.6	−14.7	−6.7	−15.1	−6.3	−7.1	−0.1	0.6	−0.2
Other developing Asia	−10.6	1.3	−11.3	−14.3	−13.7	−8.0	7.9	10.9	8.2	6.7	4.1	1.3
Middle East and Turkey	−15.7	5.8	−1.2	0.1	4.2	3.0	−9.7	5.9	19.0	16.3	8.2	5.8
Western Hemisphere	−25.2	−7.3	−25.1	−14.8	−14.6	−22.4	−31.0	−18.7	−13.4	−15.1	−9.2	−7.3
Analytical groups												
By source of export earnings												
Fuel	−13.4	11.1	−1.4	1.3	12.7	8.8	−15.0	8.6	30.4	20.5	12.7	11.1
Nonfuel	−16.2	−2.4	−5.9	−6.3	−5.9	−2.3	—	0.2	−1.0	−0.2	−0.3	−1.5
of which, primary products	−24.7	−12.6	−18.9	−19.2	−20.6	−22.0	−23.0	−11.5	−10.7	−10.0	−12.0	−12.6
By external financing source												
Net debtor countries	−15.7	−1.3	−10.2	−10.7	−8.6	−6.3	−6.7	−2.1	0.5	−0.3	−0.4	−1.3
of which, official financing	−18.7	−7.0	−21.9	−22.5	−14.9	−7.8	−17.1	−10.9	3.7	0.2	−6.7	−7.0
Net debtor countries by debt-servicing experience												
Countries with arrears and/or rescheduling during 1994–98	−14.0	−7.2	−8.2	−18.4	−15.1	−15.8	−20.8	−7.4	2.8	−2.4	−5.8	−7.2
Other groups												
Heavily indebted poor countries	−39.3	−19.7	−25.1	−26.6	−24.7	−25.8	−29.9	−22.3	−11.3	−12.9	−17.0	−19.7
Middle East and north Africa	−14.4	7.8	−6.1	−2.2	5.4	4.8	−14.2	6.1	24.8	17.9	10.1	7.8
Memorandum												
Median												
Developing countries	−18.9	−9.6	−13.6	−12.9	−14.6	−12.1	−17.0	−10.8	−10.7	−10.2	−10.2	−9.6

Table 31. Developing Countries—by Region: Current Account Transactions
(Billions of U.S. dollars)

	1994	1995	1996	1997	1998	1999	2000	2001	2002	2003
Developing countries										
Exports	716.9	862.8	965.4	1,043.7	962.5	1,055.4	1,321.4	1,278.5	1,318.9	1,412.4
Imports	731.1	868.5	949.0	1,011.0	957.9	964.3	1,149.1	1,138.0	1,190.4	1,298.7
Trade balance	−14.2	−5.7	16.4	32.7	4.6	91.1	172.3	140.5	128.4	113.7
Services, net	−43.3	−55.2	−55.7	−61.8	−51.9	−51.6	−55.7	−55.7	−58.3	−64.3
Balance on goods and services	−57.5	−61.0	−39.3	−29.0	−47.3	39.4	116.6	84.9	70.1	49.4
Income, net	−55.5	−66.2	−71.4	−72.5	−77.0	−93.1	−95.7	−94.7	−99.8	−99.2
Current transfers, net	28.4	31.6	35.9	43.5	39.2	43.5	45.8	49.4	48.6	50.7
Current account balance	**−84.6**	**−95.5**	**−74.7**	**−58.0**	**−85.1**	**−10.2**	**66.7**	**39.6**	**18.9**	**0.9**
Memorandum										
Exports of goods and services	867.9	1,036.4	1,161.4	1,262.9	1,173.2	1,260.5	1,548.9	1,510.1	1,550.4	1,664.1
Interest payments	84.9	99.0	104.3	105.6	113.3	118.3	123.5	118.1	116.1	118.8
Oil trade balance	105.4	119.3	150.0	141.5	89.9	134.0	220.1	184.4	165.9	166.7
Regional groups										
Africa										
Exports	85.1	100.1	111.2	114.3	98.7	105.5	132.8	125.4	125.2	132.6
Imports	82.4	98.8	99.8	103.9	102.9	101.1	106.9	108.4	113.3	119.8
Trade balance	2.6	1.3	11.3	10.3	−4.3	4.4	26.0	17.0	11.9	12.8
Services, net	−9.5	−11.8	−10.4	−10.6	−10.8	−10.3	−10.6	−10.2	−12.7	−12.9
Balance on goods and services	−6.9	−10.5	0.9	−0.3	−15.1	−5.9	15.3	6.8	−0.8	−0.1
Income, net	−15.0	−16.6	−18.0	−17.9	−16.5	−19.4	−22.2	−19.2	−19.1	−20.1
Current transfers, net	10.8	10.4	10.7	10.7	11.5	10.9	12.2	13.7	12.8	13.1
Current account balance	**−11.1**	**−16.8**	**−6.4**	**−7.4**	**−20.1**	**−14.3**	**5.4**	**1.3**	**−7.2**	**−7.1**
Memorandum										
Exports of goods and services	102.1	119.3	132.2	135.8	120.2	127.7	154.8	148.5	148.4	157.3
Interest payments	13.4	15.9	16.3	16.0	16.0	16.0	16.3	14.9	13.5	13.9
Oil trade balance	19.1	21.4	29.4	28.9	18.6	25.0	45.3	39.1	36.7	39.7
Developing Asia										
Exports	307.2	378.4	416.5	467.1	456.5	495.0	604.6	594.3	638.3	693.8
Imports	327.3	404.9	447.1	452.1	390.7	425.8	541.5	536.6	581.4	646.9
Trade balance	−20.1	−26.5	−30.6	15.0	65.8	69.1	63.2	57.7	56.8	46.9
Services, net	−4.6	−11.0	−6.6	−11.1	−11.8	−10.3	−9.3	−9.7	−11.7	−14.1
Balance on goods and services	−24.7	−37.4	−37.2	3.9	54.0	58.8	53.9	48.0	45.2	32.8
Income, net	−13.5	−23.4	−23.9	−23.0	−28.2	−37.9	−36.1	−37.5	−40.7	−43.5
Current transfers, net	19.2	18.3	22.3	28.0	21.5	25.0	27.7	29.0	29.0	28.6
Current account balance	**−19.0**	**−42.5**	**−38.9**	**8.9**	**47.3**	**46.0**	**45.4**	**39.4**	**33.5**	**18.0**
Memorandum										
Exports of goods and services	370.6	455.4	505.4	565.4	539.6	578.1	699.4	694.7	741.0	805.3
Interest payments	24.5	27.4	30.5	27.9	32.0	34.0	34.2	30.7	33.0	35.0
Oil trade balance	−10.4	−12.2	−18.0	−20.6	−12.7	−21.5	−38.6	−36.6	−37.7	−40.0

Table 31 *(concluded)*

	1994	1995	1996	1997	1998	1999	2000	2001	2002	2003
Middle East and Turkey										
Exports	157.2	179.8	210.3	212.5	166.6	203.9	284.2	267.5	258.1	260.9
Imports	133.3	156.7	173.8	185.3	182.5	174.1	199.2	194.7	208.1	218.5
Trade balance	23.9	23.1	36.5	27.2	−15.8	29.7	85.0	72.8	50.0	42.4
Services, net	−20.6	−24.0	−28.0	−24.3	−13.4	−19.9	−23.4	−22.3	−25.0	−27.7
Balance on goods and services	3.4	−0.9	8.6	2.8	−29.2	9.8	61.6	50.5	25.0	14.7
Income, net	9.6	14.4	14.4	16.1	19.2	17.9	17.5	18.6	17.8	19.5
Current transfers, net	−15.3	−13.3	−12.4	−11.2	−11.4	−12.8	−15.4	−17.3	−17.6	−16.0
Current account balance	**−2.3**	**0.2**	**10.6**	**7.7**	**−21.5**	**14.9**	**63.7**	**51.8**	**25.2**	**18.2**
Memorandum										
Exports of goods and services	187.7	215.4	249.5	261.4	220.5	251.4	336.2	317.6	306.4	316.2
Interest payments	10.3	11.6	11.9	12.8	12.8	12.8	14.3	14.3	14.6	16.4
Oil trade balance	81.0	91.1	113.4	109.1	68.6	106.5	174.5	153.0	137.0	135.4
Western Hemisphere										
Exports	167.4	204.5	227.5	249.9	240.7	251.0	299.7	291.3	297.2	325.0
Imports	188.0	208.2	228.4	269.7	281.8	263.3	301.6	298.2	287.5	313.5
Trade balance	−20.6	−3.7	−0.8	−19.8	−41.1	−12.2	−1.9	−7.0	9.7	11.5
Services, net	−8.7	−8.4	−10.7	−15.7	−15.8	−11.1	−12.3	−13.5	−8.9	−9.5
Balance on goods and services	−29.3	−12.1	−11.6	−35.5	−56.9	−23.3	−14.2	−20.5	0.9	2.1
Income, net	−36.6	−40.6	−43.8	−47.7	−51.5	−53.7	−54.9	−56.5	−57.8	−55.2
Current transfers, net	13.7	16.2	15.3	16.0	17.6	20.3	21.2	24.0	24.4	25.0
Current account balance	**−52.2**	**−36.5**	**−40.0**	**−67.2**	**−90.8**	**−56.7**	**−47.8**	**−52.9**	**−32.6**	**−28.1**
Memorandum										
Exports of goods and services	207.5	246.2	274.4	300.2	293.0	303.4	358.4	349.4	354.6	385.3
Interest payments	36.7	44.2	45.6	48.9	52.5	55.5	58.8	58.1	55.0	53.5
Oil trade balance	15.7	19.0	25.3	24.2	15.4	23.9	39.0	29.0	30.0	31.6

Table 32. Developing Countries—by Analytical Criteria: Current Account Transactions

(Billions of U.S. dollars)

	1994	1995	1996	1997	1998	1999	2000	2001	2002	2003
By source of export earnings										
Fuel										
Exports	166.1	188.2	226.5	229.3	168.2	216.9	326.8	293.7	277.4	279.9
Imports	111.1	125.2	129.4	141.3	141.5	137.8	151.7	166.3	175.5	180.9
Trade balance	55.0	63.0	97.1	88.1	26.7	79.0	175.2	127.3	101.9	99.0
Services, net	−37.0	−43.2	−50.2	−51.2	−41.2	−41.8	−49.0	−45.3	−45.0	−49.4
Balance on goods and services	18.0	19.8	46.9	36.8	−14.5	37.2	126.2	82.1	56.9	49.7
Income, net	2.7	5.7	4.6	5.4	9.2	6.5	4.3	7.9	7.3	9.1
Current transfers, net	−23.2	−22.8	−21.1	−20.7	−22.3	−23.8	−26.3	−26.2	−26.3	−25.2
Current account balance	**−2.5**	**2.6**	**30.4**	**21.5**	**−27.6**	**19.9**	**104.2**	**63.8**	**37.9**	**33.6**
Memorandum										
Exports of goods and services	177.4	200.5	239.3	245.1	184.4	232.7	343.2	311.8	296.9	301.9
Interest payments	11.9	14.1	14.0	15.5	15.5	14.5	15.4	13.7	13.4	13.9
Oil trade balance	116.2	131.9	168.5	164.9	107.6	155.9	256.7	222.2	202.8	206.6
Nonfuel exports										
Exports	550.8	674.6	739.0	814.4	794.2	838.5	994.5	984.9	1,041.5	1,132.4
Imports	620.0	743.3	819.7	869.7	816.4	826.5	997.4	971.6	1,015.0	1,117.8
Trade balance	−69.2	−68.7	−80.7	−55.3	−22.1	12.0	−2.9	13.2	26.5	14.7
Services, net	−6.3	−12.0	−5.5	−10.5	−10.7	−9.8	−6.7	−10.4	−13.3	−14.9
Balance on goods and services	−75.5	−80.8	−86.2	−65.9	−32.8	2.2	−9.6	2.8	13.3	−0.2
Income, net	−58.2	−71.9	−76.0	−77.8	−86.2	−99.6	−100.0	−102.6	−107.1	−108.3
Current transfers, net	51.6	54.5	57.0	64.2	61.6	67.2	72.1	75.6	74.9	75.9
Current account balance	**−82.1**	**−98.2**	**−105.1**	**−79.5**	**−57.4**	**−30.1**	**−37.5**	**−24.2**	**−18.9**	**−32.6**
Memorandum										
Exports of goods and services	690.5	835.9	922.1	1,017.7	988.9	1,027.8	1,205.7	1,198.3	1,253.4	1,362.2
Interest payments	73.0	85.0	90.3	90.0	97.8	103.8	108.1	104.3	102.7	104.9
Oil trade balance	−10.8	−12.7	−18.4	−23.3	−17.7	−21.9	−36.6	−37.8	−36.9	−39.9
Nonfuel primary products										
Exports	48.6	60.9	64.6	68.6	65.1	67.7	75.1	75.4	79.1	86.8
Imports	52.6	66.0	73.1	78.4	77.0	70.4	76.9	77.4	81.6	89.8
Trade balance	−4.0	−5.1	−8.5	−9.8	−11.9	−2.7	−1.8	−1.9	−2.5	−3.0
Services, net	−5.2	−6.4	−5.5	−6.2	−5.9	−5.6	−5.9	−5.7	−6.8	−7.1
Balance on goods and services	−9.2	−11.5	−13.9	−16.0	−17.9	−8.3	−7.7	−7.7	−9.4	−10.2
Income, net	−8.8	−9.6	−10.5	−10.7	−10.0	−10.7	−11.9	−11.6	−12.1	−13.5
Current transfers, net	6.8	6.8	8.1	8.1	9.2	9.4	9.9	10.1	9.9	10.3
Current account balance	**−11.3**	**−14.3**	**−16.4**	**−18.6**	**−18.7**	**−9.6**	**−9.8**	**−9.2**	**−11.5**	**−13.3**
Memorandum										
Exports of goods and services	59.6	74.6	79.6	84.2	81.3	83.6	91.0	92.1	96.4	105.4
Interest payments	7.7	9.1	9.2	8.8	9.2	8.9	9.3	8.3	8.6	9.8
Oil trade balance	−2.4	−3.0	−3.9	−4.3	−3.7	−3.3	−4.1	−4.0	−3.8	−3.6

Table 32 *(continued)*

	1994	1995	1996	1997	1998	1999	2000	2001	2002	2003
By external financing source										
Net debtor countries										
Exports	618.4	748.1	831.8	906.5	863.9	933.9	1,142.4	1,115.4	1,170.4	1,267.1
Imports	665.3	796.5	873.7	930.2	878.4	890.8	1,073.1	1,057.5	1,105.2	1,214.5
Trade balance	−46.9	−48.4	−41.9	−23.7	−14.5	43.1	69.3	57.9	65.2	52.6
Services, net	−18.9	−24.8	−19.0	−24.4	−23.8	−22.2	−19.4	−23.1	−26.6	−28.7
Balance on goods and services	−65.8	−73.2	−60.9	−48.1	−38.3	20.9	50.0	34.8	38.7	23.9
Income, net	−66.4	−80.9	−86.0	−88.7	−95.7	−111.2	−113.6	−113.8	−119.8	−120.4
Current transfers, net	54.5	56.1	59.0	66.6	62.7	66.4	70.3	74.7	75.2	76.9
Current account balance	**−77.7**	**−98.0**	**−87.9**	**−70.2**	**−71.3**	**−23.8**	**6.6**	**−4.3**	**−5.9**	**−19.6**
Memorandum										
Exports of goods and services	763.2	915.3	1,021.6	1,117.2	1,065.5	1,129.4	1,360.2	1,336.4	1,390.8	1,506.2
Interest payments	82.6	96.2	101.3	101.8	109.4	114.9	119.8	114.9	112.9	115.5
Oil trade balance	39.8	44.9	58.1	51.8	35.5	56.8	89.2	70.9	69.7	71.2
Official financing										
Exports	32.8	40.7	47.0	51.1	46.1	51.0	66.8	65.5	63.9	68.7
Imports	42.8	51.6	54.8	54.5	55.6	57.0	64.0	66.3	70.5	76.3
Trade balance	−9.9	−10.9	−7.8	−3.4	−9.5	−6.0	2.8	−0.9	−6.6	−7.6
Services, net	−3.1	−3.9	−3.9	−3.3	−4.4	−4.3	−3.2	−3.4	−4.2	−4.1
Balance on goods and services	−13.0	−14.8	−11.7	−6.6	−13.9	−10.3	−0.4	−4.2	−10.8	−11.7
Income, net	−5.9	−6.7	−6.9	−7.1	−6.2	−7.2	−8.0	−6.8	−6.3	−6.7
Current transfers, net	9.2	9.5	9.4	8.7	9.7	10.2	11.5	11.2	11.7	12.3
Current account balance	**−9.7**	**−12.1**	**−9.1**	**−5.1**	**−10.4**	**−7.2**	**3.1**	**0.2**	**−5.4**	**−6.1**
Memorandum										
Exports of goods and services	44.1	53.9	61.0	65.9	60.9	66.3	83.3	82.3	81.2	87.3
Interest payments	6.3	7.0	7.1	7.1	6.9	6.8	6.7	5.7	5.2	5.4
Oil trade balance	9.3	10.9	14.1	14.4	10.2	13.3	23.1	19.5	17.6	18.4
Net debtor countries by debt-servicing experience										
Countries with arrears and/or rescheduling during 1994–98										
Exports	183.3	207.4	232.0	252.6	232.3	259.2	329.2	309.0	310.5	330.0
Imports	176.3	220.9	240.2	258.9	240.9	230.5	263.9	266.9	277.7	302.5
Trade balance	6.9	−13.5	−8.2	−6.4	−8.5	28.7	65.3	42.1	32.8	27.5
Services, net	−14.8	−19.2	−24.3	−31.0	−34.7	−24.2	−25.6	−26.2	−27.4	−28.1
Balance on goods and services	−7.9	−32.7	−32.5	−37.4	−43.3	4.5	39.6	15.9	5.4	−0.6
Income, net	−26.9	−30.5	−26.8	−29.2	−32.3	−44.0	−46.3	−42.8	−45.7	−48.0
Current transfers, net	16.7	17.1	16.6	17.3	17.1	17.0	17.1	18.3	19.4	20.8
Current account balance	**−18.1**	**−46.1**	**−42.8**	**−49.3**	**−58.5**	**−22.5**	**10.5**	**−8.6**	**−20.8**	**−27.8**
Memorandum										
Exports of goods and services	220.2	250.9	283.1	311.0	281.9	303.3	376.9	357.6	361.2	384.5
Interest payments	29.2	35.5	37.8	39.2	43.3	45.6	46.9	42.9	43.7	45.1
Oil trade balance	35.3	38.3	48.6	47.5	35.7	55.2	86.8	76.4	78.7	82.2

Table 32 *(concluded)*

	1994	1995	1996	1997	1998	1999	2000	2001	2002	2003
Other groups										
Heavily indebted poor countries										
Exports	29.9	37.2	42.5	44.9	42.5	46.4	56.0	55.7	58.5	62.0
Imports	35.2	42.4	47.4	50.2	51.1	52.1	56.4	58.3	62.9	69.0
Trade balance	−5.3	−5.3	−4.9	−5.4	−8.6	−5.7	−0.4	−2.5	−4.4	−6.9
Services, net	−5.2	−7.0	−7.7	−8.4	−8.4	−7.7	−7.8	−8.0	−9.2	−9.4
Balance on goods and services	−10.5	−12.3	−12.5	−13.8	−17.0	−13.4	−8.2	−10.6	−13.6	−16.4
Income, net	−7.1	−8.2	−9.3	−8.7	−8.4	−9.1	−10.6	−9.4	−9.3	−9.8
Current transfers, net	8.1	8.0	8.7	8.1	9.4	9.7	11.1	11.2	10.8	11.2
Current account balance	**−9.6**	**−12.5**	**−13.1**	**−14.3**	**−16.0**	**−12.9**	**−7.7**	**−8.8**	**−12.1**	**−14.9**
Memorandum										
Exports of goods and services	38.1	47.0	53.1	55.4	53.6	57.8	67.9	68.2	71.3	75.8
Interest payments	6.0	6.6	7.2	6.8	7.3	6.6	6.3	5.3	5.3	5.5
Oil trade balance	3.6	4.8	6.0	6.1	3.7	6.9	12.2	10.3	11.8	11.3
Middle East and north Africa										
Exports	154.0	175.1	203.0	205.8	157.8	199.6	287.6	265.4	253.6	255.6
Imports	133.5	147.9	156.2	162.2	163.6	161.1	172.8	184.1	194.9	202.6
Trade balance	20.5	27.1	46.8	43.7	−5.8	38.5	114.8	81.4	58.8	53.0
Services, net	−22.2	−27.5	−31.1	−31.5	−23.5	−23.4	−30.1	−25.3	−26.2	−28.9
Balance on goods and services	−1.8	−0.4	15.7	12.2	−29.2	15.1	84.7	56.1	32.6	24.1
Income, net	4.6	8.9	8.5	10.4	14.0	12.1	11.2	13.5	12.4	13.8
Current transfers, net	−13.7	−13.0	−11.6	−11.0	−11.8	−13.0	−15.6	−14.9	−15.6	−14.7
Current account balance	**−10.9**	**−4.5**	**12.5**	**11.6**	**−27.1**	**14.2**	**80.2**	**54.6**	**29.4**	**23.2**
Memorandum										
Exports of goods and services	179.3	202.4	232.9	238.8	191.2	234.2	323.1	304.5	292.3	299.4
Interest payments	−11.0	−12.5	−12.9	−13.1	−12.7	−11.9	−12.4	−10.9	−10.9	−11.4
Oil trade balance	92.2	103.6	129.2	125.6	81.9	121.3	200.5	174.9	158.2	158.3

Table 33. Summary of Balance of Payments, Capital Flows, and External Financing
(Billions of U.S. dollars)

	1994	1995	1996	1997	1998	1999	2000	2001	2002	2003
Developing countries										
Balance of payments[1]										
Balance on current account	−84.6	−95.5	−74.7	−58.0	−85.1	−10.2	66.7	39.6	18.9	0.9
Balance on goods and services	−57.5	−61.0	−39.3	−29.0	−47.3	39.4	116.6	84.9	70.1	49.4
Income, net	−55.5	−66.2	−71.4	−72.5	−77.0	−93.1	−95.7	−94.7	−99.8	−99.2
Current transfers, net	28.4	31.6	35.9	43.5	39.2	43.5	45.8	49.4	48.6	50.7
Balance on capital and financial account	115.0	122.8	108.2	110.2	115.8	50.5	−27.6	−28.3	−10.8	4.9
Balance on capital account[2]	4.8	7.1	11.4	11.3	5.5	7.2	5.2	6.6	8.2	9.0
Balance on financial account	110.2	115.7	96.7	98.9	110.4	43.2	−32.7	−34.9	−19.0	−4.1
Direct investment, net	74.5	82.4	104.3	128.6	129.8	131.8	129.9	147.3	115.5	121.8
Portfolio investment, net	99.1	22.3	75.6	42.7	9.8	19.6	−13.6	−52.0	−14.1	−9.1
Other investment, net	−13.7	78.9	10.0	−9.4	−31.5	−76.3	−89.6	−49.0	−35.5	−40.8
Reserve assets	−49.7	−67.9	−93.1	−63.0	2.3	−31.9	−59.5	−81.2	−85.0	−76.0
Errors and omissions, net	−30.4	−27.3	−33.4	−52.2	−30.8	−40.3	−39.1	−11.3	−8.1	−5.9
Capital flows										
Total capital flows, net[3]	159.9	183.6	189.9	161.9	108.1	75.1	26.7	46.4	66.0	71.9
Net official flows	20.7	33.4	2.1	31.7	42.9	25.4	10.7	38.0	37.4	34.0
Net private flows[4]	139.2	150.1	187.8	130.2	65.2	49.7	16.1	8.3	28.6	37.9
Direct investment, net	74.5	82.4	104.3	128.6	129.8	131.8	129.9	147.3	115.5	121.8
Private portfolio investment, net	93.5	16.7	64.4	36.8	1.8	12.8	−17.9	−51.5	−12.8	−9.4
Other private flows, net	−28.8	51.1	19.1	−35.3	−66.4	−94.9	−96.0	−87.5	−74.1	−74.5
External financing[5]										
Net external financing[6]	174.7	229.0	249.2	258.2	202.7	183.2	169.3	156.6	168.9	188.4
Nondebt-creating flows	100.4	113.2	152.3	169.7	138.0	155.8	149.8	153.2	136.8	141.3
Capital transfers[7]	4.8	7.1	11.4	11.3	5.5	7.2	5.2	6.6	8.2	9.0
Foreign direct investment and equity security liabilities[8]	95.6	106.1	140.9	158.3	132.6	148.5	144.7	146.6	128.6	132.4
Net external borrowing[9]	74.3	115.7	96.8	88.5	64.6	27.5	19.5	3.4	32.2	47.1
Borrowing from official creditors[10]	21.5	32.9	7.7	24.0	38.4	28.4	17.8	35.2	30.9	33.7
Of which,										
Credit and loans from IMF[11]	−0.8	12.6	−2.9	0.8	8.5	1.3	−6.7	23.3	...	...
Borrowing from banks[12]	−27.8	33.7	29.9	18.6	12.4	−6.7	−5.1	−12.7	2.6	4.5
Borrowing from other private creditors	80.5	49.1	59.2	45.9	13.8	5.8	6.8	−19.0	−1.3	8.8
Memorandum										
Balance on goods and services in percent of GDP[13]	−1.4	−1.4	−0.8	−0.6	−0.9	0.8	2.2	1.6	1.3	0.9
Scheduled amortization of external debt	131.4	158.4	200.4	247.0	242.1	270.8	277.5	278.1	239.0	243.3
Gross external financing[14]	306.1	387.4	449.6	505.2	444.7	454.1	446.8	434.7	408.0	431.7
Gross external borrowing[15]	205.7	274.1	297.2	335.5	306.7	298.3	297.0	281.5	271.2	290.4
Exceptional external financing, net	19.8	22.2	20.9	18.4	21.1	18.5	4.9	14.8	24.3	7.4
Of which,										
Arrears on debt service	−14.3	−2.5	−3.5	−7.0	1.0	5.5	−28.7	3.2	...	...
Debt forgiveness	1.0	2.2	9.2	13.6	1.1	2.1	1.5	3.3	...	...
Rescheduling of debt service	25.1	20.5	14.2	10.4	5.9	8.0	29.2	6.7	...	...
Countries in transition										
Balance of payments[1]										
Balance on current account	2.4	−2.3	−16.8	−24.1	−29.4	−1.9	27.1	11.8	1.4	−1.4
Balance on goods and services	1.2	−5.2	−17.8	−30.3	−36.4	−6.3	23.0	6.8	−1.9	−3.8
Income, net	−3.1	−2.0	−4.8	0.3	−6.4	−3.6	−4.4	−3.8	−5.5	−7.3
Current transfers, net	4.3	5.0	5.7	5.9	13.3	8.0	8.5	8.9	8.8	9.7
Balance on capital and financial account	−1.8	5.9	24.6	27.4	37.4	7.8	−19.7	−5.8	−1.1	1.4
Balance on capital account[2]	10.2	0.8	1.9	10.3	2.9	−1.7	−4.5	−7.7	1.8	1.7
Balance on financial account	−12.0	5.1	22.7	17.1	34.6	9.5	−15.2	1.9	−2.8	−0.4
Direct investment, net	5.3	13.1	12.3	15.5	20.9	23.9	23.4	25.1	31.5	34.7
Portfolio investment, net	16.1	14.6	13.3	7.4	5.0	2.9	3.5	4.5	6.4	6.2
Other investment, net	−28.3	15.0	−0.7	3.7	10.1	−10.2	−20.5	−10.7	−10.2	−14.7
Reserve assets	−5.1	−37.5	−2.2	−9.5	−1.4	−7.1	−21.7	−17.1	−30.5	−26.7
Errors and omissions, net	−0.6	−3.6	−7.8	−3.3	−8.0	−5.9	−7.3	−6.0	−0.3	0.1

Table 33 *(concluded)*

	1994	1995	1996	1997	1998	1999	2000	2001	2002	2003
Capital flows										
Total capital flows, net[3]	−6.9	42.6	25.0	26.6	36.0	16.6	6.5	18.9	27.7	26.3
Net official flows	−11.2	−5.8	2.3	25.3	21.4	3.6	−3.6	−7.9	−3.6	−4.8
Net private flows[4]	4.3	48.4	22.6	1.3	14.6	13.0	10.0	26.8	31.2	31.1
Direct investment, net	5.3	13.1	12.3	15.5	20.9	23.9	23.4	25.1	31.5	34.7
Private portfolio investment, net	16.1	14.6	13.3	7.5	5.0	2.9	2.6	4.2	6.1	6.0
Other private flows, net	−17.1	20.7	−3.0	−21.6	−11.3	−13.8	−16.0	−2.5	−6.4	−9.6
External financing[5]										
Net external financing[6]	13.2	32.4	36.5	82.1	56.6	38.0	27.3	31.5	41.4	46.4
Nondebt-creating flows	16.3	15.1	14.6	30.8	26.4	23.1	22.1	18.5	34.1	37.7
Capital transfers[7]	10.2	0.8	1.9	10.3	2.9	−1.7	−4.5	−7.7	1.8	1.7
Foreign direct investment and equity security liabilities[8]	6.1	14.3	12.8	20.5	23.5	24.9	26.6	26.2	32.4	36.0
Net external borrowing[9]	−3.0	17.3	21.9	51.3	30.2	14.9	5.2	13.1	7.3	8.6
Borrowing from official creditors[10]	−5.8	−2.4	2.6	−6.9	−7.1	−6.1	−7.5	−10.2	−5.2	−9.0
Of which,										
Credit and loans from IMF[11]	2.4	4.7	3.7	2.5	5.5	−3.6	−4.2	−4.3	. . .	. . .
Borrowing from banks[12]	3.8	−0.8	4.5	3.9	4.6	−1.2	−0.8	0.8	1.7	4.0
Borrowing from other private creditors	−1.1	20.5	14.8	54.3	32.8	22.1	13.5	22.5	10.7	13.6
Memorandum										
Balance on goods and services in percent of GDP[13]	0.2	−0.7	−2.0	−3.3	−4.5	−0.9	3.1	0.8	−0.2	−0.4
Scheduled amortization of external debt	22.4	26.7	25.9	19.9	23.9	28.7	30.1	40.8	37.3	42.1
Gross external financing[14]	35.6	59.1	62.4	102.0	80.5	66.7	57.4	72.4	78.7	88.4
Gross external borrowing[15]	19.3	44.0	47.8	71.2	54.2	43.6	35.3	53.9	44.5	50.7
Exceptional external financing, net	17.3	14.9	13.6	−20.8	7.8	7.7	5.2	1.3	0.7	0.4
Of which,										
Arrears on debt service	3.8	−0.5	1.1	−24.8	5.0	1.8	1.6	−0.3	. . .	. . .
Debt forgiveness	—	0.9	0.9	—	—	—	—	—	. . .	. . .
Rescheduling of debt service	13.3	13.9	9.9	3.3	2.4	4.7	3.7	1.6	. . .	. . .

[1]Standard presentation in accordance with the 5th edition of the International Monetary Fund's *Balance of Payments Manual* (1993).

[2]Comprises capital transfers—including debt forgiveness—and acquisition/disposal of nonproduced, nonfinancial assets.

[3]Comprise net direct investment, net portfolio investment, and other long- and short-term net investment flows, including official and private borrowing. In the standard balance of payments presentation above, total net capital flows are equal to the balance on financial account minus the change in reserve assets.

[4]Because of limitations on the data coverage for net official flows, the residually derived data for net private flows may include some official flows.

[5]As defined in the *World Economic Outlook* (see footnote 6). It should be noted that there is no generally accepted standard definition of external financing.

[6]Defined as the sum of—with opposite sign—the goods and services balance, net income and current transfers, direct investment abroad, the change in reserve assets, the net acquisition of other assets (such as recorded private portfolio assets, export credit, and the collateral for debt-reduction operations), and the net errors and omissions. Thus, net external financing, according to the definition adopted in the *World Economic Outlook*, measures the total amount required to finance the current account, direct investment outflows, net reserve transactions (often at the discretion of the monetary authorities), the net acquisition of nonreserve external assets, and the net transactions underlying the errors and omissions (not infrequently reflecting capital flight).

[7]Including other transactions on capital account.

[8]Debt-creating foreign direct investment liabilities are not included.

[9]Net disbursement of long- and short-term credits, including exceptional financing, by both official and private creditors.

[10]Net disbursement by official creditors, based on directly reported flows and flows derived from information on external debt.

[11]Comprise use of International Monetary Fund resources under the General Resources Account, Trust Fund, and Poverty Reduction and Growth Facility (PRGF). For further detail, see Table 37.

[12]Net disbursement by commercial banks, based on directly reported flows and cross-border claims and liabilities reported in the International Banking section of the International Monetary Fund's *International Financial Statistics*.

[13]This is often referred to as the "resource balance" and, with opposite sign, the "net resource transfer."

[14]Net external financing plus amortization due on external debt.

[15]Net external borrowing plus amortization due on external debt.

Table 34. Developing Countries—by Region: Balance of Payments and External Financing[1]
(Billions of U.S. dollars)

	1994	1995	1996	1997	1998	1999	2000	2001	2002	2003
Africa										
Balance of payments										
Balance on current account	−11.1	−16.8	−6.4	−7.4	−20.1	−14.3	5.4	1.3	−7.2	−7.1
Balance on capital account	1.7	2.1	5.9	7.2	2.6	4.5	2.4	3.8	4.0	6.1
Balance on financial account	12.3	14.4	0.4	0.3	17.5	12.3	−5.5	−4.5	5.2	0.8
Change in reserves (− = increase)	−5.3	−2.5	−7.9	−11.1	2.5	−3.5	−13.3	−12.7	−4.7	−8.4
Other official flows, net	3.2	4.1	−3.6	2.0	3.3	0.7	1.7	1.3	1.0	0.4
Private flows, net	14.3	12.7	11.9	9.4	11.6	15.1	6.1	6.9	8.8	8.9
External financing										
Net external financing	19.8	23.9	18.8	28.3	26.9	29.7	15.9	17.1	22.2	21.9
Nondebt-creating inflows	5.9	9.9	13.4	23.2	19.5	24.3	12.2	21.1	19.0	19.5
Net external borrowing	14.0	14.0	5.4	5.1	7.4	5.4	3.8	−3.9	3.2	2.5
From official creditors	3.2	4.5	−3.1	2.1	3.5	1.1	2.1	1.7	1.3	1.4
Of which,										
Credit and loans from IMF	0.9	0.8	0.6	−0.5	−0.4	−0.2	−0.1	−0.4	. . .	. . .
From banks	2.4	0.4	0.2	0.2	−0.3	−1.1	−0.4	−2.0	0.3	0.9
From other private creditors	8.3	9.1	8.3	2.8	4.3	5.3	2.1	−3.6	1.7	0.2
Memorandum										
Exceptional financing	14.2	14.3	14.3	14.1	5.1	9.6	7.3	7.4	7.6	7.7
Sub-Sahara										
Balance of payments										
Balance on current account	−7.9	−12.6	−7.2	−10.2	−18.4	−13.7	−2.5	−6.3	−11.2	−11.8
Balance on capital account	1.6	2.0	5.7	7.1	2.5	4.1	2.4	3.8	3.9	6.0
Balance on financial account	9.1	10.4	1.5	3.3	15.8	11.4	2.2	3.9	9.0	5.5
Change in reserves (− = increase)	−3.2	−3.9	−5.2	−6.1	1.4	−3.9	−6.7	−2.3	0.4	−2.6
Other official flows, net	3.5	4.5	−3.3	3.1	3.8	1.3	2.6	2.4	1.6	1.2
Private flows, net	8.8	9.7	10.0	6.3	10.6	14.0	6.3	3.7	6.9	7.0
External financing										
Net external financing	15.4	21.7	17.4	26.6	26.1	29.3	17.1	15.6	21.1	21.2
Nondebt-creating inflows	4.5	9.2	12.2	21.3	17.8	22.5	10.8	16.7	16.0	16.7
Net external borrowing	10.9	12.6	5.3	5.3	8.3	6.8	6.3	−1.1	5.1	4.5
From official creditors	3.5	4.9	−2.7	3.1	3.9	1.7	3.0	2.8	1.9	2.2
Of which,										
Credit and loans from IMF	0.5	0.6	0.1	−0.5	−0.3	−0.1	—	−0.2	. . .	. . .
From banks	2.1	−0.1	−0.1	−0.6	−0.4	−2.5	−0.7	−2.4	0.2	0.6
From other private creditors	5.3	7.8	8.1	2.8	4.8	7.6	4.0	−1.5	3.0	1.7
Memorandum										
Exceptional financing	8.5	8.2	9.7	10.5	4.0	9.0	7.2	7.4	7.6	7.7
Developing Asia										
Balance of payments										
Balance on current account	−19.0	−42.5	−38.9	8.9	47.3	46.0	45.4	39.4	33.5	18.0
Balance on capital account	1.6	2.4	2.8	2.7	1.4	0.4	−0.4	—	1.4	1.7
Balance on financial account	29.2	61.6	66.2	23.0	−26.5	−22.1	−17.6	−27.3	−24.7	−13.8
Change in reserves (− = increase)	−43.8	−31.6	−37.6	−28.4	−20.2	−31.0	−17.2	−61.6	−66.3	−41.1
Other official flows, net	11.8	7.5	−1.0	14.1	21.3	22.3	14.1	6.4	11.5	14.8
Private flows, net	61.2	85.6	104.7	37.3	−27.6	−13.3	−14.6	27.9	30.2	12.5
External financing										
Net external financing	76.2	108.6	117.1	104.9	43.6	61.4	66.5	76.4	89.1	93.1
Nondebt-creating inflows	48.0	64.4	75.9	66.3	56.8	54.7	64.8	57.7	66.8	64.3
Net external borrowing	28.3	44.2	41.2	38.5	−13.3	6.7	1.7	18.7	22.3	28.8
From official creditors	11.2	7.5	−1.0	14.1	21.3	22.3	14.1	6.4	11.5	14.8
Of which,										
Credit and loans from IMF	−0.8	−1.5	−1.7	5.0	6.6	1.7	0.9	−2.2	. . .	. . .
From banks	10.8	29.9	28.4	14.1	−12.1	−15.4	−13.8	−4.4	2.0	5.7
From other private creditors	6.3	6.9	13.8	10.4	−22.4	−0.2	1.3	16.7	8.8	8.3
Memorandum										
Exceptional financing	1.2	0.4	0.7	0.5	14.5	6.5	−2.5	6.7	7.7	7.0

Table 34 *(concluded)*

	1994	1995	1996	1997	1998	1999	2000	2001	2002	2003
Excluding China and India										
Balance of payments										
Balance on current account	−25.0	−38.6	−40.0	−25.0	22.7	33.5	29.3	22.1	14.1	5.0
Balance on capital account	1.6	2.4	2.8	2.7	1.5	0.4	−0.4	—	1.4	1.7
Balance on financial account	27.0	40.6	49.8	33.4	−18.4	−24.9	−13.7	−14.4	−10.0	−5.8
Change in reserves (− = increase)	−3.9	−11.2	−3.2	12.0	−11.1	−16.5	−0.6	−5.6	−9.6	−5.3
Other official flows, net	3.1	3.7	−3.3	12.5	15.7	15.3	12.3	4.7	4.3	6.8
Private flows, net	27.8	48.2	56.3	8.9	−23.0	−23.6	−25.4	−13.5	−4.7	−7.3
External financing										
Net external financing	27.9	63.1	59.9	30.5	−0.8	5.0	3.8	0.4	7.5	14.3
Nondebt-creating inflows	8.8	24.6	29.3	13.5	12.0	11.5	6.7	2.1	10.1	9.6
Net external borrowing	19.1	38.5	30.7	17.0	−12.8	−6.5	−2.9	−1.7	−2.5	4.7
From official creditors	2.5	3.7	−3.3	12.5	15.7	15.3	12.3	4.7	4.3	6.8
Of which,										
Credit and loans from IMF	0.4	−0.3	−0.4	5.7	7.0	2.1	0.9	−2.2	. . .	. . .
From banks	7.1	24.2	24.4	6.8	−15.1	−13.5	−15.7	−6.2	−5.3	−1.6
From other private creditors	9.5	10.7	9.5	−2.3	−13.5	−8.2	0.5	−0.1	−1.5	−0.5
Memorandum										
Exceptional financing	1.2	0.4	0.7	0.5	14.5	6.5	−2.5	6.7	7.7	7.0
Middle East and Turkey										
Balance of payments										
Balance on current account	−2.3	0.2	10.6	7.7	−21.5	14.9	63.7	51.8	25.2	18.2
Balance on capital account	1.5	2.1	0.7	0.4	0.4	1.1	2.3	1.8	1.7	0.4
Balance on financial account	13.0	0.3	−10.6	4.9	22.3	−6.1	−52.2	−48.2	−22.3	−15.7
Change in reserves (− = increase)	−4.6	−10.5	−18.8	−10.0	11.5	−5.2	−26.5	−8.1	−10.7	−9.9
Other official flows, net	0.9	2.6	1.9	0.7	2.3	0.9	−1.6	9.2	9.1	4.2
Private flows, net	16.7	8.3	6.3	14.2	8.5	−1.7	−24.1	−49.3	−20.7	−10.0
External financing										
Net external financing	8.8	8.7	18.8	25.9	28.8	11.4	18.2	−18.9	6.1	8.5
Nondebt-creating inflows	6.8	7.5	8.6	7.7	0.1	5.2	4.5	7.0	8.7	10.0
Net external borrowing	2.0	1.2	10.2	18.3	28.7	6.1	13.7	−25.9	−2.6	−1.4
From official creditors	−1.1	−0.1	0.3	−0.7	−1.0	−1.7	2.9	8.8	9.4	4.2
Of which,										
Credit and loans from IMF	0.4	0.4	0.1	0.2	−0.1	0.6	3.3	10.3	. . .	. . .
From banks	−9.5	−1.9	−1.6	0.3	9.6	7.5	2.7	−10.9	−3.1	−5.1
From other private creditors	12.6	3.2	11.5	18.6	20.1	0.4	8.1	−23.8	−8.9	−0.5
Memorandum										
Exceptional financing	4.3	3.3	1.0	0.3	0.4	0.2	0.5	0.3	0.6	0.6
Western Hemisphere										
Balance of payments										
Balance on current account	−52.2	−36.5	−40.0	−67.2	−90.8	−56.7	−47.8	−52.9	−32.6	−28.1
Balance on capital account	—	0.6	2.1	1.1	1.0	1.3	0.9	0.9	1.0	0.7
Balance on financial account	55.9	39.4	40.7	70.7	97.1	59.1	42.5	45.2	22.8	24.6
Change in reserves (− = increase)	4.0	−23.3	−28.9	−13.5	8.4	7.9	−2.5	1.2	−3.3	−16.5
Other official flows, net	4.7	19.2	4.7	14.9	16.0	1.5	−3.5	21.1	15.8	14.6
Private flows, net	47.1	43.5	64.9	69.3	72.7	49.7	48.6	22.8	10.3	26.5
External financing										
Net external financing	69.8	87.8	94.5	99.0	103.3	80.8	68.7	81.9	51.5	64.9
Nondebt-creating inflows	39.8	31.5	54.4	72.4	61.6	71.6	68.4	67.4	42.2	47.6
Net external borrowing	30.0	56.3	40.1	26.6	41.7	9.3	0.4	14.5	9.3	17.2
From official creditors	8.2	20.9	11.5	8.5	14.6	6.7	−1.3	18.3	8.7	13.4
Of which,										
Credit and loans from IMF	−1.3	12.9	−2.0	−4.0	2.5	−0.9	−10.7	15.6	. . .	. . .
From banks	−31.4	5.3	2.9	4.0	15.3	2.3	6.4	4.5	3.4	3.0
From other private creditors	53.3	30.0	25.6	14.1	11.8	0.2	−4.8	−8.2	−2.8	0.8
Memorandum										
Exceptional financing	0.1	4.1	4.9	3.5	1.2	2.1	−0.4	0.4	8.5	−8.0

[1]For definitions, see footnotes to Table 33.

Table 35. Developing Countries—by Analytical Criteria: Balance of Payments and External Financing[1]

(Billions of U.S. dollars)

	1994	1995	1996	1997	1998	1999	2000	2001	2002	2003
By source of export earnings										
Fuel										
Balance of payments										
Balance on current account	−2.5	2.6	30.4	21.5	−27.6	19.9	104.2	63.8	37.9	33.6
Balance on capital account	0.5	1.1	3.4	0.6	0.7	1.7	2.5	1.7	2.0	2.5
Balance on financial account	21.2	4.2	−33.0	−6.7	29.1	−8.5	−87.8	−56.7	−33.7	−33.2
Change in reserves (− = increase)	1.0	−0.1	−23.0	−13.3	17.4	4.7	−41.3	−15.0	−10.2	−13.0
Other official flows, net	6.6	6.5	−0.7	5.0	6.3	2.3	−8.8	−0.3	5.3	2.4
Private flows, net	13.6	−2.2	−9.3	1.6	5.3	−15.4	−37.7	−41.4	−28.8	−22.7
External financing										
Net external financing	17.4	1.4	6.1	20.1	30.4	4.1	7.3	−11.2	−2.8	−1.8
Nondebt-creating inflows	4.1	4.4	10.5	8.6	8.8	10.8	13.1	14.0	11.8	13.4
Net external borrowing	13.3	−2.9	−4.4	11.5	21.5	−6.7	−5.9	−25.1	−14.7	−15.2
From official creditors	4.9	3.1	−0.8	2.4	1.4	1.0	0.6	−0.2	1.0	1.5
Of which,										
Credit and loans from IMF	0.4	−0.2	0.7	−0.3	−0.6	−0.5	−0.6	−0.4	. . .	. . .
From banks	−2.6	−4.5	−7.1	−3.9	3.3	1.0	−0.1	−4.9	−0.6	−6.4
From other private creditors	11.0	−1.5	3.4	13.0	16.9	−8.8	−6.4	−20.0	−15.1	−10.2
Memorandum										
Exceptional financing	11.9	12.5	8.6	8.1	6.2	5.2	2.6	1.8	1.6	0.2
Nonfuel										
Balance of payments										
Balance on current account	−82.1	−98.2	−105.1	−79.5	−57.4	−30.1	−37.5	−24.2	−18.9	−32.6
Balance on capital account	4.3	6.0	8.1	10.7	4.8	5.6	2.6	4.9	6.1	6.4
Balance on financial account	89.1	111.5	129.7	105.6	81.3	51.7	55.1	21.9	14.7	29.2
Change in reserves (− = increase)	−50.7	−67.8	−70.1	−49.7	−15.2	−36.6	−18.2	−66.2	−74.8	−63.0
Other official flows, net	14.2	27.0	2.8	26.7	36.6	23.1	19.5	38.4	32.1	31.6
Private flows, net	125.6	152.3	197.1	128.6	59.9	65.2	53.7	49.7	57.4	60.5
External financing										
Net external financing	157.3	227.5	243.1	238.0	172.3	179.1	162.0	167.8	171.8	190.2
Nondebt-creating inflows	96.3	108.9	141.8	161.0	129.2	145.0	136.7	139.3	124.9	127.9
Net external borrowing	61.0	118.7	101.3	77.0	43.1	34.2	25.3	28.5	46.9	62.2
From official creditors	16.7	29.8	8.5	21.6	37.0	27.4	17.2	35.4	29.8	32.2
Of which,										
Credit and loans from IMF	−1.2	12.8	−3.6	1.2	9.1	1.8	−6.1	23.6	. . .	. . .
From banks	−25.2	38.2	37.0	22.5	9.2	−7.7	−5.0	−7.9	3.2	11.0
From other private creditors	69.5	50.7	55.8	32.9	−3.0	14.5	13.1	1.0	13.9	19.0
Memorandum										
Exceptional financing	8.0	9.7	12.3	10.4	15.0	13.3	2.2	13.0	22.7	7.1
By external financing source										
Net debtor countries										
Balance of payments										
Balance on current account	−77.7	−98.0	−87.9	−70.2	−71.3	−23.8	6.6	−4.3	−5.9	−19.6
Balance on capital account	5.0	7.3	11.6	11.5	5.4	6.5	3.0	4.9	6.7	8.9
Balance on financial account	91.9	108.5	103.2	102.6	94.0	47.6	17.8	6.0	4.7	13.7
Change in reserves (− = increase)	−51.6	−68.0	−84.6	−55.7	−8.8	−35.6	−38.8	−74.9	−81.1	−75.9
Other official flows, net	18.5	30.6	−0.1	30.5	39.7	23.6	15.9	37.9	37.9	34.1
Private flows, net	125.0	145.8	187.9	127.8	63.1	59.6	40.7	42.9	47.9	55.5
External financing										
Net external financing	169.9	227.6	241.7	252.7	198.3	185.1	167.1	168.5	174.9	196.6
Nondebt-creating inflows	100.1	113.3	151.8	168.7	137.6	155.1	146.9	148.8	132.5	137.6
Net external borrowing	69.8	114.3	90.0	84.0	60.7	30.0	20.3	19.7	42.3	59.1
From official creditors	21.4	32.8	7.2	24.1	38.5	29.2	18.6	35.5	31.1	33.8
Of which,										
Credit and loans from IMF	−0.8	12.6	−2.9	0.8	8.5	1.3	−6.7	23.3	. . .	. . .
From banks	−27.6	33.7	30.4	18.5	10.3	−9.1	−6.3	−10.3	3.0	11.3
From other private creditors	76.1	47.9	52.4	41.3	12.0	9.9	8.0	−5.5	8.3	14.0
Memorandum										
Exceptional financing	19.8	22.2	20.9	18.4	21.1	18.5	4.9	14.8	24.3	7.4

Table 35 (continued)

	1994	1995	1996	1997	1998	1999	2000	2001	2002	2003
Official financing										
Balance of payments										
Balance on current account	−9.7	−12.1	−9.1	−5.1	−10.4	−7.2	3.1	0.2	−5.4	−6.1
Balance on capital account	3.7	5.4	6.7	9.8	3.6	5.2	2.8	4.6	5.4	7.6
Balance on financial account	5.5	6.8	2.4	−5.0	7.3	2.6	−6.2	−5.3	0.1	−1.5
Change in reserves (− = increase)	−3.1	−0.9	−3.4	−6.5	1.4	−0.8	−9.9	−7.7	−5.4	−6.6
Other official flows, net	4.2	5.7	2.6	6.9	5.5	3.4	6.2	6.5	4.4	5.4
Private flows, net	4.3	2.0	3.2	−5.5	0.4	−0.1	−2.4	−4.1	1.1	−0.3
External financing										
Net external financing	11.8	12.5	11.9	10.7	8.9	8.6	6.3	6.9	10.5	12.2
Nondebt-creating inflows	5.7	7.5	9.1	12.9	6.9	9.6	7.1	8.8	10.3	13.1
Net external borrowing	6.0	5.0	2.8	−2.2	2.0	−1.0	−0.8	−2.0	0.1	−0.9
From official creditors	4.1	5.5	2.4	6.8	5.4	3.4	6.1	6.4	4.4	5.3
Of which,										
Credit and loans from IMF	1.1	1.1	0.9	0.2	—	—	—	−0.2	. . .	. . .
From banks	−0.2	−0.1	0.5	0.7	−0.3	−1.6	−0.6	−0.6	0.7	0.6
From other private creditors	2.2	−0.4	−0.1	−9.8	−3.2	−2.7	−6.4	−7.8	−4.9	−6.8
Memorandum										
Exceptional financing	12.3	12.7	13.6	9.2	6.3	4.6	−4.9	4.6	3.1	3.1
Net debtor countries by debt-servicing experience										
Countries with arrears and/or rescheduling during 1994–98										
Balance of payments										
Balance on current account	−18.1	−46.1	−42.8	−49.3	−58.5	−22.5	10.5	−8.6	−20.8	−27.8
Balance on capital account	4.2	6.6	9.9	9.8	3.8	4.7	2.1	3.2	4.9	7.2
Balance on financial account	26.0	38.7	36.6	56.0	61.2	30.5	4.7	20.4	26.4	21.6
Change in reserves (− = increase)	−16.1	−23.4	−22.3	−3.7	8.1	1.6	−23.6	−18.6	−13.7	−25.7
Other official flows, net	2.0	3.0	−10.4	3.5	10.5	10.7	3.1	12.2	11.9	20.7
Private flows, net	40.1	59.0	69.2	56.2	42.5	18.2	25.1	26.7	28.2	26.6
External financing										
Net external financing	46.2	72.8	71.6	68.9	60.4	43.8	45.5	49.5	51.1	65.7
Nondebt-creating inflows	26.8	31.0	49.3	47.1	45.6	55.5	52.7	50.2	44.4	46.4
Net external borrowing	19.4	41.8	22.3	21.8	14.9	−11.7	−7.2	−0.6	6.7	19.3
From official creditors	1.8	2.8	−10.5	3.4	10.4	10.4	2.9	11.9	12.1	21.1
Of which,										
Credit and loans from IMF	1.0	0.5	0.7	3.9	10.9	5.6	−5.5	5.0	. . .	. . .
From banks	−36.5	3.6	7.7	13.2	7.7	−5.2	−5.9	−1.3	−0.4	2.4
From other private creditors	54.2	35.4	25.1	5.2	−3.2	−16.9	−4.2	−11.3	−5.0	−4.2
Memorandum										
Exceptional financing	18.6	21.5	20.6	17.9	19.0	13.9	0.4	9.8	10.4	9.3
Other groups										
Heavily indebted poor countries										
Balance of payments										
Balance on current account	−9.6	−12.5	−13.1	−14.3	−16.0	−12.9	−7.7	−8.8	−12.1	−14.9
Balance on capital account	3.7	5.6	11.0	9.6	3.4	4.1	1.4	3.1	5.1	7.5
Balance on financial account	6.6	6.0	−0.6	3.7	12.3	8.9	7.0	5.7	6.7	7.3
Change in reserves (− = increase)	−2.4	−1.6	−3.7	−0.9	1.2	−2.6	−3.2	−1.8	−3.9	−2.1
Other official flows, net	2.5	4.8	−2.9	4.5	4.9	2.6	4.0	4.4	2.6	2.9
Private flows, net	6.4	2.8	6.0	0.1	6.2	8.9	6.2	3.1	8.0	6.6
External financing										
Net external financing	12.3	14.9	15.4	15.5	15.9	17.4	13.3	13.3	17.9	19.2
Nondebt-creating inflows	6.6	9.1	14.8	15.1	9.3	11.8	7.2	9.8	13.2	14.8
Net external borrowing	5.7	5.8	0.6	0.4	6.6	5.6	6.1	3.5	4.7	4.4
From official creditors	2.8	5.5	−2.2	4.9	5.1	3.1	4.6	4.9	2.7	3.4
Of which,										
Credit and loans from IMF	0.5	0.6	0.3	—	0.2	0.2	—	−0.1	. . .	. . .
From banks	1.3	0.7	0.8	0.3	0.5	−1.9	−0.2	−2.0	0.7	1.0
From other private creditors	1.6	−0.4	2.0	−4.8	1.0	4.3	1.7	0.5	1.3	—
Memorandum										
Exceptional financing	9.5	8.5	11.4	8.1	1.8	6.1	−3.0	5.9	6.5	5.5

Table 35 *(concluded)*

	1994	1995	1996	1997	1998	1999	2000	2001	2002	2003
Middle East and north Africa										
Balance of payments										
Balance on current account	−10.9	−4.5	12.5	11.6	−27.1	14.2	80.2	54.6	29.4	23.2
Balance on capital account	1.6	2.1	0.8	0.5	0.6	1.4	2.3	1.9	1.9	0.5
Balance on financial account	21.5	4.9	−13.0	0.6	28.1	−5.2	−68.8	−52.1	−26.6	−21.1
Change in reserves (− = increase)	−5.8	−4.5	−17.1	−11.8	13.0	1.2	−33.3	−21.1	−11.8	−12.8
Other official flows, net	1.9	2.6	2.3	0.1	2.9	1.5	−6.7	−0.8	0.9	2.3
Private flows, net	25.4	6.8	1.9	12.3	12.2	−7.9	−28.9	−30.2	−15.7	−10.6
External financing										
Net external financing	20.6	5.1	13.6	20.3	28.4	0.7	3.8	−12.3	1.2	3.1
Nondebt-creating inflows	6.5	6.9	8.4	8.5	6.0	5.5	9.7	12.1	10.6	10.9
Net external borrowing	14.1	−1.8	5.3	11.8	22.4	−4.8	−5.9	−24.4	−9.3	−7.8
From official creditors	−0.1	−0.1	0.6	−1.3	−0.4	−1.1	−2.2	−1.3	1.2	2.3
Of which,										
Credit and loans from IMF	0.5	0.2	0.6	0.3	−0.1	—	−0.3	−0.2	. . .	. . .
From banks	−2.2	−3.4	−4.4	−1.1	6.4	6.2	−0.7	−0.8	—	−6.0
From other private creditors	16.4	1.7	9.0	14.2	16.4	−10.0	−2.9	−22.4	−10.6	−4.1
Memorandum										
Exceptional financing	10.2	9.5	6.9	5.4	2.9	2.4	2.0	1.4	1.8	1.9

[1]For definitions, see footnotes to Table 33.

Table 36. Developing Countries: Reserves[1]

	1994	1995	1996	1997	1998	1999	2000	2001	2002	2003
					Billions of U.S. dollars					
Developing countries	**380.3**	**448.4**	**541.8**	**591.7**	**606.1**	**643.7**	**692.9**	**771.1**	**886.6**	**956.7**
Regional groups										
Africa	24.7	26.3	31.4	43.0	41.3	42.0	53.1	64.8	68.0	76.2
Sub-Sahara	15.9	18.8	21.1	28.7	27.8	29.2	34.2	35.9	34.1	36.5
Developing Asia	174.3	200.8	246.5	264.9	289.8	322.9	336.9	395.3	461.9	503.1
Excluding China and India	100.4	106.2	118.0	96.3	112.1	131.3	129.7	132.6	142.5	147.9
Middle East and Turkey	75.9	90.8	107.1	113.5	113.5	124.6	147.2	152.8	195.1	199.4
Western Hemisphere	105.4	130.4	156.9	170.3	161.5	154.2	155.6	158.2	161.5	178.0
Analytical groups										
By source of export earnings										
Fuel	53.4	56.1	75.3	86.9	81.9	86.5	123.8	136.3	176.7	183.8
Nonfuel	326.9	392.3	466.6	504.9	524.1	557.2	569.1	634.8	709.8	772.9
of which, primary products	48.9	53.5	58.0	62.0	58.7	59.4	59.7	60.1	62.6	64.8
By external financing source										
Net debtor countries	355.6	419.2	504.8	553.3	568.8	599.2	636.1	710.4	790.3	866.2
of which, official financing	30.7	30.7	33.4	38.5	36.9	37.2	46.5	53.1	58.8	65.5
Net debtor countries by debt-servicing experience										
Countries with arrears and/or rescheduling during 1994–98	110.7	128.6	155.4	153.9	150.1	148.6	173.7	193.2	205.5	231.0
Other groups										
Heavily indebted poor countries	24.3	26.5	28.5	30.0	29.6	32.2	34.8	37.2	40.0	42.1
Middle East and north Africa	75.7	84.5	99.4	107.9	106.0	112.6	142.7	161.5	205.0	212.1
					Ratio of reserves to imports of goods and services[2]					
Developing countries	**41.1**	**40.9**	**45.1**	**45.8**	**49.7**	**52.7**	**48.4**	**54.1**	**59.9**	**59.3**
Regional groups										
Africa	22.7	20.3	23.9	31.6	30.5	31.4	38.1	45.7	45.6	48.4
Sub-Sahara	19.6	19.2	20.9	26.9	26.7	28.9	32.2	33.6	30.4	31.1
Developing Asia	44.1	40.7	45.4	47.2	59.7	62.2	52.2	61.1	66.4	65.1
Excluding China and India	40.9	34.4	35.4	28.4	42.7	49.2	40.6	44.2	45.0	42.2
Middle East and Turkey	41.2	42.0	44.4	43.9	45.5	51.6	53.6	57.2	69.3	66.1
Western Hemisphere	44.5	50.5	54.9	50.7	46.2	47.2	41.8	42.8	45.7	46.4
Analytical groups										
By source of export earnings										
Fuel	33.5	31.1	39.1	41.7	41.2	44.2	57.1	59.3	73.6	72.9
Nonfuel	42.7	42.8	46.3	46.6	51.3	54.3	46.8	53.1	57.2	56.7
of which, primary products	71.0	62.2	62.1	61.8	59.2	64.6	60.5	60.3	59.2	56.1
By external financing source										
Net debtor countries	42.9	42.4	46.6	47.5	51.5	54.1	48.6	54.6	58.5	58.4
of which, official financing	53.8	44.7	46.0	53.0	49.3	48.5	55.5	61.4	63.8	66.1
Net debtor countries by debt-servicing experience										
Countries with arrears and/or rescheduling during 1994–98	48.5	45.4	49.2	44.2	46.2	49.7	51.5	56.5	57.7	60.0
Other groups										
Heavily indebted poor countries	50.0	44.8	43.5	43.4	41.8	45.3	45.7	47.3	47.1	45.6
Middle East and north Africa	41.8	41.7	45.8	47.6	48.1	51.4	59.8	65.0	78.9	77.1

[1]In this table, official holdings of gold are valued at SDR 35 an ounce. This convention results in a marked underestimate of reserves for countries that have substantial gold holdings.

[2]Reserves at year-end in percent of imports of goods and services for the year indicated.

Table 37. Net Credit and Loans from IMF[1]
(Billions of U.S. dollars)

	1993	1994	1995	1996	1997	1998	1999	2000	2001
Advanced economies	—	—	**−0.1**	**−0.1**	**11.3**	**5.2**	**−10.3**	—	**−5.7**
Newly industrialized Asian economies	—	—	—	—	11.3	5.2	−10.3	—	−5.7
Developing countries	**−0.1**	**−0.8**	**12.6**	**−2.9**	**0.8**	**8.5**	**1.3**	**−6.7**	**23.3**
Regional groups									
Africa	0.2	0.9	0.8	0.6	−0.5	−0.4	−0.2	−0.1	−0.4
Sub-Sahara	0.7	0.5	0.6	0.1	−0.5	−0.3	−0.1	—	−0.2
Developing Asia	0.6	−0.8	−1.5	−1.7	5.0	6.6	1.7	0.9	−2.2
Excluding China and India	0.1	0.4	−0.3	−0.4	5.7	7.0	2.1	0.9	−2.2
Middle East and Turkey	—	0.4	0.4	0.1	0.2	−0.1	0.6	3.3	10.3
Western Hemisphere	−0.9	−1.3	12.9	−2.0	−4.0	2.5	−0.9	−10.7	15.6
Analytical groups									
By source of export earnings									
Fuel	−0.8	0.4	−0.2	0.7	−0.3	−0.6	−0.5	−0.6	−0.4
Nonfuel	0.6	−1.2	12.8	−3.6	1.2	9.1	1.8	−6.1	23.6
of which, primary products	−0.1	0.2	0.4	0.1	—	—	—	−0.2	−0.2
By external financing source									
Net debtor countries	−0.1	−0.8	12.6	−2.9	0.8	8.5	1.3	−6.7	23.3
of which, official financing	−0.5	1.1	1.1	0.9	0.2	—	—	—	−0.2
Net debtor countries by debt-servicing experience									
Countries with arrears and/or rescheduling during 1994–98	−0.8	1.0	0.5	0.7	3.9	10.9	5.6	−5.5	5.0
Other groups									
Heavily indebted poor countries	−0.2	0.5	0.6	0.3	—	0.2	0.2	—	−0.1
Middle East and north Africa	−0.5	0.5	0.2	0.6	0.3	−0.1	—	−0.3	−0.2
Countries in transition	**3.7**	**2.4**	**4.7**	**3.7**	**2.5**	**5.5**	**−3.6**	**−4.2**	**−4.3**
Central and eastern Europe	1.9	0.1	−2.7	−0.8	0.4	−0.3	—	—	−0.3
Commonwealth of Independent States and Mongolia	1.9	2.3	7.5	4.5	2.1	5.8	−3.6	−4.1	−4.0
Russia	1.5	1.5	5.5	3.2	1.5	5.3	−3.6	−2.9	−3.8
Excluding Russia	0.3	0.7	2.0	1.3	0.5	0.5	—	−1.2	−0.2
Memorandum									
Total									
Net credit provided under:									
General Resources Account	3.374	0.594	15.633	0.291	14.355	18.811	−12.856	−10.741	13.213
Trust Fund	−0.060	−0.014	−0.015	—	−0.007	−0.001	−0.001	—	—
PRGF	0.253	0.998	1.619	0.325	0.179	0.374	0.194	−0.111	0.102
Disbursements at year-end under:[2]									
General Resources Account	34.503	37.276	53.275	51.824	62.703	84.961	69.913	55.756	66.822
Trust Fund	0.157	0.153	0.141	0.137	0.121	0.126	0.122	0.116	0.111
PRGF	5.285	6.634	8.342	8.392	8.049	8.788	8.761	8.207	8.017

[1]Includes net disbursements from programs under the General Resources Account, Trust Fund, and Poverty Reduction and Growth Facility (formerly ESAF—Enhanced Structural Adjustment Facility). The data are on a transactions basis, with conversion to U.S. dollar values at annual average exchange rates.
[2]Converted to U.S. dollar values at end-of-period exchange rates.

Table 38. Summary of External Debt and Debt Service

	1994	1995	1996	1997	1998	1999	2000	2001	2002	2003
					Billions of U.S. dollars					
External debt										
Developing countries	**1,718.4**	**1,861.0**	**1,930.0**	**2,021.0**	**2,182.2**	**2,223.1**	**2,199.3**	**2,171.0**	**2,200.8**	**2,207.8**
Regional groups										
Africa	287.0	303.2	300.0	290.9	289.4	287.9	277.1	265.6	268.9	267.9
Developing Asia	509.5	565.7	600.1	653.2	683.9	687.3	661.3	673.4	682.8	704.7
Middle East and Turkey	356.4	371.7	382.6	403.9	451.5	468.8	491.6	480.4	495.3	501.7
Western Hemisphere	565.5	620.3	647.4	673.0	757.5	779.1	769.3	751.6	753.9	733.4
Analytical groups										
By external financing source										
Net debtor countries	1,678.3	1,817.8	1,882.0	1,959.2	2,106.8	2,143.7	2,118.6	2,096.6	2,126.5	2,134.0
of which, official financing	165.9	171.4	167.2	157.2	158.1	154.8	149.8	146.9	142.5	140.8
Net debtor countries by debt-servicing experience										
Countries with arrears and/or rescheduling during 1994–98	717.2	755.4	783.0	815.3	880.9	884.5	867.2	832.6	831.9	844.9
Countries in transition	**253.0**	**276.0**	**301.3**	**311.6**	**363.2**	**371.1**	**362.6**	**357.8**	**364.1**	**371.1**
Central and eastern Europe	114.7	125.5	138.7	145.3	167.8	174.5	180.6	186.4	196.3	209.0
Commonwealth of Independent States and Mongolia	138.3	150.5	162.6	166.3	195.3	196.5	181.9	171.4	167.8	162.1
Russia	127.5	128.0	136.1	134.6	158.2	154.6	140.7	127.4	121.7	114.0
Excluding Russia	10.8	22.5	26.5	31.7	37.1	41.9	41.3	44.0	46.0	48.1
Debt-service payments[1]										
Developing countries	**240.0**	**239.6**	**281.1**	**306.9**	**319.0**	**343.5**	**347.5**	**344.5**	**318.5**	**331.8**
Regional groups										
Africa	29.7	31.9	31.8	29.6	28.1	26.8	27.7	26.6	34.4	26.1
Developing Asia	65.5	75.1	78.7	83.4	98.8	94.9	96.2	98.5	100.8	103.5
Middle East and Turkey	25.7	32.9	42.5	37.5	36.3	38.0	40.6	47.4	37.7	41.3
Western Hemisphere	119.1	99.8	128.0	156.4	155.7	183.8	183.0	172.0	145.7	160.9
Analytical groups										
By external financing source										
Net debtor countries	232.7	231.0	268.7	298.7	311.1	337.0	340.6	330.8	310.5	324.0
of which, official financing	18.9	19.7	16.6	13.0	13.3	12.7	10.7	10.7	21.5	12.4
Net debtor countries by debt-servicing experience										
Countries with arrears and/or rescheduling during 1994–98	111.0	84.9	94.8	115.9	134.2	147.7	132.6	123.2	128.0	127.8
Countries in transition	**19.8**	**29.5**	**31.5**	**47.5**	**57.7**	**51.2**	**54.7**	**63.6**	**59.0**	**64.4**
Central and eastern Europe	14.8	19.5	21.6	23.5	29.3	28.7	32.4	31.6	31.7	34.3
Commonwealth of Independent States and Mongolia	5.0	10.0	9.9	24.0	28.4	22.5	22.3	32.0	27.3	30.1
Russia	4.3	6.4	6.9	20.5	24.1	17.2	16.2	26.2	22.2	24.9
Excluding Russia	0.7	3.6	3.0	3.5	4.3	5.3	6.2	5.8	5.1	5.2

Table 38 *(concluded)*

	1994	1995	1996	1997	1998	1999	2000	2001	2002	2003
					Percent of exports of goods and services					
External debt[2]										
Developing countries	**198.0**	**179.6**	**166.2**	**160.0**	**186.0**	**176.4**	**142.0**	**143.8**	**142.0**	**132.7**
Regional groups										
Africa	281.1	254.1	226.9	214.2	240.8	225.5	179.0	178.9	181.2	170.4
Developing Asia	137.5	124.2	118.7	115.5	126.7	118.9	94.6	96.9	92.1	87.5
Middle East and Turkey	189.8	172.6	153.3	154.5	204.8	186.5	146.2	151.3	161.6	158.7
Western Hemisphere	272.5	251.9	235.9	224.2	258.6	256.8	214.6	215.1	212.6	190.3
Analytical groups										
By external financing source										
Net debtor countries	219.9	198.6	184.2	175.4	197.7	189.8	155.8	156.9	152.9	141.7
of which, official financing	376.0	318.2	274.1	238.4	259.5	233.5	179.7	178.5	175.4	161.3
Net debtor countries by debt-servicing experience										
Countries with arrears and/or rescheduling during 1994–98	325.8	301.1	276.6	262.2	312.5	291.6	230.1	232.8	230.3	219.7
Countries in transition	**124.8**	**106.3**	**107.1**	**104.6**	**127.0**	**134.8**	**108.1**	**101.1**	**98.9**	**92.6**
Central and eastern Europe	119.9	100.0	103.4	99.1	107.4	116.3	108.0	100.8	100.1	97.2
Commonwealth of Independent States and Mongolia	129.1	112.2	110.4	110.0	150.6	156.9	108.1	101.3	97.5	87.3
Russia	166.1	134.2	132.4	128.2	177.3	179.3	119.1	109.1	104.6	90.9
Excluding Russia	35.5	58.0	59.5	68.5	91.8	107.4	82.1	83.9	82.6	79.7
Debt-service payments										
Developing countries	**27.7**	**23.1**	**24.2**	**24.3**	**27.2**	**27.3**	**22.4**	**22.8**	**20.5**	**19.9**
Regional groups										
Africa	29.1	26.7	24.1	21.8	23.4	21.0	17.9	17.9	23.2	16.6
Developing Asia	17.7	16.5	15.6	14.8	18.3	16.4	13.8	14.2	13.6	12.8
Middle East and Turkey	13.7	15.3	17.0	14.3	16.5	15.1	12.1	14.9	12.3	13.1
Western Hemisphere	57.4	40.5	46.7	52.1	53.2	60.6	51.1	49.2	41.1	41.8
Analytical groups										
By external financing source										
Net debtor countries	30.5	25.2	26.3	26.7	29.2	29.8	25.0	24.8	22.3	21.5
of which, official financing	42.7	36.6	27.2	19.8	21.9	19.1	12.9	13.0	26.5	14.2
Net debtor countries by debt-servicing experience										
Countries with arrears and/or rescheduling during 1994–98	50.4	33.8	33.5	37.3	47.6	48.7	35.2	34.4	35.4	33.2
Countries in transition	**9.8**	**11.4**	**11.2**	**15.9**	**20.2**	**18.6**	**16.3**	**18.0**	**16.0**	**16.1**
Central and eastern Europe	15.5	15.5	16.1	16.0	18.8	19.1	19.4	17.1	16.1	16.0
Commonwealth of Independent States and Mongolia	4.7	7.5	6.7	15.8	21.9	17.9	13.3	18.9	15.9	16.2
Russia	5.6	6.7	6.7	19.5	27.0	19.9	13.7	22.5	19.1	19.9
Excluding Russia	2.4	9.3	6.7	7.6	10.6	13.5	12.3	11.1	9.2	8.6

[1]Debt-service payments refer to actual payments of interest on total debt plus actual amortization payments on long-term debt. The projections incorporate the impact of exceptional financing items.

[2]Total debt at year-end in percent of exports of goods and services in year indicated.

Table 39. Developing Countries—by Region: External Debt, by Maturity and Type of Creditor
(Billions of U.S. dollars)

	1994	1995	1996	1997	1998	1999	2000	2001	2002	2003
Developing countries										
Total debt	**1,718.4**	**1,861.0**	**1,930.0**	**2,021.0**	**2,182.2**	**2,223.1**	**2,199.3**	**2,171.0**	**2,200.8**	**2,207.8**
By maturity										
Short-term	229.6	277.7	297.2	307.8	281.6	266.0	242.3	221.6	231.6	235.3
Long-term	1,488.7	1,583.3	1,632.8	1,713.2	1,900.7	1,957.1	1,957.0	1,949.4	1,969.2	1,972.6
By type of creditor										
Official	782.0	828.1	819.5	797.7	849.3	867.2	847.0	867.2	900.5	929.2
Banks	368.0	448.4	493.4	564.5	611.0	603.8	596.7	569.4	575.7	586.6
Other private	568.4	584.5	617.1	658.8	721.9	752.1	755.7	734.3	724.6	692.1
Regional groups										
Africa										
Total debt	**287.0**	**303.2**	**300.0**	**290.9**	**289.4**	**287.9**	**277.1**	**265.6**	**268.9**	**267.9**
By maturity										
Short-term	33.8	33.9	37.1	45.1	46.6	47.6	23.6	22.2	27.2	28.9
Long-term	253.1	269.4	262.9	245.8	242.8	240.3	253.6	243.4	241.7	239.0
By type of creditor										
Official	198.9	214.5	215.1	202.6	207.6	207.1	199.9	197.2	196.1	196.9
Banks	34.3	36.2	33.8	34.3	30.8	29.4	25.8	23.5	22.8	22.6
Other private	53.8	52.5	51.1	53.9	50.9	51.4	51.4	44.9	50.0	48.4
Sub-Sahara										
Total debt	**225.1**	**236.4**	**233.4**	**228.8**	**226.8**	**228.0**	**222.4**	**215.3**	**217.5**	**217.2**
By maturity										
Short-term	31.8	32.0	34.7	42.9	44.2	44.8	20.8	19.5	24.0	25.3
Long-term	193.2	204.4	198.6	185.9	182.6	183.3	201.6	195.9	193.5	191.9
By type of creditor										
Official	158.5	168.3	167.1	157.6	161.1	163.1	159.3	159.6	156.3	157.0
Banks	25.1	26.2	23.7	23.5	19.9	17.3	14.4	12.7	11.9	11.8
Other private	41.5	41.8	42.6	47.7	45.8	47.6	48.6	43.1	49.2	48.4
Developing Asia										
Total debt	**509.5**	**565.7**	**600.1**	**653.2**	**683.9**	**687.3**	**661.3**	**673.4**	**682.8**	**704.7**
By maturity										
Short-term	75.9	106.0	110.3	101.5	85.9	71.7	61.3	60.0	64.6	69.3
Long-term	433.6	459.8	489.8	551.6	598.0	615.6	600.0	613.3	618.2	635.4
By type of creditor										
Official	247.8	247.1	253.3	271.3	295.1	310.4	305.5	301.1	298.5	308.0
Banks	122.2	194.7	207.9	223.7	214.0	199.5	184.7	181.9	184.7	189.6
Other private	139.5	123.9	138.8	158.2	174.8	177.4	171.1	190.4	199.5	207.1
Middle East and Turkey										
Total debt	**356.4**	**371.7**	**382.6**	**403.9**	**451.5**	**468.8**	**491.6**	**480.4**	**495.3**	**501.7**
By maturity										
Short-term	40.4	42.5	43.9	49.5	57.6	58.8	62.1	46.2	44.3	48.1
Long-term	316.0	329.2	338.7	354.5	393.8	410.0	429.5	434.2	451.0	453.6
By type of creditor										
Official	161.4	173.6	173.3	166.7	168.3	168.6	173.2	183.5	197.7	200.7
Banks	90.0	91.1	110.3	148.6	175.0	188.3	202.9	190.0	190.3	193.6
Other private	104.9	107.1	98.9	88.7	108.2	111.9	115.5	106.9	107.3	107.4
Western Hemisphere										
Total debt	**565.5**	**620.3**	**647.4**	**673.0**	**757.5**	**779.1**	**769.3**	**751.6**	**753.9**	**733.4**
By maturity										
Short-term	79.5	95.3	105.8	111.6	91.5	87.9	95.4	93.2	95.5	88.9
Long-term	486.0	524.9	541.5	561.4	666.0	691.2	673.9	658.4	658.4	644.5
By type of creditor										
Official	173.8	192.9	177.7	157.1	178.3	181.1	168.4	185.4	208.2	223.6
Banks	121.5	126.3	141.3	157.9	191.2	186.6	183.3	174.0	177.8	180.7
Other private	270.2	301.0	328.3	358.0	388.0	411.4	417.6	392.2	367.8	329.2

Table 40. Developing Countries—by Analytical Criteria: External Debt, by Maturity and Type of Creditor
(Billions of U.S. dollars)

	1994	1995	1996	1997	1998	1999	2000	2001	2002	2003
By source of export earnings										
Fuel										
Total debt	**358.5**	**365.9**	**366.7**	**384.0**	**422.9**	**432.0**	**434.1**	**425.0**	**429.3**	**426.6**
By maturity										
Short-term	36.3	32.6	35.7	44.3	52.0	53.9	31.3	27.4	27.1	29.1
Long-term	322.1	333.3	331.0	339.6	370.8	378.1	402.8	397.6	402.2	397.5
By type of creditor										
Official	146.9	162.0	159.6	159.3	163.7	165.3	163.5	164.2	169.0	168.2
Banks	75.1	72.8	89.6	101.2	113.9	117.6	119.8	116.7	117.1	115.2
Other private	136.5	131.1	117.5	123.5	145.3	149.0	150.7	144.2	143.2	143.3
Nonfuel										
Total debt	**1,359.9**	**1,495.1**	**1,563.3**	**1,637.0**	**1,759.4**	**1,791.1**	**1,765.3**	**1,746.0**	**1,771.5**	**1,781.2**
By maturity										
Short-term	193.3	245.1	261.4	263.4	229.5	212.2	211.0	194.2	204.5	206.1
Long-term	1,166.6	1,250.0	1,301.8	1,373.6	1,529.8	1,579.0	1,554.3	1,551.7	1,567.0	1,575.0
By type of creditor										
Official	635.1	666.1	659.9	638.4	685.6	701.9	683.4	703.1	731.5	761.0
Banks	292.9	375.6	403.7	463.3	497.1	486.1	476.8	452.7	458.6	471.4
Other private	431.9	453.5	499.7	535.3	576.7	603.1	605.0	590.2	581.4	548.8
Nonfuel primary products										
Total debt	**185.5**	**191.1**	**187.9**	**185.5**	**191.2**	**195.2**	**198.4**	**200.5**	**198.7**	**201.3**
By maturity										
Short-term	20.4	19.8	18.9	19.3	16.5	13.4	14.8	15.2	16.5	18.1
Long-term	165.1	171.3	169.0	166.2	174.7	181.7	183.6	185.4	182.2	183.2
By type of creditor										
Official	122.9	134.9	126.1	127.9	131.7	134.4	133.6	134.8	122.6	123.4
Banks	31.7	33.3	32.2	30.1	29.3	29.6	27.5	27.4	27.1	26.0
Other private	31.0	22.9	29.6	27.5	30.2	31.2	37.3	38.3	49.0	51.8
By external financing source										
Net debtor countries										
Total debt	**1,678.3**	**1,817.8**	**1,882.0**	**1,959.2**	**2,106.8**	**2,143.7**	**2,118.6**	**2,096.6**	**2,126.5**	**2,134.0**
By maturity										
Short-term	211.6	262.2	280.5	286.6	255.1	240.0	217.4	199.7	209.9	213.4
Long-term	1,466.7	1,555.6	1,601.5	1,672.6	1,851.7	1,903.7	1,901.1	1,896.9	1,916.6	1,920.5
By type of creditor										
Official	777.2	823.2	813.8	792.1	843.2	861.9	842.2	863.0	896.4	925.1
Banks	349.2	430.7	459.3	520.9	557.3	546.9	539.0	514.1	520.4	532.5
Other private	551.9	563.9	608.8	646.2	706.4	734.9	737.4	719.6	709.7	676.4
Official financing										
Total debt	**165.9**	**171.4**	**167.2**	**157.2**	**158.1**	**154.8**	**149.8**	**146.9**	**142.5**	**140.8**
By maturity										
Short-term	10.0	8.0	5.5	5.3	5.0	3.9	4.1	4.5	4.5	4.6
Long-term	155.9	163.3	161.7	151.8	153.1	150.9	145.6	142.4	138.0	136.1
By type of creditor										
Official	130.3	145.2	141.7	138.3	141.1	140.2	137.1	135.4	124.5	124.3
Banks	13.5	12.2	9.8	9.6	8.7	7.1	6.0	5.7	4.6	3.9
Other private	22.1	13.9	15.7	9.3	8.3	7.5	6.6	5.8	13.3	12.5

Table 40 *(concluded)*

	1994	1995	1996	1997	1998	1999	2000	2001	2002	2003
Net debtor countries by debt-servicing experience										
Countries with arrears and/or rescheduling during 1994–98										
Total debt	**717.2**	**755.4**	**783.0**	**815.3**	**880.9**	**884.5**	**867.2**	**832.6**	831.9	844.9
By maturity										
Short-term	79.2	85.7	98.1	97.3	84.1	82.5	60.2	56.9	54.6	55.8
Long-term	638.0	669.7	684.9	718.0	796.8	801.9	806.9	775.7	777.3	789.1
By type of creditor										
Official	394.4	420.5	421.3	416.0	449.5	466.1	447.4	448.4	453.1	470.2
Banks	153.1	161.2	173.7	195.9	217.6	209.0	197.7	190.9	185.1	184.0
Other private	169.8	173.8	188.0	203.4	213.9	209.3	222.1	193.3	193.7	190.7
Other groups										
Heavily indebted poor countries										
Total debt	**192.9**	**194.4**	**187.4**	**173.8**	**174.3**	**174.2**	**171.0**	**168.9**	165.5	166.2
By maturity										
Short-term	11.0	9.3	8.4	8.5	5.3	4.1	3.6	3.8	3.7	3.8
Long-term	181.9	185.1	179.0	165.4	169.0	170.1	167.4	165.2	161.8	162.4
By type of creditor										
Official	155.4	167.0	156.5	146.9	150.1	151.5	148.1	147.7	136.3	137.0
Banks	22.3	21.7	19.5	19.1	15.9	13.9	11.2	9.5	9.0	9.0
Other private	15.3	5.7	11.4	7.9	8.3	8.8	11.7	11.8	20.2	20.2
Middle East and north Africa										
Total debt	**371.6**	**387.6**	**395.4**	**407.8**	**445.1**	**453.5**	**452.0**	**442.0**	453.5	456.2
By maturity										
Short-term	31.2	28.8	29.0	33.9	39.0	38.2	36.0	32.0	32.1	33.9
Long-term	340.4	358.8	366.4	373.9	406.1	415.4	416.1	410.0	421.4	422.3
By type of creditor										
Official	189.8	208.7	210.2	201.2	206.5	206.2	202.8	202.1	211.8	214.8
Banks	77.8	77.9	96.3	110.2	123.7	130.0	129.6	129.9	132.2	132.4
Other private	104.0	101.0	88.9	96.5	114.9	117.4	119.5	110.0	109.5	109.0

Table 41. Developing Countries: Ratio of External Debt to GDP[1]

	1994	1995	1996	1997	1998	1999	2000	2001	2002	2003
Developing countries	**43.1**	**41.5**	**39.0**	**38.6**	**43.2**	**44.5**	**40.6**	**40.3**	**40.9**	**38.8**
Regional groups										
Africa	77.8	73.7	68.8	65.4	67.5	67.1	63.6	62.5	62.8	58.3
Sub-Sahara	80.2	74.2	70.1	66.4	69.6	70.1	67.6	68.1	69.2	65.0
Developing Asia	34.6	32.1	30.3	31.9	36.0	33.5	30.1	29.6	27.8	26.4
Excluding China and India	51.5	51.0	49.8	57.5	81.5	70.1	63.6	63.0	56.1	51.3
Middle East and Turkey	64.7	59.3	54.5	54.9	62.8	62.2	59.1	60.7	62.3	60.8
Western Hemisphere	35.5	36.8	35.3	33.6	37.8	44.3	39.3	39.6	44.3	42.0
Analytical groups										
By source of export earnings										
Fuel	80.4	72.0	63.0	62.4	73.6	69.3	60.4	57.5	61.6	59.0
Nonfuel	38.4	37.6	35.8	35.5	39.3	41.0	37.6	37.6	37.8	35.8
of which, primary products	82.5	71.4	65.4	61.4	64.3	68.4	68.2	70.5	67.7	64.1
By external financing source										
Net debtor countries	44.8	42.9	40.4	39.8	44.1	45.7	41.9	41.6	42.2	39.9
of which, official financing	90.0	84.7	75.4	68.9	68.7	65.6	61.0	59.3	55.4	50.8
Net debtor countries by debt-servicing experience										
Countries with arrears and/or rescheduling during 1994–98	61.2	53.6	50.1	51.0	61.3	71.9	65.1	65.4	63.3	60.7
Other groups										
Heavily indebted poor countries	123.4	117.6	107.1	94.8	93.1	91.4	88.0	84.4	77.8	72.6
Middle East and north Africa	72.5	70.0	62.3	62.1	71.0	67.5	60.3	57.8	60.5	58.3

[1]Debt at year-end in percent of GDP in year indicated.

Table 42. Developing Countries: Debt-Service Ratios[1]

(Percent of exports of goods and services)

	1994	1995	1996	1997	1998	1999	2000	2001	2002	2003
Interest payments[2]										
Developing countries	**9.4**	**9.2**	**8.7**	**7.7**	**9.2**	**8.7**	**7.2**	**6.9**	**6.6**	**6.4**
Regional groups										
Africa	10.3	9.7	9.8	8.7	9.4	8.6	7.1	6.8	10.0	6.5
Sub-Sahara	8.9	7.9	8.6	7.7	8.5	8.0	6.8	6.7	11.5	7.0
Developing Asia	7.6	7.0	6.9	5.2	6.6	6.0	4.5	4.0	4.1	4.0
Excluding China and India	8.2	7.7	7.8	6.8	8.7	7.1	5.2	4.3	4.7	4.5
Middle East and Turkey	4.9	4.7	3.8	3.9	4.7	4.0	3.5	3.6	3.7	4.1
Western Hemisphere	16.2	16.8	16.0	15.4	17.1	17.8	15.9	15.7	13.0	13.2
Analytical groups										
By source of export earnings										
Fuel	4.8	5.1	4.7	4.1	4.9	3.8	2.9	2.8	2.8	3.1
Nonfuel	10.6	10.2	9.8	8.6	9.9	9.8	8.4	8.0	7.5	7.1
of which, primary products	17.0	14.4	12.9	8.4	12.6	11.6	7.2	6.8	13.2	7.9
By external financing source										
Net debtor countries	10.4	10.1	9.7	8.5	9.8	9.5	8.0	7.6	7.2	6.9
of which, official financing	23.6	19.6	17.3	10.3	15.6	12.6	5.7	5.4	13.1	6.2
Net debtor countries by debt-servicing experience										
Countries with arrears and/or rescheduling during 1994–98	13.0	13.5	13.4	11.5	14.6	13.5	10.3	9.6	11.9	10.0
Other groups										
Heavily indebted poor countries	24.7	19.0	18.0	9.2	15.1	12.3	5.1	4.9	13.7	5.8
Middle East and north Africa	4.6	5.0	4.1	3.9	4.7	3.4	2.7	2.3	2.3	2.4
Amortization[2]										
Developing countries	**18.2**	**13.9**	**15.5**	**16.6**	**18.0**	**18.5**	**15.3**	**15.9**	**13.9**	**13.6**
Regional groups										
Africa	18.8	17.0	14.3	13.1	14.0	12.4	10.8	11.1	13.1	10.1
Sub-Sahara	11.9	11.0	10.7	10.2	11.8	10.2	9.7	10.1	13.1	9.2
Developing Asia	10.0	9.5	8.7	9.6	11.7	10.4	9.3	10.2	9.5	8.9
Excluding China and India	11.0	9.7	8.7	12.0	16.0	13.3	12.4	15.9	14.8	12.7
Middle East and Turkey	8.8	10.6	13.2	10.5	11.8	11.1	8.6	11.4	8.6	8.9
Western Hemisphere	41.2	23.7	30.6	36.7	36.0	42.8	35.2	33.6	28.1	28.6
Analytical groups										
By source of export earnings										
Fuel	11.7	13.6	14.9	12.9	13.5	10.2	6.5	8.7	6.9	7.5
Nonfuel	19.9	14.0	15.6	17.5	18.9	20.4	17.8	17.8	15.6	14.9
of which, primary products	7.2	9.7	9.5	8.6	7.9	9.6	11.5	10.9	16.2	12.1
By external financing source										
Net debtor countries	20.1	15.1	16.6	18.3	19.4	20.3	17.1	17.1	15.1	14.6
of which, official financing	19.1	16.9	9.9	9.4	6.3	6.5	7.2	7.6	13.4	8.0
Net debtor countries by debt-servicing experience										
Countries with arrears and/or rescheduling during 1994–98	37.4	20.4	20.0	25.8	33.0	35.2	24.9	24.8	23.5	23.3
Other groups										
Heavily indebted poor countries	11.3	9.0	5.7	7.4	7.2	6.7	9.1	9.0	15.0	7.1
Middle East and north Africa	11.9	13.6	15.3	12.0	12.6	10.1	6.5	8.7	6.4	6.9

[1]Excludes service payments to the International Monetary Fund.
[2]Interest payments on total debt and amortization on long-term debt. Estimates through 2001 reflect debt-service payments actually made. The estimates for 2002 and 2003 take into account projected exceptional financing items, including accumulation of arrears and rescheduling agreements. In some cases, amortization on account of debt-reduction operations is included.

Table 43. IMF Charges and Repurchases to the IMF[1]
(Percent of exports of goods and services)

	1994	1995	1996	1997	1998	1999	2000	2001
Developing countries	**0.7**	**0.9**	**0.6**	**0.6**	**0.5**	**0.9**	**1.1**	**0.5**
Regional groups								
Africa	0.8	2.5	0.4	0.9	1.1	0.5	0.2	0.3
Sub-Sahara	0.5	2.8	0.2	0.7	0.7	0.2	0.1	0.1
Developing Asia	0.5	0.4	0.4	0.2	0.2	0.2	0.2	0.6
Excluding China and India	0.2	0.2	0.2	0.2	0.2	0.3	0.4	1.2
Middle East and Turkey	—	0.1	0.1	—	0.1	0.2	0.1	0.5
Western Hemisphere	1.5	1.6	1.6	1.9	1.1	3.2	4.2	0.6
Analytical groups								
By source of export earnings								
Fuel	0.4	0.5	0.3	0.4	0.6	0.4	0.2	0.1
Nonfuel	0.8	1.0	0.7	0.7	0.5	1.1	1.3	0.6
By external financing source								
Net debtor countries	0.8	1.0	0.7	0.7	0.6	1.1	1.2	0.6
of which, official financing	1.0	4.9	0.6	0.9	1.3	0.9	0.4	0.4
Net debtor countries by debt-servicing experience								
Countries with arrears and/or rescheduling during 1994–98	0.6	1.4	0.4	0.4	0.5	1.3	2.2	0.9
Other groups								
Heavily indebted poor countries	1.0	5.4	0.5	0.5	0.5	0.3	0.3	0.3
Middle East and north Africa	0.3	0.3	0.2	0.3	0.4	0.3	0.1	0.1
Countries in transition	**1.2**	**1.4**	**0.8**	**0.6**	**1.0**	**2.4**	**1.8**	**1.6**
Central and eastern Europe	2.3	2.6	0.8	0.3	0.5	0.3	0.3	0.3
Commonwealth of Independent States and Mongolia	0.2	0.3	0.8	0.9	1.6	4.9	3.2	3.0
Russia	0.2	0.3	1.0	1.0	1.8	5.8	3.0	3.7
Excluding Russia	0.1	0.3	0.4	0.5	1.2	2.9	3.4	1.4
Memorandum								
Total, billions of U.S. dollars								
General Resources Account	8.336	12.721	9.489	9.966	8.783	18.508	22.836	13.835
Charges	1.790	2.762	2.258	2.180	2.483	2.806	2.819	2.624
Repurchases	6.546	9.960	7.231	7.786	6.300	15.702	20.017	11.211
Trust Fund	0.015	0.015	—	0.007	0.001	0.001	—	—
Interest	—	—	—	—	—	—	—	—
Repayments	0.014	0.015	—	0.007	0.001	0.001	—	—
PRGF[2]	0.330	0.585	0.750	0.866	0.881	0.855	0.812	1.046
Interest	0.024	0.033	0.046	0.039	0.040	0.042	0.038	0.038
Repayments	0.306	0.552	0.703	0.827	0.842	0.813	0.776	1.009

[1]Excludes advanced economies. Charges on, and repurchases (or repayments of principal) for, use of International Monetary Fund credit.
[2]Poverty Reduction and Growth Facility (formerly ESAF—Enhanced Structural Adjustment Facility).

Table 44. Summary of Sources and Uses of World Saving
(Percent of GDP)

	Averages 1980–87	Averages 1988–95	1996	1997	1998	1999	2000	2001	2002	2003	Average 2004–07
World											
Saving	25.0	23.2	23.5	24.0	23.2	23.2	24.1	23.1	22.8	22.8	23.4
Investment	23.7	24.2	24.2	24.3	23.5	23.2	23.6	22.8	22.5	22.9	23.5
Advanced economies											
Saving	21.9	21.8	21.5	22.0	22.0	21.6	21.8	20.5	20.0	19.8	20.5
Private	21.4	21.0	20.5	19.9	19.3	18.5	18.2	17.6	18.0	17.7	17.5
Public	0.6	0.8	1.0	2.1	2.7	3.1	3.6	2.8	2.0	2.1	3.0
Investment	22.7	22.1	21.6	21.9	21.7	21.9	22.1	20.6	20.1	20.2	20.5
Private	18.2	18.0	17.6	18.1	18.0	18.0	18.5	17.0	16.4	16.5	16.9
Public	4.4	4.2	4.0	3.8	3.7	3.8	3.7	3.7	3.7	3.7	3.6
Net lending	−0.7	−0.3	−0.1	0.1	0.3	−0.2	−0.4	−0.2	—	−0.4	0.1
Private	3.1	3.1	2.9	1.7	1.3	0.5	−0.3	0.7	1.7	1.2	0.6
Public	−3.9	−3.4	−3.0	−1.6	−1.0	−0.7	−0.1	−0.8	−1.7	−1.6	−0.6
Current transfers	−0.2	−0.3	−0.3	−0.3	−0.3	−0.4	−0.4	−0.4	−0.4	−0.4	−0.4
Factor income	−0.1	−0.2	−0.2	−0.2	—	0.2	0.6	0.5	0.7	0.5	0.9
Resource balance	−0.4	0.1	0.4	0.6	0.7	—	−0.6	−0.3	−0.4	−0.5	−0.4
United States											
Saving	18.6	16.8	17.3	18.1	18.8	18.4	18.4	16.5	16.0	15.2	16.3
Private	19.6	17.7	16.5	16.2	15.7	14.6	14.0	13.9	15.2	14.5	14.6
Public	−1.0	−0.9	0.8	1.9	3.1	3.8	4.4	2.6	0.8	0.7	1.8
Investment	20.7	18.4	19.1	19.9	20.7	20.9	21.1	19.1	18.7	18.8	18.9
Private	17.1	14.9	15.9	16.7	17.5	17.6	17.9	15.7	15.2	15.3	15.4
Public	3.6	3.5	3.2	3.2	3.2	3.3	3.3	3.3	3.5	3.5	3.5
Net lending	−2.1	−1.6	−1.8	−1.8	−1.9	−2.6	−2.7	−2.6	−2.7	−3.5	−2.6
Private	2.5	2.8	0.6	−0.6	−1.9	−3.0	−3.9	−1.9	—	−0.8	−0.9
Public	−4.6	−4.4	−2.4	−1.3	−0.1	0.5	1.2	−0.7	−2.7	−2.8	−1.7
Current transfers	−0.5	−0.4	−0.5	−0.5	−0.5	−0.5	−0.5	−0.5	−0.5	−0.4	−0.4
Factor income	0.3	0.1	—	−0.1	0.5	0.8	1.7	1.5	1.9	1.3	2.2
Resource balance	−1.9	−1.3	−1.3	−1.3	−1.9	−2.8	−3.9	−3.6	−4.1	−4.4	−4.4
European Union											
Saving	20.9	21.0	20.5	21.0	21.1	20.9	20.8	20.3	20.3	20.5	21.2
Private	20.8	22.2	21.9	21.0	20.0	18.9	18.6	17.9	18.0	18.0	18.3
Public	0.1	−1.2	−1.4	0.1	1.1	1.9	2.2	2.4	2.3	2.5	2.9
Investment	21.4	21.3	19.6	19.7	20.5	20.7	21.2	20.2	19.7	20.0	20.4
Private	17.6	17.9	16.9	17.2	17.8	17.9	18.5	17.4	16.9	17.1	17.5
Public	3.8	3.4	2.7	2.5	2.6	2.7	2.7	2.8	2.8	2.9	2.9
Net lending	−0.6	−0.3	0.9	1.3	0.6	0.2	−0.3	—	0.6	0.5	0.8
Private	3.1	4.3	5.0	3.7	2.2	1.0	0.2	0.5	1.1	0.9	0.8
Public	−3.7	−4.6	−4.1	−2.4	−1.5	−0.8	−0.5	−0.4	−0.6	−0.4	—
Current transfers	−0.1	−0.3	−0.3	−0.3	−0.3	−0.4	−0.4	−0.5	−0.4	−0.4	−0.4
Factor income	−0.2	−0.6	−0.6	−0.5	−0.7	−0.4	−0.3	−0.5	−0.5	−0.4	−0.4
Resource balance	−0.2	0.6	1.9	2.2	1.7	1.0	0.4	1.0	1.5	1.4	1.6
Japan											
Saving	31.4	32.8	30.6	30.9	29.8	28.4	28.5	27.3	26.1	25.7	25.9
Private	26.4	24.7	25.9	25.8	26.0	25.9	26.7	25.9	25.2	24.7	22.3
Public	5.0	8.1	4.7	5.1	3.9	2.5	1.8	1.4	0.9	1.0	3.6
Investment	29.4	30.5	29.2	28.7	26.9	25.9	26.0	25.2	23.2	22.9	23.0
Private	21.5	23.2	20.6	21.1	19.4	18.1	19.1	18.7	16.9	17.0	17.8
Public	7.9	7.3	8.6	7.6	7.4	7.8	6.9	6.5	6.3	5.9	5.2
Net lending	2.0	2.3	1.4	2.2	3.0	2.5	2.5	2.1	2.9	2.8	2.9
Private	4.9	1.5	5.3	4.7	6.6	7.8	7.6	7.1	8.3	7.6	4.6
Public	−2.9	0.8	−4.0	−2.5	−3.6	−5.3	−5.1	−5.0	−5.4	−4.9	−1.7
Current transfers	−0.1	−0.2	−0.2	−0.2	−0.2	−0.3	−0.2	−0.2	−0.1	−0.2	−0.3
Factor income	0.3	0.8	1.1	1.3	1.3	1.3	1.2	1.6	1.6	1.5	1.5
Resource balance	1.8	1.7	0.5	1.1	1.9	1.5	1.4	0.6	1.4	1.5	1.6

Table 44 *(continued)*

	Averages 1980–87	Averages 1988–95	1996	1997	1998	1999	2000	2001	2002	2003	Average 2004–07
Newly industrialized Asian economies											
Saving	...	35.1	32.8	32.5	32.7	31.9	30.8	29.0	28.7	28.9	28.6
Private	...	28.3	25.8	25.1	26.1	25.6	22.9	20.9	21.0	21.0	20.2
Public	...	6.8	6.9	7.3	6.6	6.3	8.0	8.1	7.7	7.9	8.4
Investment	...	31.6	32.8	31.6	24.2	25.8	26.8	23.9	23.8	24.1	24.3
Private	...	25.2	26.2	25.1	17.5	19.5	21.2	18.3	18.3	18.7	19.0
Public	...	6.4	6.6	6.5	6.7	6.4	5.6	5.7	5.4	5.5	5.2
Net lending	...	3.6	—	0.9	8.5	6.0	4.0	5.0	4.9	4.8	4.3
Private	...	3.1	–0.4	—	8.6	6.1	1.6	2.6	2.6	2.4	1.2
Public	...	0.4	0.4	0.8	–0.1	–0.1	2.4	2.4	2.3	2.4	3.1
Current transfers	...	—	–0.4	–0.4	0.1	–0.2	–0.4	–0.6	–0.6	–0.6	–0.6
Factor income	...	1.1	0.8	0.7	—	—	0.3	0.5	1.1	1.2	1.2
Resource balance	...	2.5	–0.4	0.5	8.4	6.2	4.1	5.1	4.5	4.3	3.7
Developing countries											
Saving	29.2	24.6	27.1	27.6	25.9	26.0	27.4	26.8	26.7	26.9	27.3
Investment	24.0	26.7	28.4	28.2	26.7	25.8	26.2	26.2	26.1	26.5	27.3
Net lending	5.3	–2.1	–1.3	–0.6	–0.8	0.2	1.2	0.7	0.6	0.4	—
Current transfers	0.8	1.0	1.1	1.0	0.8	0.8	1.1	1.3	1.3	1.2	1.1
Factor income	5.5	–1.9	–1.5	–1.6	–1.9	–2.3	–2.2	–2.1	–1.9	–1.6	–1.4
Resource balance	–1.0	–1.2	–1.0	—	0.4	1.6	2.3	1.4	1.3	0.8	0.3
Memorandum											
Acquisition of foreign assets	0.6	1.5	3.2	4.4	2.9	3.7	4.4	3.9	3.8	3.5	3.1
Change in reserves	–0.1	1.1	2.1	1.6	0.2	0.8	1.1	2.0	2.0	1.5	1.2
Regional groups											
Africa											
Saving	18.6	16.3	17.4	16.8	15.4	16.6	18.9	19.1	18.5	18.8	19.8
Investment	21.9	19.5	19.5	19.3	20.7	20.5	18.9	19.8	20.9	21.2	21.7
Net lending	–3.3	–3.2	–2.1	–2.5	–5.4	–3.9	—	–0.7	–2.4	–2.4	–1.9
Current transfers	1.6	3.2	3.0	2.9	3.1	2.9	3.3	3.7	3.3	3.2	3.0
Factor income	–3.9	–4.5	–4.4	–4.5	–4.1	–4.5	–5.0	–4.4	–4.1	–4.0	–3.8
Resource balance	–1.0	–1.8	–0.7	–0.9	–4.4	–2.3	1.6	0.1	–1.6	–1.5	–1.0
Memorandum											
Acquisition of foreign assets	0.4	0.7	2.4	3.5	0.7	2.5	4.0	4.6	2.7	2.4	2.3
Change in reserves	–0.1	0.4	2.0	2.5	–0.6	0.6	2.7	2.7	1.1	1.7	1.8
Developing Asia											
Saving	45.3	30.4	32.5	33.4	32.1	31.3	32.4	32.3	31.6	31.3	31.3
Investment	27.0	31.7	33.9	32.8	30.0	29.4	29.9	30.3	29.9	30.2	30.8
Net lending	18.3	–1.3	–1.4	0.6	2.1	1.9	2.5	2.0	1.6	1.1	0.5
Current transfers	1.1	0.9	1.2	1.5	1.2	1.3	1.4	1.4	1.3	1.2	1.1
Factor income	19.9	–0.8	–1.1	–1.3	–1.5	–1.8	–1.0	–1.3	–1.3	–1.1	–1.0
Resource balance	–2.7	–1.5	–1.6	0.4	2.4	2.4	2.1	1.9	1.6	1.0	0.4
Memorandum											
Acquisition of foreign assets	0.6	2.4	3.7	6.0	4.4	4.9	4.9	4.8	4.8	4.0	3.4
Change in reserves	–0.6	1.4	2.1	1.9	1.0	1.4	0.9	2.8	2.8	1.6	1.2
Middle East and Turkey											
Saving	21.3	19.9	24.6	24.3	21.2	23.6	26.5	24.4	24.4	24.4	24.1
Investment	23.4	23.9	24.1	24.5	24.7	22.8	23.9	22.3	22.6	23.4	24.6
Net lending	–2.1	–4.0	0.5	–0.3	–3.5	0.8	2.7	2.0	1.7	1.0	–0.5
Current transfers	—	–0.8	–1.2	–2.7	–3.8	–4.6	–2.7	–1.2	–0.9	–0.5	–0.4
Factor income	–0.5	–1.0	1.3	0.5	–0.7	–1.1	–4.4	–2.1	—	0.5	1.0
Resource balance	–1.7	–2.3	0.4	1.9	1.1	6.5	9.8	5.3	2.6	1.1	–1.1
Memorandum											
Acquisition of foreign assets	0.6	–1.4	1.8	3.4	2.2	4.0	9.2	3.7	4.4	3.8	2.5
Change in reserves	–0.6	0.9	2.6	0.7	–1.3	1.0	3.3	1.2	2.3	2.2	1.5

Table 44 *(continued)*

	Averages		1996	1997	1998	1999	2000	2001	2002	2003	Average 2004–07
	1980–87	1988–95									
Western Hemisphere											
Saving	18.8	19.1	19.5	19.5	17.6	17.1	18.1	16.4	17.5	18.5	19.7
Investment	21.1	21.2	21.1	22.5	22.2	20.2	20.5	19.5	18.9	19.4	20.1
Net lending	−2.2	−2.1	−1.6	−3.0	−4.6	−3.0	−2.4	−3.1	−1.4	−0.9	−0.4
Current transfers	0.5	1.1	1.0	1.0	1.1	1.3	1.3	1.4	1.4	1.4	1.3
Factor income	−4.1	−3.2	−2.3	−2.2	−2.6	−3.1	−3.0	−3.2	−3.7	−3.3	−2.9
Resource balance	1.4	0.1	−0.3	−1.7	−3.1	−1.2	−0.7	−1.2	0.9	1.0	1.2
Memorandum											
Acquisition of foreign assets	0.6	1.5	3.1	1.6	0.3	0.9	0.8	1.5	1.0	2.1	3.0
Change in reserves	−0.2	0.9	1.8	0.9	−0.5	−0.6	0.1	0.1	—	1.0	0.9
Analytical groups											
By source of export earnings											
Fuel											
Saving	23.5	20.0	27.8	26.2	20.3	25.5	32.6	29.4	28.1	28.6	28.7
Investment	23.8	23.1	23.2	23.6	25.4	23.4	22.7	24.0	23.9	24.8	27.2
Net lending	−0.2	−3.1	4.6	2.6	−5.1	2.1	10.0	5.3	4.1	3.8	1.6
Current transfers	−2.4	−2.9	−2.8	−4.5	−6.0	−6.8	−4.6	−2.6	−2.3	−1.9	−1.5
Factor income	−0.3	−1.7	−0.4	−1.0	−2.3	−2.6	−6.4	−2.7	−1.2	−0.6	−0.1
Resource balance	2.5	1.5	7.8	8.1	3.2	11.5	21.0	10.7	7.6	6.2	3.2
Memorandum											
Acquisition of foreign assets	0.9	−1.6	3.8	5.5	1.6	4.0	15.1	6.8	5.2	4.8	3.5
Change in reserves	−1.0	0.2	4.2	1.7	−2.6	−0.5	6.5	2.8	2.4	3.1	2.4
Nonfuel											
Saving	30.2	25.2	27.0	27.7	26.5	26.0	26.8	26.6	26.6	26.7	27.2
Investment	24.0	27.1	29.0	28.7	26.8	26.0	26.6	26.4	26.3	26.7	27.3
Net lending	6.2	−1.9	−2.0	−1.0	−0.3	—	0.3	0.2	0.3	0.1	−0.1
Current transfers	1.3	1.5	1.5	1.6	1.5	1.6	1.7	1.7	1.6	1.5	1.4
Factor income	6.5	−1.9	−1.6	−1.7	−1.9	−2.2	−1.7	−2.0	−2.0	−1.7	−1.5
Resource balance	−1.7	−1.5	−1.9	−0.9	0.1	0.6	0.4	0.5	0.6	0.2	—
Memorandum											
Acquisition of foreign assets	0.5	1.9	3.2	4.3	3.0	3.6	3.3	3.6	3.7	3.3	3.1
Change in reserves	—	1.2	1.8	1.6	0.5	0.9	0.6	2.0	2.0	1.4	1.1
By external financing source											
Net debtor countries											
Saving	29.3	24.9	27.2	27.7	26.2	26.1	27.2	26.8	26.7	26.9	27.4
Investment	24.0	26.9	28.7	28.5	26.8	26.0	26.5	26.4	26.2	26.6	27.4
Net lending	5.3	−1.9	−1.5	−0.8	−0.6	0.1	0.8	0.3	0.4	0.2	—
Current transfers	1.2	1.4	1.3	1.3	1.0	1.0	1.3	1.5	1.5	1.4	1.3
Factor income	5.7	−2.2	−1.6	−1.8	−2.1	−2.5	−2.3	−2.3	−2.1	−1.8	−1.6
Resource balance	−1.6	−1.2	−1.2	−0.2	0.5	1.5	1.8	1.1	1.1	0.6	0.2
Memorandum											
Acquisition of foreign assets	0.4	1.7	3.1	4.4	3.1	3.7	4.1	3.8	3.7	3.4	3.1
Change in reserves	−0.1	1.2	2.0	1.6	0.4	0.9	1.0	2.0	2.0	1.5	1.2
Official financing											
Saving	13.7	14.5	18.1	18.8	17.0	19.5	21.5	21.7	20.7	21.1	22.6
Investment	19.8	19.3	22.6	21.6	22.4	22.0	21.4	22.3	23.8	24.6	25.1
Net lending	−6.1	−4.9	−4.5	−2.8	−5.4	−2.5	0.1	−0.6	−3.1	−3.5	−2.5
Current transfers	4.4	4.3	4.6	4.0	4.4	4.4	5.0	4.9	4.8	4.8	4.4
Factor income	−4.8	−3.3	−2.6	−2.8	−3.4	−2.3	−2.6	−2.2	−2.2	−2.3	−2.2
Resource balance	−5.6	−5.9	−6.4	−3.9	−6.3	−4.7	−2.3	−3.3	−5.8	−6.0	−4.7
Memorandum											
Acquisition of foreign assets	−0.1	0.4	1.4	2.3	−0.4	1.0	3.0	2.4	1.6	1.9	1.4
Change in reserves	0.1	0.6	1.4	2.5	−0.6	0.6	3.0	2.5	1.9	2.1	1.6

Table 44 *(concluded)*

	Averages		1996	1997	1998	1999	2000	2001	2002	2003	Average 2004–07
	1980–87	1988–95									
Net debtor countries by debt-servicing experience											
Countries with arrears and/or rescheduling during 1994–98											
Saving	17.6	20.2	21.7	21.0	17.7	19.3	22.6	21.3	20.6	21.1	22.3
Investment	21.4	23.1	24.4	24.5	21.7	20.0	20.7	21.3	21.4	22.1	23.4
Net lending	−3.8	−2.8	−2.8	−3.5	−4.0	−0.7	1.9	—	−0.9	−1.0	−1.1
Current transfers	0.7	1.4	1.1	0.4	0.1	−0.2	0.6	1.3	1.4	1.5	1.4
Factor income	−2.9	−2.9	−1.3	−2.1	−3.1	−3.7	−4.1	−3.3	−2.7	−2.1	−2.1
Resource balance	−1.6	−0.9	−2.5	−1.8	−1.0	3.2	5.5	2.0	0.5	−0.4	−0.4
Memorandum											
Acquisition of foreign assets	−0.3	0.4	1.4	1.7	0.9	2.9	5.8	3.6	2.6	2.7	1.8
Change in reserves	−0.5	0.8	1.4	0.5	−0.1	0.2	2.0	1.4	1.2	1.8	1.1
Countries in transition											
Saving	...	...	22.1	21.2	17.2	22.0	26.6	24.0	23.2	23.7	23.1
Investment	...	...	24.4	24.0	21.0	19.8	21.1	21.9	22.7	23.5	24.7
Net lending	...	...	−2.3	−2.8	−3.8	2.2	5.5	2.2	0.5	0.2	−1.6
Current transfers	...	...	0.7	0.7	1.7	1.1	1.1	1.1	1.0	1.0	1.0
Factor income	...	...	−0.7	—	−1.1	−0.6	−1.0	−1.0	−1.4	−1.5	−1.9
Resource balance	...	...	−2.3	−3.6	−4.4	1.8	5.5	2.1	0.8	0.8	−0.7
Memorandum											
Acquisition of foreign assets	...	...	2.0	5.7	3.1	5.8	7.7	5.2	4.5	4.2	2.9
Change in reserves	...	...	0.2	1.1	−0.3	1.0	3.4	2.3	3.3	2.6	1.1

Note: The estimates in this table are based on individual countries' national accounts and balance of payments statistics. For many countries, the estimates of national saving are built up from national accounts data on gross domestic investment and from balance-of-payments-based data on net foreign investment. The latter, which is equivalent to the current account balance, comprises three components: current transfers, net factor income, and the resource balance. The mixing of data sources, which is dictated by availability, implies that the estimates for national saving that are derived incorporate the statistical discrepancies. Furthermore, errors, omissions, and asymmetries in balance of payments statistics affect the estimates for net lending; at the global level, net lending, which in theory would be zero, equals the world current account discrepancy. Notwithstanding these statistical shortcomings, flow of funds estimates, such as those presented in this table, provide a useful framework for analyzing development in saving and investment, both over time and across regions and countries. Country group composites are weighted by GDP valued at purchasing power parities (PPPs) as a share of total world GDP.

Table 45. Summary of World Medium-Term Baseline Scenario

	Eight-Year Averages		Four-Year Average					Four-Year Average
	1984–91	1992–99	2000–03	2000	2001	2002	2003	2004–07
	Annual percent change unless otherwise noted							
World real GDP	**3.6**	**3.3**	**3.3**	**4.7**	**2.2**	**2.8**	**3.7**	**4.5**
Advanced economies	3.5	2.8	2.2	3.8	0.8	1.7	2.5	3.3
Developing countries	4.8	5.7	4.7	5.7	3.9	4.2	5.2	5.8
Countries in transition	1.2	–3.7	5.0	6.6	5.0	3.9	4.5	5.1
Memorandum								
Potential output								
Major advanced economies	2.8	2.5	2.5	2.6	2.5	2.5	2.5	2.5
World trade, volume[1]	**6.0**	**6.6**	**5.0**	**12.6**	**–0.1**	**2.1**	**6.1**	**6.9**
Imports								
Advanced economies	7.2	6.7	4.5	11.8	–1.3	1.7	6.2	6.7
Developing countries	3.1	7.1	7.0	15.9	1.6	3.8	7.1	8.5
Countries in transition	–0.3	1.6	10.0	13.4	11.7	6.9	8.0	7.3
Exports								
Advanced economies	6.5	6.4	4.3	12.0	–1.1	1.2	5.4	6.4
Developing countries	6.1	8.7	6.7	15.0	2.6	3.2	6.5	8.1
Countries in transition	0.2	1.6	7.9	14.7	5.9	5.3	6.2	6.1
Terms of trade								
Advanced economies	1.0	0.2	–0.4	–2.5	0.3	0.2	0.4	0.5
Developing countries	–3.4	0.1	0.4	6.3	–3.0	–0.6	–1.0	–0.4
Countries in transition	–1.0	–2.0	2.4	9.0	0.2	–0.8	1.3	–0.4
World prices in U.S. dollars								
Manufactures	5.8	–0.6	–0.2	–5.2	–2.3	2.6	4.2	1.0
Oil	–5.2	–0.9	7.7	57.0	–14.0	0.5	–0.8	–3.5
Nonfuel primary commodities	0.1	–0.6	1.5	1.8	–5.4	4.2	5.7	3.1
Consumer prices								
Advanced economies	4.4	2.3	1.9	2.3	2.2	1.4	1.7	2.0
Developing countries	49.0	25.5	5.8	6.1	5.7	5.6	6.0	4.2
Countries in transition	17.7	155.2	14.0	20.2	15.9	11.3	8.8	6.1
Interest rates (in percent)								
Real six-month LIBOR[2]	4.9	3.2	2.0	4.5	1.4	0.9	1.3	3.6
World real long-term interest rate[3]	5.1	3.8	2.8	2.8	2.3	3.1	2.9	3.4
	Percent of GDP							
Balances on current account								
Advanced economies	–0.3	0.1	–0.8	–0.9	–0.8	–0.8	–0.9	–0.8
Developing countries	–1.8	–1.8	0.6	1.2	0.7	0.4	—	–0.6
Countries in transition	0.1	–1.4	1.3	3.6	1.4	0.2	–0.1	–1.8
Total external debt								
Developing countries	39.3	41.7	40.1	40.6	40.3	40.9	38.8	33.9
Countries in transition	9.4	44.3	41.7	48.5	42.4	39.4	36.3	32.0
Debt service								
Developing countries	5.0	5.7	6.1	6.4	6.4	5.9	5.8	5.0
Countries in transition	2.3	5.2	6.9	7.3	7.5	6.4	6.3	4.9

[1]Data refer to trade in goods and services.
[2]London interbank offered rate on U.S. dollar deposits less percent change in U.S. GDP deflator.
[3]GDP-weighted average of 10-year (or nearest maturity) government bond rates for the United States, Japan, Germany, France, Italy, the United Kingdom, and Canada.

Table 46. Developing Countries—Medium-Term Baseline Scenario: Selected Economic Indicators

	Eight-Year Averages		Four-Year Average					Four-Year Average
	1984–91	1992–99	2000–03	2000	2001	2002	2003	2004–07
	Annual percent change							
Developing countries								
Real GDP	4.8	5.7	4.7	5.7	3.9	4.2	5.2	5.8
Export volume[1]	6.1	8.7	6.7	15.0	2.6	3.2	6.5	8.1
Terms of trade[1]	−3.4	0.1	0.4	6.3	−3.0	−0.6	−1.0	−0.4
Import volume[1]	3.1	7.1	7.0	15.9	1.6	3.8	7.1	8.5
Regional groups								
Africa								
Real GDP	2.6	2.4	3.4	3.0	3.5	3.1	4.2	4.8
Export volume[1]	5.4	4.6	3.3	6.1	2.4	0.9	3.7	6.7
Terms of trade[1]	−2.4	−1.0	2.3	13.6	−3.4	−0.5	0.3	−1.4
Import volume[1]	2.3	4.4	4.6	4.4	4.5	6.0	3.4	4.2
Developing Asia								
Real GDP	7.1	7.8	6.2	6.7	5.6	6.1	6.3	6.7
Export volume[1]	9.2	11.8	9.2	21.8	2.3	6.4	7.3	9.7
Terms of trade[1]	−1.1	0.1	−0.9	−2.2	−0.7	0.3	−1.0	—
Import volume[1]	6.0	9.7	10.1	22.5	2.5	7.7	8.5	10.7
Middle East and Turkey								
Real GDP	3.3	3.7	4.0	6.1	1.5	3.6	4.7	5.1
Export volume[1]	5.6	5.9	3.7	6.8	3.4	−0.4	5.1	4.9
Terms of trade[1]	−7.2	0.8	2.7	27.5	−8.3	−2.0	−2.8	−1.1
Import volume[1]	−0.5	2.3	6.0	14.7	−2.4	6.3	6.0	6.4
Western Hemisphere								
Real GDP	2.7	3.2	1.7	4.0	0.6	−0.6	3.0	3.9
Export volume[1]	4.3	7.9	5.8	12.6	2.5	1.3	7.3	7.6
Terms of trade[1]	−1.9	0.5	−0.3	2.5	−2.6	−0.9	−0.2	−0.4
Import volume[1]	5.6	9.4	3.4	11.1	1.9	−5.5	6.7	7.1
Analytical groups								
Net debtor countries by debt-servicing experience								
Countries with arrears and/or rescheduling during 1994–98								
Real GDP	3.1	3.4	3.9	4.6	3.3	3.4	4.3	5.0
Export volume[1]	4.5	7.8	4.5	9.6	0.4	2.3	5.8	6.9
Terms of trade[1]	−3.5	−1.7	1.1	10.5	−2.2	−1.3	−2.2	−0.6
Import volume[1]	0.2	4.9	5.8	9.9	4.7	3.7	5.0	5.9

Table 46 (concluded)

	1991	1995	1999	2000	2001	2002	2003	2007
				Percent of exports of good and services				
Developing countries								
Current account balance	−15.1	−9.2	−0.8	4.3	2.6	1.2	0.1	−2.8
Total external debt	210.1	179.6	176.4	142.0	143.8	142.0	132.7	102.7
Debt-service payments[2]	24.2	23.1	27.3	22.4	22.8	20.5	19.9	15.1
Interest payments	10.5	9.2	8.7	7.2	6.9	6.6	6.4	5.7
Amortization	13.7	13.9	18.5	15.3	15.9	13.9	13.6	9.4
Regional groups								
Africa								
Current account balance	−6.8	−14.0	−11.2	3.5	0.9	−4.8	−4.5	−3.1
Total external debt	254.1	254.1	225.5	179.0	178.9	181.2	170.4	139.5
Debt-service payments[2]	28.2	26.7	21.0	17.9	17.9	23.2	16.6	13.2
Interest payments	11.2	9.7	8.6	7.1	6.8	10.0	6.5	5.7
Amortization	17.0	17.0	12.4	10.8	11.1	13.1	10.1	7.6
Developing Asia								
Current account balance	−5.2	−9.3	8.0	6.5	5.7	4.5	2.2	−1.1
Total external debt	161.8	124.2	118.9	94.6	96.9	92.1	87.5	67.1
Debt-service payments[2]	17.3	16.5	16.4	13.8	14.2	13.6	12.8	9.1
Interest payments	7.9	7.0	6.0	4.5	4.0	4.1	4.0	3.7
Amortization	9.4	9.5	10.4	9.3	10.2	9.5	8.9	5.4
Middle East and Turkey								
Current account balance	−39.4	0.1	5.9	19.0	16.3	8.2	5.8	−3.9
Total external debt	180.6	172.6	186.5	146.2	151.3	161.6	158.7	137.5
Debt-service payments[2]	15.2	15.3	15.1	12.1	14.9	12.3	13.1	12.3
Interest payments	6.0	4.7	4.0	3.5	3.6	3.7	4.1	4.0
Amortization	9.1	10.6	11.1	8.6	11.4	8.6	8.9	8.3
Western Hemisphere								
Current account balance	−10.0	−14.8	−18.7	−13.4	−15.1	−9.2	−7.3	−5.8
Total external debt	278.9	251.9	256.8	214.6	215.1	212.6	190.3	145.8
Debt-service payments[2]	40.2	40.5	60.6	51.1	49.2	41.1	41.8	31.3
Interest payments	18.2	16.8	17.8	15.9	15.7	13.0	13.2	11.3
Amortization	22.0	23.7	42.8	35.2	33.6	28.1	28.6	20.0
Analytical groups								
Net debtor countries by debt-servicing experience								
Countries with arrears and/or rescheduling during 1994–98								
Current account balance	−17.2	−18.4	−7.4	2.8	−2.4	−5.8	−7.2	−6.8
Total external debt	341.1	301.1	291.6	230.1	232.8	230.3	219.7	170.6
Debt-service payments[2]	35.2	33.8	48.7	35.2	34.4	35.4	33.2	23.7
Interest payments	14.5	13.5	13.5	10.3	9.6	11.9	10.0	8.6
Amortization	20.7	20.4	35.2	24.9	24.8	23.5	23.3	15.1

[1]Data refer to trade in goods and services.
[2]Interest payments on total debt plus amortization payments on long-term debt only. Projections incorporate the impact of exceptional financing items. Excludes service payments to the International Monetary Fund.

WORLD ECONOMIC OUTLOOK AND STAFF STUDIES FOR THE WORLD ECONOMIC OUTLOOK, SELECTED TOPICS, 1992–2002

I. Methodology—Aggregation, Modeling, and Forecasting

II. Historical Surveys

III. Economic Growth—Sources and Patterns

IV. Inflation and Deflation; Commodity Markets

V. Fiscal Policy

VI. Monetary Policy; Financial Markets; Flow of Funds

VII. Labor Market Issues

VIII. Exchange Rate Issues

IX. External Payments, Trade, Capital Movements, and Foreign Debt

X. Regional Issues

XI. Country-Specific Analyses

***Staff Studies for the
World Economic Outlook***

World Economic and Financial Surveys

This series (ISSN 0258-7440) contains biannual, annual, and periodic studies covering monetary and financial issues of importance to the global economy. The core elements of the series are the *World Economic Outlook* report, usually published in May and October, and the quarterly *Global Financial Stability Report*. Other studies assess international trade policy, private market and official financing for developing countries, exchange and payments systems, export credit policies, and issues discussed in the *World Economic Outlook*. Please consult the IMF *Publications Catalog* for a complete listing of currently available World Economic and Financial Surveys.

World Economic Outlook: A Survey by the Staff of the International Monetary Fund

The *World Economic Outlook,* published twice a year in English, French, Spanish, and Arabic, presents IMF staff economists' analyses of global economic developments during the near and medium term. Chapters give an overview of the world economy; consider issues affecting industrial countries, developing countries, and economies in transition to the market; and address topics of pressing current interest.

ISSN 0256-6877.

$49.00 (academic rate: $46.00); paper.
2002. (Sep.). ISBN 1-58906-179-9. **Stock #WEO EA 0022002.**
2002. (April). ISBN 1-58906-107-1. **Stock #WEO EA 0012002.**
2001. (Dec.). ISBN 1-58906-087-3. **Stock #WEO EA 0172001.**
2001. (Oct.). ISBN 1-58906-073-3. **Stock #WEO EA 0022001.**
2001. (May). ISBN 1-58906-032-6. **Stock #WEO EA 0012001.**
2000. (Oct.). ISBN 1-55775-975-8. **Stock #WEO EA 0022000.**
2000. (May). ISBN 1-55775-936-7. **Stock #WEO EA 012000.**

Official Financing for Developing Countries
by a staff team in the IMF's Policy Development and Review Department led by Anthony R. Boote and Doris C. Ross

This study provides information on official financing for developing countries, with the focus on low-income countries. It updates the 1995 edition and reviews developments in direct financing by official and multilateral sources.

$25.00 (academic rate: $20.00); paper.
2001. ISBN 1-58906-038-5. **Stock #WEO EA 0132001.**
1998. ISBN 1-55775-702-X. **Stock #WEO-1397.**
1995. ISBN 1-55775-527-2. **Stock #WEO-1395.**

Exchange Rate Arrangements and Currency Convertibility: Developments and Issues
by a staff team led by R. Barry Johnston

A principal force driving the growth in international trade and investment has been the liberalization of financial transactions, including the liberalization of trade and exchange controls. This study reviews the developments and issues in the exchange arrangements and currency convertibility of IMF members.

$20.00 (academic rate: $12.00); paper.
1999. ISBN 1-55775-795-X. **Stock #WEO EA 0191999.**

World Economic Outlook Supporting Studies
by the IMF's Research Department

These studies, supporting analyses and scenarios of the *World Economic Outlook*, provide a detailed examination of theory and evidence on major issues currently affecting the global economy.

$25.00 (academic rate: $20.00); paper.
2000. ISBN 1-55775-893-X. **Stock #WEO EA 0032000.**

Global Financial Stability Report: Market Developments and Issues

The *Global Financial Stability Report,* published four times a year, examines trends and issues that influence world financial markets. It replaces two IMF publications—the annual *International Capital Markets* report and the electronic quarterly *Emerging Market Financing* report. The report is designed to deepen understanding of international capital flows and explores developments that could pose a risk to international financial market stability.

$49.00 (academic rate: $46.00); paper.
September 2002 ISBN 1-58906-157-8. **Stock #GFSR EA0032002.**
June 2002 ISBN 1-58906-131-4. **Stock #GFSR EA0022002.**
March 2002 ISBN 1-58906-105-5. **Stock #GFSR EA0012002.**

International Capital Markets: Developments, Prospects, and Key Policy Issues (back issues)
$42.00 (academic rate: $35.00); paper.
2001. ISBN 1-58906-056-3. **Stock #WEO EA 0062001.**
2000. (Sep.). ISBN 1-55775-949-9. **Stock #WEO EA 0062000.**

Toward a Framework for Financial Stability
by a staff team led by David Folkerts-Landau and Carl-Johan Lindgren

This study outlines the broad principles and characteristics of stable and sound financial systems, to facilitate IMF surveillance over banking sector issues of macroeconomic significance and to contribute to the general international effort to reduce the likelihood and diminish the intensity of future financial sector crises.

$25.00 (academic rate: $20.00); paper.
1998. ISBN 1-55775-706-2. **Stock #WEO-016.**

Trade Liberalization in IMF-Supported Programs
by a staff team led by Robert Sharer

This study assesses trade liberalization in programs supported by the IMF by reviewing multiyear arrangements in the 1990s and six detailed case studies. It also discusses the main economic factors affecting trade policy targets.

$25.00 (academic rate: $20.00); paper.
1998. ISBN 1-55775-707-0. **Stock #WEO-1897.**

Private Market Financing for Developing Countries
by a staff team from the IMF's Policy Development and Review Department led by Steven Dunaway

This study surveys recent trends in flows to developing countries through banking and securities markets. It also analyzes the institutional and regulatory framework for developing country finance; institutional investor behavior and pricing of developing country stocks; and progress in commercial bank debt restructuring in low-income countries.

$20.00 (academic rate: $12.00); paper.
1995. ISBN 1-55775-526-4. **Stock #WEO-1595.**

Available by series subscription or single title (including back issues); academic rate available only to full-time university faculty and students. For earlier editions please inquire about prices.

The IMF *Catalog of Publications* is available on-line at the Internet address listed below.

Please send orders and inquiries to:
International Monetary Fund, Publication Services, 700 19th Street, N.W.
Washington, D.C. 20431, U.S.A.
Tel.: (202) 623-7430   Telefax: (202) 623-7201
E-mail: publications@imf.org
Internet: http://www.imf.org

For Reference

Not to be taken from this room